East of Delhi

SOUTH ASIA RESEARCH

Series Editor

Martha Selby

A Publication Series of
The University of Texas South Asia Institute
and
Oxford University Press

DHARMA
Its Early History in Law, Religion, and Narrative
Alf Hiltebeitel

POETRY OF KINGS
The Classical Hindi Literature of Mughal India
Allison Busch

THE RISE OF A FOLK GOD
Viṭṭhal of Pandharpur
Ramchandra Chintaman Dhere
Translated by Anne Feldhaus

WOMEN IN EARLY INDIAN BUDDHISM
Comparative Textual Studies
Edited by Alice Collett

THE RIGVEDA
The Earliest Religious Poetry of India
Edited and Translated by Stephanie W. Jamison and Joel P. Brereton

CITY OF MIRRORS
The Songs of Lālan Sãi
Translated by Carol Salomon
Edited by Saymon Zakaria and Keith E. Cantú

IN THE SHADE OF THE GOLDEN PALACE
Alaol and Middle Bengali Poetics in Arakan
Thibaut d'Hubert

TO SAVOR THE MEANING
The Theology of Literary Emotions in Medieval Kashmir
James Reich

THE OCEAN OF INQUIRY
Niścaldās and the Premodern Origins of Modern Hinduism
Michael S. Allen

A LASTING VISION
Dandin's Mirror *in the World of Asian Letters*
Edited by Yigal Bronner

EAST OF DELHI
Multilingual Literary Culture and World Literature
Francesca Orsini

East of Delhi

Multilingual Literary Culture and World Literature

FRANCESCA ORSINI

OXFORD
UNIVERSITY PRESS

OXFORD
UNIVERSITY PRESS

Oxford University Press is a department of the University of Oxford. It furthers the University's objective of excellence in research, scholarship, and education by publishing worldwide. Oxford is a registered trade mark of Oxford University Press in the UK and certain other countries.

Published in the United States of America by Oxford University Press
198 Madison Avenue, New York, NY 10016, United States of America.

Library of Congress Cataloging-in-Publication Data
Names: Orsini, Francesca, author.
Title: East of Delhi : multilingual literary culture and world literature / Francesca Orsini.
Description: 1. | New York : Oxford University Press, 2023. | Series: South Asia research series | Includes bibliographical references and index.
Identifiers: LCCN 2022060626 (print) | LCCN 2022060627 (ebook) | ISBN 9780197658291 (hardback) | ISBN 9780197658314 (epub)
Subjects: LCSH: Oudh (India)—Civilization. | Oudh (India)—History. | Hindu literature—History and criticism.
Classification: LCC DS485.O94 O77 2023 (print) | LCC DS485.O94 (ebook) | DDC 954/.2—dc23/eng/20230103
LC record available at https://lccn.loc.gov/2022060626
LC ebook record available at https://lccn.loc.gov/2022060627

DOI: 10.1093/oso/9780197658291.001.0001

Printed by Integrated Books International, United States of America

To Allison, Aditya, and Sunil
who will always be missed

Contents

List of Figures and Tables ix
Acknowledgments xi
Note on Transliteration xv
Map of Purab qasbas *and cities* xvii

1. Introduction: A Multilingual Local in World Literature 1
   No Paris Consecration 1
   Located and Multilingual 4
   Why Purab? 9
   The Linguistic Economy in the Region 14
   But Is This World Literature? 20
   This Book 22
2. Following Stories across Scripts, Languages, and Repertoires 24
   The Emergence of a Genre 28
   Sumptuous Romances 34
   Hindavi *Kathas* in the Mughal World 50
   Hindavi *Kathas* into Persian 62
   Kathas in the World of Print and in Literary History 69
3. Making Space for Sant Texts: Orature, Literary History, and World Literature 74
   Making Space for Sant Orature 79
   Poetry and the Idiom of Caste 83
   The Aesthetics of Sant Orature 87
   Religious Dialogism in Sant Orature 94
   Both Mobile and Located 100
   Sant Orature into Print: Booklets and World Literature 108
4. Local Cosmopolitans: Poetry and Distinction in the *Qasbas* and Small Courts of Awadh 116
   Reconstructing a Multilingual Archive 119
   Studying and Strolling 130
   Practices of Distinction 135
   Strategies of Local Inscription 139
   Parallel Cultivation 142
   Urdu and Amnesia 147
5. Colonial Impact and Indian Response 152
   Awadh as a Colonial Center 154

Colonial Effects and the Vernacular Problem 159
Separate Canons 165
Colonial Folklore and the Invention of Folk Literature 172
Forget the Novel 179
Beyond (and through) English 187
Shifting the Lens 188

Conclusions: Thinking through Space 192

Notes 201
Bibliography 251
Index 277

Figures and Tables

Figures

2.1 Lorik enters Chanda's palace bedroom 29

2.2 Two folios from a Jayasi *Padmāvat* copied in Persian script in Gorakhpur in 1697 44

2.3 Folio of a *Padmāvat* copied in Nagari script in the eighteenth century 45

2.4 Folio from a *Padmāvat* copied in Kaithi script 46

3.1 Malukdas's seat in Kara and the remaining wall of his original home 102

3.2 The mausoleum of Khwaja Karak Shah, Kara 103

3.3 A ghat in Kara 104

3.4 Collected and bound Belvedere *Santbānī* booklets from the 1920s 112

3.5 Belvedere Press Sant Bani booklets 114

4.1 Detail of Bhanupratap Tiwari's autobiography with his translation of a Persian couplet into Brajbhasha on the side 146

4.2 The bazaar of Faizabad with performers 149

Tables

2.1 Manuscript History 47

2.2 *Kathas* in the Eastern Region 48

2.3 Translation to transcodification 63

2.4 Avadhi Romances into Persian 64

3.1 Sants in the Eastern Region 78

3.2 *Santbānī Pustakmālā* 111

Figures and Tables

Figures

Tables

Acknowledgments

When, back in 2004, I decided that it was not enough to keep critiquing the modern paradigm of Hindi and its monolingual literary history and that I needed to try to propose alternative paradigms, I knew that even equipping myself with the tools necessary for the task would be a long and daunting process. It has indeed been so, but it has also been exciting and pleasurable. By 2004 I had been working on Hindi literature for twenty years, on Urdu for less than ten, and studied Farsi for just two (wishing, in my late thirties, that I had done so in my early twenties as a university student in Venice, since Ca' Foscari boasted a fine Persian Department, unlike the quarrelsome and less distinguished Hindi one I was in). By 2004 I had also taught Brajbhasha and Avadhi texts, but still felt I knew too little about their broader historical and literary context—the pegs I could hang the texts on, so to speak, were far too blunt. Italian literary historiography, combining material and social history with semiotics, provided an excellent model (for which I am still grateful to my excellent high school teacher, Ambrogio Barbieri), whether Remo Ceserani and Lidia de Federicis's pathbreaking high school textbooks *Il materiale e l'immaginario* or the thick, encyclopaedic tomes of the *Storia della letteratura italiana* edited by Alberto Asor Rosa and published by Einaudi. But the question was, how to envisage a similar history for north India?

An Arts and Humanities Research Council grant for a project titled North Indian Literary Culture and History from a Multilingual Perspective (1450–1650) enabled me to travel to libraries in Europe, India, and Pakistan; bring together at SOAS the very best scholars in the field, from the most distinguished doyens to new PhD students; and learn from them all. The project ran between 2006 and 2009, and since it was multilingual and interdisciplinary—taking in, besides literature, music, art, and book history, history of religion, and social history—all of us felt that we were always learning something new. And since a core group got together year after year, we felt we were building a conversation and a cohort together. This book is therefore the result of a collective endeavor, which included twelve series of lecture and text readings, two small workshops, three conferences (and two conference volumes: *After Timur Left*, co-edited with Samira Sheikh, and *Tellings and Texts*, co-edited with Katherine Schofield), all facilitated by Jane Savory and Rahima Begum in the Office for Regional Centres at SOAS. Of course, all errors of judgment or fact in this book are mine.

After thanking the AHRC for its financial support, I want to start thanking all the librarians—Dr. Ata Khurshid of the Maulana Azad Library in Aligarh, and the helpful staff in the Asian Readings Room of the British Library in London, the Bibliothèque Nationale in Paris, the Allahabad Museum and Hindi Sahitya Sammelan in Allahabad, Bharat Bhavan at Benares Hindu University, the Rajasthan Oriental Research Institute in Jodhpur and Jaipur, the Abhay Jain Pustakalay and Anup Sanskrit Pustakalay in Bikaner, the Rampur Raza Library, Khuda Bakhsh Library in Patna, and the Library of the Asiatic Society in Kolkata—who gave me access to their collections and allowed me to copy or scan far more material than I was able to process. Marina Chellini, curator of North Indian languages at the British Library, and Jonathan Loar, South Asia reference librarian at the Library of Congress, helped with images at a crucial time. I next want to thank all the scholars who agreed to take part in the project and share their knowledge, many of whom became good friends (what my husband, Peter, called "our gang"): Muzaffar Alam, Imre Bangha, Amy Bard, the late Aditya Behl and Allison Busch, Katherine Butler Schofield, Eva de Clercq, John Cort, Françoise "Nalini" Delvoye, Thibaut d'Hubert, Richard Eaton, Supriya Gandhi, Walt Hakala, J. S. Hawley, Monika Horstmann, Aparna Kapadia, Dilorom Karomat, Pasha M. Khan, the late Sunil Kumar, Allyn Miner, Christian Novetzke, Shantanu Phukan, John Seyller, Sunil Sharma, Samira Sheikh, Ramya Sreenivasan, Richard Widdess, and Richard Wolf. It is indeed heartbreaking that Aditya Behl, Allison Busch, and Sunil Kumar left us all too soon. Whitney Cox was an intellectual companion throughout the project, and I also benefited from the scholarship of the late Simon Digby, Winand Callewaert, Polly O'Hanlon, the late Shyam Manohar Pandey and Robert Skelton, and Andrew Topsfield. For invaluable help with Persian texts, I must first and foremost thank Sunil Sharma for his timely assistance with reading texts and translation queries over the years, and Narges and Hashem Sedqamiz for hosting me in Shiraz in 2005 while Hashem and I read Mir 'Abd al-Wahid Bilgrami's *Haqā'iq-e Hindī*. I must also thank the members of the weekly Persian Reading Group that met at Harvard in 2013–2014, including Sunil Sharma, Abhishek Kaicker, Shahrad Shahvand, Neelam Khoja, Abe Naofumi, and Nicolas Roth. And Imre Bangha, Richard Williams, the late Shyam Manohar Pandey, and the other members of the Braj reading group who read with me parts of Alam's *Mādhavānal Kāmkandalā*. For anything about Arabic in India, I am indebted to my brilliant former PhD student Simon Leese. In India, I am deeply indebted to Professor Azarmi Dukht Safavi and to Fawzia and the late Farhan Mujeeb for hosting me in Aligrah and enabling my library work there, and in Allahabad to my very dear friends Alok and Rajul Rai, Raghoo and Maya Sinha, Arvind Krishna and Vandana Mehrotra, and Sara Rai and Muhammad Aslam, who have shared all the steps of this very long project, indeed of my entire career. Alok, Arvind, and Sara accompanied me on a memorable trip to Jais, and Sara and Aslam to Kara, where Muslim Miyan was a gracious guide. In Delhi, I must thank my dear friends Vasudha Dalmia and Kumkum Sangari for their encouragement, and Professors Harbans Mukhia and the late Sunil Kumar for arranging several talks before knowledgeable Delhi audiences. Professor Mazhar Hussain arranged for a talk at the Centre for Indian Languages at Jawaharlal Nehru University a few years ago, after which a Hindi student asked, "Madam, *iski kya prasangikta hai?*," What is the relevance of this?—a question that this book has taken seriously and has tried to answer. In the United States, I am particularly indebted to the late Allison Busch for inviting me to Columbia to teach a short course on bilingual texts in 2008, and to Ramya Sreenivasan for inviting me to the University of Pennsylvania to try out the chapters of this book at the South Asia Center in 2017.

But this book also tries to address readers interested in world literature, and I have collected quite a few debts in this field, too. The year I spent as Mary I. Bunting Fellow at the Radcliffe Institute at Harvard, 2013–2014, was tremendously stimulating, and I learned so much from the other fellows, particularly Elaine Freedgood, Mary Franklin-Brown, and the fearsomely clever Lucia Allais, Caroline Jones, Ewa Lajer-Burcharth, Ruth Mack, and Sophia Roosth (thank you!); Vivek Narayanan, Krassimira Daskalova, Linda Gordon, and the late Frances Gouda provided much needed company, and Vivek some terrific translations, while Sunil Sharma (yes, again) and Sanjay Krishnan gave me the chance to present the first ideas of this book at Boston University. The year at Radcliffe laid the foundation for the project on Multilingual Locals and Significant Geographies, which was generously funded with an Advanced Grant by the European Research Council (2015–2021). While the conception of this book predates that project, the arguments regarding world literature were developed as part of it in conversation with the project team: my dear friend and former colleague Karima Laachir, our brilliant postdoctoral researchers Fatima Burney, Itzea Goikolea-Amiano, and Sara Marzagora, and PhD scholars July Blalack, Jack Clift, and Ayele Kebede Roba. I must thank them all for providing such wonderful intellectual collaboration and support, broadening my horizons, and sharing a real adventure in world literature. I must also thank Professor David Damrosch for inviting me to teach at the Institute of World Literature in Copenhagen in 2017 (and, more recently, to join the editorial board of the *Journal of World Literature*), Debjani Ganguly for inviting me to contribute to her wonderful *Cambridge History of World Literature* and join the adventure of the *Cambridge Studies in World Literature*, and my SOAS colleague Wen-Chin Ouyang for being such a great partner in crime. Finally, Neelam Srivastava, Galin Tihanov, and Imre Bangha generously read the book manuscript and offered great comments and useful corrections.

Note on Transliteration

A volume of this kind inevitably contains a large number of transliterated words in several languages. But to make the text readable without sacrificing its scholarly appeal, I have chosen to keep diacritical marks to a minimum and to use them only for book titles and direct quotations. For Devanagari, the transliteration follows R. S. McGregor, *The Oxford Hindi- English Dictionary* (New Delhi: Oxford University Press, 1993), with the exception that nasalized vowels are transliterated with a ṃ instead of ṁ, soft *c* (च) and its aspirate *ch* (छ) with *ch* and *chh*, and ś (श) and ṣ (ष) with *sh*. For Persian and Urdu words, I have slightly adapted existing systems as below:

ا A	ب B	پ P	ت T	ث S̱	
ج J	چ CH	ح Ḥ	خ KH		
د D	ذ Z̤	ر R	ز Z	ژ ZH	
س S	ش SH	ص Ṣ	ض Ż		
ط Ṭ	ظ Ẓ	ع ‘	غ GH	ف F	ق Q
ک K	گ G	ل L	م M	ن N	

و W, V, Ū (O only if specified as majhul) ه H

ی Y, Ī (E only if specified as majhul)

short vowels: a, i, u

Map of Purab *qasbas* and cities

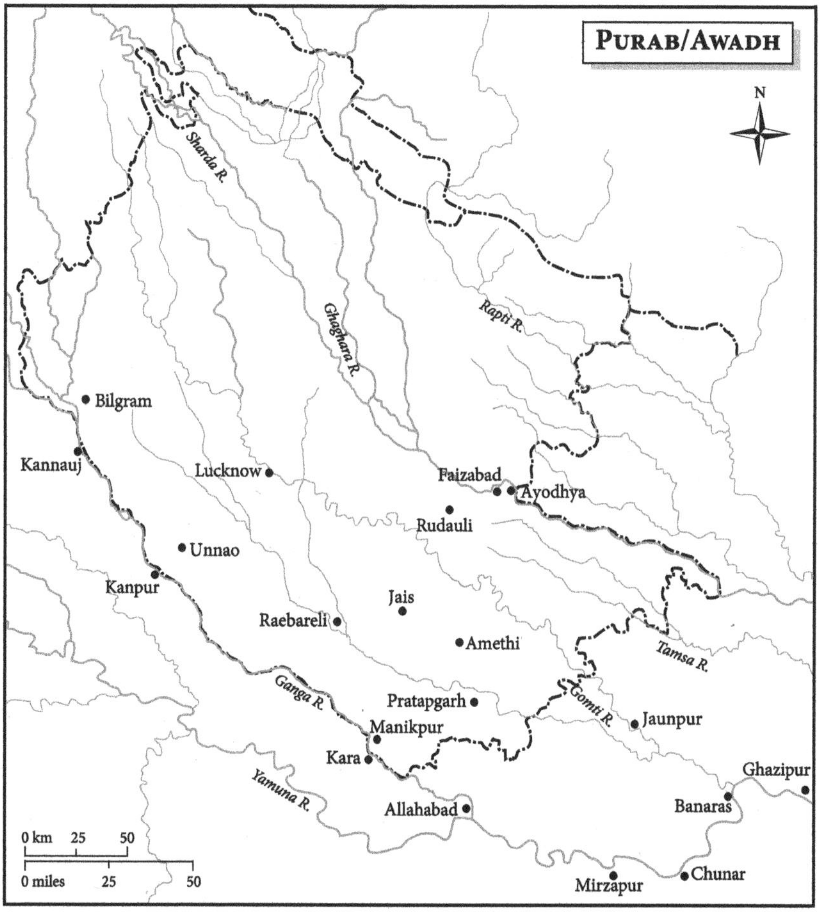

1
Introduction
A Multilingual Local in World Literature

No Paris Consecration

In 1865, the French travel writer and Orientalist Théodore Pavie published in Paris *La Légende de Padmanî, reine de Tchitor, d'après les textes hindis et hindouis*, using manuscripts in the collection of the great Orientalist Joseph H. Garcin de Tassy (1794–1878), professor of Hindustani at the École spéciale des langues orientales. "Padmanî, Queen of Tchitor," Pavie wrote, "is famous throughout India for her beauty and her heroic demise (*dénouement héroïque*).... The bards of Rajasthan and Hindu poets converted to Islamism have told with equal enthusiasm, in the old idioms of the country as well as in Persian, the history of this beautiful princess, daughter of the King of Ceylon and wife of the râṇa of Tchitor, who excited the covetousness of Sultan Alâ-ud-dîn" (5).[1] Pavie's translation was picked up by the poet and sinologist Louis Laloy (1922) for a libretto he wrote for Albert Roussel's ballet-opera *Padmâvatî*. Laloy concentrated on the final dramatic events of the capture of Chittor by Sultan Ala'uddin Khilji and added a few gory touches of his own: in the temple crypt of the besieged city, the Brahman priests tell Padmavati that the god Shiva demands a "royal sacrifice." Padmavati is ready to immolate herself, but a second victim is needed. When her husband, Ratansen, asks Padmavati to give herself up to Ala'uddin in order to save the city and its people, she stabs him to death and both die together on the funeral pyre.

Neither Pavie's French translation nor Roussel's opera, both now largely forgotten, made Padmavati's story, so famous in India, famous in Europe, too. Why not? Orientalists carried news and often physical manuscripts of "Oriental" texts to Europe, and it was the curiosity they aroused about "Oriental literatures" that had made the idea of world literature thinkable in the first place.[2] Yet too many obstacles stood in the way of recognizing many of these works "*as* literature" (Damrosch 2003: 6).[3] Thanks to enterprising book importers, many *more* books in Indian languages circulated in nineteenth-century Europe than do now, yet apart from very few exceptions these books remained what I call an "absent presence:" physically there in library repositories, but absent, even when translated, from the readers' and critics' imagination of world literature (Orsini 2020c). In other words, the migration of books per se is not enough if mental categories

East of Delhi. Francesca Orsini, Oxford University Press. © Oxford University Press 2023.
DOI: 10.1093/oso/9780197658291.003.0001

make texts invisible as literature.[4] This problem of mental categories was not confined to Europe. Even within South Asia, particularly as fundamental categories of language, literature, and religion were reformulated in the context of colonial modernity, the earlier texts of the Padmavati story became problematic.

The oldest version of the Padmavati story is a sumptuous and accomplished vernacular romance in verse that combines a love quest with a martial narrative. It was written around 1540 by the Sufi poet Malik Muhammad Jayasi in the small town (or *qasba*) of Jais in northern India, in a language that he called Hindi.[5] As Jayasi tells it, when Prince Ratansen of Chittor in Rajasthan hears from a wise parrot about the beautiful and accomplished Princess Padmavati, who is a "lotus woman" (*padminī*) or a woman of the most excellent kind, in faraway Lanka (Sri Lanka), he becomes a yogi ascetic and leaves home on a quest for her. After undergoing several trials and tests, Ratansen becomes indeed worthy of Padmavati and they marry. But further trials await him on the way home and in Chittor, where Padmavati and Ratansen's first wife, whom he had left behind, quarrel spectacularly. The Delhi Sultan Ala'uddin hears of Padmavati's beauty and decides to besiege Chittor in order to seize her—this forms the second part of Jayasi's narrative, which combines and adapts historical elements (Sreenivasan 2007). When Ratansen is tricked and imprisoned by Ala'uddin, Padmavati calls upon two valiant subordinate warriors, Gora and Badal, who free Ratansen but die fighting. Ratansen himself is killed by a rival Rajput king. When Ala'uddin finally enters Chittor to capture Padmavati, only dust awaits him—she has immolated herself with Ratansen's first wife on his funeral pyre. Jayasi's *Padmāvat* is a wonderfully rich and dense work. Jayasi uses the common vernacular stanzaic form of verse tales (*kathas*; see Chapter 2) but embellishes it with poetic set pieces, spirited dialogues, and a dense web of metaphors to encode both the quest and the martial narrative in order to convey both spiritual and didactic meanings (de Bruijn 2012; Behl 2012a).

Jayasi's *Padmāvat* was well-known and admired in India in the early modern period and circulated widely in re-creations and translations into several Indian languages as well as Persian (see Sreenivasan 2007; Chapter 2 in this volume). But for Orientalists and colonial administrators, religion (alongside caste) was the fundamental category of identity in South Asia.[6] So Jayasi puzzled modern scholars: Why would a Sufi poet, a Muslim, write *in Hindi* (rather than in Persian or Urdu) and favor Hindu Rajput heroes over the Muslim Sultan of Delhi? For the towering colonial linguist and scholar-administrator George A. Grierson (1889: 18, emphasis added), who first brought Jayasi's *Padmāvat* within the purview of Hindi literary history, the work stood "as a conspicuous, and almost solitary, example of what the *Hindū mind* can do when freed from the trammels of literary and religious customs."[7] The greatest Indian Hindi literary historian, Ramchandra Shukla ([1929] 1988: 71, emphasis added), praised Jayasi because, like other Sufi poets of Avadhi romances, "*though a Muslim* he told *Hindu stories in the speech of the Hindus* and with full empathy; he set his liberal heart in perfect tune with the touching realities of their lives" and strove to remove any estrangement between "Hindu and Muslim hearts" by laying them simply before one another (see also Chapter 5). Underlying this warm praise lie strong assumptions about language, authorial intention, and "birth determinism," which held that a Muslim-born poet in Hindi must be "choosing" this language and tale with a specific motivation, like that of overcoming religious fault lines and promoting social harmony, because Hindi and a "Hindu" tale naturally "belong" to Hindus.[8]

In a similar vein, although Pavie knew and acknowledged Jayasi's as the earlier and more extensive text, the one he chose to translate was a later, shorter, and simpler version that cut out the quest and concentrated on the Rajput heroics of Gora and Badal against the mighty Sultan Ala'uddin—a version in which, by the way, Ratansen is ready to compromise with the Sultan and let him become Padmavati's "brother." Written around 1623 in a "mixed Hindoo provincial" language that Pavie (1865: 7n) identified as Rajasthani, Jatmal's text appeared to him more authentic.[9] The story, a legend of "Rajput valour," "belonged" more, in Pavie's eyes, to the Hindu Jatmal than to the Muslim Jayasi, who in order to know the story must have been a "Hindu convert to Islam" who only borrowed it.[10] Colonial ethnic categories inform Pavie's characterization of languages, too. Jatmal's language is one of "people who know better how to fight than how to narrate; energy replaces delicacy and the choice of words; the crude and harsh patois of the mountain clans has replaced the perfect speech [= Sanskrit] of the Brahmans. Though unformed this patois may be, it is worthy of respect" (Pavie 1865: 7).

Unlike other early Hindi authors such as Kabir and Mirabai, whose poems now appear in the *Norton Anthology of World Literature* (Puchner et al. 2018), or Tulsidas's Hindi retelling of the *Ramayana*, the *Rāmcharitmānas*, Jayasi's (1995) *Padmāvat* has even now failed to "enter world literature." Grierson's own unfinished translation—completed by A. G. Shirreff (1944) of the Indian Civil Service—has not found literary readers, and the only other modern translation is into Italian (Jayasi 1995). Why so? Is it because the words and works of Kabir, Mirabai, and Tulsidas, translated over and over by many hands, speak more directly to modern devotional or radical sensibilities? Or because short song-poems (like short stories) are easier to anthologize than long and elaborate romances? Or because the single and incomplete Grierson-Shirreff translation is almost unreadable, whereas there are eleven complete English translations of the *Rāmcharitmānas* to choose from?[11]

There are other puzzles, too. Many manuscripts of Jayasi's *Padmāvat* exist, in different scripts, and it was translated into Persian (and later Urdu) several times. But although an early seventeenth-century Persian editor called him the "chief of the poets" (*malik al-shuʿarā*), an appellative usually reserved for the imperial poet laureate, Jayasi is nowhere mentioned in the biographical dictionaries of either poets or Sufis—only in a few local histories.[12] What does this silence of the Persian archive tell us about the circulation of texts across scripts, languages, and audiences, and about the "technologies of recognition" of early modern literary archives? If ethnoreligious and monolingual understandings of identity, language, literature, and script are problematic, what we need, as I will argue in this book, is a different approach altogether.

Located and Multilingual

The questions arising from the early circulation yet patchy recognition of Jayasi's *Padmāvat*, from the friction in modern literary histories between the text's language and content and the author's religious identity, and from its invisibility within world literature take us to the core of this book. Its basic proposition is that in order to properly *see* this work and others like it, to account for their power and significance, but also more broadly to appreciate the life of literature in regions of the world that have long been multilingual—not only India but also Latin America, Italy, the Balkans, the Caucasus, Central Asia, the Middle East, Africa . . . indeed, most of the world!—we need to challenge ethnolinguistic categories that align script, language, community, and nation and ignore the multilingualism inherent in people, places, and texts. And we need to turn world literature, with its technologies of recognition, on its head.

What we need instead, this book suggests, is an approach that is both located and multilingual. Location means not simply a geographical, historical, or cultural context but also a position, an orientation, a necessarily partial and particular perspective, a standpoint from which one inhabits and views the world. In other words, in this book Purab, the region east of Delhi (hence its name, "East") in the north Indian Gangetic plains later better known as Awadh, is not another macro-category, nor is it a region as a bounded territory, or an "ecology" with a set of characteristics, but a standpoint from which to consider the different scales and ecologies at work *in the same space* and, often, *in the same person and text.*[13]

Following Doreen Massey's ([2005] 2012: 9) understanding, a located approach views space as "the product of interrelations; as constituted through interactions, from the immensity of the global to the intimately tiny." Massey asks us to consider space "as the sphere of the possibility of the existence of multiplicity in the sense of contemporaneous plurality; as the sphere in which distinct trajectories coexist; as the sphere therefore of coexisting heterogeneity." For her, space and plurality are co-constitutive: "Without space, no multiplicity; without multiplicity, no space" (9). To apply this understanding to literature means that, even if the texts and stories we have are limited, and some are more powerful or prominent than others, a located approach will always look for plurality and ask: What *other* stories and *other* gazes are there, and what other stories and actors does *this* story make invisible? In Chapter 3, I go to the small town of Kara to look for the Hindi devotional saint-poet Malukdas, and discover the nearby tomb of a much earlier Sufi saint, then a Persian hagiography about him, and an Urdu local history. Kara becomes a "multilingual local," where "local" as a noun refers to a locale. As I show, a located approach that shifts back and forth between these different language texts and the geographical site where they were composed opens up our imagination and alerts us to dialogic qualities and multilingual traces in the texts that we would otherwise miss.

A located approach is particularly important for world literature as the new, expanded version of the field of comparative literature that seeks to shed its Eurocentric past. "For any given observer," David Damrosch (2003: 27) argued in *What Is World Literature?*, "even a genuinely global perspective remains a perspective *from somewhere*, and global patterns of the circulation of world literature take shape in their local manifestations." Yet in world-system or field theories like those of Pascale Casanova's ([1999] 2004) *The World Republic of Letters* or the Warwick Research Collective's *Combined and Uneven Development* (2015), and in approaches that focus on "global" circulation, this important insight gets forgotten or sidelined. Too quick to assert that literature has indeed been assimilated into universal categories, a global system of value, and a single global market, world literature acquires an objective reality, like a map spread out before our eyes, an epiphenomenon of the objective history of globalization. Yet both the single map and its implicit bird's-eye view from nowhere are a fiction, a variety of "one-world thinking" that we should be suspicious of, or at least cautious about.[14] In such models, those sitting in the putative centers on the world literary map appear implicitly endowed with a better or wider field of vision, as if they were standing on a hill: "*They* can recognize literary value and bestow recognition, and *they* are implicitly more 'universal,' worldly or innovative than their counterparts in the so-called literary peripheries" (Orsini and Zecchini 2019: 2). In fact, this book argues, their view (and their literary taste) is as located and partial as that of others elsewhere, often *more* partial because less curious and less aware of its own biases and limitations. They think they know, but they don't know what they don't know. A located approach eschews the easy binary of local vs. global in which the world is always elsewhere, wholly stacked on the side of the global, and where the distant gaze of editors and critics at the "center" determines who and what is or is not "world."[15] Moreover, unlike other approaches to world literature, a located approach believes in the necessary incompleteness of any account and neither wishes nor aims for totality.[16]

The corollary to the notion of the "multilingual local" is what I call "significant geographies." Unlike "world" or "globe"—singular terms that tend to unify and assimilate—"significant geographies" suggests that for each text, story, individual, or group, the world actually consists of a number of crisscrossing geographies that are significant *to them*, whether these geographies are real or imaginative (see Laachir, Marzagora, and Orsini 2018). Moreover, whereas "world" and "globe" (or "global") make us assume that we already know what we are referring to without needing to describe their contours, "significant geographies" forces us to ask: What are the specific geographies, conceptual categories of space, toponyms, places, landscapes, and horizons that are significant to, say, Jayasi's *Padmāvat*, Tulsidas's *Rāmcharitmānas*, or Malukdas's hagiography? Though these poets lived within a two-hundred-kilometer radius and within a hundred years from each other and wrote in roughly the same language—and thus appear to be part of the same world—their "significant geographies" only partly overlap, as we shall see. In other words, the notion of significant geographies helps us disaggregate and demystify "world" and reintroduces agency in the equation: Which geographies matter *to whom* and *when*? We are back to Massey's "possibility of the existence of multiplicity in the sense of contemporaneous plurality."

Moreover, the fact that a person, a space, or a society has more than one language necessarily produces a plurality and heterogeneity of geographical imaginings. Given that each language, genre, and poetic idiom encodes particular ways of looking at the world, "significant geographies" makes us think about geography and space in ways that foreground literary mediation.[17] Though Urdu *ghazal* poetry and verse narratives, or *masnavis,* share the same language and may be composed or enjoyed by the same person, their imaginative geographic notions of "world" are quite different. The *ghazal* world is typically generic: the tavern, the desert, the alley leading to the beloved's house. "*Dunyā*, the word most commonly used to mean 'world,' often carries a connotation of lack; it is something which is simply worldly rather than eternal, like the divine," Fatima Burney (2019: 158) reminds us: "Accordingly, to be fully concerned with the world is to have lost sight of the ultimate and eternal truth(s) which go beyond the physical realm of perception."[18] By contrast, in *masnavis* the world is valorized as a realm of action. In historical *masnavis* commemorating campaigns or victories, toponyms and dates are often quite specific. Narrative (or "*dastan*-like;" Suvorova 2000) *masnavis* combine the tangible and the fantastic. They are quite able to incorporate local realia, but they also transport readers or listeners into parallel worlds of humans and supernatural beings, mixing distant toponyms of Islamic lands with those of Persian literature (Suvorova 2000; Pritchett 1991).[19] "Significant geographies" makes us think about the specific uses of spatial concepts and images: How do authors in India inscribe themselves within the Perso-Greek cosmology of the "seven climes," or in the cosmic time of the four ages of the world? What does a Mughal map do in a story like Puhakar's (Chapter 2) and in Malukdas's poem about how God created different people out of the same clay (Chapter 3)?

Finally, "significant geographies" (in the plural) highlights multiplicity, openness, and disjuncture and discourages easy technologies of recognition and complacent distant gazes. It makes us think about actual (and always limited) trajectories of circulation. Echoing Massey, we can think of world literature, the "immensity of the global," as a tapestry of crisscrossing significant geographies, a "coexisting heterogeneity" that never becomes a single totality. Each view of the world and of world literature, after all, makes some parts of them visible but *invisibilizes* others (another term that will recur in this book). One only needs to think of how Orientalists magnified Sanskrit while making Persian and Persianate literatures practically invisible within Indian literary history. Or of how in the early twentieth century a reorientation toward the East and the new literary geographies made visible by pan-Asianism de-emphasized India's long links with Central and West Asia. Or we may think of the competing geographies of Cold War literary networks, or the near-invisibility of non-Anglophone and -Francophone African and South Asian literatures in world literature today.

In comparative and world literature we are used to thinking of the movement across languages as always involving a spatial move and a crossing of boundaries (typically national ones), and of the relation between languages as strongly hierarchical. Moreover, literary histories typically focus on only one language and on what people *wrote* in that language, and primarily on "great works" or literary innovations. This regularly makes what they also spoke, sang, read, or studied in other languages drop out of focus. Moreover, translingual traffic is considered only in terms of (formal) translation, something that again fails to capture the many other ways in which multilingualism shapes literary cultures.

Instead, my located and multilingual approach explores the ways in which people and literature operate *ordinarily* across languages in the same multilingual location. It considers the hierarchies but also the aesthetics and affective power of languages and artistic forms, the meanings with which people endow them, and the world or worlds they imagine and to which they connect. The result is also a different kind of literary history, one that focuses on literary practices and multiple "communities of taste;" on the *transmission* of tastes and stories across languages and communities rather than the *translation* of texts; on genres that are locally significant; and on nonlinear narratives of change that trace realignments and new configurations rather than drastic epistemic and aesthetic breaks (Chapter 5). It is a comparative or world literature from the ground up, located and looking outward for connections rather than making sweeping global or transnational gestures. Let me draw out these points a little.

A multilingual literary history cannot be simply a process of adding different language texts and archives (Persian + Sanskrit + Hindi + Urdu, etc.), for this would not capture how people engage with literature within a multilingual society. Archives, even early modern ones, can be surprisingly monolingual and normative, so one must take them seriously but also challenge them for what they don't say and what they invisibilize. Persian and Urdu biographical dictionaries of poets and notable people (*tazkiras*) are a wonderful and rich archive, but their world is almost exclusively one of elite Muslims—Sayyids and shaikhs (Chapter 4). Moreover, *tazkiras* almost never mention or quote verses in the other languages in which poets composed (unless it is Persian for Urdu poets and vice versa), nor do they say if there were other poets composing in other languages in the city or court they describe.[20] If monolingual/national literary history (say, Italian or Russian) takes language as the subject of its narrative, multilingual literary history must refrain from doing so. Instead, it must consider the available range of languages (the "linguistic economy;" see below) at a given time and what people did with them. It must assess the relative importance (or "capital," to use Bourdieu's term) of languages, how the balance between them changed over time, and the written and aural access different groups had to each language.[21]

Then the multilingual literary historian must look at *individuals* and ask: What literary education or *habitus*, if any, did they get, and in which language? What *other* languages and traditions did they have command of or access to? What tastes did they cultivate, and with whom? Did multilingual poets mix poetic languages and tastes, or did they practice them separately, in parallel? Did they set up equivalences between tropes and poetic elements in different languages or not (Chapters 3 and 4)? And do their practices and tastes match their pronouncements (Chapter 5)?

Texts, in this approach, are the results of generic choices, acknowledged genealogies, and intertextual references, but also possibly of unacknowledged dialogism with other languages and archives.[22] It pays to be attentive to even the smallest traces of multilingualism within texts and to ask what they are traces of: Are they the products of chance, familiarity, interest, or something else? The material aspects of texts, even minute details of script, format, quality of paper, or illustration, can also point to significant historical shifts in taste and in the ambitions of patrons—as when Hindi tales got first written in codex format and illustrated—or pose interesting historical puzzles (Chapter 2).

As already discussed, and as this book itself shows, a *spatial* approach that explores and brings together textual production and literary practice in different languages by actors active in a single area produces a rich and textured literary history, whether or not the actors in question acknowledge one another. For example, while Purab did not become a center of Krishna devotionalism (or bhakti) in the sixteenth century, unlike Bengal or the Braj area, thanks to cross-over evidence from Persian and Hindi Sufi sources we now know that in Purab, too, singers, storytellers, and devotees sang and narrated Krishna's marvelous exploits before mixed audiences (see Orsini 2015b).

Paying attention to literary practices in different languages, spaces, and communities of taste also produces a heterogeneous sense of *historicity*, attentive not just to the different understandings of time and history within specific texts, genres, and repertoires but also to the overlap of old and new tastes. Such an approach is as attentive to continuities as to innovations and, e.g., explores whether literary innovations spread across languages (Chapter 4). In terms of continuity of taste, devotional bhakti poetry is arguably most striking: fifteenth-century Kabir and late sixteenth-century Tulsidas are still the most popular poets from the region and the most likely to figure in anthologies of world literature (see Hess 2015; Mehrotra 2011; Lutgendorf 1991).[23] But Kabir's once disputed poetic status (Chapter 3) shows that thinking of literary culture and history as comprising not one but several parallel layers helps us acknowledge that multiple value systems were (and are) involved. Perhaps the most problematic aspect of applying Pierre Bourdieu's model of fields to world literature is the insistence on the establishment of a single value of literary capital with universal recognition, a kind of global literary currency, which leaves little or no space for multiple systems of value and functions of literature.[24]

Let me now turn to the particular region in north India that is my location and standpoint in this book, delineate it in both space and time, and show how its linguistic economy changed over time. I chose it because it was a region where power remained contested and Persian did not acquire the hegemonic status it acquired at the Mughal court. I then argue that the multilingual and located approach I have sketched complements and helps correct current top-down and macrosystemic approaches to world literature.

Why Purab?

The region of Purab lies in the middle of the Indo-Gangetic plain, crossed by its great rivers (Ganges, Yamuna) and by long-distance trade routes that for centuries ran from Bengal all the way to Afghanistan. It extends in the north to the Tarai tract of southern Nepal, and in the south to the hills and ravines of Bundelkhand (see map of Purab/Awadh). The site of ancient empires, yet still densely wooded in the first half of the second millennium CE, the region takes its names from its location relative to the political center of Delhi and from the ancient Kosala capital of Ayodhya, which became known as Awadh in Persian sources, and Oudh in British colonial ones. Awadh was one of the *subahs*, or administrative provinces, of the Mughal Empire, but in this book I take a broader view to encompass the area where Avadhi was and is spoken.[25] In this more expansive sense, Awadh includes also the adjacent Mughal province of Allahabad and overlaps with the other historical name for the region, Purab, or "the East."[26]

A region of early Islamic conquest in the eleventh and twelfth centuries CE, Purab had many small towns (*qasbas*) but no large city (Wink 1990). The exception was Jaunpur, which was founded by a local governor who declared himself Sultan and started a dynasty that lasted for a century (1380–1480). In the fifteenth century the region was caught in the tussle between the Sharqi dynastic rulers of Jaunpur and the Lodi Sultans of Delhi, and later between the early Mughals and the Suris of Bihar. It was at this time, intriguingly, that some of the more sumptuous vernacular romances were composed and that the taste for illustrated books took hold (Chapter 2). Under the Mughals, the region was administered through the two provinces (*subahs*) of Awadh (i.e., Ayodhya) and Allahabad, as already mentioned. Banaras and its learned Brahmans enjoyed the patronage of high Mughal officials like the finance minister Todarmal and the general and governor Man Singh, whose palaces dominated the city, and pilgrimage and temple construction made it a wealthy town.[27] Already toward the end of the Delhi Sultanate, in the fifteenth century, but even more from the time of Emperor Akbar in the second half of the sixteenth, local Hindu service groups also began to learn and cultivate Persian as a language of education, opportunity, and culture. Craftsmen made up about a third of the urban population and must have provided a substantial audience for vernacular poetic gatherings of all kinds (see Chapter 3).

The *qasba* towns that dotted the region were garrisons and trade marts along trade routes that led from Bengal to Delhi and all the way north to Afghanistan, or to Agra and southwest toward Gujarat; horses, precious stones, slaves, perfumes, and fine cloth were among the commodities traded (Digby 2004). These towns were also administrative and religious outposts of the north Indian Sultanates (late twelfth to early sixteenth century), where Muslim religious and service families received lands as grants-in-aid to support their livelihood and to populate, develop, and control the territory.[28] Members of these families occupied local administrative positions and reproduced themselves culturally by teaching Persian to their children. While bearing the name of one's local *qasba* as part of one's own name (e.g., Amrohi, Bilgrami, Kakorvi, Khairabadi) gradually became a mark of distinction, ambitious individuals had to migrate in search of higher positions. Local Sultanate administrators and Sufi communities in the *qasbas* sponsored the first substantial works in the local vernacular (Chapter 2); they also cultivated a taste for vernacular songs and, later, for courtly poetry in Brajbhasha, which became the cosmopolitan poetic vernacular in the late sixteenth century. A biographical dictionary of poets from the *qasba* of Bilgram gives a clear sense of the shifts in poetic tastes (Chapter 4).

From the time of the north Indian Sultanates and throughout the Mughal period (sixteenth to eighteenth centuries CE), the *qasbas* were surrounded by a countryside largely controlled by armed chieftains in their mud forts. These Hindu as well as Afghan and Turk chieftains provided military labor to a succession of rulers, from the Sultans to the Mughals, and later still to the East India Company. Purbiya (i.e., from Purab) soldier-cultivators remained famous until the great Rebellion of 1857 (Kolff 2002). These rural chieftains resisted imperial extraction and subordination whenever they could, and competed and clashed with each other. Sufis who were given land grants often found themselves at the receiving end of the chieftains' raids, Mughal sources report (Alam 1991).

Muslim rural chieftains, also called "rajas," were an ethnically and linguistically heterogeneous lot: Turk, Afghan, Mughal, and Indian. Hindu chieftains, their narratives recount, remained largely mobile until the seventeenth century; in other words, they were unable to retain hold of a tract as their homeland. Allochthonous origin often bolstered claims to high status anyway, and some Rajput groups traced their entry into the area to the time of the Delhi Sultanate conquest (Bennett 1870: 83). Unlike the Rajputs of north-western India, Awadh Rajputs were not co-opted into the Mughal Empire as military-administrative officials (*mansabdars*) and did not rise in the imperial ranks or become connected to the imperial house, though they occasionally served in the Mughal armies. Significantly, they did not cultivate Persian. Only in the general increase of wealth in the Mughal heyday were they able to garner enough strength to settle and set up small local courts, for which they began to employ poets of courtly Hindi (Brajbhasha) alongside bards-cum-genealogists (Chapter 4).

Power in the region therefore remained contested and was never completely centralized, nor were there powerful local dynasties or military clans to be subdued and incorporated at a high level, as was the case in Rajasthan. It was perhaps for this reason that the Sultanate and Mughal imperial language of Persian did not become completely hegemonic, as it did in the Mughal centers. One consequence of this lack of Persian hegemony was precisely a thriving multilingual literary culture, for the Persophone elite also cultivated poetic and musical tastes in the vernacular. Paradoxically from the point of view of modern literary histories, it was Sufis who first composed literary texts in Hindavi in the late fourteenth century (Chapter 2), and it was Sultans, their local notables, and later Mughal grandees who first patronized local Brajbhasha poets like Narhari and Gang (Chapter 4) (see Busch 2011).

The lack of centralization and the *qasba*-rural dynamics make Purab an ideal case to observe the diffuse, on-the-ground workings of literature in a multilingual, multiethnic, and multireligious society, unlike imperial or local courts, where courtly culture becomes synonymous with the culture at large. For the point of this book is not to argue about a specific Purbi or Awadhi regional identity, and Awadh as a distinct political entity emerged only in the eighteenth century.[29] Rather, Purab/Awadh highlights the "multiplicity of stories and trajectories" (Massey): of *qasba* literati and state officials, craftsmen, and holy men; of urban merchants, rural landlords, strongmen, and armed peasants who doubled as foot soldiers; of rivers and routes, fields and ponds, fairs and festivals. Whether people primarily identified as Purbi or as Awadhi is not the point; the point is to map the multilingual world out of which modern north India grew with its specific linguistic identities.

Toward the end of the Sultanate period, the first radical, vernacular voices of saint-poets (called Sants in Hindi) Kabir and Raidas burst upon the city of Banaras. Banaras had long been a center of Sanskrit Brahmanical scholarship, which received a fresh wave of patronage from patrons at the Mughal court, and it was here that Tulsidas, the poet of the devotional Hindi Ramayana, moved from Ayodhya in the late sixteenth century. Later Sants in the seventeenth and eighteenth centuries founded establishments in the countryside and in the *qasbas* (Chapter 3). Devotional Sant poetry is important to our story because it assembled large "communities of taste" and of worship across social divides; it also represents a substantial share of poetic practice in the region.

With the post-Mughal state of Awadh (or Oudh, as it was often spelled in English), which lasted a little over a century, from 1732 to 1856, and whose borders constantly shifted, the region and its glittering capital Lucknow became a center of Urdu literary culture, music, theater, and crafts. Indeed, Awadh has become identified with Lucknow under the Nawabs, its courtesans, polite sociability, and lively street culture—an identification heavily laden with nostalgia, with the result that other, older cultural layers (Hindavi, Brajbhasha) have become largely invisible (Chapter 5). In parallel with Lucknow, Banaras also became a semi-autonomous polity and a thriving commercial and literary center, with merchants and religious establishments competing with the rajas as significant patrons (see Dalmia 1997). Unlike Lucknow, the main poetic language in Banaras was Brajbhasha (and later modern Hindi) but also Bhojpuri, whose vibrant oral literature circulated across the region east of Banaras. Whereas the two cities epitomize very different cultures—Urdu and Muslim Lucknow and Hindu and Sanskrit/Hindi Banaras—Chapter 5 argues that culturally there was much that they shared.

While modern Hindi and Urdu languages and literatures were first promoted and codified in the early nineteenth century in colonial Calcutta, at Fort William College, for the sake of East India Company recruits, it was in the cities of Awadh—Lucknow, Banaras, Kanpur, and Allahabad—that Urdu and Hindi print cultures exploded later in the nineteenth century (Chapter 5). Their many schools and colleges attracted students and teachers—hence readers—in large numbers from the nearby *qasbas* and villages, while magazines, publishers, and associations gathered talented writers and established literary networks running all the way from Calcutta to Delhi and beyond. The Lucknow publisher Naval Kishore, whose paper mill was the biggest industrial concern in the region, published books in at least nine languages and dispatched them as far as Europe and Iran (see Stark 2007). Urdu remained the primary print language in the nineteenth century for a growing, heterogeneous, and cosmopolitan middle class, while English replaced Persian as the language of the higher echelons of colonial administration, and hence of higher education and professional mobility. Awadh was rocked by the Great Rebellion of 1857, which broke out in the Kanpur cantonment, had Lucknow (which the East India Company had taken over in 1856, exiling the last king to Calcutta) as one of its epicenters, and saw a landowner from an old Purbiya family in rural Bhojpur become a popular leader. Like Delhi, Lucknow suffered and was transformed in the repression that followed, though it remained a center of Urdu literature, print culture, and politics (see Talwar Oldenburg 1984; Dubrow 2018; Sikander 2021). Allahabad became the regional colonial capital and a growing center of English education, print, and Anglicized public culture; it was here, while working at the *Pioneer* newspaper, that Rudyard Kipling wrote *Plain Tales from the Hills* (1888), gazing back upon life in the Punjab and Simla.

Awadh was central to nationalist politics, whether of urban associations or of rural peasant protests like the no-rent movement of 1919–1920. The Nehru family resided in Allahabad, and so did several other leaders of the Indian National Congress, while Banaras and Kanpur became socialist and communist strongholds. It was in Banaras and Allahabad that the Hindi movement emerged in the 1870s, with its strong critique of Urdu as a language "alien" to Indian culture. It was also in Banaras, Lucknow, and Allahabad that scholars connected with literary associations and the new colleges and universities wrote the first literary histories of Hindi and Urdu, which became the cornerstone of the literary curriculum (Chapter 5). Yet Awadh—or rather the United Provinces of Agra and Oudh, as it was renamed in 1902—was not the presidency cities of Calcutta or Bombay but "upcountry." Local elites and older tastes were not swept away by English education. Rather, they developed their own distinct amalgams of old and new literary tastes, even as they looked to literary developments and activities in Bengal as models. Some *qasbas* printed their own newspapers and were important nodes of Muslim political activism (see Robinson 1974; Rahman 2015; Khan Mahmudabad 2020; Robb 2021). They also continued to produce generations of fine Urdu poets, many of whom, like Majrooh Sultanpuri and Kaifi Azmi, would later find fame in Bombay as versatile film lyricists. For this reason, Chapter 5 will argue, Awadh provides a useful setting to assess the impact of colonial culture in the subcontinent beyond the presidency capitals.

Independence and Partition in 1947 decimated the Muslim service and landed elites, who migrated in large numbers to Pakistan and became part of the new administrative elite there. In what now became eastern Uttar Pradesh, or U.P., their position was further weakened by the Abolition of Zamindari Act of 1950—which features prominently in Vikram Seth's novel *A Suitable Boy* (1993). Yet whereas in Seth's novel—set in a university town that partly resembles Allahabad—it is the Anglophone middle class that inherits the nation, the region in the 1950s had a thriving Hindi literary culture of magazines, publishers, and poets. Though this goes beyond the scope of this book, the heated debates within Hindi circles in Allahabad and Banaras between leftist Progressives and more liberal Experimentalists grafted themselves on competing Cold War internationalisms and reflected competing versions of world literature (see Orsini 2022a).

Qasbas and the culture of Nawabi Lucknow continued to loom large in the cultural imagination as sites of nostalgia for a lost Urdu and Persianate world. While Urdu was disempowered in post-Independence U.P., as in the rest of India, Hindi magazines testify to their readers' continued familiarity with and interest in Urdu fiction and poetry. With time, Hindi writers gravitated toward Delhi (a few to Bombay), and Allahabad, Banaras, and Lucknow became provincial centers, each with its distinctive cultural identity, local intelligentsia, and active student culture and politics. In the current metro-centric Indian public imagination, though, even cities with over a million inhabitants, like Allahabad and Banaras, count as "small towns," while the Awadh countryside appears in Hindi cinema largely as a "badland," the backdrop for caste- and violence-ridden films.

The Linguistic Economy in the Region

The linguistic economy of north India in the early modern period can be summarily called one of multiple diglossia, with several high languages (Persian, Sanskrit, Arabic) and one undifferentiated vernacular.[30] A simplified form of Persian also seems to have been a spoken lingua franca, while individuals and groups maintained their own spoken languages (e.g., "Turki") for generations (see Karomat 2014; Péri 2017). Literacy was limited, and education and the *written* cultivation of poetry were restricted to only a few administrative and religious professionals, teachers, and merchants and traders, usually men (Chapter 4).

Persian was the backbone of education and of Sufi textuality, and Persian authors from the region date back to the fourteenth century (Hadi 1995; Rizvi 1983).[31] Reading the Qur'an was part of primary education for Muslims, and some Arabic was part of common prayers and rituals (and could thus be heard and overheard), but knowledge of Arabic poetry and other forms of textuality was much more limited, though it experienced a revival in the eighteenth and nineteenth centuries (see Leese 2019). It has been difficult to find evidence of widespread cultivation of Sanskrit in Purab after the "Islamic conquest," but this might be more because this has been the traditional cut-off point for scholarship, apart from that on the city of Banaras. There is at least one Sanskrit narrative of King David and Bathsheba, the *Sulaimanacharitra* (ca. 1500), written for a Sultanate Lodi patron in the region (see Minkowski 2006; Malla 2015), and references to Sanskrit education and texts crop up regularly in autobiographical accounts by Brahman and other authors, suggesting that Sanskrit must have been more current than we know.[32]

The vernacular was simply called "Indian" (*hindi, hindavi*) in Persian sources, and "speech" (*bhakha,* i.e., *bhasha*) in the others, and it was written in whatever script one had learned or was familiar with, whether Persian (or Perso-Arabic), Nagari (or Devanagari), or the cursive Kaithi used by local scribes (Chapter 2). The generic terms *bhakha* and "Hindavi" seem to have denoted not just a lack of grammatical interest toward the vernacular but also a continuum of circulation, so that vernacular songs and tales could travel and be understood across the whole of north India. Oral performers and performance contexts were crucial in making a flexible vernacular accessible across north India. Though "eastern" and "western" (i.e., Rajasthani and Punjabi) manuscript recensions of Kabir's songs and poems vary greatly, as performers and scribes inverted, added, or subtracted lines and replaced terms, the fact that these variants are *not* linguistic suggests that their language was not too local to require changing (see Vaudeville 1974; Callewaert and Lath 1989; Callewaert, Sharma, and Taillieu 2000; Bangha 2010a).

To avoid confusing this early nomenclature with modern Hindi (which is grammatically Khari Boli, the mixed speech of the area around Delhi), I will use Hindavi for the umbrella language that was used in early modern vernacular, including Avadhi, texts. When around 1500 a koine based on a vernacular further west, from the Braj area between Agra and Delhi, became a distinct poetic idiom that found favor at courts and in devotional circles alike, it acquired a separate name, Brajbhasha. Brajbhasha became a "cosmopolitan vernacular" (Pollock 1998a), with a standard poetic language that needed to be properly learned through manuals and teachers, and eastern poets started writing it, too (see Busch 2011).[33] Even a devotional poet like Tulsidas who had been writing in Avadhi started to compose songs and poems in Brajbhasha.[34]

The popularity in the eighteenth century of another idiom of vernacular poetry, Rekhta, a kind of Persianate poetry in Khari Boli, helped crystallize a separate linguistic identity for what became known as Urdu in the nineteenth century. By then the dominant public vernacular of the region, Urdu became the official language of the courts and the lower echelons of the East India Company administration in the North-Western Provinces in 1835.

Meanwhile, new ideas of natural language inspired by European knowledge systems coalesced separate and mutually exclusive clusters of script-language-community for Urdu (i.e., Persian-Urdu-Muslims) and Hindi (Nagari-Hindi-Hindus) that went against the grain of this multiscriptual and multilingual world. Discourses and literary histories based on these clusters traced Hindi and Urdu as the languages of Hindus and Muslims *from the earliest beginnings*, while implicitly or explicitly accusing the other language of being a latecomer. A key document of the Hindi movement, Madan Mohan Malaviya's (1897: 1) *Court Characters and Primary Education in the N.-W. P. and Oudh*, begins with the statement, "When the Muhammadans came to India, Hindi was the vernacular of Hindustan, and the Nagri character, or its variations, the medium through which all business was carried on." By contrast, Urdu scholar Hafiz Mahmud Sherani viewed early occurrences of Hindavi words and phrases in Persian texts as evidence of the development of Urdu as a *Muslim* language (Chapter 5). The Hindi-Urdu controversy is a textbook case of the intractability of language debates and has generated copious scholarship.[35] Although the arguments are formulated in "objective" terms of linguistic traits and historical evidence, each position produces its own partial and selective view of the literary past, excluding large swaths of literary production and ignoring the evidence of multilingual practices and tastes. For, in David Lelyveld's (1993: 202) deft formulation, "People did not have languages; they had linguistic repertoires that varied even within a single household, let alone the marketplace, school, temple, court, or devotional circle. These codes of linguistic behaviour took on the same characteristics of hierarchy that other sorts of human interaction did."

In order to understand how multilingualism works in practice, rather than taking languages as stable signifiers and subjects of history ("the history of Hindi," "English came," etc.), it is therefore more useful to think about what people do *with* languages. One way of looking at it is to consider a multilingual individual's linguistic repertoires as just "language" or interlanguage. This underlines the way individuals seamlessly shift between repertoires and that, in practice, different repertoires are "someone's language." It is a position sometimes taken by linguists or by those who emphasize just how ordinary multilingualism was and is—e.g., the fact that vegetable sellers, rickshaw drivers, religious preachers, etc. adapt their pitch or use an interlanguage with their customers or audience without a second thought. Ganesh Devy (1999: 185) has called it "translating consciousness," and has argued that "in India several languages are simultaneously used by language communities as if these languages formed a continuous spectrum of signs and significance." Yet interlanguage performance does not rule out the consciousness of languages as distinct, and of different languages and repertoires as each carrying their own aesthetics—an awareness that partly comes with education and cultivation.

This discussion of languages raises four points that are relevant for a multilingual literary history. First, education involved learning literary texts and acquiring familiarity with poetic idioms, which became part of one's body till they "stayed in the throat" (as the Hindi/Sanskrit expression *kaṇṭhastha* goes); a multilingual education therefore entailed stacking up literary tastes, as Bhanupratap Tiwari's autobiography in Chapter 4 shows: Persian and Urdu poetry, Brajbhasha, Avadhi, and Sanskrit. But did people who acquired multiple literary tastes mix them or not? This is an important question for a multilingual literary culture, and as we shall see, the Sufi writers of Avadhi romances in Chapter 2, the Sants in Chapter 3, and Persophone intellectuals in Chapter 4 all provide different answers.

Second, if we switch from a focus on people to one on spaces, even before the coming of loudspeakers, public and domestic spaces and sites of worship and leisure were saturated with sounds and voices—from Sanskrit chanting to the Arabic call for prayer, from devotional circles singing in the vernacular to the songs and tales of itinerant performers, poetry competitions, etc. Indeed, "making sound and hearing or listening to music, songs, speeches, sermons, and stories have been equally constitutive of South Asian social and cultural history" (Orsini and Schofield 2015: 1). Emphasizing oral performance and transmission blurs the boundaries between literature and orature (or oral literature), at least at the point of reception.[36] It shows that, given the wide currency of "oral-literate" genres like tales (Chapter 2) and songs (Chapter 3), script and literacy were only partial obstacles to access and to the circulation of tastes and tropes across languages and "socio-textual communities" (Pollock). It was precisely these oral-literate genres that fed the boom of commercial publishing and theater in the second half of the nineteenth century, proof of the resilience and indeed modernity of orature even after written literatures went their separate ways (see Orsini 2009). Conversely, even those unschooled in Sanskrit or Persian would have been aware of and have picked up words or phrases in these languages—much as is the case with English now—even without acquiring full command over them. This explains verses in "quasi-Sanskrit" (called *sahaskritī*) or the "quasi-Persian" songs of the Sants, which sound like Persian without adhering to Persian grammar or prosody (Chapter 3).[37] *Why* poet-singers engaged in these language performances is another question worth asking. Overhearing is important also because it forces us to think of the reach of texts or performances beyond their intended audiences. Particularly for tales, songs, and ritual recitations in public spaces, others could stand by and listen, too.

Third, we may expect a multilingual literary culture like that of Purab to be overflowing with translations, but this is actually not the case. While translation plays a crucial symbolic role in comparative and world literature, within this multilingual literary culture there was arguably considerable poetic traffic, but translations took place only under special conditions (see Orsini 2019b).[38] In this situation of prolonged and intense language contact (so intense that "contact" does not seem the right word, and "coexistence" may be better), words were absorbed across languages—many everyday terms in Hindi come from Persian or even Arabic—but their use in poetic idioms tended to be more conscious and should count as "marked." I will distinguish in this book between poetic *idioms* (Brajbhasha, Persian, Rekhta/Urdu), i.e., used according to specific meter and poetics, and linguistic *registers*, which denote a more limited employment of terms, tropes, and phrases (Chapters 3 and 4).[39]

Finally, and this goes back to the emphasis on multilingualism as pervading bodies and spaces, familiarity and even preference for aesthetic tastes persisted even when competitive language ideologies "othered" them—whether it was Urdu *ghazal* poetry among Hindi readers, or Krishna songs among Muslims. This contradiction between the force of ideology and the pull of aesthetic taste is evident not just in historical figures like Bharatendu Harishchandra (Chapter 5) but also in fictional characters like Topi's grandmother in Rahi Masoom Raza's (1969, 2005) Hindi novel *Ṭopī Śuklā*, who hates Muslims but loves Persian poetry. To keep sight of this contradiction is very important. In post-Independence India, the dialogic and multilingual religious and literary culture of Purab/Awadh is usually called "Ganga-Jamni culture," from the two rivers that run through it and meet at Allahabad (the ancient Prayag, or Prayagraj under the recent dispensation). This "composite culture" (the other term used) stands for a spirit of peaceful coexistence that has overtones and mystifications, similar to the *convivencia* in medieval Spain. But just as unpacking the different elements of multilingualism within the Christian and Muslim polities of medieval Spain—as Maria-Àngeles Gallego (2003) has done—helps demystify the *convivencia,* unpacking the multilingual literary culture of early modern Purab and colonial Awadh helps us avoid the pitfalls of either positing Hindus and Muslims as eternal strangers and enemies or assuming that a plurality of languages and tastes leads to pluralism as an attitude.[40] Culture, as Antonio Gramsci, Raymond Williams, and Stuart Hall taught us, is always a domain of struggle, though it is not a domain of struggle *alone*. For this reason, in this book I rather take Mikhail Bakhtin's (1986, 1992) notion of dialogism as a guide. Thinking of languages and utterances as dialogic stops us from thinking that they "belong" to any particular group. It also means paying close attention to how different participants accent and re-accent utterances, and whether or not they acknowledge their antecedents and interlocutors.

One final point. At first glance, the multiple diglossia of Purab matches Sheldon Pollock's definition of cosmopolitan and vernacular.[41] Pollock narrates the relationship between the two in terms of *vernacularization*, in which the vernacular becomes literary by taking on the apparatus of the cosmopolitan language. After all, Brajbhasha and Urdu did become "cosmopolitan vernaculars" when they adopted Sanskrit and Persian poetry and poetics. Yet while Pollock plots the relationship between cosmopolitan and vernacular in terms of a historical zero-sum game, with the vernacular language and literature gradually taking the place of the cosmopolitan, in Purab as in other parts of the world the story is arguably one not of substitution but of continuing and in fact expanding multilingualism. Thus, the expansion of Hindavi and Brajbhasha in religious, urban, and courtly circles in the fifteenth and sixteenth centuries was matched by the parallel geographical dissemination and rooting of Persian (its "provincialization") and by its social expansion after it became the administrative language of the Mughal Empire.[42] Sanskrit, too, received a fillip from Mughal and other patronage, as we have seen.

It is possible to take the polarity and hierarchy between cosmopolitan and vernacular too far, however. In practice we know that cosmopolitan languages were not always used for their "universal reach;" they could also work to obscure communication and as coterie languages (e.g., Irish Latin), for local practices, or to score local points and in local polities (see Kapadia 2018). Conversely, literary vernaculars such as Brajbhasha and Rekhta/Urdu seem to have been cosmopolitan from the start and circulated across polities over wide geographic areas.[43] Indeed, the programmatic statements prefacing medieval vernacular translations speak of dissemination, not localization (Kabir's "flowing water" of Hindi vs. the stagnant "well water" of Sanskrit). Pankaj Jha's (2019) recent study of the fifteenth-century polymath Vidyapati, who composed works in Sanskrit, Avahatta, and Maithili, traces Vidyapati's calibrated choices of language and genre for his multilingual audience.

The aesthetics and affective power of the vernacular(s) undercut the language hierarchy, too. Shantanu Phukan (2001) has shown that Hindavi songs sounded particularly "sweet" and pregnant with emotions to Persophone ears. Some Persian Sufi texts set up equivalences between Arabic, Persian, and Hindi poetic thoughts (through the phrase *dar īn ma'ni,* "with the same meaning" or "i.e.") (see Orsini 2014a), while proficiency in Brajbhasha poetry and poetics was proudly displayed by Awadh Persophone elites till the eighteenth century (Chapter 4).

In order to avoid reifying "cosmopolitan" and "vernacular" and tying them to specific cultural and political orientations that in many cases would be anachronistic, I reserve these terms for languages—while remaining mindful of the range of registers within each of them (Shankar 2012). I then also use "cosmopolitan" and "local" as locations and orientations.[44] For the same reason, I prefer to use "diglossia" only when a clear hierarchy is involved, and "multilingualism" otherwise. Indeed, in such complex contexts avoiding generalizations is imperative. To say that "every language is heteroglossic" or that "everyone was multilingual" or that Persian and Sanskrit were cosmopolitan and Hindavi vernacular/local does not help beyond a point. Rather, we need to look for clues about how people understood and used the different languages.

But Is This World Literature?

But is this world literature? you will wonder. The way we conceptualize world literature, I always think, has much to do with the way we view the world. Does "world" mean only those people or texts that travel or have a cosmopolitan, global vision even without traveling? Or is "world," to paraphrase Ngũgĩ wa Thiong'o's (1993) definition of "center," always "from here," i.e., it always includes the subject and is always located? One of the hurdles in opening up comparative literature into world literature has been that early models and theorizations were too preoccupied with demarcating the territory of what world literature is and what it is not: "[W]orld literature cannot be literature, bigger; what we are already doing, just more of it. It has to be different," was Franco Moretti's (2000: 2) opening salvo. But if Moretti rightly posited that "world literature is not an object, it is a *problem*" (55), the anxiety of coping with what seems an impossibly large body of material quickly led to models that sought to *contain* and manage world literature, falling back on a familiar economic narrative of global expansion and unification.[45] In the process, complexity, disjuncture, and texture were sacrificed to clarity and manageability. As always, the question has to be *Qui prodest?* Who gains by this move?

Paradoxically, while world literature is supposedly interested in and open to literatures beyond Europe and the Americas, so far it has actually recognized only those that correspond to its own categories (the novel, the lyric, modernism) or that clearly speak to the "world" because of their expansive, transnational imagination (e.g., Walkowitz 2015; Ganguly 2016). That these literatures speak to world literature is unmistakable, but what about the rest? What if it uses different genres and voices other concerns, or simply fails to reach the so-called world reader at the center? Where has the openness, the "multiplicity of stories and trajectories" gone? Ah, but world literature cannot be the *totality* of literature in the world, is the trenchant reply.

Here world literature can learn from other disciplines that have engaged with the "problem" of the world, like anthropology and history. We can learn from the efforts of global historians to discard "container-thinking" and *explore* spatial entities (in my case, Awadh) rather than presuming fixed ones (Conrad 2016: 136).[46] As Sebastian Conrad puts it, "[G]lobal histories experiment with alternative notions of space. They typically do not take political or cultural units—nation-states, empires, civilizations—as their points of departure" (65). One of their strategies is to trace or "follow" the trajectories of circulation of an object—in the case of literature, a trope, text, or genre—along its significant geographies, without a priori privileging one network (the transnational) or one center as "the" center of "the world." This kind of work has indeed been done in literary studies, too, particularly for genres like the *qasida*, the *ghazal*, and indeed by Moretti for the novel, and for the satirical magazine *Punch*.[47]

For global historians, no spatial scale or unit of analysis is by definition best suited to study global processes, and one rather needs to shift scales and units.[48] In this book, I have highlighted positionality and tried to shift the gaze back and forth between local and distant views, in other words between the *Padmāvat* in Purab, Bengal, and Paris—*without* privileging Paris as the point of arrival or assimilation into world literature. Time-wise, too, new global historians try to resist the single Eurocentric timeline, either by combining multiple "layers" or "scales" of time or by highlighting plural trajectories through synchronic studies (see Conrad 2016: 146–147, 150).[49] This is something that literary history can do remarkably well, shifting from the microlevel of words and phrases to the broader level of genre, from individual utterance to discourse, from debates within a local coterie to the shifting fortunes of texts over the longue durée. In other words, I contend, world literature need not only be transnational and found at the highest level of circulation; it can be intranational, cross-regional, located in a place or a person, or formed by the intersection of different layers of production, circulation, and reception.[50] Finally, global historians recognize the fallacy of the "neutral" global gaze and acknowledge that every account of the global is necessarily located.

So far, historical accounts of world literature have acknowledged the earlier existence of world regions with their own specific literary cultures, but have then posited the unification of the literary world as a result of imperial expansion, global capitalism, and the assimilation of the world's literatures into a single system or space.[51] This simplified vision of a unified literary globe, I have argued elsewhere, owes too much to the cartographic imagination and the historical narrative of triumphant capitalism and empire (Orsini 2015b). "World," Debjani Ganguly and Pheng Cheah, among others, argue, always exceeds the material and territorial category of the "globe."[52]

The multilingual and located "ground-up" approach of this book can act as a useful complement (or antidote) to world literature approaches that are top-down or, quite simply, never look down from the top, and which risk being too selective in their choice of genre (the novel) and language (English), effectively closing off the possibilities of world literature even before the field has properly opened. As already stated, the two "problems" this book grapples with are multilingualism and location. In particular, this book seeks to "bring back together" the languages and archives that colonial/modern literary histories have carved apart in the name of language identities (Chapter 5). Despite the long history of multilingualism roughly outlined above, the histories of Sanskrit, Persian, Hindi, Urdu, and English literatures in the subcontinent have all been written as if the "other" languages were not there, thereby making connections, parallels, and overlaps invisible. This is not a problem peculiar to north India or South Asia alone. While multilingual literary cultures have been the norm rather than the exception across the world and throughout history, in most cases literary history and pedagogy still focus on a single language and treat multilingualism as an add-on or a phase on the way to the national language, and not as a "structuring structure," as Pierre Bourdieu (1984) would put it. In other words, whether it's the Maghreb, the Horn of Africa, Iran, Russia, Italy, England, the Balkans, the Caucasus, Latin and North America, East and Southeast Asia (the list could go on), multilingualism has inhered and continues to inhere in the structures of social and cultural life and in systems of reproduction that ensure the unequal distribution of social, economic, and cultural capital among people. Multilingualism informs the logic of distinction and the social arrangement of spaces, and inflects behavior and even bodily posture and accent (Bourdieu 1984).

Oral and written multilingualism have been an enduring feature of literary life throughout history. For this reason, the methodological approach used here and the insights generated by exploring the region of Purab or Awadh can be applied to other regions where languages also need to be "brought back together" in order to produce other examples of "comparative literature in one place."

This Book

My aim in this book is not to write a comprehensive literary history of north India at large.[53] Rather, each chapter focuses on a particular genre, phenomenon, and problem that helps illuminate the ordinary life of literature in this particular "multilingual local:" how new trends and fashions appeared over time; what "significant geographies" found expression and how they overlapped or combined with one another; which texts and tastes circulated widely; how fashions coming from elsewhere were appropriated; and which local forms did *not* travel yet still mattered to the people involved.

My next chapter takes up one of the strategies suggested by Conrad (2016): it "follows" a genre in its written transmission, oral performance, circulation, and trans- or recodification across languages and periods, mostly within Purab but also out of it. It uses the emic term *katha* (story, tale, narrative) to connect texts that have been considered to belong to different traditions, and interrogates manuscripts for the clues they can give us about their social location.

The third chapter takes up orature, which has been conspicuously absent from discussions of world literature (see Barber 2006; Levine 2013; Gunner 2018). This chapter focuses on the songs of the Sants, which are useful for world literature because they invite us to reflect on songs as both very located and intensely mobile and far-reaching. In north India the songs of the Sants were carriers of religious ideas and of poetic idioms and aesthetics beyond the court, and traveled quickly thanks to singers across a range of different audiences and regions—as the popularity of Kabir's songs in Punjab and Central India testifies.

The fourth chapter discusses literary education and the multilingual cultivation of Persian and Brajbhasha poetry in small towns (*qasbas*) and villages. This allows us to address questions of local elite patronage and tastes, of the economic value and function of poetry, and of the local cultivation of cosmopolitan poetic tastes. Once again, instead of thinking of poetic idioms and aesthetics as *belonging* to specific languages and groups (Persophone scholar-administrators, Sufis, Hindu rajas, merchants), we will see that the same idioms and genres were cultivated by different groups within the culture of Mughal and post-Mughal elites, generating an "intermedial culture" that combined and connected music, poetry, and the visual arts.[54] But did individuals cultivate poetic idioms in different languages separately, in parallel as it were, or did they combine them, either conceptually or in terms of metrical forms and poetic vocabulary?

Finally, the fifth chapter considers the impact of colonialism on the multilingual literary culture of the region, the institutionalization of literature in education, and the creation of separate canons and literary histories for Hindi and Urdu, a process in which European and Indian intellectuals both took part. The result was a gap between ideas of language, literature, religion, and community on the one hand, and literary *tastes and practices* on the other hand. As we shall see, the modern monolingual literary histories of Hindi and Urdu came at the expense of many exclusions—of the "other" language, of the multilingual world, and of contemporary orature.

By shifting the point of view and making visible the "plurality of stories" that together make up the multilingual space of Purab or Awadh, this book seeks to participate and intervene in world literature. If, as Pheng Cheah (2015: 2) has argued, world literature is "both a site of processes of *worlding* and an agent that participates and intervenes in these processes," this book seeks to make a located and multilingual approach more commonplace in world literature.

2

Following Stories across Scripts, Languages, and Repertoires

माल भाँड नट नाटक नाचहिं पंडित बैठि सासतर बाँचहिं।
Doha: गीत नाद रस कथा भल होई बिसराम
    गढ़कै लोग भएउ सुखी दान देहिं भल दाम
Wrestlers, mimes, actors dance and perform,
Pandits sit and read out the scriptures.
Songs, sounds, tales to savour (*rasa kathā*) are good pastimes,
People from the fort are happy and give good rewards.

—Malik Muhammad Jayasi, *Kanhāvat*, 1540: v. 24.7
and *doha;* Jayasi 1981: 146

तब घरमैं बैठे रहैं जांहि न हाट बाजार ।
मधुमालति मिरगावती पोथी दोइ उदार ॥
ते बांचहिं रजनीसमै आवहिं नर दस बीस।
गावहिं अरु बातैं करहिं नित उठि देंहि असीस ॥
I stayed at home and did not set foot in the bazaar.
At night I read out (*bāṃcahiṃ*) *Madhumālatī* and *Mirigāvatī*,
those two large books (*pothī udār*), ten-twenty people came,
I sang and talked, they blessed me as they left.

—Banarsidas, *Ardhakathānak*, 1641: vv. 335–336;
translated by Lath in Banarsidas 1981: 249

Whether recited by professional storytellers (called *kathavachak*) at courts or in front of mixed audiences in the open settings of city squares, village assemblies (*chaupals*), or people's courtyards, or by talented individuals in the more intimate settings of people's homes like the one Banarsidas mentions, it is good to think of the *katha* (*kathā*) as an oral-literate genre. Literate, because what we have in hand are the texts, and books are indeed often mentioned or depicted.[1] Oral, because *kathas* were meant to be read aloud (*bāṃchahiṃ*) or sung (*gāvahiṃ*), thus reaching out to and drawing in audiences beyond the limits of literacy or even language, as performers accompanied and translated the main text, interspersed with an exposition that, in some cases, would become the main performance.[2]

East of Delhi. Francesca Orsini, Oxford University Press. © Oxford University Press 2023.
DOI: 10.1093/oso/9780197658291.003.0002

Katha is an emic term, meaning "story" or "tale" (lit. "something told"). It is a term used for a wide range of narratives on religious and nonreligious topics that are now associated with quite different traditions—Sufi, Hindu devotional, heroic.[3] In Hindavi, *kathas* stabilized from the start on a pattern of several four-unit couplets (lit. *chaupai*, "four feet," with sixteen beats for each foot) interspersed with one longer two-unit couplet (called *doha* or *sortha*, with twenty-four beats for each line). This pattern did not change whether the *katha* was about Krishna and Rama, a woman's trials, or a battle. In Persian and Urdu, narratives are usually called *qissa* or *dastan* whether they are in verse or in prose; verse narratives are also called *masnavis* if they follow a metrical pattern of rhyming verses (AA, BB, CC, etc.) and generic characteristics that go back to the model set up by the twelfth-century Persian poet Nizami of Ganja (in modern Azerbaijan), a model followed by Amir Khusrau of Delhi, among many others.[4] In this chapter I consciously stick to the term *katha* rather than the terms introduced by modern Hindi scholars to distinguish between romances by Sufi authors (*premakhyan*) and narratives by Hindu authors (*prabandha kavya*) in order to break down modern ethnogeneric boundaries (see Shukla [1929] 1988). Instead, this chapter highlights the circulation of stories and texts, their particular inflections in register and taste, and the commonalities and dialogism among them. This commonality is suggested not just by the use of the same metrical pattern—in Hindavi at least—but also by the familiarity that poets, storytellers, and audiences display with the *range* of stories and by the dialogism inherent in so many *katha* texts, whether they draw explicit intertextual connections or we can perceive overlapping repertoires of themes, characters, and tropes. Another reason I prefer to use the emic term *katha* rather than the European ("universal") genre equivalent of "romance" is to avoid the historical and historiographical associations that romance carries within European literary history and the historical study of narratives. In European literature "romance" is usually identified with the medieval courtly romance, "a self-portrait of feudal knighthood with its mores and ideals" (Auerbach [1946] 1953: 131). It is usually juxtaposed to the Greek and Roman epic and, of course, to the bourgeois novel because of its "clear and conscious reduction of the radius of the sociosphere" and its limited or absent polyglottism (Segre 1997: 389; see Lukàcs 1971; Bakhtin 1992; Moretti 1987). Some scholars have questioned this division by calling attention to the romance's tendency to "swallow up the other genres somehow, becoming, more than a guide-genre, a 'total' genre," or by highlighting the etymological continuum between *roman* and romance (Segre 1997: 395). Others have pointed to the dialectic and dialogism between early novels and romances in terms of values and other features (McKeon 2002). Nonetheless, using the term "romance" for *kathas* risks loading them with universalist genre expectations in terms of social form, aesthetics, and teleology. Instead, I will use "romance" more specifically for texts that call themselves "tales of love" (*pemkathas*).

The circulation, adaptation, and reuse of texts, stories, and poetic tropes and forms across languages and cultural and religious domains were very much the norm in medieval Europe and the medieval and early modern Mediterranean, whether this process involved a movement across spaces or across different languages and sociotextual communities within the same location.[5] The study of these transfers, which typically "follows" the permutations of a story or a text or a form—whether it is the story of the Buddha, the *Pañchatantra*, the Alexander romance, or the *Arabian Nights*—has been paradigmatic of world literature, and rightly so, for what can express more eloquently the dynamic worldliness of texts?[6] Translation is a cornerstone of these studies.

"Following" is the main strategy of this chapter, too. It allows us to connect texts that have been classified as part of different traditions in different languages and to explore the conditions under which they were transmitted, orally and in writing, and the audiences they reached. But, as we shall see, translation features only marginally in this exploration. Moreover, taking genre, loosely defined, as our chief parameter allows us to trace the shifting contours of its imagination and the mediation that texts performed between narrative, aesthetics, and the social world. "Following" the genre of the *katha* in the longue durée and across languages (Hindavi, Persian, and Urdu) allows us to address questions of changing taste and patronage and of archiving and canonization—why, e.g., did Hindavi *kathas* not enter Hindi print culture in the nineteenth century? Worldliness in this case does not necessarily mean reaching distant readers but intervening confidently in the local world.

As we shall see, this is not an entropic story of vernacularization or the simple transfer of literary resources from high languages to an emerging vernacular (see Pollock 1998a, 1998b; Chapter 1). Nor does considering each version as belonging to either a "cosmopolitan," "local/vernacular," or intermediate "epichoric" literary ecology help us beyond a point (see Beecroft 2015). Rather, we need to tell this as a story of several parallel and overlapping processes (Massey's "multiplicity of stories and trajectories"). These include the development of a trilingual Islamic-Sufi culture (Arabic, Persian, and Hindavi); the cultivation of vernacular tales and songs among regional Sultanate rulers, their administrators, and local rural chieftains; the parallel emergence of *kathas* about Krishna and Ram in eastern towns; a shift in taste in the Mughal period toward Persian and toward Brajbhasha poetics; the renewed vernacularization of the genre in Urdu in the nineteenth century; and its difficult position in modern Hindi and Urdu literary histories. By carving out separate traditions for Hindavi Sufi and bhakti, Persian, and Urdu narratives, modern histories have obscured the interconnected history of the genre.

Methodologically, "following" the *katha* genre involves paying attention to both the material aspect of texts and to their narrative and rhetorical strategies. At one level, there are the material clues that *katha* manuscripts provide about their social and religious location and circulation: these clues include script, format, quality of paper and calligraphy, and whether or not the manuscripts are illustrated.[7] As it happens, most *katha* manuscripts from this region turned up during early twentieth-century manuscript searches in private homes rather than courtly collections, and they are incomplete or lack colophons. But even when what we have is the bare text without a colophon telling us where it was written or copied, by whom and for whom, the material aspect still tells us something. It often throws up interesting puzzles, as we shall see, that force us to inquire about, rather than assume, the social location of that text.

At another level, the *kathas'* narrative strategies and textual features also provide clues about their location and circulation. Notable features that get inflected are the social location of the protagonist (is he a soldier or a prince?) and the emphasis on particular characters. References to local flora, fauna, foods, or toponyms "localize" a story, while conversely referents and tropes related to cosmopolitan Sanskrit or Persian poetics "cosmopolitize" it. The inclusion of religious elements, sometimes in combination, tells us whether the tale was supposed to speak to a particular religious community or to several at once. Other clues include linguistic register, the presence or absence of literary ornamentation and "set pieces," and the acknowledgment of (or silence about) sources, whether they were read or "overheard" (see Chapter 1). Does the text establish any intertextual relations? And finally, does it carry any multilingual traces, and if so, what are they traces of?

Kathas are particularly important to the study of the multilingual literary culture of north India for the familiarity with narratives and aesthetics that the traffic of stories *both* produced *and* assumed. To take the example of Persian tellings of Hindavi *kathas:* Were they translations? Had the Persian authors *read* the Hindavi texts? And did writing in Persian entail a shift from a local to a cosmopolitan position, with an accompanying transçodification of local or Indic references (nightingales instead of mynahs, cypresses instead of *kadamba* trees)? Were *kathas* remolded to sound like *masnavis* and *qissas*? How much familiarity with vernacular and Sanskrit *kathas* could Persian authors assume in their readers and listeners? Within South Asia, the critical paradigm of "many Ramayanas" (Richman 1991) has provided a blueprint for approaching different tellings of the "same" story without positing an ur-text. The "many Ramayanas" approach gives equal value to each telling and acknowledges that authors or storytellers consciously play with the audience's familiarity with other tellings because there is a "common pool" of signifiers which every author "dips into" and from which she "brings out a unique crystallization, a new text with a unique texture and a fresh context (Ramanujan 1991: 46)."[8] But whereas such an approach *assumes* the tellers' and audiences' familiarity with the story, in our case, as I already suggested, we need to consider that *kathas* produced as well as assumed familiarity with narratives and aesthetics across several different communities of taste.

As in the following chapters, my aim here is not to provide a comprehensive account of all the *kathas* written east of Delhi. Rather, the chapter brings together a dozen texts from different archives in order to illuminate some key aspects, connections, and shifts in the genre and in the regional multilingual literary culture between the fourteenth and the early twentieth centuries.

The Emergence of a Genre

The first Hindavi *katha*, Da'ud's *Chandāyan* (1379), stands out for the number of innovations and social and aesthetic mediations it performed. Whereas other early vernacular *kathas* drew on familiar episodes from the *Rāmāyaṇa* and *Mahābhārata* epics or on characters from the Jain or Purana repertoires, Da'ud's *pemkatha* (lit. "love story," romance) "entextualized" an oral narrative, one that is in fact still current as oral epic in the region.[9] Da'ud "literarized" the story of Lorik and Chanda by adding literary conventions from both Persian and Apabhramsha, as well as from oral folk traditions.[10] By doing so he created a new genre, that of Hindavi (Avadhi) *pemkathas*, or romances.

Chandāyan established a metrical template (regular stanzas of *chaupais* and *dohas* strung together) and narrative building blocks. These included a prologue and narrative sequences that involved the awakening of love, the transformation of the hero into a yogi, and his elopement with the beloved or quest in search for her, leaving his first wife behind; the hero's return home with his second wife after the first wife's pitiful message; his difficult reintegration (including a quarrel between the two wives); and the narrative resolution with the disappearance and/or death of the protagonist. This proved to be a winning combination, and the *Chandāyan* became the template for the whole long tradition of vernacular romances (*pemkathas*) in the region and, more broadly, for the definition of the romance in South Asia (see Behl 2012a: 23; d'Hubert 2018: 249–250).

Lorik, the hero, is a brave warrior of undistinguished lineage with only "fifty-two unnamed followers" (Sreenivasan 2014: 264). Chanda, the heroine who falls in love with him when she watches him return victorious from battle, is of higher status; it is her father's city of Govar that the text describes in lavish terms as a splendid city with a tall palace (*dhaurahara*) and an abundance of groves, shrines, water tanks, cattle, and bazaars full of traders and entertainers.[11]

Figure 2.1 Lorik enters Chanda's palace bedroom, decorated with wall paintings of gods and characters from the epics.
Source: Rylands Collection, The University of Manchester Library, Hindustani MS 1, f. 160r.

The four-storied palace was covered in red lac,
with pictures coloured in golden wash:
a drawing of Lanka with Vibhishan,
the body of big-headed Ravan;
the seizing of Sita, who was with Ram the king,
the Pandavas at the place of Kurukshetra. . . .
Many lines from tales, poems, Sanskrit verses, and play prologues were inscribed. (*Chandāyan* v. 193, Da'ud 2018: vol. I, 281)

Elephants, horses, chariots, and sterling horsemen and archers adorn her father's army, while her bedroom walls depict scenes from the epics (Figure 2.1), and a celebratory meal is described in lavish detail over ten stanzas with a profusion of meat, vegetable, and rice dishes.[12]

If the description of Govar follows established Sanskritic conventions with its list of shrines, water tanks, bazaars, and thirty-six castes (*bābhan, khatarī, bais, guvārā, khāṇḍaravāra au agaravārā*), by comparison the lists of trees and foods—fried *kāchara* and *pāpaṛa, bhāṇṭā* and *ṭīṇḍasa, kaddū, chachīṛa, turaī, sītāphala,* etc.—evoke a much more familiar world.[13] *Chandāyan,* Thibaut d'Hubert has recently argued, shows the emergence of vernacular literature not as some unmediated expression of the people but as a careful "staging of the familiar" that creates reality effects (2018: 228). This is particularly clear with respect to descriptions and dialogues, which can be highly poetic and symbolic or draw upon the everyday register of women's squabbles, something that later Sufi romances particularly relish.

Da'ud's *Chandāyan* differs from modern oral epics in what it adds, what it leaves out, and what it focuses on (Pandey 1985).[14] It adds a prologue mirroring that of Persian *masnavis,* with their praise of God and his creation, of the Prophet Muhammad as the perfect man and of his four companions, of the poet's Sufi guide (*pir*), of the "ruler of the time," and of the local governor or patron. It also adds elaborate descriptions of the town of Govar, as we have seen, and of the heroine Chanda, which mirror the stock conventions of Sanskrit and Apabhramsha poetics. The lament of Lorik's first wife, Maina, is instead a set piece taken from the oral tradition of women's songs, the "song of the twelve months," in which a woman laments the absence of her distant beloved. In other words, rather than simply transferring or translating a high literary model into the vernacular, Da'ud combines resources from multiple written and oral literary traditions. What he leaves out from the oral narratives are battles, and more battles, as well as the particular caste-centric focus on Ahir pastoralists, on whom more below.[15] Moreover, compared to the oral narratives, the characters in Da'ud's romance are wealthier, the milieu more courtly, and the geographical references broader.[16]

Da'ud focuses on the love between Lorik and Chanda and shifts the meaning of the characters and of the story. Chanda's nurse, who bears the enigmatic name Brihaspat (Jupiter), acts as advisor and guide. Chanda herself is constantly compared to the moon (her name means "moon"): she lights up the earth when she is born (lit. *autārī,* descends like an avatar); she is a perfect "lotus woman" like Padmavati, and is waited upon by constellations (Da'ud 2018: I, 135).[17] Key terms like *rasa* and *viraha* (the pain of longing and separation from one's beloved) are re-accented so as to convey coded meanings about the progression of the Sufi disciple's "ordained love" toward God.[18] At significant moments the rather fast narrative pace slows down and "thickens," as Behl puts it, as when a wandering musician describes Chanda's beauty to the neighboring king Rupchand. This stock description of the heroine's beauty, with a whole stanza devoted to each detail of her body, from her hair to her toes, turns into an effective narrative device. Each stanza increases Rupchand's desire till he swoons and is ready to give all his wealth to the musician: on hearing of Chanda's red lips, Rupchand loses blood; when he hears of her lovely tongue, he can only scream "Catch her, catch her;" and upon hearing of her beautiful mole (*tila*), he burns to ashes (*tila tila jarai bujhāi*; see below) (Da'ud 2018: I, 174).[19] This ability of Hindi verses describing the heroine's beauty to ignite desire was much admired (see Behl 2012a; Phukan 2000).

Da'ud was a local Sufi, depicted in a (later) manuscript as a pious, bare-breasted shaikh sitting cross-legged before a ledger with his book (see Brac de la Perrière 2008: table 23). He wrote *Chandāyan* in Dalmau, which was then one of the military checkposts of the Tughluq Sultanate, a brick and mud fortress overlooking the River Ganges about six hundred kilometers east of the Sultanate capital, Delhi.[20] This geographic and social location is important. The military governors and local chieftains who controlled small but strategically important towns like Dalmau, Ramya Sreenivasan (2014) suggests, aspired to be part of the north Indian political elite of the Delhi Sultanate but lacked the material resources to do so through lavish construction of palaces, fortresses, or mosques and temples.[21] One thing they could and did do, though, was to patronize local poets and performers. Given that the ability to gather and control military manpower among local agriculturalists and pastoralists was crucial for these chiefs, it is hardly surprising that it is these local rajas and their agriculturalist-pastoralist soldiers (*bīra*) who are the protagonists of *Chandāyan* (see Kolff 2002).

One more thing about location. In *Chandāyan* the initial praise of God and the Prophet employs Hindavi rather than Arabic or Persian religious vocabulary.[22] Religious markers in the *katha* belong to the "diegetic religion," i.e., to Lorik and Chanda's world of temples, ascetics, gurus, and Hindu rituals. Hindi scholars have tended to wonder at and commend this knowledge of Hindu religion and customs by a local Sufi and view it as a syncretic gesture bridging cultures (e.g., Shukla [1929] 1988; see Chapter 1). Others have instead spoken of "competitive dialogism," a tendency to assimilate Hindu elements and make them part of Sufi discourse (Behl 2012a: 63). But dialogism need not be viewed as competitive. It can also mean acknowledging that language is shared, that one's utterance is not the first or last word on a subject, and that other speakers may accent it and listeners hear it differently.[23] As with other Sufi romances, this re-accenting and double accenting spoke of the value placed on the ability to extract multiple meanings from words and images—an ability that distinguished the talented poet and patron-connoisseur (lit. a *rasika*, endowed with *rasa*). It also spoke of the coded nature of these texts—no "mere" romances—and their ability to address multiple audiences at once, as we shall see. After all, while ordinary listeners would perceive only that there was "more" to the story, the initiated or the connoisseurs would hold the key to its hidden meanings. Da'ud wrote of Chanda's mole:

> *naina savana bicha tilu iku parā, jāna biraha masi bindu kā dharā*
> *mukha ke suhāga bhaye tila sangū, pirima puhupa janu baiṭha bhuvangū*
> *bāsu lubadha tiha baiṭho āī, kāḍhi rahā hara jāna uḍāī*
> *biraha dagadha hauṃ marana sanehā, ragata nahīṃ kuilā bhaī dehā*
> *tila birahai bana ghuṅghachī jarī, ādhī kāri adhī rāturī*
> *doha*: *tila sañjogi bājuri siru kīnhā aughaṭa bhā pari jāī*
> *rājā hiye āgi parajār tila tila jarai na bujhāī.* (*Chandāyan*, stanza 74, Da'ud 2018: I, 174)

> Between her eye and ear lies a mole,
> a spot of blackest ink,
> as if placed there by separation incarnate.
> Her face is fortunate because the mole is there,
> like a snake[24] sitting in the flower of love,
> drawn by its scent,
> sweating poison till its life flies away.
> I am singed by longing, dying of love
> I have no blood left, burnt to a cinder!
> Trees of *ghuṅghachī* berries, burnt,
> Are now half black, half crimson.
> *doha*: When that arrow struck the singer, he lay stunned, tossed to one side.
> And the king burnt by a terrible flame, a fire that none could extinguish.
> (translated in Behl 2012a: 79, slightly changed)

According to a Persian Sufi treatise from the region, disciples were told to interpret the word as follows:

> I.16 And if among Hindavi words one finds mention of ***alaka*** [= lock of hair] or other nouns for it, or of ***tila*** [= mole], they indicate anything which causes confusion (*ḥairānī*) to the mystics, distraction to the seekers, and disarray (*bī-sar-o-sāmānī*) to the lovers. At times they indicate their restlessness in front of the veil (*ḥijāb*),[25] at times they mean sin, and at other times they indicate also the [sin of] forgetting God for one's whole life.
> verse: "If you knew the worth of each one of your hairs
> Would you waste even one of your musk locks?" (Bilgrami, *Haqā'iq-i Hindī*, f. 8)[26]

Already in Da'ud's description, Chanda's mole leads to confusion, distraction, and disarray. But for the Sufi disciple, it could also lead, on a different level of interpretation and of reality, to the expulsion of poison through fire.

Apart from inaugurating the genre of Hindavi romances, *Chandāyan* is notable for two more things. First, its popularity, which seems to have lasted for two or three centuries.[27] Second, it was the first vernacular Hindavi tale to be made into a book, a codex written in Persian script (a form of *naskh*). Not only that, but the earliest available manuscripts of *Chandāyan* are all copiously illustrated, though unfortunately none of them is complete or coeval with the text's composition. Iconographic and codicological analysis has assigned them to two or possibly three distinct regions, which suggests that the tale spread well beyond Awadh.[28] Even if, frustratingly, we don't know who the patrons of these manuscripts were because no colophon has been preserved, that *Chandāyan* became a valued book-object and in fact inaugurated the tradition of illustrated books in Hindavi and that it traveled so far *without translation* are historically deeply significant facts.

The first fact speaks of a community of taste that was familiar with Persian writing and the Persian "art of the book" and extended that taste to the vernacular, in this case a vernacular literary tale that in many ways mirrored the Persian romantic *masnavis* of Nizami or Amir Khusrau but told a local story.[29] Though *Chandāyan* is clearly indebted to Persian models, its language is a vernacular resolutely devoid of Perso-Arabic vocabulary. While I have cautioned against the danger of overinterpreting authorial intentions on the basis of religious identity, this linguistic choice suggests that Da'ud, his patron, and those who commissioned copies of the manuscript in Persian script envisaged and valued the vernacular as a *parallel* poetic idiom and sphere of literary cultivation to Persian. The second fact, that *Chandāyan* circulated widely without translation, speaks of the mobility of its patrons and/or the wide currency and understandability for this vernacular, which appears less local or localized as a result. Who, among the Sultanate elites, were the mobile carriers and patrons of these vernacular books in Persian script?[30] Possibly those military governors and Indo-Afghan chieftains who could and did invest in such new symbols of conspicuous consumption as lavish clothes, perfumes, large feasts, poets and bards—and now illustrated books. The compulsion to move, because of war or because they were displaced by stronger claimants, recurs often in the genealogies and narratives of these military groups, both Dirk Kolff (2002) and Simon Digby (2014) have shown, and it is not surprising that their prized *katha*, *Chandāyan*, should have traveled with them as far as Bengal to the east and the Deccan to the south.

But if *Chandāyan* was so popular for so long, why are there no other Hindavi romances extant before the early sixteenth century? There is a political explanation: for much of the fifteenth century Purab was a battleground between the rulers of Delhi in the west and Jaunpur in the east. In one of these periodic raids, Shaikh ʿAbd al-Quddus Gangohi's complete Persian rendering of the *Chandāyan*, the first Persian version of a Hindavi *katha* text, was destroyed.[31] But if we take a broader definition of the *katha* genre beyond Sufi romances, we notice that other, non-Sufi *kathas* were in fact written in and survive from the long fifteenth century, composed in other, comparable milieus.[32] Despite political strife, people did not stop telling or listening to tales.

Sumptuous Romances

While *Chandāyan* established the vernacular literary *pemkatha* as a genre, the next, and truly dazzling, set of Sufi romances dates from over a century later, in the first half of the sixteenth century, between the tail end of the north Indian Sultanates and early Mughal rule, a period that saw the second Mughal ruler, Humayun, defeated by the Indo-Afghan Sher Shah Suri, who expanded his reign from his base in Bihar to the whole of north India between 1538 and his death in 1545; Humayun then returned from his exile in Iran and defeated Sher Shah's son Islam Shah before himself dying in 1556. Afghan military elites scattered to other parts of the subcontinent or were absorbed into the Mughal military-administrative system (see Digby 2014). Two *kathas* by Jayasi dated 1540 mention, in quick succession, Humayun and Sher Shah as "rulers of the age."[33]

Despite their individual specificities, Qutban's *The Magic Doe* (*Mirigāvatī*, 1503), Jayasi's *Padmāvat* and his lesser known *Kanhāvat* (both 1540), and Manjhan's *Madhumālatī* (1545) share a similar expansiveness, a similar set of main characters, and a similar plot and narrative arc that include the princely hero's quest, his travels, obstacles, and trials.[34] They follow *Chandāyan*'s template in the prologue, but their narratives are more complex and include talking parrots, adventures with monsters, fairies, and almost fatal shipwrecks, among other events. They are punctuated with more symbolism, philosophical musings, and enigmatic references in the form of key terms, speeches, and dialogues. They also delight in intertextual references to an unprecedented degree, and although they draw extensively upon preexisting motifs, they are all original stories.[35]

The scholarship on these and similar works is now vast and sophisticated.[36] Their striking literary and religious dialogism, together with linguistic and material clues from the manuscripts, signal a shift in the genre and its social location and circulation. They point to the sophistication of a *vernacular* culture of storytelling and music, and a social compact between (mainly Afghan) elites and local chieftains (rajas), in which Sufis played a mediatory role.

To start with, the early sixteenth-century (or late Sultanate) romances weave wide intertextual nets, both Persian and Sanskritic. The prince's ordeals in Qutban's *The Magic Doe* (*Mirigāvatī*) are modeled on the Persian poet Fariduddin Attar's *Conference of Birds*, Behl (2012b: 120ff.) has shown, while the episode of the cannibal in the cave blinded by the hero trying to escape echoes Sindbad's travels. But Qutban, Jayasi, and Manjhan display an intimate knowledge of stories and characters from the Puranas, the *Rāmāyaṇa*, and *Mahābhārata*, too. This is only one of countless examples, which amplifies the pain of the prince's father through the examples of Ram's father, Dasharath, in the *Rāmāyaṇa*, the pious son Shravan Kumar in the Puranas, and Abhimanyu's father, Arjun, in the *Mahābhārata*:

> The prince set out, disguised as a yogi.
> When the king [his father] heard, his breast was on fire.
> Just as **Daśaratha** died, separated from his son,
> he also wished to leave his life that instant.
> As **Arjuna** cried when **Abhimanyu** was killed,
> just so the king began to weep and wail. . . .
> "As the blind parents of **Śravana**, agitated without him, died screaming,
> if I die without meeting him alive again, even in heaven will I regret it!"
> (Qutban, *Mirigāvatī*, translated in Behl 2012b: 81)[37]

In *Padmāvat*, not only does Jayasi engage in a pervasive intertextual dialogue with the characters and story of the *Rāmāyaṇa*, but he also uses a typical Puranic device of having the gods Shiva and Parvati intervene in the story: they facilitate the meeting between Ratansen and Padmavati and celebrate their wedding.[38] While, as we have seen, Sufi adepts could decode these references in their own way, there is no doubt that Hindu listeners would also have responded to the familiar referents. Jayasi's self-embedding in the epic-Puranic world while maintaining his identity as a Muslim and a Sufi extends to his imagination of time. In *Padmāvat* he praises his hometown of Jais as a "religious center" since the Golden Age (*satajuga*). In his version of the story of Krishna, *Kanhāvat,* he expands this idea using the timeframe of the four ages: Jais has been a religious place since the Golden Age, the home of sages (*rishi*) in the Second Age and of ascetics in the Third Age; when they abandoned it in the Fourth Age of Kaliyuga, it was resettled by Turks, who turned it once again into a beautiful town.[39] Not only is the coming of the Turks framed as a resettlement and a restoration rather than a violent upheaval; their presence turns the usually dystopian picture of Kaliyuga into a happy one.

These romances also mention each other as part of an ever-expanding repertoire of stories. When Padmavati in a letter warns Ratansen about the perils of love, she quotes both *Mirigāvatī* and *Madhumālatī* as well as other Puranic love stories:

bahutanha aisa jīu para khelā, tūṃ jogī kehi māṃha akelā
***bikrama** dhaṃsā pema ke bārāṃ, **sapanāvatī** kahaṃ gaeu patārāṃ*
***sudaibacchha mugudhāvatī** lāgī, kaṃkana pūri hoi gā bairāgī*
***rājkuṃvar** kañchanpura gaeu, **mirigāvatī** kahaṃ jogī bhaeu*
*sādhā kuṃvar **manohara** jogū, **madhumālatī** kahaṃ kīnha biyogū*
***pemāvati** kahaṃ **sarasura** sādhā, **ukhā** lāgi **anirudha** bara bāṃdhā.*
(*Padmāvat*, 233.2–7, Jayasi [1956] 1998: 223)

Many have risked their lives, you are not the only one, yogi!
For the sake of love **Vikrama** plunged into the underworld to fetch **Sapnavati**.
For **Mugdhavati**, **Sudaivaccha** [Sadavriksha] traveled as renouncer to Kankanpuri,
Rajkunwar went to Kanchanpur and became a yogi for **Mirigavati**'s sake,
Manohar practiced yoga and renounced the world for the sake of **Madhumalati**.
Sarasura practiced austerities to gain **Premavati**, and for **Usha Aniruddha** waged war.

Qutban, Jayasi, and Manjhan also dwell at much greater depth on the topic of love, both as a cosmic force but also as a path to self-transformation, something that the hero needs to learn under the heroine's guidance. This is the *rasa* of love (*prema-rasa*), an innovation by the Sufi poets on the existing classification of *rasas* in Sanskrit poetics. Mirigavati's stern rebuke to Rajkunwar when he first tries to grasp her in the pond echoes Shirin's reproof to Khusrau in Nizami's *masnavi*:

"O Prince, control yourself!
I will tell you something, if you will follow it!
You are a king's son, and desire me
but I am of noble birth myself. . . .
Force does not count; only through *rasa*
can you enjoy the savor of love.
Count that as true, in both the worlds.
Rasa cannot be enjoyed through violence.
It is a savor that only comes through *rasa*.
If you talk of enjoying *rasa*, I have told you gently what *rasa* means.
Only those who are colored with *rasa* can savor it now or hereafter."
(Qutban, *Mirigāvatī*, v. 86, translated in Behl 2012b: 73–74)

In narrative terms, learning the *rasa* of love requires a "constant deferment of desire in order to draw the seeker into the process of self-realization" (Behl 2012a: 81). When Rajkunwar and Mirigavati finally meet again, he has to debase himself as a supplicant and overcome her coquettishness (Hindi *māna*, Persian *nāz*) with his entreaties (Persian *niyāz*), until they come to dwell one inside the other (Qutban, *Mirigāvatī* v. 292, translated in Behl 2012b: 147).[40]

Love in the romances has more than an individual or spiritual meaning, and its centrality echoes the role of love as a code to signify and cultivate loyalty and attachment between rulers and courtiers (see Behl 2012a; d'Hubert 2018; de Bruijn 2012). Learning to love selflessly, to love well, to balance love commitments, and to recognize and reward love were all skills widely valued and cultivated in polities during and after Timur's time. "The presence of true lovers allows the creative and beneficial power of love to manifest its 'effect' [*ta'thīr*] on society and generate a just rule," as d'Hubert (2018: 238) puts it.

Language in these later romances is always sumptuous and rich in compact metaphors and similes, some of which will sound familiar. When a distraught Prince Rajkunwar describes to his nurse the beauty of Mirigavati's mole, he compares it to a black bee, a spot of ink, and the cause of cosmic confusion (see Chanda's mole above):

> Between her eye and her ear lay a mole.
> God had created a black bee on a lotus!
> Enmeshed in scent, it could not fly away.
> What can the clever man do when caught by love?
> Separation itself broke forth as ink, and was
> Put there in this guise to enchant the world! (Qutban, *Mirigāvatī*, v. 56.1–3, translated in Behl 2012b: 61)

At times metaphors extend over a whole scene, as in the night of love between Rajkunwar and Mirigavati that gets coded as battle, with each bodily part or item of clothing compared to a military item:

> The night's struggle had been incomparable.
> She had set elephants [her breasts] in battle array,
> and ranged against him Tocharian horses [long of neck].
> Her curling locks she arranged on the crown of her head,
> and in place of armor she wore her blouse.
> She wore bracelets and armbands and bangles on her wrists.
> Her sari was wound tight at the line of battle.
> Her eyes shot the arrows of [Death,] the sun's son, from the bows of her eyebrows.

Her breasts were circular battle formations—with their strength she'd conquered her lord [239].
The *tilaka* of our hero, his sword,
struck the crown of her head. Her curling locks
were scattered, her parting disordered.
With his nails, sharp spears, he assailed her armor.
Her blouse, ripped to tatters, fled from the scene.
Her bracelets broke when her lord took her hand.
Her armbands snapped, slipping off her arms.
The sari she'd wound tight around the line of battle
was torn to shreds, attacked by a mad elephant.
They came to the encounter and stayed locked in combat,
till the sun rose to intervene and caught them.
If the sun had not risen to make peace, who knows what would have happened?
Trampled in this battle of two mad elephants, the earth gushed forth in a stream. (Qutban, *Mirigāvatī*, translated in Behl 2012b: 240)

At other times a passage can be read—like a Sanskrit pun, or *shlesha*—according to two different codes, yielding two sets of meaning.[41]

The later romances continue and extend Da'ud's religious dialogism and re-accenting of Indic terms. One of the most interesting instances, starting with Da'ud, involves the hero temporarily turning into a yogi.[42] This transformation of the prince into a renunciant with a begging bowl and other yogic insignia marks his rejection of his previous existence and his resolve to concentrate on his quest for the heroine until he finds her.[43] It is also a physical manifestation of the pain of *viraha*, or longing for the absent beloved, and as we have seen, the metaphors of self-consummation and self-annihilation work for both ascetic penance and love longing. In some cases the transformation is quite brief.[44] Mostly, though, the prince-as-yogi sets out alone or in a group (*khaṭaka*) and undergoes several adventures and trials along the way. That this is a temporary state is apparent to the keen-eyed. When Rajkunwar saves a local princess, Rupmini, from a demon, she muses:

"You are not a yogi.
I'll ask you, but you must promise to tell the truth!
What is your name? Where is your home?
Why have you taken the path of yoga?" (Qutban, *Mirigāvatī*, v. 131, translated in Behl 2012b: 90)[45]

Even more dangerously, when Padmavati's father, the Raja of Sinhala, is informed that Ratansen tried to enter the palace and must therefore be a thief in a yogi's disguise, he is ready to have Ratansen pierced on a stake. At the very last moment a bard (*dasaundhi bhāṭa*) steps in and warns the raja, "He is no *jogi*, he belongs to the world. Only one who knows the difference is a true seeker" (*Padmāvat*, v. 264, Jayasi [1956] 1998: 251). The implication is that, unlike the raja, the bard is a "true seeker" because he recognizes that Ratansen's yogi look is only a disguise.[46] The expression the bard uses literally means "to him belongs enjoyment" (*āhi so bhojū*), and Sufi romance writers play extensively on the binary of yoga and *bhoga*, asceticism and worldly enjoyment. Unlike true yoga, in these romances the yogi does get to enjoy *bhoga* once he is perfected and has overcome all the trials. Once the ordeal is over, Ratansen tells his companions:

> You practiced yoga for my sake then,
> Now don't nurse abstinence in your hearts.
> Whoever you did penance for (*tapai jogū*)
> Now take pleasure (*mānai bhogū*) with them. (*Padmāvat*, v. 331, Jayasi [1956] 1998: 330)

One of the most striking interpretations of the yoga-*bhoga* binary and of religious re-accenting (in fact multi-accenting) occurs in Jayasi's take on the Krishna story.[47] Given Krishna's personality it would have been difficult to turn him into a steadfast advocate of asceticism! But Jayasi manages to both transform Krishna into a lovesick yogi and to advocate enjoyment (*bhoga*) as a spiritual path (*bhoga-bhagati*). Through the term *rasa-bhoga*, "the enjoyment of *rasa*," Jayasi presents the story of Krishna as equivalent to the mutual desire, longing, and union between God and humans, in contrast to his wicked uncle Kamsa's pride-sickness (*garaba roga*).

When Krishna falls sick with love for Chandravali, who in the Vaishnava tradition is one of the important milkmaids in love with Krishna and here becomes the second heroine, his old nurse suggests that ascetic penance (*tapa*) will bring him the *bhoga* he desires. Disguised as a yogi, Krishna sits in Chandravali's garden for fourteen nights repeating (*japa*) her name till finally she comes. To her he appears a strange creature—why is he dressed like a beggar if he claims to be a king? Krishna reveals that he is actually not a yogi but Gopala, Vishnu's avatara and an enjoyer of pleasure (*rasa-bhogī*):

> Listen Gaura [i.e., Chandravali] this is my knowledge,
> I am untouched by pleasure or pain.
> Nothing comes, nothing goes,
> I sit alone quietly throughout.
> This is what you call one who knows the core (*mūla gyānī*),
> Who does not smile at pleasure or weep in pain.

This is the game of the creator,
and it's me, like a shadow inside the ancestral offering (*piṇḍa*).
Outwardly I look (*pragaṭa rūpa)* like Gopala Gobinda,
the hidden knowledge (*kapaṭa gyāna*) is: neither Turk nor Hindu.
Murari's embodied form (*rūpa*) comes in different guises:
sometimes a king, sometimes a beggar.
Sometimes a pandit, sometimes a fool,
sometimes a woman, sometimes a man.
For the sake of my *rasa*, it's all a game after all.
Many shades and guises, only one (*akelā*) taking pleasure in all.
(*Kanhāvat,* stanza 177, Jayasi 1981: 217)

Krishna is addressing Chandravali, but extradiegetically Jayasi is formulating a statement that can be interpreted in different ways at once. According to the theology of Krishna bhakti, Krishna has created his beautiful form—in fact any form—for the sake of his cosmic play, or *līlā* (the term used here is *rasa*), and he is at one time ineffable Being and God with visible attributes. At the same time, according to the Sufi theology of the "unity of existence" (*waḥdat al-wujūd* in Arabic), this is Allah, the only God, revealing that he is immanent in all things and that a hidden realm exists in which no outward difference matters; the enlightened seeker knows this and remains unmoved by appearances and events because he can see through them. "Neither Turk nor Hindu," a stock phrase in religious discourse at the time to articulate different positions, here refers to this hidden knowledge, a stage or state of deep understanding where all external differences fall away.[48]

A further explanation of the path of *bhoga* occurs in the final section of the *katha,* in the debate (*goshthi*) staged between Krishna and the great yogi Gorakhnath. To Gorakhnath, who is disappointed to see Krishna enveloped in *bhoga*, Krishna replies with a number of objections: Yoga is "outward knowledge and outward form," but a true ascetic remains detached at home (i.e., in the body). What do *jogis* like Gorakh know of *bhoga* anyway? And what is the point of human birth if one does not experience it? Death will come for everyone, whether *bhogi* or *jogi* (*Kanhāvat,* stanza 348, Jayasi 1981: 317). After the debate, Krishna and Gorakh fight briefly and then come to an accommodation: "Yoga is best for the *jogī*, and *bhoga* best for the *bhogī*." Whereas elsewhere yoga is a stage in the lover's preparation, in this debate it stands for an outward form of religion.[49] This kind of religion, which values spiritual exercises for the sake of personal benefits, is blind to the true, secret essence of things, so that Krishna's critique comes to echo the Sufi's critique of *shari'ah* Islam. Jayasi is brilliantly making two religious statements at the same time—one about the superiority of Krishna bhakti over Nath yoga, and the other about the superiority of the Sufi path to the *shari'ah*!

As already noticed about *Chandāyan*, the linguistic register that Sufi romance poets employed to achieve these literary and religious effects was not a mixed one—unlike the Sant poets in the following chapter. Rather, they translated Sanskrit and Persian metaphors into a uniform register in which even Sanskrit and Persian words are written according to the phonology of Hindavi.[50] This led early scholars either to assume that they had "translated" Persian texts into the vernacular or, conversely, that since they used hardly any Persian and Arabic terms they must not have known Persian at all.[51] A multilingual paradigm allows us to envisage a different scenario, one in which these clearly educated and talented poets had most likely studied Persian (and Arabic) as well as Sanskrit and Apabhramsha poetics but produced a sophisticated vernacular literary idiom.

This chimes with Qutban's description of his patron, Sultan Husain Shah Sharqi, as a connoisseur, and of himself as a sophisticated vernacular Hindavi poet who, by the time of writing, had already been displaced from his capital, Jaunpur:

> Shāh Ḥusain is a great king.
> The throne and parasol adorn him well.
> He is a pandit, intelligent and wise.
> He reads a book and understands all the meanings. . . .
> He reads the scriptures, difficult of access,
> and speaks the meanings aloud and explains them.
> A single word can have ten meanings:
> pandits are struck dumb with amazement. . . .
> In his reign I composed this poem,
> when it was the year nine hundred and nine.
> In the month of Muharram by the Hijri moon,
> the tale was finished and I read it out loud!
> I have used the meters *gāthā, dohā, arill,* and *arajā*,
> and the *soraṭhā* and *caupā'ī* to adorn my poem.
> Many classical letters and words came into it,
> and I also chose all kinds of *desī* words.
> It's beautiful to recite, listen with care!
> When you hear this, you will not like any other.
> Two months and ten days it took me to put it together and to finish it.
> Each word is a pearl I have strung. I speak with heart and mind. . . .
> First, this was a Hindavī story,
> then some poets told it in Turkī. [?]
> Then I opened up its multiple meanings:
> asceticism, love, and valor are its *rasas*.
> When it was the year 1503,

> I composed this tale in *caupāīs*.
> If you read its six languages without a wise man,
> evening will fall and you'll still be reading! (Qutban, *Mirigāvatī*, stanzas 20–21, translated in Behl 2012b: 195)

As Aditya Behl has pointed out, Qutban did not actually *use* all the meters he mentions here, nor is the tale in six languages, but this inscription of multilingualism and reference to his multilingual knowledge set him up as a sophisticated and learned poet, and his *katha* as something inviting, even requiring, careful and guided exposition.

The other Sufi romances do not seem to have been composed at court but in *qasbas*. Sources also point to the proximity between these Sufi poets and Hindu chieftains, such as between Jayasi and the raja of nearby Amethi, whose undoubtedly very small "court" Jayasi was said to frequent (Khan n.d.: 15–16). Jayasi's unusual choice of subject—a historical narrative about the valor of Rajput rajas and their loyal subordinates against the lust and pride of the Delhi Sultan—not only played to his favorite theme of earthly pride chastised (as in *Kanhāvat*) but may have had resonance for his Amethi audience at a time when another Sultan, this time Mughal, loomed from Delhi (see Sreenivasan 2007).

The material evidence of manuscripts, script, and format further suggests a mixed audience and patronage for these romances. First, they are often found in manuscript collections bundled together with non-Sufi tales, tangible evidence that they became part of a common repertoire, thereby confirming the internal intertextual evidence.[52] Second, these *kathas* were copied in *both* the Persian script and Kaithi (the cursive script scribes in the region used for documents), suggesting two parallel networks of transmission.[53] In fact, the earliest extant manuscript of Qutban's *Mirigāvatī* is written in the Kaithi script, in a rough hand on thick, coarse paper, and it is *the first vernacular north Indian text not in the Persian language and script to be illustrated.*[54] Though it carries no colophon, this material clue suggests that possibly some local chieftain—like the Raja of Amethi—had by this time acquired a taste for illustrated books to be recited and displayed at his gatherings.[55]

If in the *Chandāyan* food is the centerpiece of the festive celebrations for the pastoralist warrior Lorik, Qutban's *Mirigāvatī* includes a glittering music and dance performance at a royal court, with a complete list of musical *ragas* (Qutban, *Mirigāvatī*, vv. 246–252, Plukker 1981: 52–53).[56] For some the courtly sophistication narrated in these early sixteenth-century romances may have reflected their own, as was the case of Sultan Husain Sharqi, but for others it may have worked as a shared imaginative aspirational, or even an exotic horizon. In terms of social characterization, the protagonists of these romances, Ratansen, Manohar, Rajkunwar, are all royal princes of the highest Solar or Lunar dynasties.

Gora and Badal, the social equivalents in the *Padmāvat* of Lorik, the *Chandāyan*'s hero, are not the heroes but Raja Ratansen's loyal subordinates.

If the *Chandāyan* traveled far, how far did these Hindavi romances travel? Though there are no early manuscripts of the *Padmāvat*, we know that it spread quickly, for only fifty years later its first vernacular courtly retellings were composed in Dakkhini by Hans Kabi at the court of Ibrahim 'Adil Shah of Bijapur, and in Bengali by Alaol at the court of Mrauk-U in Arakan.[57] As we have seen, when the story traveled westward to Rajasthan it became the standard historical narrative of Padmini of Chittor and the basis for later tellings such as Jatmal's, which Theodor Pavie considered "authentic" because Jatmal was a Hindu.

Within the Mughal world, Jayasi's *Padmāvat* seems to have retained recognition within Sufi milieus, though with the rise of Brajbhasha as a cosmopolitan vernacular its language may have started to sound obsolete. The first extant dated manuscript of *Padmāvat*, copied in 1675 by the Chishti Sufi Shaikh Muhammad Shakir in a *qasba* five hundred kilometers northwest of Jais, calls Jayasi *malik al-shu'arā'*, see p. 4 [22], or "king of poets," the title bestowed on poet laureates in the imperial court. The manuscript shows the utmost editorial attention to Jayasi's text, vocalizing it carefully and glossing each and every Hindavi word, even the most common, with a Persian equivalent. Such extensive glossing may be evidence of editorial care or of Shaikh Muhammad Shakir's struggle with the language.[58] A later Urdu version calls Jayasi's language Eastern, or Purbi (Ishrat n.d.).

The Persian glosses also show that Shaikh Muhammad Shakir was not interested in Jayasi's wealth of epic-Puranic and floral references: every mountain—Meru, Sumeru, Kailasa, etc.—becomes a generic "mountain" (*kūh*). The enchanting lists of fruits, flowers, and musical instruments become "name of fruit," "name of flower," "name of instrument." Cities such as Ayodhya are glossed simply as "toponym" (*nām-i jā-st*), and even a key character like Ratansen's first wife, Nagmati, is glossed as "woman" (*'aurat*), while the goddess Parvati becomes "wife of Mahadev (Shiva)" or simply "a woman" (*'aurat-i mahādev, 'auratī bud*). So while this particular manuscript is evidence of Jayasi's recognition among Persianate north Indian Chishti Sufis, it also arguably marks a loss of its social relevance and aesthetic appreciation, a point I'll return to when discussing Persian versions.

Outside the Sufi milieu, beyond Purab, even Jayasi's name seems to have been forgotten in late Mughal circles. When in 1738 the Persian-educated Delhi *littérateur* Anandram Mukhlis heard the *Padmāvat* recited by his "eastern" (*purbi*) servant and composed a Persian version of his own, the tone he employed suggests that the tale was new to him, that its eastern language sounded exotic, and its aesthetics needed the refinement of Persian garb:

> My servant told the colorful tale that Jayasi, the author of the Hindi *Padmāvat*, had written entirely in the eastern dialect—as though it were an eastern melody

Figure 2.2 Two folios from a Jayasi *Padmāvat* copied in Persian script in Gorakhpur in 1697.

Source: © The British Library Board, MS Hindi B 11.

brimming over with pain. Jayasi had based its wording on uncommon ideas and rare metaphors; however, since the work contains the bewitchments and marvels of love, it compels the heart to feel pain. And I said to myself: "if this Hindi beloved (*maʿshūq*) were to be displayed in the robes of a Persian writer then it is possible that this work of art might appear elegant and permissible in the estimation of those who possess taste (*dar naẕar-i ahl-i ẕauq īn fan mustaḥasan numāyad*). Therefore, my pen laid the foundations of this literary project and, having completed it within the span of a week, called it

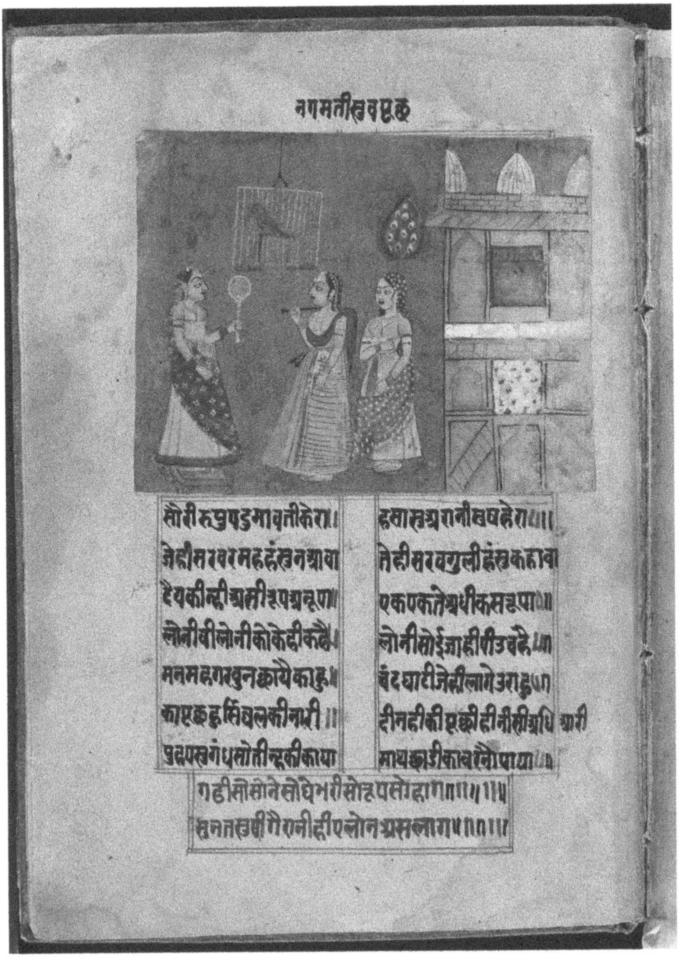

Figure 2.3 Folio of a *Padmāvat* copied in Nagari script in the eighteenth century.
Source: © Library of Congress, Asian Division's South Asian Rare Book Collection.

Hangāmah-ye 'Ishq [The Clamour of Love]." (Anand Ram Mukhlis, *Hangāma-ye 'ishq*, Phukan 2001: 34)

Mukhlis appears unaware of the wider popularity of Jayasi's tale, which was still being copied and illustrated in north India, or of earlier Persian versions (see Figures 2.2–2.4 and Table 2.1).

This mixed evidence raises historical and geographic questions about the fortune of this sophisticated vernacular genre. Should we consider *pemkathas* mainly a Sultanate genre, whose popularity waned as the cultural tastes of the

Figure 2.4 Folio from a *Padmāvat* copied in Kaithi script, a rare example of a calligraphic and illustrated Kaithi manuscript: the iconography and cartouche suggest a patron and artist familiar with Mughal Persian miniatures.
Source: Courtesy Bharat Kala Bhavan, Banaras, Acc. N. 10862.

Mughal elites shifted toward courtly poetry in Persian and Brajbhasha (see Busch 2011; Sharma 2015)? Or should we consider them a regional, eastern (*purbi*) genre that remained largely confined to the region? Most of the scholarship so far has focused on romances from the Sultanate period, merely mentioning the later texts. Yet a closer look (see Table 2.2) reveals not only a substantial continuing tradition, at least within the region, but also significant reverberations as well as shifts within the genre and in its social locations.

Table 2.1 Manuscript History

Qutban's *Mirigāvatī* (1505)		
1520–1570?	K	Handmade paper, full illustration with each leaf, found in Thakur Omprakash Singh's house in Ekadla in 1950s, Bharat Kala Bhavan
end 17c/ early 18c?	P	Found at Sufi hospice of Hakim Ajmal Khan
early 18c?	P	Sufi hospice, Maner Sharif
n.d.	K	Colophon missing, Bharat Kala Bhavan, Banaras Hindu University
1771	K	No colophon, National Archives, Nepal
Jayasi's *Padmāvat* (1540)		
17c?	P	Maner Sharif library, with texts by Burhan, Sadhan, etc.
1675	P	Amroha, copied by Muhammad Shakir, with P interlinear glosses
1685	K	Leiden University library
ca. 1696	P	British Library
1696	P	Gorakhpur, copied by 'Ibadullah Khan, ill. British Library
1697	P	Copied by Rahimdad Khan, British Library
1701	K	Baitalgarh, copied by *Krishna Brahman Baruva ke Dube Hariram putra* [NPS Khoj]
1702	P	British Library
early 18c?	P	British Library
1710	K	Folios in Bharat Kala Bhavan, Banaras
1719?		Bibliotheque Nationale, Fonds Gentil 32
1724	P	Sufi hospice, Bihar Sharif
ca. 1729?		Edinburgh University Library
1734	K	Selected scenes, ill. for Muh. Sultan Khan, at Bharat Kala Bhavan, Banaras
1747	K/D	With Babu Krishna Baldev Varma, Kaiserbagh, Lucknow [NPS Khoj]
1764?	D	Library of Maharajas of Banaras [NPS Khoj]
ca. 1780	P	Kartarpur, Bijnor
1785	K	Manje Shahr, Salempur dist., copied by Dayalal Kayasth Basondi
1786	K	Royal Asiatic Society Calcutta
early 19c?	D	Mirzapur, illustrated, copied by Than Kayastha, British Library
Manjhan's *Madhumālatī* (1545)		
1587	D?	Copied by Madhodas Kohli in Kashi; Bharat Kala Bhavan
1687	K	Copied by Rammalu Sahay; from Ekadala, in the house of Rawat Om Prakash Singh in 1955
1719	P	Copied by Miyan Abdul Rahman in Agra during the reign Muhammad Shah; "faux Chinese paper with wide brush strokes of gold," Rampur Raza Library
n.d.	P	Banaras

P = Persian script, K = Kaithi, D = Devanagari

Sources: Sreenivasan 2007; Das 1903; Plukker 1981.

Table 2.2 *Kathas* in the Eastern Region

Da'ud, *Chandāyan* (1379), Dalmau

- **Persian:** lost translation by 'Abd al-Quddus Gangohi (15c)

? Damo's *Lakṣmansen-Padmāvatī kathā* (1459)

Ishvardas, *Satyavatī kathā* (1501), born in Banaras, settled in Ghazipur; also wrote *Ekādasī kathā, Svargārohaṇ; Bharata milāp, Aṅgadpair, Sītā vanvās*

Sadhan, *Maināsat* (early 1500s?), ms together with Maner *Chandāyan*

- **Persian:** Hamid Kalanauri (d. 1619), *'Iṣmatnāma* (includes long praise of Emperor Jahangir, turns Indian months into Persian zodiac signs)
- **Bengali:** Daulat Kaji and Alaol, *Satī Maẏnā Lor -Chandrāṇī* (1659)

Qutban, *Mirigāvatī* (1503), Husain Shah Sharqi, Kahalgaon (Bhagalpur district, Bihar)

- **Persian:** *Anon. Rājkunwar* (1604), ill. prose version of Qutban's *Mirigavati* at Salim's Allahabad court

Lalach Kavi, *Haricharit* (1530), incomplete but popular, Hathgaon (near Rae Barelli), Kayasth or sweetmaker by caste

Jayasi, *Padmāvat* (started 1540), *Kanhāvat* (finished 1540), *Ākhirī kalām, Akahrāvaṭ, Chitrarekhā, Kahrānāmā, Maslānāma,* Jais

- **Persian:** Mulla 'Abd al-Shakur Bazmi (1590–1662), Deccan, *Rat Padam* (1618), *masnavi* (*hazaj* metre) *Tuḥfa al qulūb* (1651) dedicated to Shah Jahan
- 'Aqil Khan Razi (d. 1696), *Sham' wa parwāna* (1658–1659, *masnavi*)
- Lachman Ram, Ghazipur, *Farah-bakhsh* (completed 1723), mixed prose and poetry
- Anandram Mukhlis, *Hangāma-yi 'ishq* (1739–1740, *masnavi*)
- 'Imaduddin Khan, Rampur, *Bustān-i sukhan* (1808)
- Khwaja Muhammad Zakir, Banaras, *Padmāwat-i Ẕakīr* (1807, several mss)
- *Anon.* prose *Padmāwat* (1894)
- **Bengali:** Alaol, *Padmāvatī* (1651)
- **Urdu:** Mir Ziauddin 'Ibrat, *Padmāwat wa Ratan sen* (1838)
- *Maṯnavī sham 'o parwāna qissa Ratan o Padam*

Manjhan, *Madhumālatī* (1545), Sarangpur

- **Persian:** S. Ahmad Muh. Husaini Kashifi (d. 1648), *Gulshan-i ma'ānī,* Kalpi
- 'Aqil Khan Razi (d. 1696), *Manohar wa Madhūmāltī* (date?)

Tulsidas, *Rāmcaritmānas* (begun 1574), started in Ayodhya, moved to Banaras

Alam, *Mādhavānal-Kāmakandalā* (1584), mentions Todarmal

- **Persian:** Haqiri, *Maḥż-i ijāz* (1680)

Usman, *Chitrāvalī* (1613) and *Indrāvatī* (date?), Ghazipur

Puhakar, *Rasaratan* (1618), from Bhumigaon (Doab)

Shaikh Nabi, *Gyāndīpak* (1617). Baldemau village, near Dospur, dist. Jaunpur

Dharnidas (fl. 1656?), from Saran dist. in Bihar, *Prem-pragās*

Surdas, *Nal daman* (1657), father settled in Lucknow from Gurdaspur region

Table 2.2 Continued

Dukhharandas, *Puhupāvatī* (1669), Ghazipur, a follower of Malukdas
Newaj (Tivari Brahman from the Doab), *Śakuntalā* (1680) for Aurangzeb's son Azam Shah; also wrote *riti* verses
Husain Ali, *Puhupāvatī* (1731), "Harigaon," disciple of poet Keshavlal of Kannauj
Qasim Shah, *Haṃsa Jawāhara* (1736, Muhammad Shah's reigh), Daryabad, Bara Banki district
Kunwar Mukund Sing, *Naladamayantī* (1741)
Nur Muhammad "Kamyab," *Indrāvatī* (1754), *Anurāga bānsurī* (1764), Azamgarh region; also wrote in Persian
Ghulam Ashraf, known as **Shaikh Nisar,** *Yūsuf Zuleikhā* (1790), Rudauli, uses *chaupai, kavitt* and *savaiya*
Shahnawaz "Ali 'Saloni," *Prem chingārī* (1833), Rai Bareilli, then moved to Rewa, patronized by Raja Vishwanath Singh
'Ali Muras, *Kunwarāvat kathā* (date?); praise-description of Banaras at the beginning
Khwaja Ahmad (1830–1904), *Nūr Jahān* (of Khutan, 1904), Babuganj, dist. Pratapgarh
Shaikh Rahim Ansari (d. 1921), *Bhāṣā prema rasa* (1903–1915), worked in govt service in Bahraich; also wrote in Urdu and Persian
Kavi Nasir, *Prem darpaṇ* (1917), b. village Jamaniyan near Ghazipur; moved to Calcutta

Sources: Pandey 1982b; McGregor 1984; Hadi 1995; Sreenivasan 2007; Perso-Indica website.

What do these later texts tell us about the Mughal life of the *katha* genre? In the late Sultanate period, Hindavi *kathas* had crucially mediated local social and political relations and religious idioms and articulated a sophisticated vernacular taste. What happened with the coming of a new imperial polity, and a new cultural climate? Can we detect any significant shifts in plot, characterization, or geographical imagination? Do *kathas* register the consolidation of devotional bhakti groups and the new cosmopolitan vernacular taste in Brajbhasha poetry and poetics? And if the Sultanate *kathas* had expressed a vernacular cosmopolitanism and had become a model for courtly vernacular romances elsewhere, how did Persian authors deal with them? Did they transcodify the tales according to generic Persian literary conventions, or did they retain Hindavi characteristics?

The next section discusses four Hindavi (or should we now say *purbi*?) texts that show the impact of the Sufi romances and, in different ways, register the new cultural, political, and religious developments. The section after that explores how the Hindavi romances were transported into Persian, again along a spectrum of possibilities.

Hindavi *Kathas* in the Mughal World

The Perso-centric and Iranophile cosmopolitan and elite culture of the Mughal imperial court of the late sixteenth to eighteenth centuries has long stood for Mughal culture at large, and only in recent years has the image of this elite culture broadened to acknowledge the Mughal emperors' and their elites' involvement with Indian music, Sanskrit textuality, and poetry other than Persian. It was partly thanks to its success at the Mughal court that Brajbhasha became a "cosmopolitan vernacular."[59] We also now recognize that Mughal sub-elites, like the Rajputs who rose in the ranks of the Mughal administrations or stayed at its fringes, adopted aspects of Mughal culture, like court etiquette, dress, or architecture, but inflected them with their own tastes and preferences in, say, food, poetry, or religion (see Chatterjee 2009). Finally, while scholarship on bhakti devotion—which boomed in this period—for a long time followed the bhakti archive in ignoring the Mughal imperium, a recent historical turn in religious studies has explored the accommodation between at least some powerful bhakti establishments and the Mughal state, particularly in the Braj region, which was after all very close to the Mughal capital of Agra (see Hawley 2005; Burchett 2019). But what about Purab?

As Chapter 1 showed, Purab was incorporated into the Mughal state as two provinces, of Awadh and Allahabad, and while the political center of gravity shifted westward, a steady movement of governors, administrators, and poets in their accompanying entourages connected this and other provinces to the center.[60] Local Sufis, who had enjoyed close relations to the north Indian Sultans, may have struggled to reach the Mughal imperial ear, but some managed to do so (Alam 2009). *Qasbas* retained and possibly increased their local importance as centers of Persian education, which was now a requisite for employment in the imperial administration, and Allahabad grew as a provincial capital. In fact, it was here that Prince Salim, the future Jahangir, rebelled against his father, Akbar, in 1599–1604 (see below), and several original *kathas* in Hindavi and Persian specifically mention Jahangir as the "king of the age."[61] Investment in Persian education certainly grew, but so did cultivation of Brajbhasha poetry and poetics (Chapter 4), which in turn foregrounded the importance of Sanskrit language and poetics. And although Purab has so far remained marginal to the story of Krishna bhakti devotionalism in the sixteenth and seventeenth centuries, there is plenty of evidence of the active presence of devotional singers, poets, communities, and leaders once we look for it, though we still need to piece the evidence together.

The *kathas* discussed in this and the following section register the shifts in Mughal cultural tastes, though in different ways. For their sophistication and expansive geographical imagination they can all be called cosmopolitan, though they come from different social locations. The first text, Alam's *Mādhavanal-Kāmakandalā,* is by a poet who was perhaps close to one of Akbar's ministers. Though not a Sufi romance, it displays several characteristics of the genre. The second, Usman's *Chitrāvalī,* is a Sufi romance by an urban poet and displays considerable continuity with earlier *kathas,* but also a distinctly novel geographical imagination. The third *katha,* Puhakar's *Rasaratan* (Jewel of *rasa*), is by a local Hindu poet who claims some distant connection to the Mughal court and bends the genre in the direction of Sanskritic "poetic science" and away from Sufi romances. The fourth and most famous *katha*—indeed the most famous text of early modern Purab—Tulsidas's *Rāmcharitmānas,* rewrites the genre for a devotional audience and inscribes it into a Sanskrit genealogy that also leaves out any dialogism with Sufi texts.[62] In terms of themes, one revolves around musical virtuosity and two around another Mughal interest, painting, and portraiture in particular. Two incorporate the expansive geographical imagination and ethnic pluralism of the Mughal Empire, marking their date in both Islamic Hijri and Hindu Vikrama calendars.[63] The last *katha* turns resolutely away from the present to evoke a perfect Hindu cosmos. In modern literary histories they belong to different categories: Sufi (*Chitrāvalī*), bhakti (*Rāmcharitmānas*), and not much anywhere (*Rasaratan*) (Chapter 5). But we can see them as representing the "multiple stories and trajectories" (Massey [2005] 2012) of Mughal vernacular culture: urban Sufi, courtly Brajbhasha (Chapter 4), and bhakti devotionalism (Chapter 3).

There is in fact only one Hindavi romance, or *pemkatha,* that can be directly linked to the Mughal courtly milieu, and it tellingly revolves around music. We know that, like the Sharqi Sultans of Jaunpur before them, the Mughals enthusiastically cultivated north Indian music, and central to the love story between the Brahman musician Madhavanal and the courtesan dancer-singer Kamkandala (an already existing story) is musical connoisseurship (*guna, guṇa*)—a polysemic term referring generically to "talent" and more specifically to aesthetic and musical connoisseurship. Alam's *Mādhavānal-Kāmakandalā* (1582) praises the third Mughal emperor, Akbar (r. 1556–1605), and then, with greater fervor, his powerful Hindu finance minister Todarmal, who may have been the patron of the work (*Mādhavānal,* v. 4.5, Alam 1982: 3–5).[64] Todarmal was from Laharpur, in today's Sitapur district (in the Mughal province of Awadh) and had worked for Sher Shah Suri before moving into the heart of the Mughal administration.

Alam's praise of *guna* suggests its importance in a world of opportunities but also instability:

> No one questions high or lowly status,
> if you have *guna* you sit high up.

A talented man going abroad
sells his wares at a higher price.
Just as a mother rears her son,
guna always bestows happiness.
Without talent, your ancestors fall from heaven,
without talent, your mouth utters lowly words.
Without talent, you are like a sightless man,
without talent, you are a wingless bird.
doha: When you fall into bad times and lose your wealth,
    if talented, your talent stays with you.
    If there is talent in your body,
    wealth will come by you again. (*Mādhavānal,* v. 33, Alam 1982: 25)

Musical performances at court play a crucial role in Alam's tale and, as was already the case with Qutban's *Mirigāvatī,* allow him to display his technical musical knowledge.[65] In fact, reading Qutban's and Alam's *kathas* together helps us trace a continuity of tastes and connoisseurship between Sultanate and Mughal culture—though this was not a debt that the Mughals themselves necessarily acknowledged.[66]

Alam says nothing about himself. In contrast, Usman, the author of *Chitrāvalī* (1613), describes with some pleasure his family and hometown of Ghazipur, further east from Banaras on the Ganges. Usman follows Jayasi in inscribing Ghazipur in the paradigm of the four ages, or *yugas,* but his description moves between a conventional depiction of the ideal city (*nagara-varṇana*) and a more realistic one of Hindu and Muslim groups:[67]

Ghazipur is an excellent place,
famous from the start as an abode of the gods.
The Yamuna and Ganga touch it together,
with lovely Gomti in between.
By the river is a fine bank,
in the *dvāpara* age a godly ascetic (*devatana*) came here to practice.
It was resettled in *kaliyuga,*
like a second Amarapuri.
A fort on top, god's river below—
seeing it washes sins away.
People of great learning live here—
Sayyids and wise shaikhs
who speak nothing but knowledge (*gyāna*);
you long to see them and are happy to listen.

Godly in knowledge and meditation, heroic in battle,
Silent in contemplation, clever in assemblies, lions to their enemies.
(*Chitrāvalī*, stanza 24, Usman 1981: 7)

The local Muslim elites—Sayyids and shaikhs—are listed first. But then come dagger-carrying *mogals* and Pathans, warlike Rajputs and musicians (*gunījana*), bards (*bhāṭa*) who expound on prosody (*piṅgala*), and musical specialists (*kalāvanta*): "Everyone is a king in his own house," and people ride Tajik and Turkic horses "as if they were noblemen (*umrā* and *mīra*)" (*Chitrāvalī*, 26.1, Usman 1981: 7). Usman also mentions lower-caste people (*sudranha*) who "spread out trade in every house and practice religion day and night. They hold discourses about knowledge, while young women sit and recite all the *rasas*" (*Chitrāvalī*, 26.1, Usman 1981: 7). Is this perhaps a reference to the upwardly mobile Sant devotees who were active in the Ghazipur region (see Chapter 3)?

About himself, Usman says that he studied a little (lit. "four syllables," *acchara chāri*) and then realized that poetry is the only immortal thing in the world.[68] And since "those who sing *kathās* full of *rasa* savor that nectar (*amirita*) and make others savor it," he decided to compose one himself (*Chitrāvalī*, 28.6–7, Usman 1981: 8). Usman praises the Sufi master Shah Nizam Chishti and his own *pir* Baba Haji for their transformative look of love (*mayā diṣṭi*) and the churning they produced in him. In the tradition of earlier Sufi *kathas*, he uses Indic vocabulary for spiritual truths and concepts: "[A]s I churned and churned, one day the churning stick broke. Then the realization 'you are that' (*tatvamasi*) came out of the matter, and hell fell away."[69] The prologue ends nicely gesturing to the polysemy of the *katha* and the mystery of oneness and multiplicity:

I created a *kathā* in my heart,
sweet to tell and happy to hear.
I crafted it as it came to my mind,
but each will grasp it in their own way.
A child will find *rasa* for his ears,
young men will increase bodily desire.
An old man will listen and realize
that the world is empty business (*dhandhā*).
A *jogi* will find the path of yoga,
a *bhogī* will find pleasure and joy.
This story is a happy wish-fulfilling tree,
you find the fruit you wish for.
I wrote a lovely, spotless mirror—
if you look you'll find yourself.

> Everyone tells and listen about worldly honor and manners;
> Sweetness is found in what one prefers. (*Chitrāvalī*, stanza 32, Usman 1981: 9)

The plot of Usman's *Chitrāvalī*, like Puhakar's *Rasaratan*, on which more later, hinges on portraits and painting, possibly refracting the burgeoning Mughal courtly interest in the genre. In the prologue Usman praises god as the supreme *chiterā* (painter) and cleverly develops the metaphor: god created the world as a picture of himself (*yaha jaga chitra kīnha jehi kerā*, 1.1), he painted a picture of Man and Woman, he created all the colors, he created form (*rūpa*) and color (*barana*) though he himself has neither, etc. Usman's (1981: 8) romance contains many motifs familiar from other romances, and in fact it mentions their protagonists Mirigavati and Rajkunwar, Padmini and Ratansen, Madhumalati and Manohar when discussing embodiment (*rūpa*), love, and longing (*viraha*)—clearly placing itself in the tradition of Hindavi Sufi romances. The story is full of twist and turns. The Nepali prince Sujan chances upon a small forest shrine while hunting, and while he sleeps the temple deity takes him to the picture gallery of Princess Chitravali, a motif that echoes Manjhan's *Madhumālatī*. When Sujan wakes up he admires her portrait and paints his own picture before the deity takes him back. Smitten by love, Sujan returns to the shrine and undertakes austerities. In turn, Chitravali has found his picture and, smitten by love herself, sends out eunuchs in yogi garb to look for him—a variation on the *jogi* motif. Her mother's devious maid finds Sujan's portrait and informs her; aghast, the mother orders the maid to wash the portrait away. In revenge, Chitravali shaves the maid's head and dismisses her, turning her into an enemy.

Meanwhile, one of the yogis finds Sujan, takes him to Chitravali's city, and arranges a meeting at Shiva's temple—another staple motif. But the maid finds Sujan first, blinds him, and throws him into a cave, where he is eaten by a giant snake, who, however, spits him out, scorched by Sujan's fiery unhappy love. Sujan's sight is restored by a collyrium given by a mysterious "forest man" (*banamānusa*). Still wandering in the forest, Sujan is then picked up by an elephant, which in turn is carried off by a flying "king of the birds" (*pakshīrāja*). Dropped on the ocean shore, Sujan reaches nearby Oceantown and is found resting in the garden of the daughter of the local king. Sujan helps defeat the neighboring king who wanted to abduct her and is rewarded with her hand. (She becomes his first wife, like Rupmini in *Mirigāvatī*.) Together, they undertake a pilgrimage to Girnar, a real pilgrimage site in western India, where one of Chitravali's yogis finds him. Meanwhile, Chitravali's father decides to get her married and sends painters to make portraits of all the available princes, a motif that reappears in Puhakar's

Rasaratan as well. The yogi informs Chitravali, who gives him a letter for Sujan to come to the ceremony, where she herself will choose her husband (*svayaṃvara*). Her mother learns about it, though, and Sujan finds himself in jail, till one of the painters returns with his portrait and vouchsafes for his standing and lineage, and Chitravali and Sujan can finally get married. Echoing earlier *kathas*, the first wife's lament eventually reaches Sujan and convinces him to return home. After a shipwreck (another echo from the *Padmāvat* and *Madhumālatī*), Sujan and Chitravali finally manage to reach Jagannath Puri, another important sacred site, and here the tale ends.

A striking novelty in *Chitrāvalī* which, rather surprisingly, we also find in Usman's contemporary, the Sant poet Malukdas (Chapter 3), is its geographical imagination. I can only call it Mughal imperial, since it encompasses both the provinces of the Mughal Empire and other political and imaginative "significant geographies," like Kabul and "Alexander's Russia." Compared to the other Sufi romances, this *katha* innovatively combines contemporary political geographies with imaginative and conceptual "Hindu" and Islamicate ones. For example, it mentions Ceylon by its multiple names—Lanka, Singhaldip, Sarandip, Ceylon—and as the place where Adam first set his foot on earth.[70] The servants Chitravali sends out searching for Sujan cover the main routes of the Mughal Empire and beyond: it is worth tracing the details of these journeys, because for over ten stanzas they provide a sense of the "world" from the perspective of a provincial Mughal Sufi vernacular poet.

One servant travels to Multan, Sindh, the city of Thattha (full of Baluchis), Ghakkhar, and Peshawar—where "he saw the whole world." He then travels to Kabul ("the country of the *mogalas*") and further into Central Asia, to Badakhshan, Khurasan, and "Alexander's Rus, where everything is dark," Mecca ("God's place," *vidhi asthānā*), Medina with the pilgrims on *haj*, then Baghdad, Istanbul, and Ladakh (Usman 1981: 101). The servant traveling south goes all the way to Lanka and Sarandip, passing through "happy and rich" Gujarat, Jamnagar in Kacch, Ceylon ("the place of father Adam," *bābā ādama kā asthānā*), crossing the bridge from Rameshwaran. He then goes to Balandip, where he sees the English, *aṅgrejā*.[71] He then goes to Karnatak, Kukhar (?), Odisa, and Tailanga (Telangana). He sees black Africans (*habshīs* and *jaṅgis*), Tamils and foreigners (*firaṅgīs*). From Orissa he travels to the port of Hooghly, then turns back to go to Berar and the Deccan (102). The servant going east first visits Mathura, then Vrindaban—where he looks for Sujan in the same way as the milkmaids search for Krishna. He visits Delhi and sees the imperial throne, then Agra, Prayag, and the sacred confluence of the three rivers (*tribenī*). He worships Shiva in Banaras (called by its Hindu name, Kashi) and undertakes the *panchkosi* pilgrimage around it, then leaves disappointed for Rohtas. After Magadha (*maggaha*) he travels to northeast Bihar and to Tirhut, where he hears of the famous poet Vidyapati (102). Finally, one servant travels to Bengal, beyond the Brahmaputra to Sonargaon, where he visits the holy site (*tīratha*) of the famed Five Pirs (*pañchpīra*). From there he goes to Malwa, Sondip, Pegu and Manipur, Makharhanga, until he turns back to Girnar (in Gujarat), where he finally finds Sujan (103). The imaginary geography of earlier *kathas* had remained limited to diegetic toponyms. In *Chitrāvalī*, too, Chitravali's capital is Rupanagar, the City of Beauty. Yet here it is compounded by a real geography of truly imperial proportions, a startling innovation.

Chitrāvalī projects a very Mughal combination of Persianate cosmopolitanism and Indic markers. In his praise of Jahangir, Usman writes that Arab, Iraqi, Egyptian, Khotanese, and Chinese visitors all come bringing gifts, and the Persian festival of Nawruz is celebrated at court. At the same time, he uses the Indic motif of the six seasons (*shaḍṛtu*) to compare Jahangir to the sun and the seasons' natural elements to his court (Usman 1981: 4–5).

If we turn to the next *katha*, Puhakar's *Rasaratan* (1618), we find similarities but also significant differences. Puhakar writes proudly of his scribal Kayastha family, which served the local king, and of his grandfather and great-uncle, who had earned respect at Akbar's court.[72] About himself he tells us that he studied scribal technologies (*vṛtti kāistha*), studied Hindi (here probably already meaning Brajbhasha) prosody and poetics thoroughly, and learned from the classical Sanskrit poets and from the Rajasthani poet Chand Bardai; he also mentions that he "strolled through Persian poetry" (Puhakar 1963: 5; see Chapter 4). Though Puhakar clearly values the family connection to the Mughal imperial court, the fact that he does not mention a Mughal patron and that his *katha* was copied in the Nagari script suggest a more local, Hindu patron.[73]

While Puhakar must have known the Hindavi *pemkathas*, as will become clear, he pointedly does not mention them and sets his story entirely in a Puranic world of gods and human princes. *Rasaratan* tells the story of the love between Princess Rambhavati and Prince Surasena, orchestrated by the god of love Kama and his wife Rati, who want to bring together the most beautiful man and woman on earth. Like *Chitrāvalī*, its plot hinges around portraits and the search for the real person they represent. The goddess Rati takes Surasena's semblance and appears to Rambha in a dream, causing her to fall sick with love, though she does not know with whom—Puhakar here stops to explain nine of the ten states of love, complete with definitions and examples (*lakshaṇa*). In order to save Rambha, her clever and "mature" (*prauṛha*) maid Mudita, who has guessed that her illness must be due to love, arranges for the queen to send painters (*chitrakāra*) to make portraits of all the princes, just as in *Chitrāvalī*—the mysterious man must be among them. Meanwhile, a contest in which Rambha will choose her husband, a *svayaṃvara*, is arranged. One painter finds Surasena, realizes that this must be the man since he has also been pining for an unknown beloved, and makes him fall in love by painting Rambha's picture for him. Surasena then leaves his parents in order to take part in the groom-selection contest, but bored nymphs see him asleep and decide to make him marry Champavati, a nymph (*apsarā*) who was banished from god Indra's heaven. In a scene strongly reminiscent of Manjhan's *Madhumālatī*, they bring their two beds together while they sleep, and Champavati becomes Surasena's first wife. Surasena nevertheless leaves her and manages to reach Rambha's contest in time, traveling with a group of yogis. After further trials Surasena and Rambha finally marry.

While the plot devices will sound familiar by now from the Sufi romances, Puhakar's *Rasaratan* also articulates Mughal culture in terms of courtly (*riti*) Hindi—so much so that we can call it a *riti katha*. *Riti* poetry was sophisticated poetry in Brajbhasha that was informed by Sanskrit poetics and systematically detailed the many types of heroine (*nayika-bheda*)—all elements we find here. Instead of the simple *chaupai-doha* stanzaic structure of most *kathas*, Puhakar displays his knowledge of prosody by using a dazzling array of meters.[74] Even his initial invocation to Shiva and praise of Jahangir resemble a typical freestanding and highly alliterative praise verse (*praśasti*) in Brajbhasha:

timira vaṃsa avataṃsa sāhi akabara kula nandana
jagata gurū jagapāla jagata nāika jagavandana
sahinasāha ālamapanāha naranāha dhurandharai
tega vṛtti dillī nareśa triya chāri jāsu ghara
ardhaṅga aṅga pañcama gharani tarani teja mahi chakkavai
nara rāja manahuṃ pañchama sahita supañcha mili mahi bhuggavai.
(*Rasaratan*, Puhakar 1963: 7)

Crest of Timur's lineage
child of King Akbar's family.
Lord and protector of the world,
world hero praised by the world.
Shahanshāh, ālampanāh,
lord of men and hero.
You rule Delhi by the sword,
with four wives in the house.
Your fifth and clever mistress bedazzles the earth with sunlike radiance;
The lord of men, as if with a fifth [?,] enjoys the earth with all five.[75]

Several systems of knowledge, or *shastras*, underwrite Puhakar's *katha* and infuse its description and dialogue. There are three types of encounter (*darasana*): dream, picture, and face to face (Puhakar 1963: 30; see Insler 1989);

Rambha's palace companions are modeled on the various types of heroines, and Rambha's own experience of longing (*viraha*) follows step by step the classification of love states in the Sanskrit tradition: from desire to memory, restlessness, incoherent speech, the inability to move—Puhakar stops just before the last stage, death.[76] Each description of hero and heroine—and of their portraits—becomes an elaborate head-to-toe inventory (*nakha-shikha*). Courtly performances of music and dance feature in the tale mostly as accompaniment to royal processions (see Busch 2015). Music, astrology, palmistry, erotic science—the Indian knowledge systems valued in Mughal culture—are all given due space.[77]

At the same time, Puhakar by and large disregards the Sufi conceptual vocabulary of the *pemkatha* tradition. Usman (1981: 8) still used the key term *rasa* in the Sufi understanding (e.g., "the *rasas* of knowledge," or *gyāna rasana*). For Puhakar, *rasa* is not the *rasa* of love, or *prema-rasa*, but one of the traditional nine *rasas* of Sanskrit poetics;[78] *viraha* is only one of the two classical forms of erotic love (*shringara rasa*) rather than the path of self-purification and self-transformation, as in Sufi romances. Only once does *Rasaratan* mention the "difficult path of love" (*kaṭhina pema-panthu*),[79] and when Prince Surasena becomes a yogi, it is less to divest himself of his worldly attachments and more to reach Rambha's town with a group of yogis. Rambha plays no transformative role for the hero, unlike in Sufi romances, but is simply a courtly princess.[80]

Bedecked—or rather beladen—with the ornaments of *riti* poetry, *Rasaratan* moves at a stately pace, with comparatively little dialogue and action and few trials and adventures, unlike the other romances. Its language mirrors Puhakar's attempt to transform the Hindavi *pemkatha* into a recognizable Brajbhasha courtly genre—perhaps closer to the Rajasthani tradition of Chand Bardai's *Rāsau*.[81] Even more striking, given its debt to Sufi romances and similarities with Usman's *Chitrāvalī*, intertextual references in *Rasaratan* include none of the famous Sufi romances but only mention epic-Puranic characters. For this very reason Hindi literary historians from Ramchandra Shukla onward have saluted *Rasaratan* as a "completely Indian" romance, unlike the "non-Indian" ones by Sufi poets.[82] In fact, it makes better sense to consider *Rasaratan* part of the same tradition and note that Puhakar did not acknowledge such connection. What Puhakar's *Rasaratan* also shows is that, when poets moved away from the Sufi template, they tended to remove the coded language, leading to a loss of polysemy. In the case of Tulsidas's *Ramkatha,* the code became that of bhakti theology, and both in Tulsi's *Rāmcharitmānas* and in *Rasaratan* intertextual references include only the epics and the Puranas.

It may seem churlish to squeeze a discussion of Tulsidas's (ca. 1530–1623) masterpiece, the *Rāmcharitmānas* (Holy Lake of the Deeds of Ram, ca. 1574), into the rubric of Mughal *kathas.* No Hindi work has been as cherished and canonized, and more has been written in Hindi about Tulsidas than any other poet. But the reason I discuss it here rather than in a separate chapter is because in the *Mānas*, as the work is familiarly called in Hindi, Tulsidas expanded the possibilities of the *katha* genre in a completely new direction. Clearly well-versed in Sanskrit and familiar with the earlier Sanskrit versions of the *Rāmāyaṇa*, Tulsidas sacralized the narrative through elaborate Sanskrit and vernacular invocations that frame and pepper the story. He fashioned an artful and pliable vernacular language and a narrative that instructed, entertained, and moved the listeners and brought them again and again to realize Ram's love for his devotees and the salvific power of devotion, bhakti. Its early renown shows that it found an echo among an existing and growing devotional community of taste.[83]

In fact, Tulsidas's *Ramkatha* was not the first devotional *katha* to be written, nor the first in the region. A few decades earlier, a poet called Lalach had written a *katha* about Krishna adapting the tenth book of the Sanskrit *Bhāgavata Purāṇa*.[84] Incidentally, this was only ten years and forty miles away from where Jayasi saw a performance of Krishna's story in Jais in 1540 and decided to write it in his own way (see Orsini 2015b). Lalach's rather plain and swift-moving *Haricharit,* in *chaupai-dohas,* follows quite closely the Krishna narrative of the *Bhāgavata Purāṇa*. He mentions no specific sectarian affiliation but generally praises devotion, the Sants, and the gathering and singing of devotional songs (*satsang*). Though unremarkable in artistic terms and therefore neglected by literary historians, Lalach's early *Harikatha* circulated widely and for a long time—his unfinished text was completed by another poet a hundred years later, and scores of manuscript copies of this text have been found as far afield as eastern U.P., Bihar, Malwa, and Gujarat, most in the cursive Kaithi script.[85] The text is worth noting for us because it signals the substantial presence of textual communities gathering around devotional texts, as well as the mixed nature of entertainment and edification that storytelling was supposed to bring. The reward (lit. "fruit," *phala*) that telling and listening to a *katha* brought was held to be as great as pilgrimage or Vedic sacrifice (see Orsini 2015d).

Tulsidas's monumental *katha* about Ram is quite a different enterprise in both complexity and scale. A lengthy and elaborate prologue opens with ritual invocations to various gods in Sanskrit and Hindavi, dwells on the poet's doubts before the daunting task of following the footsteps of Valmiki, his claimed though not only intertext, before laying out the scheme of seven "stairways" that lead down to the lake, while four sets of divine and mythological narrators narrate the story of Ram. The result of this complex edifice is a narrative that dizzyingly exists at multiple levels and multiple temporalities: it takes place after, during, and before it is being told on earth, and it is told at the same time in various celestial realms.[86] Listening to it means entering another time-space and being enveloped by a narrative of all-powerful devotion.

Tulsidas appears less interested than Valmiki's narrative in Ram's slaying of demons or in describing rituals but expands every possible opportunity to detail Ram's loving encounters with relatives, helpers, and foes, who all emotionally declare their devotion to him. He also skillfully alternates between swift narrative sections—as when Ram, his brother Lakshman, and wife Sita travel through the forest in exile—and slow "episodes" (*prasanga*) about pivotal emotional encounters, ecstatic descriptions of Ram's beauteous appearance, discourses on bhakti theology, and pithy statements that have become proverbial wisdom (see Lutgendorf 1991).

Tulsi's best-known poetic devices are alliteration and extended similes that develop over the course of one or more stanzas, binding together multiple abstract and concrete elements into causes and effects. This is an example from the prologue, which builds a mental picture of the Lake of Ram continuing from the previous stanza:

> The seven books are its stairs,
> which, seen by wisdom's eye, please the heart.
> The Lord of Raghus' [Ram's] fame is transcendent and limitless—
> its narration is the water's profound depth.
> The glory of Ram and Sita makes it nectar-like,
> sparkling with the wave-play of similes.
> *Caupāī* verses are its dense lily-pads,
> its poetic devices, pearl-bearing oysters,
> and its lovely lyric verses and couplets (*chanda soraṭhā sundara dohā*),
> a multitude of many-colored lotuses.
> Matchless meaning, mood, and eloquence (*aratha anūpa subhāva subhāsa*)
> are their pollen, nectar, and fragrance.
> Right actions are lines of honeybees,
> and wisdom, detachment, and discrimination are *haṃsa* birds.
> Allusion, ambiguity, and varying verse forms
> are many kinds of charming fish.
> The four aims—success, virtue, pleasure, and release—
> expounded with knowledge and wisdom,
> the nine poetic moods, and the spiritual disciplines (*nava rasa japa tapa joga virāgā*)
> all are water creatures, living in this lovely lake.
> Praise of the upright, the holy, and the divine name
> are like colorful waterfowl.
> The assembly of saints (*santasabhā*) is a mango grove on all sides,
> and their faith is likened to the season of spring. . . .
> Restraint and discipline (*sama yama*) are flowers, yielding fruits of wisdom,

whose nectar is love for Hari's feet, as the Veda declares.
And the many supplemental stories here (*aurau kathā aneka prasaṅga*)
are multicolored parrots and cuckoos.
These gardens and groves of ecstasy,
where birds of happiness sport,
are watered by tears of love
from the eyes of the heart's gardener. (*Mānas* 1.37, Tulsidas 2016: 85–89, translated by Philip Lutgendorf)

Traditional poetic objects like flowers, bees, and groves are here combined with religious and philosophical concepts, brought together by the overarching image of the lake surrounded by stepped landings, gardens, and water fowl. This description continues for another six stanzas and paints a narrative of fortunate and happy folks who manage to bathe in the lake and sing and tell the story, and unhappy ones who keep away or belittle the lake.[87] It then turns to a celebration of the River Ganges, which "surges toward the sea of Ram's reality," and a brief summary of the story (*Mānas* 1.40, translated in Lutgendorf 2016: 93).

Formally, Tulsidas employs the established *chaupai-doha* pattern of other *kathas*, regularly enriching it with other meters (*chhanda*), while linguistically his Hindavi moves effortlessly between demotic and Sanskritized vocabulary according to the effect he wants to create. Critics have noted his inclusion of (a few) Arabo-Persian words, but in fact even more than Puhakar's *Rasaratan*, Tulsi's *Ramkatha* demarcates a separate and self-contained, Hindu-only space and makes no acknowledgment of the existence of the Sufi romance tradition (Stasik 2009).[88] Unlike the Sufi romance authors discussed in this chapter, or the Sants discussed in the next one, Tulsi does not try to speak across religious divides. In early Hindi scholarship, this has been viewed as Tulsidas's heroic defense of Hindu culture against the Muslim onslaught. Ramchandra Shukla hailed Tulsidas as the savior of Hindu culture, and he was canonized as "the" Hindi classic poet par excellence (see Orsini 1998). A multilingual and located approach instead views Tulsidas's *katha* as expressing a specific position of religious and cultural demarcation, which was made possible by the expansion of devotional culture in Awadh towns and villages and the protection of pilgrimage routes to sites like Prayag (Allahabad), Banaras, and Chitrakut under the Mughal imperium.[89] In Tulsidas's Banaras, Madhuri Desai (2017) shows, from the late sixteenth century Hindu Mughal grandees like Akbar's finance minister Todarmal and Raja Mansingh of Amber built mansions (*havelis*) and supported Brahman communities and the construction of two large temples dedicated to Shiva Vishweshwar and Bindu Manav and several monasteries (*maths*) in the heart of the city. Desai notes that the Mughal state owned large swaths of land in Banaras and ratified all private ownership along the river's edge and elsewhere in the city.[90]

The textual sophistication of texts like *Chitrāvalī, Mādhavānal-Kāmakandhalā, Rasaratan,* and the *Rāmcharitmānas* and the continuous copying of the earlier Sufi *pemkathas* suggest that Hindavi *kathas* remained a lively genre, at least in the region, as the profusion of copies in Kaithi script also indicates.[91] But unlike the late Sultanate *kathas* discussed in the previous section, and apart from Tulsidas's *Mānas* and, to a lesser extent, Alam's *Mādhavānal*, Hindavi *kathas* written in the Mughal period do not seem to have found further echo. Why did *kathas* like *Chitrāvalī,* which delights the reader with its originality and sophistication, not travel more?[92] The answer seems to lie in the change of poetic fashion and the greater attraction exercised by Brajbhasha poetic genres (see Chapter 4). Mughal poetic culture was a Persian-Brajbhasha one, and *kathas* mostly became raw material for Persian poets to turn into Persian narratives rather being patronized as a Hindavi genre, as I show in the next section. Later Hindavi *kathas* became local affairs, largely restricted to devotional and Sufi audiences (see Table 2.2).

Hindavi *Kathas* into Persian

Persian retellings and translations of Indic stories have become a rich and growing field of scholarship in the past few years, thanks to the burgeoning interest in Mughal multilingualism and cultural exchanges.[93] The trend took off in the sixteenth century during Akbar's reign, continued with his son Jahangir (r. 1605–1627),[94] and lasted until the nineteenth century.

Much of the scholarship has so far tended to focus on cultural exchanges at the imperial court and to view these translations as part of an imperial project to "know" and "incorporate" Indian lore. Yet the archive shows a wider range of impulses and motivations at work. There were Iranian and Central Asian literati curious about Indian themes and tales, and Persian literati with local roots, Sufi affiliation, or from Hindu backgrounds keen to validate their regional and/or spiritual tradition within the cosmopolitan idiom of Persian literature (see Pellò 2018). Paying attention to these differences helps delink Persian writing from a stable cosmopolitan position that identifies the cosmopolitan with the center or the transnational.[95] Instead, Persian in India occupied an ambivalent position as both an Indian and a transnational language, and as we shall also see in Chapter 4, one could be a local cosmopolitan.

Nor, as Chapter 1 argued, can we simply consider the high languages as cosmopolitan and the vernaculars as local and unsophisticated. In the case of Persian rewritings of Avadhi *kathas*, it would indeed be easy to consider the Mughal trend of rewriting them as Persian *qissas* and *masnavis* as turning a local vernacular form into a cosmopolitan one. For some, like Anandram Mukhlis, quoted above, this was indeed the case: *Padmāvat* was a charming tale but needed to be improved by re-dressing it in Persian garb. However, this chapter so far has shown that Avadhi *kathas* were actually cosmopolitan texts—whether in terms of literary sophistication and confidence, expansive intertextuality, or broad reach—in the vernacular. In other words, it is more useful to think of cosmopolitan and vernacular (or indeed local) as two positions along a spectrum of possibilities within each language, as Subrahmanyam Shankar has argued (2012). This is the argument I pursue in this section: Persian in India covered a broad spectrum of social locations and levels of sophistication, so that in different circumstances one could write (and certainly speak) a kind of "vernacular Persian" or a cosmopolitan one, or indeed both. With respect to Persian retellings of Avadhi *kathas*, this spectrum is reflected in different authorial stances, which range from respect for the vernacular text to complete transcodification into the Persian *masnavi* code. We can call these two poles *genre localization* and *genre cosmopolitism*, with several intermediate positions, shown in Table 2.3.

At one end, and in rarer cases, we have a more or less iconic translation and an attitude of admiration and respect for the vernacular source text and author; the Persian author/translator acts as part–"local informant," knowledgeable about Indian lore and cultural details, and part–Persian *littérateur*, displaying his mastery of Persian codes and ability to set up poetic equivalences between Hindi and Persian tropes. This is the case of the first text I consider, the anonymous *Rājkunwar*. We then slide into the mere mention of the original author or text and an abridged retelling of the story, with the Persian author inhabiting an ambivalent position as both insider and outsider, familiar with the story's cultural referents but translating them for a presumed unfamiliar audience. At the other pole we have a more or less drastic transcodification, which uses a few details of the Hindavi tale to produce a variation on the Persian template of a romantic *masnavi*. In this case the balance shifts decidedly toward the display of Persian literary codes and its already long-standing repertoire of Indian tropes.[96] It is difficult to map a historical trajectory in the movement from one pole to the other. Rather, they appear to have been different simultaneous possibilities within the Indo-Persian literary field. Table 2.4 shows that only a few Avadhi *kathas* were rendered into Persian, and only Jayasi's *Padmāvat* more than twice.

Table 2.3 From Translation to Transcodification

Translation	Mention of source author/text	Retelling with more or less significant changes	Transcodification

Table 2.4 Avadhi Romances into Persian

Qutban, *Mirigāvatī* (1503)	
	Anon. Rājkunwar (1604), ill. Persian prose narrative for Prince Salim in Allahabad
Jayasi, *Padmāvat* (1540)	
	Mulla 'Abd al-Shakur Bazmi (1590–1662), Deccan, *Rat Padam* (1618)
	'Aqil Khan Razi (d. 1696), Delhi, *Sham' wa parwāna* (The Lamp and the Moth, 1658–1659, *masnavi*)
	Lachmi Ram, Ghazipur, *Farah-bakhsh* (Splendid, completed 1723, prose version of *Shamā' wa parwāna*)
	Anandram Mukhlis, Delhi *Hangāma-yi 'ishq* (Tumult of Love, 1739, 1742, *masnavi*)
	Khwaja Muhammad Zakir, Kashmir, Lahore, Banaras, *Padmāvat-i Ẕakīr* (Zakir's Padmavat, H 1222/CE 1807, several mss.)
	'Imaduddin Khan, Rampur, *Bustān-i sukhan* (Garden of Speech, H 1223/CE 1808)
	Rai Gobind, *Tuḥfat al-qulūb* (Gift of the Heart, n.d., prose *dastan*)
Manjhan, *Madhumālatī* (1545)	
	S. Ahmad Muh. Husaini Kashifi (d. 1648), Tirmiz, then Kalpi, *Gulshan-i ma'ānī* (Flower-garden of Meaning)
	'Aqil Khan Razi (d. 1696), *Masnavī miḥ-o māh* (Love and the Moon)

In terms of textual analysis, this approach entails looking out for the presence or absence of Hindavi terms and Indic referents and the amount of explanation provided for them; checking the repertoire of intertextual references; and noting whether characters, episodes, and cultural practices are maintained or recoded. Let us consider two of these Persian retellings that show different articulations within the two poles of genre localization and genre cosmopolitism, beginning with the anonymous translation of Qutban's *Mirigāvatī*, a true literary-historical puzzle.

Written and profusely illustrated for Prince Salim, the future Emperor Jahangir, when he rebelled against his father, Akbar, and established his own capital with his own atelier (*karkhana*) in Allahabad, this is definitely an imperial object.[97] Yet it is also the closest to the Hindavi text, in fact decidedly simpler in its Persian prose than the sophisticated original Hindavi verse romance. This suggests that the anonymous author was a local man who was familiar with the Hindavi text and its wealth of intertextual references and who respected Qutban's text as a literary work. I then turn to Mulla 'Abd al-Shakur Bazmi's *masnavi Rat Padam*, which significantly edits Jayasi's narrative and rewrites the characters according to a more generic Persian template.

In contrast to all the other Persian adaptations of Hindavi texts that I have seen, the Persian prose *Rājkunwar* actually *is* a translation—not literal or complete, but a translation nonetheless, which struggles bravely to reproduce the Hindavi even when it thickens into dense allusive language, as in the description of Mirigavati and Rajkunwar's lovemaking, coded (as we saw above) as a battle:

> The Rani attacked with the help of her elephant and horse and with her own fancy she arranged her hair, and in place of an armor she wore a *kanchukī*, which is a piece of clothing of Indian women, and made a *dastāna* out of her bracelets, and she tied her *sari*, which is a dress of Indian women, tightly around her waist. And with the force of her glance, which was like Raja Karna's arrow, and of her eyebrows, which were like Arjun's bow, and her breasts, which you'd think were Kishan's discus, she gained the upper hand in the battle of pleasure. Rajkunwar, despite the sword of his *qashqa* [mark on the forehead] was defeated by the Rani. He scattered her hair like deadly snakes, and with the spears of his nails he tore the armor of her blouse to shreds, and the threads of her sari were torn in the battle of the two elephants. The two armies showed their mettle in the battlefield of pleasure. When the sun, the great light, rose again, he did not attempt a truce. He knew what would happen when the two *mast* elephants met: streams would gush forth. (*Rājkunvar, f.* 80r)

After the lost translation of the *Chandāyan* by the fifteenth-century Awadh Sufi ʿAbd al-Quddus Gangohi (see Digby 1975; Shahbaz 2020), this is the first time that a Hindavi vernacular *katha* was rendered into Persian, and even more impressively accorded the status of a literary work rather than treated as raw material. Arguably, the absence of Qutban's prologue and of his signature verses that round off many stanzas offsets this recognition of vernacular textuality and authorship, but there is in fact one trace when the Persian author translates in prose a couplet with Qutban's signature:

> *kutubana tavana tẽ gābhīrā ati sara sukkai ativaṃta*
> *subhara naina nahi sukkahī jala bhari āvaṃta.*
> Quṭban says, "Far deeper streams have evaporated quite completely.
> But eyes that well up do not dry up, for water continues to flow from them."
> (Qutban, *Mirigāvatī*, 276 *doha*, translated in Behl 2012b: 141)

> ***Ai Quṭb ke nām-i shāʿir ast,*** *tālhā-yi āb az tābash-i āftāb khushk mīshawad, ammā chashmahā-yī ke bisyār pur-ast hargiz khushk namīshawad o sāʿat ba-sāʿat pur shuda.*

> **Oh Quṭb, which is the name of the poet,** ponds of water dry up from the heat of the sun, but eyes that are overfull never get dry, since with every hour they fill up. (*Rājkunwar,* fol. 92r, emphasis added)

As I argue throughout this book, these small "traces" are important and invite us to read them as clues of broader tendencies—in this case I would say of the presence and recognition of a vernacular *text* by a cosmopolitan author. By contrast, in his own rendering of the *Padmāvat*, the Deccani 'Abd al-Shakur Bazmi talks of "copying" from a "Hindavi manuscript" and follows the story pretty faithfully but fails to mention Jayasi's name.[98] Haqiri, who wrote a Persian version of the story of Madhavanal and Kamakandala, despite claiming that he "told a story no one had told before," mentions Alam's name at the end,[99] and the same is true of Anandram Mukhlis, as we saw earlier.

As I have already suggested, what Persian writers (and in this case the master in charge of illustrations) included and left out of their retellings offer important clues about their perception of what Persian readers needed to know or would be interested in, and also about shifts in taste. In the case of *Rājkunwar,* the Persian translator included the list of musical modes (*ragamala,* which is, however, not illustrated) but omitted the plaintive twelve-months lament (*barahmasa*), a folk set piece that had been an important and stable element of Hindavi Sufi romances. Prince Rajkunwar's temporary transformation into a yogi, his trials and encounters are the most intensely illustrated sections, probably because they matched Salim's interest in ascetics and wonders. By contrast, the elaborate musical performance, Rupmini's separation, and the fight between the two wives are not illustrated at all. The Sufi code is greatly simplified: Rajkunwar's trials are overcome by trust (*tawakkul*) in God, while the densely coded exchange between Rajkunwar as the "supplicant" and Mirigavati as the "coquette" who needs to be wooed before she grants her favor retains its depth.

What about Qutban's many epic-Puranic references? As in many other Indian Persian texts, the Persian translator envisages his Persian readers as *both* cosmopolitan *and* local, both potentially ignorant of anything Indian and familiar with Indian words and things. As a result, many Hindavi words are left untranslated and unexplained, like the names of musical ragas or, in no particular order, the eleventh-day fast of *ekadasī,* auspicious signs (*sagun/śakuna*), an itinerant ascetic (*jangam*), a demon (*rakkas*), a discus (*chakkar*), women friends (*sakī/sakhī* and *sahelī*), and a cup (*pyāla*), while an equal number that would have been familiar are glossed, like the "*kanchukī,* which is a piece of clothing of Indian women," or epic-Puranic characters and episodes. When translating the passage in which city-dwellers celebrate Rajkunwar after he has saved Rupmini from the demon (see above), in some cases the characters are not glossed, while in other cases a little backstory is given (in bold), as with the black snake Kali Nag:

> Without doubt this is a second Ramchand, who slayed Ravan and freed Sita from captivity. It must be the same Ramchand who extinguished the powerful Bali. He is Kanh who defeated Kans in battle and killed him. He must be another Kanh, who vanquished **Kali Nag, which is the great snake that had come and settled in the midst of the Jamna. [Kanh] entered the water and defeated him. And after placing a *mahār* in its nose he dragged it out like a camel.** And he is Bhim who killed Kichak and broke Dusasan's arms to pieces. And he is just like Narsingh, who tore open Hirankasap the demon's (*dait*'s) chest. (*Rājkunwar*, f. 39v, emphasis added)

In this way, the Persian *Rājkunwar* remains a richly intertextual text that both presumes and increases familiarity with epic-Puranic lore. However, it survives in only one copy, which suggests that despite the lavish illustrations this simple prose version did not find favor in Mughal elite circles.

By comparison, the only slightly later *Rat Padam* (1618) by 'Abd al-Shakur occupies a middle ground between the two poles of genre localization and genre cosmopolitism. Most likely an Indian rather than Iranian émigré poet, Bazmi presents himself as someone versed in Persian poetry and used to composing in the courtly genres of *ghazals* and *qasidas* who was asked by his father, also a connoisseur of Persian and Hindi poetry, to compose "a fresh *masnavi*" on the love of Ratan(sen) and Padam(vati). Bazmi declares himself unequal to the task but sets to it in a filial spirit (*Dāstān-i Padmāwat* vv. 291–292, Bazmi 1971: 49).[100]

Although he never mentions Jayasi's name, Bazmi in fact retells the *Padmāvat* story quite faithfully, though he streamlines and shortens it. He also removes much of its enigmatic code or transforms it into magic (*saḥr, fusūn).*[101] What the parrot Hiraman teaches Padmavati is mostly magic, and he is called "a Brahman magician" (*barahman-i fusūn-sāz*) (*Dāstān-i Padmāwat*, vv. 372, 378, 446, Bazmi 1971: 54, 58). As with Muhammad Shakir's Persian glosses on the *Padmāvat* manuscript, mentioned above, Jayasi's detailed lists of birds, trees, flowers, scents, etc. that evoke a sensuous presence are flattened into generic "birds" and "flowers."[102] Even more striking, particularly when compared with *Rājkunwar*, all the intertextual references in Bazmi's work are not to the epics or the Puranas but to the Qur'an.[103] The weakening of the Hindavi romance template is visible elsewhere, too. Though Padmavati is first introduced through a symbolic epithet as "the light of rulership" (*chirāgh-i pādshāhī*) (*Dāstān-e padmāwat*, v. 339, Bazmi 1971: 54), she is then described in typical Persian poetic terms—as an unbored pearl—rather than in the extended metaphors of light in Jayasi's work.[104] Bazmi's most sweeping change is to do away with Ratansen's first wife, Nagmati, and her powerful expression of longing, or *viraha:* instead of her twelve-months lament, a crow delivers a similar summons from Ratan's mother. Moreover, the fight between the two wives, which was crucial to the Sufi romances as an expression of the hero's struggle for reintegration into the world, is also left out. Gora and Badal, the two valiant warriors who in Jayasi's *Padmāvat* and other Rajasthani versions help free Ratan from Sultan Ala'uddin and perform an important political mediation between lower- and higher-level Rajputs, here become clever ministers and do not fight at all (Bazmi 1971: 209). Clearly, that particular political mediation has become irrelevant to this Persian Deccani version.

It is fair to say that most retellings of the great sixteenth-century Hindavi *kathas* follow Bazmi's model rather than *Rājkunwar*'s. In other words, Persian "translations" largely transcodify Hindavi romances into generic tales about "Indian beauty" and "Indian love," with smoldering suffering and great devotion. The poets did stress in some way the "Indian" peculiarity of the story or the characters ("Indian beauty," "Indian sweetness"), but they typically did away with the elements that pertained to the complex aesthetic, religious, social, and political mediations that Hindavi *kathas* had enacted. This may well be the price of becoming more cosmopolitan.

Did these Persian "translations" of Avadhi romances travel far across the Persian cosmopolis, which stretched from the Balkans to Central Asia and all the way to China? As it happens, they did not. In fact, they don't seem to have circulated beyond the subcontinent. True, translation is usually a necessary *but not sufficient* condition for a text to circulate "beyond its sphere of origin," according to Damrosch (2003: 4), and it could well be that these texts were just not considered good enough to be transmitted and translated. But there are also other reasons why they did not circulate as widely as, say, the Persian version of the *Mahābhārata* undertaken at Akbar's court, or Amir Khusrau's early fourteenth-century *masnavis* that became part of the standard Persian literary canon even outside India.

One reason, we have seen, has to do with the multiple social locations of Persian literature within India; not all Persian authors were linked into cosmopolitan networks. Another reason has to do with literary fashions at the Mughal imperial court. As Sunil Sharma (2015) has noted, Emperor Akbar preferred literary gatherings that involved storytelling, particularly the story of Amir Hamza, and commissioned translations of the Sanskrit epics. His son and successor Jahangir was more fond of listening to and discussing Persian poetry, particularly *ghazals*; his own son and successor Shah Jahan was keener on works of contemporary history, while the next Mughal emperor, Aurangzeb 'Alamgir, was especially fond of Jalaluddin Rumi's spiritual *Masnavī* (see Sharma 2015). During much of this time, it was *émigré* Iranian poets who dominated the Persian literary scene at the Mughal court, and only very rarely did Indian Persian poets reach fame outside India (see Sharma 2017).[105] By and large the Persian versions of Avadhi romances were undertaken by lesser poets outside the orbit of the Mughal court. This of course does not mean that they are less interesting or do not deserve our attention, only that their authors were less likely to find an echo in the wider Persian world.

Kathas in the World of Print and in Literary History

Within Purab, *kathas* continued to be written and copied until the early twentieth century. The Raja of Banaras sponsored a Persian *Padmāwat* by the Kashmiri poet Zakir as late as 1807, and an Urdu *Padmāwat* by Mir Ziauddin 'Ibrat was composed in Rampur in 1838 and printed by the famed Naval Kishore Press in Lucknow later in the century.[106] However, in the eighteenth and early nineteenth centuries Urdu prose and verse narratives (*masnavis, qissas,* and *dastans*) mostly veered away from the Indic geographies of Hindavi *kathas* and toward Persianate geographies—their heroes traveled to the enchanted lands of Qaf instead of Lanka, and in search of the flower of Bakawali instead of a lotus-woman.[107] At the same time, even when their stories were set in imaginative distant or "otherplaces," Urdu *masnavis* like Mir Hasan's *The Magic of Eloquence* (*Siḥr al-bayān*, 1774) encoded the sophisticated courtly and urban culture of Lucknow under the Nawabs, by which I mean that material details of food, musical entertainment, domestic rituals, and clothing—or what Ruth Vanita (2012: 67) has called "the pleasures of dress"—rooted these texts into a world familiar to their readers. The result was a thrilling combination of material familiarity and fictional enchantment—a very different kind of realism from that of modern novels.

It was these Persian or Persianate narratives that were translated or freshly composed in Urdu prose at Fort William College in Calcutta—works like Nihalchand Lahori's prose narrative *Gul-e-bakāwalī* (The Bakawali flower, 1804) or Mir Bahadur 'Ali's *Nasr-e-benażīr* (Incomparable prose, or The prose of Benazir, 1803), which retold Mir Hasan's *The Magic of Eloquence* in poetry-mixed prose. And it was these prose texts, and the verse and stage versions they inspired, that became staples of Urdu publishing in the nineteenth and early twentieth centuries. As set texts for examinations for the Indian Civil Service, these prose texts soon also acquired English translations and annotated editions. For example, Major Henry Court (1889: n.p.) advertised his English translation of the prose version of *The Magic of Eloquence* as useful for giving "an English student a thorough insight into Eastern customs, modes of speech, and etiquette." This was not entirely inappropriate, for the characters in these narratives did behave and speak according to contemporary manners. At the same time, though, the label "Eastern" or "Oriental" pushed these texts into an unescapably nonmodern and noncoeval realm.[108]

As for the Hindi print market, apart from Tulsidas's classic, which was one of the earliest Hindi texts to be printed despite its voluminous size, and which has remained a bestseller and an object and medium of devotion, Hindavi *kathas* struggled to enter the print market and Hindi literary history. Most of the *kathas* discussed in this chapter in fact only surfaced after 1900 during the searches for Hindi manuscripts undertaken by the prominent Hindi association Nagari Pracharini Sabha (Society for the Promotion of the Nagari Script) (see King 1974; Dube 2009; Chapter 5).[109] This is how Qutban's *Mirigāvatī*, Usman's *Chitrāvalī*, Puhakar's *Rasaratan*, and others came to notice—in short, almost the whole tradition. Several of these manuscripts were found in the libraries of local rajas and prominent literati (including the Maharaja of Banaras and Bharatendu Harishchandra; see Chapter 5), so *physically* they had been there all along. But they did not form part of the burgeoning Hindi literary historical consciousness, which pivoted around other genres, such as the short Brajbhasha poem, or *kabitta* (see Chapters 4 and 5).[110] "This unprecedented ancient text (*prāchīn granth*) lay idle for a long time (*bahut dinoṃ se nirarthak paṛā thā*), Babu Avinash Lal unearthed it with great effort and had it printed at Babu Gopinath Pathak's behest at the Benares Light Press," reads the frontispiece of Newaj's *katha Śakuntalā nāṭak* (1864), to my knowledge the only Hindavi *katha* printed in the nineteenth century before G. A. Grierson "discovered" and printed Jayasi's *Padmāvat*. For example, Babu Ramkrishna Verma's Bharat Jiwan Press in Banaras published hundreds of Brajbhasha poetry collections—contemporary as well as classics—but not a single *katha*.[111] True, Jayasi had already been mentioned by the "father of modern Hindi," Bharatendu Harishchandra, and *Padmāvat* was included as part of Hindi literature by Grierson (1889) and Sudhakar Dvivedi, who edited it in 1896 and published it as part of the *Bibliotheca Indica*, one of the few volumes in the Asiatic Society of Bengal's series devoted to a vernacular text. Even the seminal Hindi literary historian Ramchandra Shukla enthusiastically championed the *Padmāvat* and edited Jayasi's collected works.[112] And yet Sufi romances—or *premākhyāns*, as Shukla called them and as they are known in Hindi criticism—remained suspect on account of their "un-Indianness," i.e., their Sufi orientation.

As a matter of fact, apart from Tulsidas's *Rāmcharitmānas* and Jayasi's *Padmāvat*, *kathas* have remained strangely peripheral to the narrative of Hindi literary historiography, which has remained focused more on devotional and courtly traditions. The Hindi literary histories that were informed by the Nagari Pracharini Sabha Search Reports, like those by the Mishra brothers or Ramchandra Shukla, did begin to insert the Hindavi *kathas* into the general narrative of Hindi literary history, and a number of scholarly editions and studies were undertaken by the next generation of great Hindi scholars in the 1950s and 1960s,[113] while Agarchand Nahta brought to light the connections with Jain and Rajasthani manuscripts and traditions. Yet although scholars' introductions and monographs drew a more and more complete picture of the tradition, the critical assessment of the genre did not go beyond generic categories of Sufi vs. "Indian" (*bhāratiya*) or beyond an appreciation of the Sufi poets' "love for Hindi" and openness to Hindu characters and rituals. With the studies of S. M. Pandey and particularly Aditya Behl and Thomas de Bruijn, the richness and depth of the early, Sultanate Sufi *kathas* have come into sharper focus, but not the later tradition or the non-Sufi tales.[114]

What are the advantages of taking a historical and multilingual longue-durée view of the genre and—where possible—of the material evidence of individual manuscripts, as I have attempted to do in this chapter? For one thing, if we move away from considering Sufi and non-Sufi and Hindavi and Persian as separate traditions, we become more sensitive to the dialogic and intertextual characteristics of the *katha* as a genre. We notice the many mediations that *kathas* were called upon to perform: between oral genres and codified aesthetic and prosodic systems; between heterogeneous audiences and patrons; between local and cosmopolitan, and "Indian" and Persian, tastes and imaginaries. We stop thinking of imperial and royal court culture as synonyms of "Mughal culture" and become sensitive to other, parallel domains even within Persian. We are able to use generic variations to trace the changing fashions of this multilingual literary culture and its multiple and coexisting publics. This is the work of comparative literature "in one place."

So in the period of the north Indian Sultanates of Delhi and Jaunpur the Hindavi Sufi romance (*pemkatha*) emerged as *the* premier genre of vernacular literary expression and sophistication, and it traveled to the Deccan and Arakan as a template for further vernacular courtly romances; in the Mughal period the effort to transport some of that mediation and sophistication into Persian (*Rājkunwar*) did not catch on, and simpler attempts at inserting them as "Indian stories" within Persian cosmopolitan literariness (like Bazmi's) were more common. Paying attention to change at the scale of specific narrative elements pays dividends, too: in some Hindavi *kathas* (*Chitrāvalī*, *Rasaratan*) Mughal "real" geography overlay the imaginative Indic geography, and painting replaced music as a focal narrative device. Moreover, even when elite literary tastes turned to other genres, such as short Brajbhasha poems (*kabittas*) and poetic manuals (*riti-granths*; see Chapter 4) in the seventeenth century, or Urdu verse *masnavis* and prose *qissa* and *dastans* in the eighteenth and nineteenth, Sufi and regional literati continued to write and copy *kathas* in Avadhi. Puhakar's *Rasaratan* is a somewhat awkward attempt at bringing the *katha* template and Brajbhasha poetics together.

In the nineteenth century, the story of Padmavati and Ratansen became the epitome of "Hindu resistance" against "Muslim aggression." Ironically, the fact that it had been created by the Awadhi Sufi Malik Muhammad Jayasi was forgotten. Colonel James Tod included it in his *Annals and Antiquities of Rajasthan* (1914 [1829]) as "history" but drew upon Jain and Rajasthani versions and seems to have been unaware of Jayasi's work. Based on Tod's phenomenally successful book, new nationalist versions of the Padmavati-Ratansen-Ala'uddin story began to be composed in Bengali in the form of narrative poems, plays, and historical novels (see Sreenivasan 2007). Several manuscript and printed copies reached British and European libraries in the nineteenth century. As we have seen, in 1856 the French Orientalist Théodore-Marie Pavie anachronistically translated Jatmal's later text as the authentic, patriotic, original one, and summarized Jayasi's as a more fanciful version. With ethnolinguistic identities mapped onto literary archives, Sufis praising Rajputs instead of Sultans just did not make sense!

In parallel, manuscripts of Jayasi's and other *katha* texts continued to be copied in Purab, and the oral epic of Lorik and Chanda went on circulating orally thanks to itinerant storytellers. One performer whom Shyam Manohar Pandey interviewed and recorded in 1966 had traveled extensively along the networks of eastern or Purbi migrant labor from U.P.-Bihar to Bombay, Karachi, Calcutta, Berar, Rangoon, Sindh, Delhi, Multan, Mathura, Agra, Nagpur, Jabalpur, Bhusaval, Rameshwaran, Puri, and many other places. Pandey (1982a: 20) admits that he "was the only singer who had travelled so extensively."

From the perspective of multilingual literary history, and of a multilingual and located approach to world literature, all these forms of circulation across languages, scripts, and written/oral domains deserve attention. Taken together, they give us a sense of the texture of this literary culture and its social, political, and spatial imaginaries. Only a comparative approach allows us to illuminate the interrelationships and the plural and overlapping histories, trajectories, and tastes that, following Massey, make up space. Wouldn't it be churlish to consider only Pavie's French translation, or Laloy and Roussel's slight opera, as "world literature," just because they were done in Paris?

This chapter has focused on narratives of romance, adventure, or devotion that were meant, through their artistry, to act upon the listener and produce a transformative experience—a deep quest toward ordained love (Sufi romances) or awe and devotion (*Mānas*). The following chapter explores another kind of verbal performance, experience of literature, and sociotextual community by focusing on the orature of the Sants, or poet-saints of the eastern region. Sant poems, sung in a group with drum and cymbals in communal sessions, have provided perhaps the most widespread spiritual *and* artistic experience for people in north India and beyond. For this reason, they are particularly suited for expanding what "literature" means in world literature studies.

3

Making Space for Sant Texts

Orature, Literary History, and World Literature

In the 1920s, the Hindi poet Nirala (1896–1961), who had grown up in Bengal and worked in Calcutta, was spending some time between jobs in his ancestral village in the Unnao district of central Awadh. Nirala's education had been patchy, in a mixture of Bengali, Hindi, and Sanskrit, but this did not stop him from considering himself the (as yet unacknowledged) equal of Rabindranath Tagore, whom he admired and envied to the same high degree. In the Hindi literary world of the 1920s, Nirala and his fellow Chhayavadi, or "Shadowist," poets were trailblazers of free verse and introduced a new individual sensibility. They were also viewed with suspicion by conservative critics. Nirala was the most radical of the group, and his story-memoir *Chaturi the Chamar* (*Chaturī chamār*, 1934) delights in displaying his own radicalism as a meat-eating Brahman who befriends the local low-caste cobbler, teaches his son, and consorts with other low-caste men.

Chaturi is an "old inhabitant" (*qadīmī bāshindā*) of the village, and his ancestral house had stood for generations at some distance behind Nirala's. Though younger in age, in terms of village caste kinship Nirala counts as Chaturi's uncle (*kaka*). Nirala has heard that in his knowledge of the devotional saint-poets called Sants, "Chaturi was a greater expert than the various Chaturvedis [i.e., high-caste Brahmans], only he didn't know how to write the alphabet." One day he asks Chaturi to sing Sant poetry for him; that evening Chaturi arrives with a full complement of singers and accompanists for a night of devotional (*bhajan*) singing, "Kabirdas, Surdas, Tulsidas, Paltudas and several other well-known and unknown Sants." Chaturi's singing of the Sants' songs about the absolute reality beyond any attribute (*nirguṇ*) is a revelation for Nirala:

> Earlier I used to think of Nirgun only as a word and used to laugh when people praised the music and called them "Nirgun songs" (*nirguṇ pad*). Now I got serious—understanding grows with the ravage of age. Sitting on a stool, I began to listen to the *bhajans*. With a magisterial voice, Chaturi would remind the others of forgotten songs. I realised that Chaturi was an expert of Kabir's poetic corpus. He said to me, "*Kaka*, those great scholars do not understand these Nirgun songs." Then, perhaps placing me in the same category as those

East of Delhi. Francesca Orsini, Oxford University Press. © Oxford University Press 2023.
DOI: 10.1093/oso/9780197658291.003.0003

> scholars, he said, "The meaning of this song poem is . . ." I stopped him in a deadpan voice, "Chaturi, just sing today, tomorrow morning you can come to explain the meaning. Explanations now would still the thirst for the songs." (Nirala 1983: 380)

Chaturi complies, but the manner in which he and his companions sing these song-poems makes Nirala (1983: 380) realize that "they understood the meaning of those songs of such high quality. . . . [M]any songs had literary ornamentation, and they understood that, too." The next morning Chaturi shows Nirala how he explains the songs—he belongs to the community of Kabir's followers, and their tradition of singing and commentary involves singing one line and then drawing out the meanings of words and images. His commentary is so sophisticated that it puts to shame those found in Hindi literary and religious magazines, Nirala observes, though unfortunately for us he does not reproduce any of it. In this sketch, Nirala's presumed literary superiority and greater understanding as a sophisticated poet are trumped by Chaturi's deep embodied knowledge. While Chaturi sings the songs of Kabir and other Sants for their spiritual and philosophical messages, he is nonetheless fully cognizant of their literary qualities.

Sants (lit. "good people") is the name given to a whole host of charismatic saint-poets whose powerful voices burst into almost all Indian vernaculars in the second millennium CE.[1] Their song-poems (in Hindi often called *pad*, lit. "foot," or *sabad*, "word") and pithy utterances (*sakhi*, "witness") speak of their inner realization and strong devotion (bhakti) and longing for the absolute or for a particular god, often couched in familiar, intimate terms and in a rhetoric of direct, urgent address. These songs became the means through which whole communities of devotees could channel their own devotion, either individually or in singing circles. Some Sants created or joined communities, or *panths* ("paths"), like Guru Nanak in the Punjab or Malukdas in Awadh. In other cases, like Kabir's, it was their followers who, after their death, established communities with monasteries (*maths*), gurus and initiates, rituals, etc. It was typically out of these *panths* that written archives of anthologies, compilations, and hagiographies (called *parchai*, lit. "introduction," and *bhaktamal*, "garland of devotees") emerged that came to dominate the collective memory of the Sants. And it is this proliferation of discourse that supports the idea of a "bhakti public sphere," i.e., the idea that the idioms, practices, and institutions of bhakti provided a physical and discursive space for nonelite subjects to come together and make themselves heard (see Novetzke 2007; Agrawal 2009). Although, as we shall see, the caste profile of Sants differed, it is nevertheless clear that they provided a powerful poetic voice and a focus for lower-caste individuals and groups to articulate a sense of self, of social and religious hierarchies and exclusions, and of the nature of things (see below). This still held true for Chaturi in the 1920s.

The repertoire of bhakti oral and written texts forms one of the largest poetic repertoires in South Asia and constitutes a major part of poetic experience for audiences beyond literate groups. Within bhakti, devotion trumps appearances and social norms and ties; and particularly women and lower-caste Sants were trenchant in their critique of caste and family norms.

The largely oral textual tradition of Sant saint-poets ("Kabirdas . . . Paltudas and several well-known and unknown Sants") embodied in Chaturi the cobbler and revealed to the high-caste Hindi poet Nirala through their local encounter raises several issues that are crucial to the proper recognition of oral textuality, not just within the literary history of the region East of Delhi but also within world literature. Songs, storytelling, and other forms of oral verbal art play a determinant role in literary expression around the world, yet unwritten verbal arts are usually explicitly excluded from definitions of world literature.[2]

The first obstacle to the recognition of oral literature pertains to the category of literature per se, its socially and culturally constituted nature and the critical discourse that decides what is, and isn't, literature. This is a point that world literature theorists often initially acknowledge before they slip into "universal" genre terms and "global" visions of the world literary system that park the issue and exclude oral literature.[3] "Literature" is therefore the first "technology of recognition" (Shih's 2004 term) that we need to unpack. Here I use the term "orature" not to juxtapose it with (written) literature but rather, following Ngũgĩ wa Thiong'o (2007), to emphasize that written literature is only a small part of the totality of expressive, aesthetic discourses circulating in the world. Nirala "used to laugh" when people praised the songs of the Sants and called them literature, yet there is no doubt that more people in India are familiar with Kabir's poetry than with Nirala's! In fact, Sant texts were probably born orally, though not necessarily so, since several Sants were literate, and circulated in both oral and written forms. In using "text" for both oral and written texts I follow Karin Barber, who avoids linking "text" with writing and adopting a literacy/orality split right at the start; rather, she takes W. F. Hanks's definition of text as "any configuration of signs that is coherently interpretable by some community of users" (Hanks 1989: 95, quoted in Barber 2007: 21). Text emphasizes form, artistry, and interpretation—all aspects Nirala recognized in Chaturi's singing of Nirgun songs.

The second, related obstacle to the recognition of orature in world literature involves the (narrow) definition of aesthetics that prevents the recognition of parallel literary practices to the ones officially recognized as "literary," practices that see songs or tales carrying religious or didactic functions. As Kabir put it, poetry *was* his theology, and gatherings like Chaturi's (*satsang*, lit. "company of the good") were a crucial part of spiritual practice.[4] Sant song-poems exhort, unveil, warn, bear witness, lament, rejoice, adore. While they generally do not follow the rules of "poetic science" (*kavya-shastra*), they do not lack ornamentation, as Nirala noted, and rely on vivid imagery and direct address. Critical discourse recognizes this feature of Sant orature, but often to the detriment of an appreciation of the aesthetics of these utterances and forms, as we shall see. For this reason, apart from Kabir, in Hindi literary histories most Sant poets feature as what I call "three-line poets," acknowledged but not appreciated as poets and carvers of imaginative language.[5] When we focus on Sant song-poems as "texts" and on their aesthetics and artistry—their poetic idioms, imagery, rhetoric, language, and address—rather than only on their spiritual or social message, we realize that we need to relativize courtly aesthetics and broaden the realm of aesthetics (rather than "corrupting" or "lowering" it). A section of this chapter looks for a critical vocabulary to do justice to the aesthetics of Sant song-poems and shows how they "ventriloquize" current poetic genres and transfigure the everyday world. Since bhakti orature has been the domain in which nonelites, including women and lower-caste and "untouchable" saint-poets and groups of devotees, have left their mark and made their voices heard, attending to the aesthetic value of this poetry means recognizing, as Nirala did with Chaturi, that nonliterate individuals and groups have been carriers of ideas, aesthetic knowledge, and understanding.

Third, while circulation in world literature is usually predicated on the technologies of print and the written word, orature pushes us to ask what technologies allow it to circulate, often very widely indeed.[6] These technologies include performance and memorization, but also chapbook printing, radio, audio-cassettes, and now digital technologies.[7] As we shall see, it was chapbook publishing that ensured the continued and widespread diffusion of Sant orature in the twentieth and twenty-first centuries, and the same is true of other oral traditions.[8] The circulation of printed chapbooks follows different—both regional and transnational—pathways from those of book publishing, and once again requires us to expand our biblio-centric understanding of world literature.[9]

Finally, it pays to consider Sant orature as highly mobile but also located. Already Hindi scholar Ramchandra Shukla noted that the poems of Sant Malukdas contain many Persian and Arabic words and phrases.[10] A later section of this chapter shows how a methodology that moves back and forth between Malukdas's texts, the actual locale of Kara, the Muslim-majority *qasba* near Allahabad where he lived in the seventeenth century, and a Persian-language text concerning another, much earlier celebrated local Sufi saint, helps explain this characteristic of Malukdas's idiom as part of a dialogic exchange. Malukdas's imaginative use of Sufi poetic idiom or more generally Islamic vocabulary was a dialogic strategy (Bakhtin) through which this Sant addressed the Muslim devotees and fellow preachers around him in a language that they understood and that he re-accented (see also Chapter 2). Within a multilingual literary history, this dialogism and the use of elements from a different religious-poetic idiom are important because they show the traffic between languages and poetic idioms even *in the absence of translation*. Unlike the parallel and distinct cultivation of different poetic idioms that we'll encounter among more courtly *qasba* poets in the next chapter, within the multilingual religious context of the cities and *qasbas* of the eastern region, instead, Sant poets like Malukdas displayed their knowledge of Islamic and Persianate idioms by incorporating "nuggets" of them and re-accenting their utterances in their own song-poems.[11] This poetic traffic makes a significant point for world literature, too, which imagines monolingual speakers and readers and foregrounds translation as the necessary means of circulation across languages and audiences. Among multilingual literary practitioners and audiences, these textual clues reveal, circulation can happen routinely without translation and despite varying degrees of linguistic command.

Within the broad range of songs that circulated across north India, this chapter focuses particularly on Sant orature because it usefully encapsulates all the questions raised above. Among the Sants of Purab, only Kabir and Raidas became famous and were canonized in their own time. The others (Table 3.1) are "three-line poets." Yet, as I hope to demonstrate, Sant poetry provides one more fruitful and located viewpoint from which to observe the workings of this multilingual and multilayered literary culture. For this reason, rather than focusing on the more famous Kabir, who already has a place in world literature, I focus on other Sants, such as Malukdas, Gulal, and Paltudas. Let me first, though, dwell further on the obstacles to recognizing Sant orature before turning to the important issue of caste and going on to discuss the aesthetics, linguistic strategies, locatedness, and mobility of Sant orature in the eastern region.

Table 3.1 Sants in the Eastern Region

Banaras	Gulal (d. 1700)
Kabir (15c)	Bhikha (19c)
Raidas (15c)	Ayodhya
Kara	Paltudas (18c)
Malukdas (17c)	Barabanki Satnamis
Bhurkura (dist. Ghazipur)	Jagjivandas (18c)
Yari Sahab	Nevaldas
Bulla Sahab	Dulandas
Kesodas	

Making Space for Sant Orature

Why has it been so difficult to value Sant orature for its aesthetics as well as its religious and social message? Delving more into the obstacles—those "technologies" that have stood in the way of its recognition—will hopefully help remove them. First, within South Asia the Sanskrit "science of literature" (*sahitya* or *kavya-shastra*) conceived of "literature" (*kavya*) as a highly regulated set of genres and discourses *in the cosmopolitan languages*, primarily Sanskrit but also other translocal languages such as Prakrit and Apabhramsha (see Pollock 2006; for Prakrit, see Ollett 2017). Pollock (2006: 299) reproduces the view of Sanskrit pandits when he writes, "By contrast, the world of the 'un-cultured,' that is, of the uncourtly and uncosmopolitan languages of Place was subliterary: a domain of the sung, the unwritten, the oral." Pollock acknowledges the long and complex interplay between orality and literacy in Indian literary culture, but as part of his strong argument about the centrality of *kavya* and of writing in contrast to earlier fetishizations of pure orality centered around Vedic chanting, he argues provocatively that "the oral poet stands entirely outside of history," and that "such oral culture is not only unknowable in its historicity, it is excluded from the literary history made by committing texts to writing. . . . It is no redundancy to say that a *literary work does not exist until it becomes literate*" (317, 318, emphasis added). Not only does Pollock posit a sharp distinction between orality and the world of writing that echoes Jack Goody's; he also sets writing as a condition for entry into literature and into history.

Here, instead, my position aligns with that of scholars who understand orality and writing as part of a single continuum. They point to the uses of written texts in performance and how, in many contexts, literacy and the presence of books have coexisted with a valorization of orality both "as a fact and an ideal" (Blackburn 2006: 20; see Novetzke 2015). Flipping Pollock's perspective, we can argue that the highly regulated field of *kavya* existed within a wider field of orature with multiple aesthetic registers.[12] It is also simplistic to view Sant orature as completely separate from the realm of vernacular courtly poetry (i.e., *riti kavya* in Brajbhasha; see Chapters 1 and 4): particularly from the sixteenth century onward, Sant poets often saw themselves as "poets" (*kavi*) and used some of the same poetic forms (*kabitta, kundaliya*, etc.) as courtly poets, though with different results.[13]

A second obstacle, particularly in the age of the old textual philology, has been the instability of the Sant archive. There are often no early manuscript sources anywhere near the time or place of composition.[14] And over the centuries the corpus of several of the most popular saint-poets, like Kabir, or Surdas or Mirabai further afield, grew enormously, often with few overlaps between the various textual traditions (see Hawley 1979; Callewaert, Sharma, and Taillieu 2000). Thankfully, the early categorically negative statements ("none of the Kabir texts are original") and the dismissals of large swaths of the bhakti corpus as "spurious" and of bhakti hagiographies as completely unreliable have given way to more judicious and sensitive approaches, what we may call "bhakti philology" (e.g., Callewaert, Sharma, and Taillieu 2000; Bryant and Hawley 2015; Novetzke 2015). Bhakti philology has developed a sophisticated theory of "corporate authorship" that neither naively assumes a single psychological self as the author of the poems nor dismisses these texts positivistically as nonhistorical, but recognizes the existence of a collective sense of distinct poetic personae and of what an authentic Kabir or Mira poem sounds like, whatever their historical status (Hawley 1988, 2005; Mukta 1994). Bhakti philology continues to pay attention to chronology and to value early manuscripts but incorporates later additions and unattested oral texts as part of what it calls the "Kabir (or Sur, or Mira) tradition," or what Purushottam Agrawal (2009) in Hindi calls *up-rachnaen*, or secondary texts. It also values manuscript textual variation as evidence of the life of the texts and their multiple constituencies. Thus in "Kabir's Most Popular Songs," David Lorenzen (1996) cheerfully notes that only one of them appears in the early manuscripts; Callewaert's critical edition of Kabir places variant texts side by side rather than trying to reconstruct an *ur*-text (Callewaert, Sharma, and Taillieu 2000); and Linda Hess (2015) studies the Kabir oral tradition in Malwa.[15]

The observations by bhakti philologists on the relationship between physical texts and performance also have bearing on the status of the text as a material object. Christian Novetzke (2015: 22) has noted the constitutive difference between the orderly and canonizing *pothīs* (lit. "books") compiled by theologians and copied by scribes, and the notebooks (*baḍas*) scribbled by performers, "loosely organised and often hastily constructed with lots of margin corrections, lines crossed out, and other emendations." For these performers, the written book is a prop, an aid to oral performance, so that it would be wrong to consider the performance a variation on a stable written text. In the case of the Sant poets in particular, the high degree of variation in the order of song lines has prompted Winand Callewaert and Mukund Lath (1989) to posit an "oral-scribe archetype." Particularly in the case of Sants who did *not* leave a community of followers who quickly assembled and stabilized their words into a corpus, as was the case with Guru Nanak's successors and the Sikh community or of Dadu Dayal and the Dadu *panth*, the earliest generations of transmission were oral, by singers, and "manuscripts of the seventeenth century that have been preserved are copies of early [traveling musicians'] notes, now lost." This means that the "inversions, different lines and omissions" are not scribal "errors" but rather "proof enough that most variants in the manuscripts were brought about by singers, not by scribes" (62).

Although the Sants that I discuss in this chapter did in fact create or were part of lineages that preserved their compositions in writing, their manuscripts did not attract the attention of modern scholars, who relied instead on printed booklets. These booklets, as we shall see, were crucial in preserving and circulating Sant texts, but they also flattened and standardized them. As a result, apart from Kabir the Sants exist more as a collective than as individual voices, something that may have hampered their recognition as poets.

The third obstacle in recognizing Sant orature has been the critical tendency to focus on their religious message and ideas rather than on their poetry. Already missionaries and colonial scholar-administrators were attracted by their religious position and message—particularly that of Kabir—and by their popularity with the north Indian masses. Orientalists held religion as the key to understanding India, but in polemic with Orientalists who focused on the early Sanskrit corpus the scholar-administrator George A. Grierson believed that vernacular bhakti yielded a better understanding of modern India and earned the subjects' trust.[16] As we saw in Chapter 1, Grierson was not only a phenomenal linguist but also a key mediator of Hindi literature in Britain and Europe, the author of the first history of Hindi literature in any language, the editor of several early Hindi texts, and a collector of oral texts. Grierson shared with Bishop Westcott and other missionaries the belief that bhakti—Kabir's included—derived from the spread of early Christianity.[17] And even when that particular theory was disproved, Christian vocabulary permeated Grierson's and others' descriptions of bhakti and its poet-saints, whose poems they called hymns. For Grierson (1920: 101, 102, 120), bhakti taught "the fatherhood of God and His infinite love and compassion;" Krishna worship taught "the first, and great, commandment of the law (the second—thou shalt love thy neighbour as thyself—it hardly touches);" Tulsidas's devotion "is directed to a loving, all-powerful God, who offers Himself to His worshippers as the Great Example." Following Westcott's (1908) description of Kabir in *Kabīr and the Kabīrpanthīs* as "the Indian Luther of the 15th century" (quoted in Vaudeville 1974: 22), Grierson spoke about Kabir in the idiom of the European Reformation, and argued (1920: 119), "That some of [Kabir's] ideas, nay, many of his actual phrases, were borrowed either directly or at second hand from the Gospels cannot be doubted."[18]

Even Hindi scholars who did not share these Christian views shared some of the same epistemological premises. In order to prove that bhakti was a "real religion," they described it as a derivation and combination of notions and elements from earlier, established philosophies and religions.[19] Particularly in the case of Kabir, "birth determinism" meant trying to match his birth and upbringing with his ideas—how could he know Hinduism and Vedanta so well if he was born a Muslim?[20] Another premise that British and Indian scholars shared was the historical view of bhakti as a direct product or consequence of Islamic "invasion," and the words they used almost exactly mirror each other's. According to Grierson (1920: 101), bhakti had come from the South and "rapidly spread into

Northern India, then gasping in its death-throes amid the horrors of alien invasion;" it "came at this time as balm and healing to a suffering people, and we see this reflected in . . . lyric poetry." Ramchandra Shukla famously opened his chapter on the Age of Bhakti with a bleak picture of Muslim destruction and Hindu despair.[21] In his monograph on the Nirguna School of Hindi poetry, Pitambar Datt Barthwal ([1936] 1978: 8) drew a similarly gloomy picture of "Mohammadan conquest" and a stark polarity between polytheist, idol-worshiping Hindus and monotheist, idol-breaking Muslims: "There was thus a vast gulf of hatred separating the two races, that still needed being bridged." Sants and Sufis alone were "above all race-prejudices" and "viewed this state of things with grave concern" (8). The Sants therefore had answered the need of the hour; theirs was a reform movement that Medieval India "urgently needed," which "would aim at sweeping away all ignorance and superstition, that gave rise to Mohammadan superstition and fanaticism on the one hand and iniquitous social fetters on the other and that stood in the way of communal rapprochement and social equities" (17).[22] Contemporary echoes would not have been lost on readers who had witnessed the violent communal riots in north Indian cities in the 1920s.

Religious and political questions have therefore dominated critical discussions of bhakti and of the Sants, and even for literary scholars they have tended to overshadow serious engagement with their poetry. Even when critics did discuss the poetry, they did not find it to their liking. "Didactic religious treatises" was Grierson's (1920: 119) verdict on Kabir's poems. "Crudeness of expression," "ruggedness," "didacticism," echoed Shukla ([1929] 1988: 63), who added, "[H]ere and there you can find [in Malukdas] poetic construction (*pad vinyās*) and *kavitt* as in good poets." Even when Hindi critics meant to applaud the artistry of Sant poets, they damned them with faint praise. For other critics, like the Mishra brothers, it was a simple matter: Sant poets did not follow the established formal rules (*riti*) of poetry and did not know, or care, to play that poetic game. Barthwal, whose Romantic ideals underwrote his views of poetry, praised Sant poetry and its direct "experience of inner life" for its "artlessness" as "natural poetry." He also approved of their "observation of nature," of some "delightfully melancholy images," of the symbolic love songs, but this ideal not only pushed Sants' poems toward Tennysonian maudliness but also made Barthwal distinguish between "true poetry" and "mere didacticism." As a result, he surgically divided their good verses from bad ones (see Barthwal [1936] 1978: 227, 228).[23] The combination of deep philosophical-religious meanings and aesthetic appreciation that Nirala heard in Chaturi's illiterate yet perceptive understanding of Sant poetry went unrecognized before these strongly held ideals of what poetry was and should be like.

Critical reception, particularly for Kabir, has changed dramatically (see Dvivedi 1964; Singh 1982). Kabir is the one precolonial Indian poet foreign readers may have heard about and who may therefore count as a world poet.[24] In India, his poems are sung both by those who embrace their spiritual message and those who value his critique of caste and organized religion.[25] Yet this focus on Kabir has tended to obscure the other Sants from the region, who remain "three-line poets." As I have already suggested, the booklets brought out by Belvedere Press in the early twentieth century, which played a crucial role in spreading these Sants' words, turned them into a collective rather than individual voices and may have hampered their recognition as poets. Before we explore their aesthetics, though, it is important to emphasize the role they played in articulating a subordinate and critical position.

Poetry and the Idiom of Caste

Although poems critiquing or referring to caste form only a relatively small part of Sant orature, they are nevertheless important for the argument about the multilayered and multilingual literary culture of Purab that this book makes. They are important because they make caste visible, debunk its importance, and make low caste a position from which one can speak in strong, confident, at times sarcastic, tones. The Brahman pandit is berated for caring about caste and pollution and thereby missing the true nature of things, the Muslim priest for his literal adherence to ritual practices. Any low-caste devotee singing through the signature of "Kabir" or "Raidas the Chamar" can inhabit that bold and outspoken position. Because even when Raidas refers to himself as low-born in self-abasing terms, it is to marvel, through a set of oppositions, at the power of bhakti and of the absolute, which has raised one like him to honor and fame:

Nāgara janāṃ merī jāti bikhiāta chamāra
Townsmen! My caste is known as *chamār*
In my heart I dwell on Ram Govinda's name.
. . .

> The palmyra palm-tree is thought impure—
> yet when thought of as paper,
> inscribed with words of devotion for the lord
> it is worshipped and honoured.

Townsmen! My caste is known as *chamār*
In my heart I dwell on Ram Govinda's name.

> My caste is *kuṭabāṇḍhalā*
> I cart carcasses around Banaras.
> Now Brahmans and headmen stretch out before me

> It's your name, my refuge, says your servant Raidas. (Raidas 47, translated in Callewaert and Friedlander 1992: 132–133, slightly modified)[26]

This, Raidas says, is true not only of him but of other low-born Sants, too, like Namdev the calico-printer and Kabir, whose family revered Sufi shaikhs and *pirs*.[27]

The body is a central object of attention in the yogic idiom of Sant poetry anyway, which often speaks of its nine doors and three channels. Caste-related song-poems emphasize its materiality, the inevitable elements of impurity, touch, and decay, often using the metaphor of a clay pot molded by hand:

> Eighty-four hundred thousand vessels
> decay into dust, while the potter
> keeps slapping clay
> on the wheel, and with a touch
> cuts each one off.
> We eat by touching, we wash
> by touching, from a touch
> the world was born.
> So who's untouched? asks Kabir
> Only he
> who has no taint of Maya. (Kabir Śabad, 41, translated by Linda Hess in Kabir 1983: 55)

Or

> A wall made of water, air the pillar,
> blood and semen its mortar,
> a skeleton of bones, flesh, and veins—
> the cage where the poor bird lives.
>
> Creature, what is yours and what is mine?
> A perch on which the bird rests. (Raidas 101, translated in Callewaert and Friedlander 1992: 163, slightly modified)

Beside these poems that throw the universally impure body back at the listener and defy caste distinctions, caste features in Sant orature also as part of what I call their "stamping the everyday." Here caste is neither defied nor rejected but rather used as a metaphor. Drawing upon an oral genre of (usually satirical) caste-specific poems, such poems employ the acts or qualities associated with a particular caste or profession figuratively to define truth, virtue, and their absence, or Sant practice. "A Kayastha" or scribe, "an Ahir" or cattle herder, a Baniya or trader "is one who . . ."—such caste poems begin, sometimes tautologically, by defining what a true representative of the caste is and does:[28]

बनिया पूरा सोई है जो तौलै सत नाम
A proper Baniya is one
    who weighs the true name.

He weighs the true name and
    spreads out a carpet of mercy,
using scales of love and
    trust as a stamping stone.
He sets up the shop of discernment
    and trades knowledge back and forth.
Sitting on top of contentment, he
    whets the stone of the name,
loads and unloads songs of devotion and
    speaks words that are sweet.
He carries the key of pleasure (*surata*)
    to unlock the word.
Paltu says, I only deal with those
    who behave like this. (Paltudas 2008: vol. 1, 93).

A goldsmith, or *sonar*, is someone "who gives currency to truth and lets no counterfeit into his *dharma*;" a warrior, or *chhatri* (Kashtriya), "establishes the country of the Impassable and the Unseen (*agama agochara*) and harasses no one through force or violence" (*jora jabara kāhū na satāvai*) (Gulal, in Lal 1933: 355). A Kayastha or scribe "teaches the soul and saves Time writing without letters:"

सुन्य किताब कलम मन केरी । दम दावात मसल मसि फेरी
The book (*kitāba*) is the void, the pen (*kalama*) his mind,
breath the inkpot (*dāvāta*) in which ink is ground.
With a steadied mind, he draws out letters
and fills copies by writing the name. (Gulal 869, in Lal 1933: 351)

In this way, everyday actions and objects—inkpots, scales, whetstones—become the stuff of poetry, and ordinary language becomes a poetic idiom. In the process, Sant poets claim the authority to redefine what caste truly is.

Chaturi, a low-caste Chamar, sang not only the poems of Raidas the Chamar but also poems by Sants of other castes. In fact, apart from Raidas and Kabir (who would be impure because of his Muslim birth), poet-saints in the eastern region came from what we would call middling or higher castes: Malukdas belonged to a family of Khatri traders who sold blankets; Paltudas was a trader from a different community (*baniya*); Gulal was a high-caste Thakur or Kshatriya; and his successor Gulal was a Brahman. Yet even they spoke a language that challenged caste and considered caste hierarchies ultimately irrelevant. Whatever the caste of their followers, their voice or *bani* provided an idiom and a space for people like Chaturi to inhabit a dignified self.

Is bhakti about existential liberation or about social dignity and freedom from caste and religious restrictions? While in modern times these two aspects have been seen in opposition and people come to Sant orature for one reason or the other, it is important to recognize that singing Sant poems has been a way of accessing both (Hess 2015). Praising the salvific power of the Name, cutting the tie of Maya or illusion, and dwelling in "Painlesstown" (*beghampura*) speak to both freedoms, even if those freedoms last only for the duration of a song:

> Painlesstown is the name of that city
> where pain or distress find no place.
> No anxiety, no taxes, no property,
> no fear of failure or dread of loss.
>
> I have found a great place to live,
> it's always good there, my friend.
>
> Rule (*patisāhī*) there is strong and stable,
> no one is second or third, all are one.
> Settled and prosperous, forever famed
> Rich and wealthy live there in great number.
>
> I have found a great place to live,
> it's always good there, my friend.
>
> They stroll around wherever they please,
> no inner court or palace stops them.
>
> I have found a great place to live,
> it's always good there, my friend.
>
> Says Raidas, the freed Chamar,
> whoever inhabits that city is my friend.

I have found a great place to live,
it's always good there, my friend. (Raidas, 36, translated in Callewaert and Friedlander 1992: 126, slightly modified)

Beghampura, "Painlesstown," may be a utopian place where people who have become free of worldly ties go and live but, particularly with its Persianate vocabulary of rulership, taxes, and, slavery (*patisāhī, tasavīsa, khirājū, khalāsa*), it also speaks to worldly concerns and aspirations of peaceful living without the fetters and humiliations of caste.

The Aesthetics of Sant Orature

"How earnestly one wishes that these Nirguṇīs knew and cared for the ordinary rules of grammar and prosody if not of rhetoric. Even a little bit of polish would have immeasurably enhanced the charm of their utterances," lamented the author of the first monograph on them, Pitambar Datt Barthwal.[29] "After acknowledging the greatness of [Kabir's] personality, when it comes to his poetic art the pen hesitates a little," wrote the influential Mishra brothers, who placed Kabir among their "nine jewels" of Hindi literature, though after the less harsh and more melodious bhakti poets Tulsidas and Surdas. They admitted that about "a hundred pages" of Kabir's poems are of high quality, while the rest were, from the poetic point of view, repetitive and dull. Echoing Barthwal, they conceded that "[h]ad Kabir Sahab composed books (*granth*) from a literary perspective, there is no doubt that given the level of his composition he could have written excellent ones. He had all the qualities of a good poet (*satkavi*), he only lacked the will. He did not even want to be a good poet, he was a sermon-giver and a religious preacher" (Mishra (1910) 1924: 511, 512). Intriguingly, both Barthwal and the Mishra brothers stated that Tagore's 1915 English translation had bestowed recognition as well as literariness on Kabir's verses. "Though naturally enough poetic ideas cannot be faithfully translated into a foreign tongue, yet in fact most of the poems of the Nirguṇī poets appear grander in translations than in the original, for it is not only poetic 'aroma' but also crudeness of expression that evaporates in the process," wrote Barthwal ([1936] 1978: 223).[30]

Thus early Hindi scholars chose to think that Kabir and the other Sants *could* have been poets if they had wanted, but that poetry was not their aim. By contrast, more recently Purushottam Agrawal has argued strongly that Kabir's poeticity—his poetic vision, voice, and creativity with language in his songs and utterances—not only carried but produced his message. Kabir, in Agrawal' words, "sees everything with a poet's eyes," and while "a preacher uses language for his message, through language a poet attains his truth" (2009: 395, 407).[31] And whereas Kabir's texts consist mainly of song-poems (*sabad* and more expository poems called *ramaini*, "small Ramayanas") and icastic couplets (*sakhi*), later Sants employed the poetic forms of courtly poets, though they eschewed their dense ornamentation.[32] Their artfulness consists rather in extended metaphors drawn from everyday life, a knowing use of rhythm, repetition, and progression toward the denouement in the final line, and an artful ventriloquizing and re-accenting of voices and of "nuggets" of language from a wide range of idioms and genres (see also D. Gold 1992). In fact, Sants like Malukdas, Paltudas, Bhikha, and Gulal used practically *all* the oral and written poetic idioms then available in north India—from women's seasonal songs to children's alphabet songs—a strategy I call "ventriloquism." Besides, unlike courtly (*riti*) poetry that laid out the ground of poetry and peopled it with a specific set of human and nonhuman characters, settings, situations, and emotions and carefully monitored the amount of everyday words and items that could enter it, Sant poetry embraced the everyday and made everyday language and the everyday spaces, activities, and transactions of the home, the field, and the bazaar the stuff of poetry. Take this poem, which uses fishing ponds to establish a connection between the dryness of the earth and that of the unawakened human:

Jyoṃ jyoṃ sūkhai tāla tyoṃ tyoṃ mīna malīna
The more the ponds dry up,
the more fish fret.

The more fish fret,
Jeth grows parched.
Three waters have run by,
the song's sense's escaped you.
Lotuses wither,
ruddy geese fly abroad,
Fish get killed,
the ground cracks up.
So the human body wastes away,
unknowing,
the call goes unanswered,
you spoil everything yourself.
Paltu says, years, months, days,
watches, hours, minutes, seconds,
the more the ponds dry up,
the more fish fret. (Paltudas 2008: vol. 1, 25–26)

This single-image poem works through an extended metaphor and refigures the familiar natural phenomena of the hot summer month of Jeth, taking the listener on a destabilizing journey of cause and effect before snapping the image at the end to make us see through and beyond the material and the mundane.[33] The song is an "event" that takes place in time and seeks to effect an experience and a transformation of vision and of the heart. The contrast between the two levels of signification—the mundane and the hidden—running in parallel throughout the poem works to produce what Kenneth Bryant (1978) called an "epiphany." This is the function of bhakti poetry more generally: to produce effective spiritual experiences and realizations through the experience of sounding in one's body words that teach and transform while enchanting you. Take another poem by Paltudas, a "coiling verse" or *kundaliya* composed of a single *doha* line (13 + 11 instants or *matras*), "Take your shawl and wash it, the washerman will die" (*Dhubiyā phira mara jāyagā, chādara lījai dhoya*) to be used as a refrain, followed by a quatrain in the *rola* meter (11 + 13 *matras*) that "coils" into the second half of the *doha* line ("take your shawl and wash it," *chādara līјai dhoya*), over the first half of the first *rola,* and then repeates that first line in the second line of the last verse. The poem uses everyday (soap or *sābuna*, saltwort or *saunda*) vocabulary pertaining to the impure and low-caste activity of washing dirty clothes to speak about the need to cleanse one's mind and soul with practice and devotion. Together with the clear delight in using everyday words, the song transfigures a familiar, mundane experience into a gradual experience of self-purification:

Dhubiyā phira mara jāyagā
chādara līјai dhoya.
The washerman will die,
take your shawl and wash it.

Take your shawl and wash it,
so much dirt has gathered.
Walk to the satguru's bathing steps
where clean water abounds.
Your shawl has gone shabby,
why fold it every day?
Scrub it first
with the saltwort of good company (*satsaṅg*)
and the soap of knowledge,
the stains of unrest will wash away.
Starch it next with the name, then
wrap it all around you:
the sea of existence won't rebound.

Make sure, Paltu says,
your mind is not soiled again.
The washerman will die then,
take your shawl and wash it. (Paltudas 2008: vol. 1, 7)

With the right attitude, by singing and listening attentively to this song, one can trace within one's heart the experience of gradually cleansing one's dirty shawl, lingering on the stubborn stains, until the same restless and tainted mind, the shawl, can accompany one toward a death that will avoid rebirth.

In a song-poem by Malukdas, the obsessive anaphoric repetition of the word "dead" (*muvā*) in the first two verses and the refrain turns this scene of sociability into a ghostly one—a ghostly marriage, a ghostly funeral, a ghostly battle. "The whole world's dead, I have seen it" perfectly expresses the Sant's inner vision that reveals human striving to be ultimately pointless. The second half of the poem turns to the listener and dwells for a while on the body's physical decay in order to induce disaffection and disgust. The poem strikes a restless note for most of its duration—"I am still looking for the Lord's threshold"—before coming to rest on the final assertion: "I have found him!"

Muvā sakala jaga dekhiyā,
maĩ to jiyata na dekhā koy
The whole world is dead, I've seen it;
not one I see alive.

Dead are the bride and bridegroom, yes,
dead is the one who marries them;
dead are those in the *barāt*
and a dead man gives the official blessing.
The dead fight the dead,
the dead overpower the dead,
dead and dead have fought and died,
and a dead man regrets it.
In that one day you'll die,
the skin will melt or wither.
And so the false body
chants the true name;
death to the dying is always the same
and whoever dies comes to know this.
The one who dies at Ram's door
again and again, never dies at all
Knowing this is how it goes,
I wander sadly here and there.

I've found the lord who doesn't decay and doesn't die,
Says Malukdas. (Malukdas 2011: 13, *śabda* 7, translated by Vivek Narayanan)

While songs like this have immediate impact, they also invite exegesis, as Chaturi's vignette showed, particularly when they contain technical words. Several songs transfigure worldly transactions of service, like the following one in which, ironically, Paltu appears in the Lord's court to respond to the accusation of having "killed illusion." Hari's name, knowledge, *riddhi* and *siddhi* (prosperity and success, but also key words in Sant vocabulary), discernment (*bibeka*), *mukti* (liberation), Maya—all these are technical terms whose role in this little courtroom scene would require explanation and exposition:

Santa darbāra tahsīla santoṣa kī
In the Sant court in the district (*tahsīl*) of contentment
the kettledrum (*ḍaṅkā*) booms, calling out Hari's name.

In the courtroom of knowledge
riddhi and *siddhi* stand watch with folded arms,
discernment pushes and shoves, while
mukti pleads with her head bare,
scolded in this rough court.
You killed Maya, why did you do that?
Paltudas is a fierce fiend. (Paltudas 2008: vol. 2, 7)

Other single-image poems elaborate on the theme of the dangers of travel, of life as a perilous boat crossing, or a trade transaction in which you need to recognize the true gem. The range of occupations, activities, and everyday objects—acrobats, colors, cooking, cows, dancers, dogs, drinking, horse riding, medicine, music, service, taxes, thieving, trade, travel, and warfare—has no equivalent in courtly poetry.

As already mentioned, Malukdas, Paltudas, Bhikha, Gulal, and other Sants drew eclectically from practically all the oral and written poetic forms then available in north India. These included seasonal songs sung at particular times—like spring Phag and monsoon swing Hindola songs—or for specific festivals like Holi or Tij; songs of the twelve months (*barahmasa*) and women's wedding songs; children's syllabaries, ordered according to either the Nagari (*ka-kha-ha-ra*) or the Arabic (*alif-be*) alphabets; songs about the pain and madness of love in the Persianate Sufi poetic idiom of love; songs about service in the court of the master or Pir and God, or in the language of Islamic preaching and of bhakti and yogic practice; Sanskrit-like hymns (*stotra, sahasranama*) and ritual songs (*arati*). I call this strategy "ventriloquizing" since in each case the Sant voice inhabits that of the woman, or the preacher, and re-accents their words, to use Bakhtin's term, to convey a new meaning relating to devotion or self-awakening. While the next section discusses re-accenting Sufi/Islamic vocabulary as a form of dialogism, here I dwell on some of the other songs.

Thanks to their emotional intensity and urgency, women's songs were a particular favorite, and *viraha*—a woman's longing for her absent beloved—easily channeled spiritual longing. The following song-poem by Malukdas is in the voice of a *virahini*, a woman desperate because her beloved has gone off as a yogi (*jogiya*). Only at the end does the poet, like a guru, redirect her understanding toward herself for the final "epiphany:"

> *Kauna milāvai jogiyā ho,*
> *jogiyā bina rahyo na jāya*
> Who will bring me my jogiya?
> I cannot live without him.
>
> I thirst for my love, I
> repeat "*piu piu*" day and night.
> If I cannot find my jogiya now,
> life will take leave of me.
> My guru is a hunter, I a doe,
> he strikes me with love's arrow.
> When you are struck, you know it,
> it's a pain no one else knows.
> Says Maluk, listen jogini,
> He's inside your mind and body.
> It's your love that will bring the jogi to you, easily. (Malukdas 2011: 6)

The poem begins like a typical song in which the female subject longs after her wandering beloved. While usually the melodious and onomatopaeic call of the black cuckoo (*piu piu,* meaning "beloved, beloved") heightens her suffering, a literal and metaphorical thirst, here she herself becomes the bird who keeps calling *piu piu.* But already in the second verse the woman's song gets twisted: her painful love has in fact been caused by the guru's piercing eyes or words, a point elaborated through a Sant re-accenting of the common saying "Only one who feels pain know what it's like." The pain of love, a fire lit by the guru's word, as Kabir would say, is necessary to purify and transform the devotee's heart. In the third and final verse (the refrain is still "Who will bring me back my jogiya? I cannot live without him"), the voice shifts to Maluk, who instructs the woman (called jogini since she is herself undergoing the yoga of love) that she is wrong in perceiving pain as separation. Unlike other *viraha* songs, this one offers a resolution: the pain of love is necessary but can be extinguished by correct understanding.

Sant songs ventriloquize not only women's songs of longing but also the songs calling for "presence and presents" that women sing together on ritual occasions or simply when they meet.[34] In the following example, women praise a married woman who is fortunate (*sohaginī*) because her husband is Ram, who will always indulge her and will never bring upon her the curse of widowhood. As singer and listener turn to Ram, the penultimate verse becomes a micro-hymn, or *stotra*, in his praise (*nā upajai nā bīnasai santana sukhadāī*):

> *Sadā sohāgina nāri so, jā ke rāma bhatārā*
> *mukha māṃge sukha deta haĩ, jagajīvana pyārā*
> Happy is the woman whose husband is Ram,
> the world's beloved, who gives her all the happiness she asks for
>
> She'll never be a widow, everybody knows
> he will never grow old, die, or be killed—he's immortal.
> A human body lasts two days, listen to me you gurus,
> if you love someone who dies, tragedy strikes.
> Unborn, he will never die, he brings joy to good people,
> Maluk says, that's why I fell for him! (Malukdas 2011: 3)

The poem pivots around the terms *sadā* (ever, eternal) and *sohāg* (good fortune) and shifts between ordinary expressions of blessing and homely happiness (the world's benevolence, a husband who gives his wife everything she asks for) to a philosophical vocabulary in order to contrast wordly temporality ("two days") with the timeless absolute who bestows real joy.

Stamping and piercing the everyday, a bold mix of everyday and esoteric imagery, ventriloquism and the re-accenting of current poetic idioms and voices—these are the main elements of Sant poetics. Key to the rhetoric and power of this poetry is its direct address—or rather, assault, as Hess has written about Kabir's poems (in Kabir 1983). This direct address ("Listen fellow sadhus!" or simply "Listen!") makes "you" the object, who needs to look deep, stop sleeping, scrub the shawl clean of impurities, etc.[35]

Kenneth Bryant (1979) once contrasted devotional poetry to Krishna and Ram as "dramatic"—because it sets up scenes in which the devotee looks on or takes part—with Sant poetry as "dialectical." This definition does not apply to all Sant poems, but it does to this extended syllogism by Paltudas:

> बिना सतसंग ना कथा हरि नाम की
> Without the Sants' company, no *katha* of Hari's name

> without Hari's name, illusion won't flee.
> without illusion fleeing, you'll get no release (*mukti*)
> without release, passion (*anurāga*) won't arise
> without passion, you won't get bhakti
> without bhakti, love won't stir up in your heart.
> without love no name, without name no Sant.
> If you ask for a boon, Paltu says,
> ask for the Sants' company. (Paltudas 2008: vol. 2, 21)

Together with its eclectic ventriloquism and density of signification, this use of poetry to conduct a robust discourse about reality, caste, religion, and the path to freedom ensured that even ordinary, illiterate, low-caste people like Chaturi the Chamar became, to use Purushottam Agrawal's felicitous phrase, "well-listened" (*bahushrut*), acquired the confidence to argue and philosophize, and became experts at singing, recognizing, and decoding a wide range of idioms.

Religious Dialogism in Sant Orature

> Any utterance reveals to us many half-concealed or completely concealed words of others with varying degrees of foreignness. Therefore, the utterance appears to be furrowed with distant and barely audible echoes of changes of speech subjects and dialogic overtones, greatly weakened utterance boundaries that are completely permeable to the author's expression. (Bakhtin, "The Problem of Speech Genres," in Morson and Emerson 1990: 138)

"Dialogism" is a key term in Mikhail Bakhtin's linguistics and poetics, and he used it in different contexts and with multiple meanings. While in literature Bakhtin considered dialogism to be peculiar to novelistic discourse, in fact it works very well to explain the presence and use of words, images, and phrases of Sufi and more generally Islamic discourse within Sant orature, one of its peculiar features.[36] Three aspects of Bakhtin's concept of dialogism are particularly relevant here. First, his notion that every utterance is dialogic because it is addressed to someone.[37] Second, the notion that words come to us already dialogized, already "spoken-about" (Morson and Emerson 1990: 138). The Sants' use of yoga and Nath technical vocabulary relating to the body as a microcosm has been much commented upon by critics (e.g., Dvivedi 1964; Vaudeville 1974). But their use of words, images, and expressions typical of Sufi love poetry and Islamic preaching is equally noteworthy. A third, related, aspect is what Morson and Emerson (1990: 146) call dialogic utterances with "quotation marks," that is, when one can hear deliberate echoes of other people's utterances.[38] In the case of Sant poems, I would argue that we can distinguish between those that contain Persianate words as part of an unmarked or mixed register and those in which we can hear the quotation marks around Persianate words and phrases because they appear as "nuggets of speech" that deliberately contrast with the Hindavi morphology encircling them.

As the next section goes on to argue, the context for this dialogism with Sufi and Islamic poetic and rhetorical discourses was provided by the Muslim-majority *qasbas* or towns of Awadh where Sants like Malukdas and Paltudas lived and where assemblies of poetry, storytelling, and singing at Sufi hospices (*khanqahs*), Friday sermons at the local mosque, and orations for the birth and death of the Prophet or for the martyrs at Karbala were part of the local soundscape. Attention to oral recitation and performance once again helps us move away from assumptions about the specific audiences of genres and limited access to written texts, particularly if written in high languages, and edge toward an appreciation of how much people heard and overheard what was being sung, said, or recited, however limited their formal literacy may have been. Mindfulness to spatial location also helps us appreciate that the Sants knew they were speaking to audiences who were familiar with those discourses (the first kind of Bakhtin's dialogism)—just as Sufi romance writers in Purab knew that their audiences were familiar with the epics and Puranas (Chapter 2).

There is no better evidence of the conscious re-accenting of Sufi discourse than in the small but striking number of Sant compositions in what we may call "spoken Persian."[39] These consist almost exclusively of Persian words and phrases (in the example below, *pura nūra, hamā jā*) with minimal or no grammatical elements. In the following example, there is only one Persian verb, *osta* (< P *ast*); the other verbs are either absent or are in Hindavi, as are the few words **in bold:**[40]

> ***Hai** hajūra **nahī̃** dūra, hamā-jā **bhara pūra***
> *zāhirā jahāna, **jā kā** zahūra pura nūra*
> *besabūha, benamūna, bechagūna osta*
> *hamā osta hamā azosta, jān-jānāṃ dosta*
> *shabo roza zikara fikara**hī maĩ** mashgūla*
> ***tehī** dargāha **bīcha, paṛe haĩ** qabūla*
> *sāheba **hai merā** pīra, qudrata **kyā kahiye***
> ***kahatā** Malūka bandā, **taka** panāha **rahiye**.* (Malukdas 2011: 19)

> The Presence **is not** far, **it fills** everywhere,
> manifest in the world, **its** appearance is full of light.
> Without place, shape or sample, he is ineffable,

He is all, all is from him, a friend of all creatures.
I spend night and day repeating his name, meditating on him
I lie in the middle of his court, seeking his favor.
My pir is my lord, what to say of his power?
Says Maluk, my friend/the slave, dwell in his refuge.

The effect created is one we may call "quasi-Persian"—the composition *sounds* like Persian, though it is ungrammatical and eschews the rules of Persian prosody. In the process, Sufi technical terms and phrases (e.g., *besabūha, benamūna, bechagūna, hamā osta, hamā azosta*) become part of Sant vocabulary, encouraging equivalences (e.g., *pīr* = guru) and stretching Sant language. As to the intention behind this gesture, we can only speculate: Was it meant to display Persian competence, however limited? To play with phrases and concepts overheard? Does it reflect simplified communication in the high language? The fact that Malukdas happily reconciles two positions—"He is all" (*hamā osta*) and "all is from Him" (*hamā azosta*)—that Sufis would read in opposition to each other, i.e., "unity of existence" (*waḥdat al-wujūd*) and "unity of witnessing" (*waḥdat al-shuhūd*), suggests that he is not interested in the finer points of Sufi doctrine.[41]

In another song-poem, Malukdas ventriloquizes Sufi discourse by taking the position of the servant or slave (*bandā*) who is devoted to his master or *pīr* and whose practice is internalized rather than ritualistic. This song begins with a typical utterance about passionate love (*'ishq*); the familiar expression "drinking the cup of love" is first voiced with a Persian term (*almasta*, "drunk") and then translated into Hindavi (*piyā prema piyālā*, "I drank the cup of love"). While the refrain insists on the subject's intense desire to see the lord (in a quasi-Persian compound, *dīdār-divānā*), the song next visualizes him as an old house servant (*bandājādā*, P. *bandīzāda*) "standing in the court of the Lord." Yet this is not an external form of service but an internalized one: Malukdas has forgotten how to pray, fast, and rattle off the rosary and will not resume these ritual duties, but he wears the "cap of honesty" and undertakes the pilgrimage to Mecca within his own heart. Perfectly readable within a Sufi understanding of internalized devotion, the song-poem expresses Sant practice and emotion-work just as well.[42]

I'm crazy for the sight of you

Moment by moment I long to glimpse you,
        merciful sahib, listen to me!
Drunk and oblivious to my body,
        I drank from the cup of love;

I stumble and fall and fall again,
enraptured in your colours.
Forever standing in your court
like an in-house bonded servant,
I wear on my head a cap of honesty,
a jacket and a cape.
Tauzi and namaz I know nothing about,
nor do I know about fasting;
The call of zikr I completely forgot
the moment I found this heart.
Says Maluk, I won't resume namaz now,
heart has been taken by heart;
Mecca and Haj I saw in my heart,
I found my supreme guide. (Malukdas 2011: 26,
translated by V. Narayanan)

In fact, it's not just Sufi poetic idiom that Malukdas reaccents. A song warning the listener not to waste their life sleeping but to wake up before death comes ventriloquizes the warning of a Muslim preacher to his congregation about the Day of Judgment, "when Jibreel [Gabriel] comes mace in hand." The warning against the sin of indifference (*gunāha, gāphila*) is directed as much at oneself as at the listener, creating a sense of common human failing:

Gāphila hai bandā
This slave, ignorant,
sins and sins again,
How will the lord be pleased
if and when He calls?
My heart fears the last day when
Jibreel comes mace in hand.
In this world of dreams,
do no doubt, my heart,
Else the angel will glare
raging at you,
Maluk says, and you will have
no country where to hide.
Have mercy on me,
only then will I rejoice.[43]

It is easy to imagine that Malukdas would have heard such preaching or poems of warning in the *qasba* of Kara (see the next section), but what is remarkable is that he makes this language his own without registering it as a translation. A century later, in the capital of Nawabi Awadh, Faizabad, Paltudas will even refer explicitly to an Arabic Hadith (*laham kullahum*) in order to remind Muslims of what the Prophet had said and to urge them not to eat meat:

Laham kullahum, "all flesh,"
so the Prophet said about the body.
So the Prophet (*nabī*) said in the *ayat* of the Hadith.
The same life in everyone. There is no other.
Blood and flesh are one, it's unseemly to eat it, Maulvi.
The same light (*rosana*) of the Prophet shines in everyone.
Callous, Paltu says, is only a wretched *kafir*.
Laham kullahum, "all flesh,"
so the Prophet said about the body.[44]

For a study of multilingual literary culture, all these usages are significant because they highlight the traffic of poetic and religious idioms *without the mediation of translation.* Moreover, it's not only the Persianate vocabulary that reveals the dialogism between Sant orature and Sufi discourse; it is also the ideas expressed. Sometimes the particular location of the utterance within the larger discourse of a text is revealing. Let's take, for example, Malukdas's work *Bhakti viveka* (Discernment of devotion), which contains questions and answers between a disciple and his guru (Vanshi 2006: 144ff.). To the disciple's question of how one can reach the highest being and snap the thread of rebirths, or *samsara*, the guru first offers a brief conceptual explanation and then a longer exposition on the unity of being.[45] A couplet and a poem elaborate on the idea that God can be seen in everyone despite the diversity of appearances:

Saba ghaṭa merā pīu khālī kahūṃ na dekhie
baṛa bhāgī hai jīu jehi ghaṭa paragaṭa hoi [soī].
My lover is in every body, see,
nowhere is empty.
Happy is the one in whose body he appears.

Jahā̃ dekhaũ *tahāṃ sāhib merā*
Wherever I look I see my sahib:
In one body as a lord, in another a servant.
In one as Ram, in another Rahman.
One eats the Hindu way, the other the Muslim,
One rattles the *tasbih*, the other the *mala*,
One belongs to Allah Miyan, the other to Krishna Gopal. . . .

> Maluk says, it's a story that cannot be told
> One's a fool, the other knows it in the body.[46]

This idea that God is everywhere and in everyone ("nowhere is empty") and that someone who has true knowledge ("in the body") can perceive this reality echoes and re-accents the words Sufi poets often used to explain the same idea. In fact, Malukdas's poem echoes almost verbatim a Hindavi couplet that a fifteenth-century Sufi of Awadh, 'Abd al-Quddus Gangohi, had used to "translate" a Persian utterance (which appears first in his text):

> ***Dar har chi badīdīm*** *nadīdīm bajuz-i dūst*
> *ma'lūm chunīn shud ki kasī nīst magar ūst*
> Wherever I looked, I saw none but the friend;
> thus I learnt that nothing exists but him.
>
> ***Jidhara dekhūṁ*** *he sakhī tidhara aura na ko'ī*
> *dekhā būjhi bicāra men sabhī āpana so'ī*
> Wherever I see, there is no one else.
> I realised that everything is He himself. (Gangohi 1898: 3; see Orsini 2014a: 427)

While "translating" the Persian verse, the Hindi utterance reaccents it by bringing to it the emotional trope of vernacular poetry of the woman searching for her beloved (see Pauwels 2021). Malik Muhammad Jayasi, too, had Krishna reveal a similar truth in the *Kanhāvat*: "[S]ometimes a king, sometimes a beggar. Sometimes a pandit, sometimes a fool, sometimes a woman, sometimes a man . . . Many shades and guises, only one (*akelā*) who takes pleasure in all" (Jayasi 1981: 217; see Chapter 2). Malukdas uses almost the same words here, adding a nice touch about Hindus and Muslims praying and eating in different ways (*kehũ jaivẽ kehũ khātā khānā*). Clearly, by the time Malukdas used them, these words had been "already spoken" many times and were "furrowed with distant and barely audible echoes of changes of speech subjects and dialogic overtones." Jayasi's "hidden truth" becomes Malukdas's "highest state." While Sufis and Sants in the *qasbas* and villages of Awadh followed their own practices and beliefs and in fact did not record conversations with each other, *language itself appears as a dialogic site of interaction*. Sants and Sufis, and no doubt other preachers and speakers, too, accented and re-accented words and expressions and used and reused nuggets of language (or, more rarely, incorporated stories about each other, as the next section shows) in ways that "weakened utterance boundaries." The result was a widespread familiarity with religious ideas across religious communities and paths. Jayasi, Gangohi, and other Sufi poets and masters display their familiarity with Vaishnava and yogic ideas and vocabulary, Malukdas and Paltudas with Islamic and Sufi ones. Dialogism is a better frame for this display than syncretism, because it acknowledges that each speaker accented the same utterance in their own particular fashion, to make their own particular point (see Orsini 2018).

Sant orature traveled widely and quickly. In the next section, drawing mainly on existing research and, for Malukdas, on internal textual references, I try to heed Isabel Hofmeyr's (2004: 25) suggestion to "uncover empirically the complexity of circuits" and then "ask what the theoretical import of such journeys might be." Taking a located and multilingual approach pays, I suggest: traveling to Kara to explore Malukdas's "place" (*sthan*) as well as neighboring Sufi shrines, reading his works and hagiography together with Persian sources about nearby Sufis and an Urdu local history, and shuttling back and forth between the site and the texts all support this understanding of dialogism.

Both Mobile and Located

Discussions of circulation, particularly in the context of world literature, tend to create an opposition, and a hierarchy, between texts that circulate and those that do not. After all, in David Damrosch's formulation, only the former qualify as world literature. But throughout this book, and particularly here, I suggest that we need to pay attention to both location and circulation as constitutive of, informing, and informed by literary texts.

That Sant orature circulated quickly and widely has long been recognized. Considering that hardly any vernacular manuscript has survived from the fifteenth and sixteenth centuries, it is striking to find songs by both Kabir and Raidas included in one of the earliest manuscripts, comprising a range of bhakti poets and compiled in 1582 in Fatehpur, a thousand kilometers west of Banaras; in other words, both Sants became part of the Hindi manuscript tradition from very early on. Around the same time, poems by Kabir ad Raidas were also incorporated into the vast collections compiled further away, in Rajasthan and Panjab, within the communities of Dadu Dayal and Guru Nanak's successors.[47] Further evidence of early circulation and recognition can be found in the biographical verses and stories of the genres called "garland of devotees" (*bhaktamal*) and "introduction" (*parchai*) and in poems that respectfully string together the names of saint-poets and renowned devotees, cutting across religious and denominational differences.[48] Navnit Ram Soni's *Bhagatmāl*, composed in Persian in Ghazni, Afghanistan, in 1682, shows the wide spread of bhakti orature and networks, sustained by pilgrimage and trade routes.[49] The bhakti archive itself shows gurus traveling to make new disciples or renew ties with them and to visit pilgrimage sites, and disciples traveling to see their masters.[50] Already in his lifetime, Malukdas established additional "seats" (*gaddis*) in nearby Allahabad and Lucknow, but also in Multan, Kaul, and Nepal, and had disciples further east and south (Dikshit 1965: 28).

Interestingly, this broad geography is reflected in one of Malukdas's poems that continues the discussion between the disciple and the guru mentioned in the previous section. Using the familiar image of the potter as the creator to say that people from all these different regions are made of the same clay, Malukdas launches into a staggering geographic tour de force that includes Uzbekis, Chaghatais, Khurasanis, Kabulis, Kashmiris, people from Balkh and Bokhara, from Thatta and Bhakhar in Sindh, (Iranian) Iraq, Rumi (Ottomans), Shami (Syrians), Habshi, Firangis, people from the Deccan, Jangar (Bikaner) and from the more familiar Purab (Awadh and Bihar), Bengalis, Khasis of Assam, and people from the western to the eastern corners of the central region. Malukdas wonders how a single potter could have molded all these different kinds of people![51] This expansive geographical imagination, which goes from Transoxiana in Central Asia to northeast Assam and to the Deccan in the south, is an ethnic map that closely matches the Mughal geographical and ethnic imagination, as well the actual geography of Malukdas's network of disciples.[52] It is a trace that shows that even less-traveled Sants were cued into much wider geographies.

At the same time, it pays to consider location as well as mobility. As the previous section showed, locating Malukdas in Kara, the Muslim-majority *qasba* on the banks of the Ganges about seventy kilometers west of Allahabad, where he was born and lived, helps us to catch the not so "distant and barely echoed tones" of Sufi utterances. In the same way, locating Paltudas, a century and a half later, in Ayodhya, next to Faizabad, which had become the capital of the Nawabi state, helps us hear the dialogism with the Urdu poetry that was developing there. I end this section with my experience of going back and forth between Kara and the Hindi, Persian, and Urdu textual material in an attempt to gain a less generic and more located understanding of Malukdas's orature or *bani*. Allow me to shift to a more personal tone as I narrate this experience.

The first time I went looking for Sant Malukdas to Kara in 2014 with my Allahabad friends, armed with only a modern printed edition of his verses, a booklet published by the Belvedere Press (more on it below), there was not much to find. His compound is an empty modern courtyard with a modern, rather generic white marble statue of Maluk sitting; on the whitewashed walls, a few older and some definitely new sayings and painted scenes illustrate his life; and there is an underground bricked cell where—we were told—Malukdas used to meditate. Nearby, a plain modern marble cenotaph, or *samadhi*, stands next to a piece of old brick wall that was the most tangible remnant of Maluk's home (Figure 3.1). Even the priest was new, recently brought in by the latest active

Figure 3.1 Malukdas's seat in Kara and the remaining wall of his original home.
Photograph by author, August 2014.

guru in Malukdas's direct lineage. No devotees or pilgrims come anymore, he told us, and when locals meet once a week it's not Maluk's songs they sing but a common prayer. When I asked the priest if he had any old manuscripts, what he unwrapped was the bound photocopy of a modern text handwritten on a large copy book. Kara is a historic *qasba*, but there was little evidence of its having been densely inhabited.

On the way back to Allahabad we stopped at the tomb and impressive compound of Khwaja Karak Shah (Figure 3.2). But without stories, Kara looked rather empty and disconnected, with large empty spaces in between.

It was only when I was back in London, armed with a copy of Malukdas's *parchai* written by his nephew Suthradas that was given to me in Allahabad, a better edition of some of his works printed in Delhi, and a Persian work written in 1370 containing anecdotes about Khwaja Karak Shah in the British Library (*Asrār al-makhdūmīn*, The secrets of the lords, Lahauri 1893), that both figures started to acquire some depth and texture.[53] I was also lucky to get hold of an early twentieth-century short local history of Kara Manikpur written in Urdu, and a typically insightful concise essay by Christopher Bayly (1980) on Kara as a typical "Muslim gentry" *qasba* in the eighteenth and nineteenth centuries.[54] The

Figure 3.2 The mausoleum of Khwaja Karak Shah, Kara.
Photograph by author, August 2014.

local history filled Kara's empty spaces with the names of the various localities, bathing steps, and places of worship—tombs, temples, Sufi "seats"—the names of governors during the Sultanate and Mughal periods, local notables, and communities of inhabitants. Bayly's economic and social history provided a context in which the lone buildings left could be inserted (Figure 3.3). It was only after having been to Kara, and in the effort to connect these very different texts spanning seven centuries to the spaces I had seen and to each other, that a more dynamic and less generic sense of the place slowly began to emerge.

Historical sources tell us that Kara was an important political center from the early Sultanate period, a provincial capital since 1193, associated with the early Sufi martyr of the region, Mas'ud Ghazi, and particularly with Ala'uddin Khilji (r. 1296–1316), who was governor here before he became the Sultan of Delhi. By Malukdas's time, though, Kara had been downgraded by the Mughal emperor Akbar from provincial capital (as Kara-Manikpur) to district headquarters.

Kara was also an entrepôt for down-river and long-distance road trade. (The Ganges is fordable nearby during the dry season, and this was an important crossing between Awadh and the lower Doab.) By 1600 it had a large *sarai* for travelers (Bayly 1980). Local production included paper, printed cloth, and brass

Figure 3.3 A ghat in Kara.
Photograph by author, August 2014.

pots; Malukdas's Khatri family sold blankets. Afghans seem to have long retained control of the district, and the names of the localities and of the patrons of local monuments testify to a varied population of shaikhs, Kayasths, Gujarati traders-bankers, Pathans, and so on. At the beginning of the twentieth century, the town's Muslim population was still one-third larger than its Hindu (Manikpuri 1916: 18).

Like other *qasbas*, Kara had its fair share of Sufis, but its most famous holy man was an ascetic "intoxicated with divine love" (*majzub*) named Khwaja Karak Ahmad Shah, who had come with his brother from Transoxiana to trade and had settled first in nearby Bhamrauli and then in Kara, where he died in 1301. The tombs of several Khilji princesses and nobles crowd the compound of his shrine, and many other tombs, mosques, and gardens dot the town and its environs (Manikpuri 1916: 52ff., 92). *Asrār al-majẕūbīn*, more a collection of anecdotes than of sayings, shows us Karak Shah sitting in the bazaar or in the local wine shop (though the wine he drinks smells of rose water), responding to visitors' queries and requests, performing miracles, redistributing the gifts he receives, and occasionally composing Persian verse or engaging in musical sessions with Hindi singers (Lahauri 1893: 3, 16).[55]

Intriguingly, Khwaja Karak figures directly in Malukdas's hagiography, though the two are divided by almost four centuries. This is even more remarkable since usually Sufi and Sant archives pointedly do not mention each other: Sufi hagiographies abound with anecdotes of encounters with yogis, while Sant hagiographies feature Brahman pandits and Muslim governors or judges.[56] Before we come to this remarkable textual encounter, let us go over the rest of Malukdas's hagiography, written by his nephew Suthradas (Dikshit 1965).

In the hagiography, Malukdas is presented as an avatar sent by the Original Creator (*ādipuruṣa kartāra*) as a particle (*aṃśa*) of himself. Other details are quite homely (Dikshit 1965: 45). As mentioned, Malukdas was born into a family of Khatris whose business was to sell blankets. Already as a child he enjoyed the company of wandering sadhus and would steal from the family storeroom to cook for and feed them. Two of the four miracles in the hagiography involve the god Ram refilling the emptied storeroom when Malukdas's mother gets angry, and delivering Malukdas's load of blankets safely home when Malukdas foolishly sends them home with un unknown porter (*majūra*), who turns out to be none else than God himself. Malukdas had earlier married (parents' usual attempt to turn a young man toward worldly matters) but is relieved when both wife and daughter die.[57] And when he announces to his parents that he has become a devotee (a *baisno*, Vaishnava) they make their peace with it, give him some capital, and tell him to sell blankets and spend all the proceedings for sadhus if he wants to:

सिख दई बेटा बेचो कमरी पैदा करके जोरहु दमरी।
पैदा करि खरचो सब मांहीं हम तुम ते कछु चाहैं नाहीं।
पैदा करिकै खर्चिये पूंजी राखै मान।
नाही पूंजी घटे जग बानिये न सनमान॥ (Dikshit 1965: 47)

Sikha daī beṭā becho kamarī paidā karake jorahu damarī.
Paidā kari kharacho saba māṃhīṃ hama tuma te kachhu chāhaiṃ nāhīṃ.
Paidā karikai kharchiye pūñjī rākhai māna.
Nāhī pūñjī ghaṭe jaga bāniye na sanmāna.

They told him, son, sell blankets and make money (*damarī*, coins),
spend all the money you make, we want nothing from you.
doha: Spend *after* you earn. Capital maintains honor.
Else, your capital will shrink and the world won't honor you as a
trader.

This is exactly what Malukdas proceeds to do,[58] all the while beginning to exhibit the emotional extremes of loving devotion (*prema bhakti*), so that people think he's gone mad—the term used is one applied to Sufi lovers, too (*divānā*):

sākhī pada jo āpu banāvahī,
loga divānā [kā] kahi gāvahī (Dikshit 1965: 47)

He composed couplets and song-poems,
people sang them and thought him mad.

Once Malukdas's name spread and people started to come for *darśan* and initiation, his main activity seems to have been to feed and provide for all and sundry—no one was turned away empty-handed. The empty compound we now see contrasts with the bustling crowds the words evoke:

ब्राह्मण भाट परोसी जेते, लेहिं रोज भूखे सब तेते
Brāhmaṇa bhāṭa parosī jete, lehī roja bhūkhe saba tete.
Brahmans, bards and neighbors
daily come to eat their fill.
Travelers come from many countries, disciples
bring their offerings.
Hungry dogs and animals come, and
they get their fill, too.
Hindu and Turk [Muslim] widows get
food and bedding.
Any stranger who comes gets
food and travel expenses.
The sick and maimed get treatment.
Nobody expects anything.
Hari collects, the people spend and eat. (Dikshit 1965: 50)

It is in the context of another miracle (*Rāma kī kalā*, God's play) that Maluk comes into direct contact with Karak Shah. Khwaja Karak Shah was "praised by all Muslims," Suthradas tells us, and he was famous for his learning and miracles (*karāmātī*). One day he staggers in the local bazaar and drops the amphora full of wine and the cup in his hands. When the cup breaks he kicks a stone in anger. This creates a very deep channel (*panārā*) that nobody, neither the local government official nor the headman, can dam. Water starts to flood the town, and when it reaches Malukdas's own compound a couple of days later, he decides to stop it. First he throws in a lot of stones and then he pays laborers to do, collecting stones and bricks that are lying around.[59] Local Muslims tell Malukdas that there is no point since it's the Khwaja's curse; in fact they complain to the local state official (*hakīma*) that this dam work is hurting them because, as a later line says, the stones come from Muslim mosques and tombs. Malukdas retorts that no ill can come from a *pir*, and that Karak himself has told him that he will not cause anyone harm. The official dismisses the complaint, chiding the plaintiffs that they are not good Muslims anyway because they never pray, whereas Malukdas is generous and has been doing good works. The Khwaja himself appears in a dream to the local Muslims and reproaches them for challenging Malukdas, who is "a friend of the same hue, kept close by God."[60] The next morning at dawn the Muslims go to Malukdas to pay their respects; even the "obedient" official cannot remain in the town if Malukdas opposes him.[61] This story is about a local contest over space and means at a time of crisis, which is solved when Karak Shah shows his support for Malukdas's intervention. Malukdas appears able to attract considerable crowds and funds, which he redistributes locally; he commands influence over the local Mughal official and acknowledges on easy and familiar terms the *qasba*'s most famous Muslim ascetic.

This hagiographical story brings together Karak Shah and Malukdas, who are separated by centuries but whose shrines lie only two kilometers apart. Moving back and forth between the different textual traditions and the physical spaces, dotted with the remains of Sufi tombs and establishments, helps us to better understand not just the story but also all the many Sufi echoes and dialogism of Maluk's poetry noted in the previous section. After all, Sufis and their utterances were all around him! One could perform a similar exercise with the later Awadh Sant Paltudas. Although I have no hagiography or intersecting source for him, the images in his poems of street performances, dancing girls, and rich foods, and the play between lover and beloved (*'ashiq* and *ma'shuq*) so typical of Urdu poetry—all elements that characterized the culture of Nawabi Faizabad—clearly provide an intertext for his poetry, as in these few examples of warning poems:

Gone are the acrobat's drum, the tamashas (*tamāse*)
when all that are left are dancing girls (*nāch nachaniyā*),
Paltu says, all is gone. (Paltudas 2008: vol. 1, 67)

The miracle actor (*kārāmātī naṭa*) performs,
he'll regret it later.

He struts and shakes his hips
in four days he'll be in hell. (Paltudas 2008: vol. 1, 66)

And

Gorged on *qāliyā* meat and *nān-pulāo,*
drunk on glass chalices of wine (*sarāb*) at lamplight,
he sleeps, wrapped in a colored turban (*chīreband*).
Just hear the angels (*firiste*) cry when they come. (Paltudas 2008: vol. 1, 69)

Dig your grave first,
then become a lover (*āsika* < *'āshiq*).
First wrap a shroud around your head,
then step out.
A lover sleeps neither day nor night.
Paltu says, Hey, when does the
cruel beloved (*bedardī māsuka*) ever feel distress? (Paltudas 2008: vol. 1, 69–70)

Located and at the same time very mobile, the words of these comparatively minor Sants would probably not have even reached us had it not been for the remarkable enterprise of one individual, Bhaleshwar Prasad, the editor of the *Santbānī Pustakmālā* (Sant Voices book series) and owner of the Belvedere Press in Allahabad. The enduring success of this series demonstrates that if we really want to consider the circulation of orature as part of world literature, we need to go beyond the book and consider booklets as an important medium with its own parallel network of circulation. While early missionary, Orientalist, and Indian literary interest in Kabir gave rise to a profusion of printed editions, translations, and selections, in the case of the other Sants, including Raidas, Malukdas, and Paltudas, it was thanks to the Belvedere Press that they entered the world of print.

Sant Orature into Print: Booklets and World Literature

In manuscript form, Sant orature (*bani*) was copied and transmitted as part of larger anthologies and as separate works; both appear in the first catalogues of old Hindi manuscripts as belonging to the collections of private individuals.[62] Its transfer from the oral and manuscript traditions into print took place at the crossroads of quite different trajectories and at the hands of multiple actors—European and Indian Christian missionaries, British Orientalists at Fort William College in Calcutta, Hindi scholars and literary institutions in Banaras, commercial publishers like the Belvedere Press in Allahabad and the Venkateshwar Press in Bombay, lineage holders, and Bengali literary figures such as Kshitimohan Sen and Rabindranath Tagore. Unsurprisingly, the material product of these interventions also differed, though we see similarities in format and agenda emerge, partly because these actors were responding and reacting to one other.

For missionaries and colonial scholar-administrators, it was the *religious position* and message of the Sants, and of Kabir in particular, that drew their attention, as well as their popularity with the north Indian masses.[63] Already the Italian Capuchin friar Marco della Tomba, who was active in north Bihar in the late eighteenth century, had undertaken two (unpublished) translations of "Cabirist" texts and had sought to understand their religious philosophy (Vaudeville 1974; Lorenzen 2006). But the first time Kabir's poems appeared in print was in a lithographed anthology published in Calcutta aimed at providing teaching material for East India Company recruits, William Price's (1827) *Hindee and Hindostanee Selections*. Other early translations and print editions were by missionaries: E. Trumpp's 1877 translation of the *Guru Granth*; the 1890 Hindi edition of the *Bījak*, the core text of an important branch of the Kabir *panth* by Rev. Prem Chand, a convert and Baptist missionary in Munger (Bihar), and its 1917 English translation by Rev. Ahmed Shah. Nineteenth-century bazaar editions by Indian commercial publishers instead consisted of compilations of the works of several saint-poets for devotional purposes, with little editorial intervention.[64]

The main Hindi literary institution, the Nagari Pracharini Sabha of Banaras (est. 1893; see Chapter 5), was another major force: its *Search for Hindi Manuscripts* reports alerted Hindi scholars and the Hindi public to the existence of many texts and traditions and provided the building blocks for Hindi literary histories, while its scholarly editions of Hindi classics like Shyam Sundar Das's *Kabīr Granthāvalī* (Collected works of Kabir), based on two manuscripts preserved in the Sabha's library, provided new standards of publication (Das 1928).[65] At the same time, Ramchandra Shukla's ([1929] 1988) famously disparaging comments on Kabir and the Sants in his *History of Hindi Literature* (*Hindī Sāhitya kā Itihās*) provided the impetus for several more positive reevaluations. Outside the Hindi-speaking world, the Bengali scholar Kshitimohan Sen collected sayings and poems of Kabir from contemporary oral sources and published them in Bengali in the early 1910s, and it was from them volume that Tagore (1915) selected the poems for his influential translation *A Hundred Poems of Kabir*.[66] The result of this publishing activity was an overwhelming focus on Kabir, with an array of printed books at both the top and bottom of the price range—English translations, scholarly editions, and cheap bazaar anthologies. This has remained the case. After Tagore's, other influential translations by both scholars and poets have included those by Charlotte Vaudeville into French and English (*Au cabaret de l'amour*, 1959; *Kabir*, 1974), by Robert Bly (*The Kabir Book: 44 of the Ecstatic*

Poems of Kabir, 1977), by Linda Hess and Shukhdev Singh (*The Bījak of Kabir*, 1983), by Vinay Dharwadker (*The Weaver's Songs*, 2003) and, most recently, by Arvin Krishna Mehrotra (*Songs of Kabir*, 2011).

It is against this publishing landscape that Baleshwar Prasad's commercial-devotional printing effort at Belvedere Printing Press in Allahabad from 1903 onward (he died in 1920, and his sons took over the concern) appears remarkably wide-ranging and systematic. His *Santbani Series*, or *Pustakmālā*, which remains in print to this day, includes almost fifty titles. In the case of the "lesser Sants" of Awadh (in boldface in Table 3.2), in most cases it has remained until recently the *only* printed edition of their works.[67]

Compared to the miscellaneous books of Sant songs and verses that had been on the market since the 1860s, the scholarly editions brought out by the Nagari Pracharini Sabha, or the voluminous collections brought out by the lineages themselves,[68] the *Santbānī Pustakmālā* occupies a distinctive middle ground. These are booklets with a *modern look*, printed with movable type in codex format, with margins, indents, and first-line indexes for easy retrieval of individual poems (unlike some ritual books, such as the stories accompanying ritual fasts, which still imitate horizontal manuscript format even today).

We do not know much about the founder-manager of the Belvedere Press, Baleshwar Prasad, who belonged to an Agrawal service and business family that had moved from Punjab to Farrukhabad and then to Banaras in the nineteenth century. After serving as deputy collector to the Raja of Banaras and junior secretary to the colonial Board of Revenue, in 1902 Prasad retired and moved to Allahabad, where he set up a steam press in Belvedere House, next to the university, in the Civil Lines area.[69] Prasad belonged to the Radhasoami community, a devotional sect centered around a line of gurus who advocated meditation on a *nirgun* deity and who saw all the Sant poets as their inspired precursors, and while his publishing efforts clearly reflect the catholic and inclusive approach of the movement, their diffusion went far beyond it (see Juergensmeyer 1987). (The business is still in the family.)

Prasad's introduction to the series, which appeared behind the cover of every volume, spoke of the need to save this orature, or *bani*, from disappearing.[70] He stressed the effort and investment he put into finding, copying, and collating the manuscripts in proper editorial fashion as a form of service to the general public (*sarvasādhāraṇ*).[71] The term he favored for the Sants was the generic *mahatma*, or "great soul" (the title also given to Gandhi), and while his statement and the short biographies within each booklet talk at length of the Sants' different communities (*sampraday*, *panth*) and provide tables with lineages, the statement also reveals a strong standardizing and generalizing impulse, so that any theological difference or specificity of focus, or competition among Sants and communities, is erased.[72] This move mirrors the Radhasoami belief in an

Table 3.2 *Santbānī Pustakmālā*

Kabīr Sāhib' collection of *sakhis*
Kabīr Sāhib's collection of *sabads* and biography (4 parts)
Kabīr Sāhib's bundle of knowledge, *rekhtas*, and swing songs (*jhūlne*)
Kabīr Sāhib's syllable poem (*Akharāvatī*)
Dhanī Dharmadās's *Vocabulary* (*Shabdāvalī*) and biography (4 parts)
Tulsī Sāhib's (of Hathras) *Vocabulary* (*Shabdāvalī*) and biography (4 parts)
Tulsī Sāhib's (of Hathras) *Jewel Ocean* with biography
Tulsī Sāhib's (of Hathras) *Ghaṭ Rāmāyaṇ* in two parts, with biography
Guru Nānak Sāhib's *Prāṇ-Saṅgalī* with notes and biography (2 parts)
Dādū Dayāl's *Bānī*, part 1, with biography
Dādū Dayāl's *Bānī*, part 2, with biography
Sundar-Bilās and biography of Sundardās
***Palṭū Sāhib** part 1—kundaliyas* and biography
***Palṭū Sāhib** part 2—rekhtas, jhulnas, arills, kabittas,* and *savaiyas*
***Palṭū Sāhib** part 3—shabd* or *bhajan* and *sakhis* in various ragas
***Jagjīvan Sāhib's** Vocabulary* (*Shabdāvalī*) and biography (2 parts)
Dūlan Dās's Bānī and biography
Charandāsjī's *Bānī* and biography (2 parts)
Gharībdās's *Bānī* and biography
Raidāsjī's *Bānī* and biography
Dariyā Sāhib's (from Bihār) *Dariyāsāgar* (Dariya's ocean) and biography
Dariyā Sāhib's (from Bihār) selected *padas* and *sakhis*
Dariyā Sāhib's (from Marwar) *Bānī* and biography
Bhīkhā Sāhib's *Bānī* and biography
Gulāl Sāhib's (**Bhīkhā Sāhib**'s guru) *Bānī* and biography
Bābā Malūkdās's *Bānī* and biography
Gusaīṃ Tulsīdās's *Twelve Month Song* (*barahmasi*)
Yārī Sāhib's *Collection of Gems* (*Ratnāvalī*) and biography
Bullā Sāhib's *Extract of Words* (*Shabdasār*) and biography
Keśavdās's *Ambrosial Sip* (*Amīghūṃṭ*) and biography
Dharnīdās's *Bānī* and biography
Mīrā Bāī's *Vocabulary* (*Shabdāvalī*) and biography (4 parts)
Sahjo Bāī's *Light of the Natural State* (*Sahaj-Prakāsh*) and biography
Dayā Bāī's *Bānī* and biography
Selection of Sant Orature (*Santbānī Saṅgrah*) (2 parts)
Selection of Sant Orature (*Santbānī Saṅgrah*) with biographical sketches

immemorial Sant philosophy (*sant-mat*), which they claim to represent and into which they incorporate many poet-saints.

While Prasad shared the widespread perception of the fragility and perishability of oral and manuscript traditions and appeared keen to echo the Nagari Pracharini Sabha's search efforts and scholarly standards of publication, his intended audience was not the Hindi *literary* public but the general public, who would benefit from reading and singing these works as part of their individual or collective spiritual discipline, or *sadhna*. The rearrangement of the manuscript works of the Sants into individual portable booklets along a standard thematic pattern and with a handy apparatus was well suited to and successful in reaching out to modern devotees far beyond those who belonged to the Sant's specific community.[73] Indeed, arguably the very doctrinal blandness of the enterprise facilitated diffuse and border-crossing readership. You did not need affiliation, initiation, or commitment to a Sant lineage to use and enjoy the poetry.

Similarly, despite the fact that we can see some Sants inclining toward particular oral forms, language registers, and poetic strategies rather than others—Gulal toward Holi and spring songs, Bhikha and Bula toward Bhojpuri, Malukdas toward single-metaphor poems—the *Santbānī* booklets de-emphasized any such specificity. All the Sants fit the same pattern, all the volumes followed the same arrangement (first thematic and then by genre), and all their verses are presented as "attractive, devotion-arousing, and beneficial to the general public" in a similar way. These very portable booklets could circulate singly and inexpensively—they still do—or be bound by readers into more durable volumes (Figure 3.4). Astonishingly, they have remained the main source even for scholarly studies of north Indian Sants—including this one.[74]

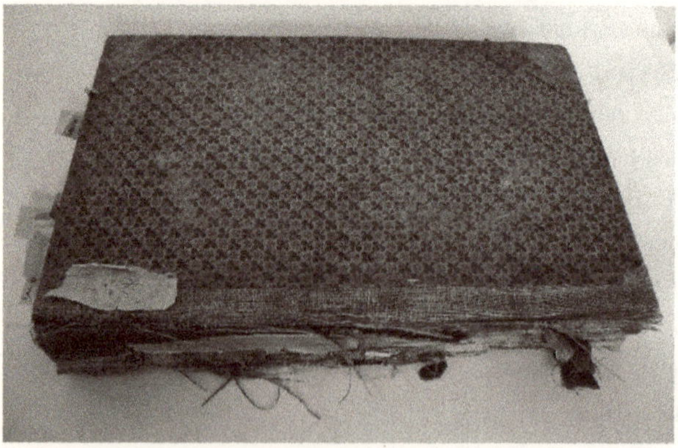

Figure 3.4. Collected and bound Belvedere *Santbānī* booklets from the 1920s.
Source: Courtesy of Vasudha Dalmia. Photograph by author.

Booklets or chapbooks have been crucial to the dissemination not just of Sant orature but of other forms of orature as well. This is well documented by the work of Catherine Servan-Schreiber on chapbooks of Bhojpuri songs and oral epics. As with the Sant booklets, this kind of publishing involves enterprising printer-publishers who, in her case, collect (often in exploitative fashion) oral texts from performers and distribute them to a mobile network of peddlers and itinerant singers. In the case of the Belvedere Press booklets (Figure 3.5), even now the family speaks of individual *sadhus* and devotees from distant regions dropping in to buy individual booklets, bulk orders from bookstores and monasteries, and of the brisk commerce taking place at religious fairs and railway stalls. This is a varied and diffuse distribution circle that extends all over north India, far beyond the domain of Hindi literary books.[75] Visually, these chapbooks appear printed on cheap, low-quality paper with bright and colorful plasticated covers and reproduce older typeset editions, only with the date and price changed. Intriguingly, the prices of these booklets are comparable to those of Hindi literary paperbacks, but they represent quite a different book object. Moreover, like Servan-Schreiber's Bhojpuri songs and oral epics, Sant orature has found favor with later cheap and decentralized technologies, whether the audio-cassettes that boomed in the 1980s or YouTube channels now (see Manuel 1993). If Chaturi the cobbler's descendants are literate today and still sing Sant songs, they would purchase Belvedere Press booklets and listen to YouTube video performances.

There are at least two implications of the phenomenon represented by the *Santbānī* booklets and other orature-related chapbooks for orature and world literature. First, if we really want to acknowledge and make space for orature within world literature, we need to take into account the technologies through which it circulates, often equally—if not more—widely than "official" or legitimate literature. These are technologies which run parallel to and are usually quite distinct from book publishing—as scholars working on Brazilian *literatura do cordel* (Slater 1982) or West African *onitsha* chapbooks (Newell 2000) have shown—and usually involve different actors and agents. Recognizing the multiplicities of circuits, actors, and economic models involved is therefore crucial. The trajectory and story of Sant orature in Purab in the age of print intersects with that of legitimate Hindi literary culture but is neither defined nor contained by it. It it both intensely local and intensely mobile.

Second, booklets and chapbooks highlight a different kind of reading and use of the text as an aid for practice. Rather than considering this mode as "nonliterary," we do well to attend to its specific forms and character and to the fact that it is not devoid of aesthetic expectations. These texts do provide aesthetic experiences, though not *only* aesthetic ones. This means that we have to attend to the quality and characteristics of their aesthetics, but also (though this is not something I do in this chapter) to people's modes of engagement with the

Figure 3.5 Belvedere Press Sant Bani booklets in the office of Belvedere Press, Allahabad.
Photograph by author.

texts. In the case of other forms of orature, such as the performance of oral epics or singing at spiritual sessions, scholars have noted the performers' active engagement with and manipulation of the text, their selecting and rearranging lines and passages, "knotting together" verses from different compositions, etc. (see, e.g., Pandey 1982a; Lutgendorf 1991; Viitamäki 2015). If David Damrosch's definition of world literature is any text that enters a literary culture beyond its own and is read as literature, the catch here is "as literature": literature defined by whom?

As for this book's concern with multilingual literary history and the "multiplicity of stories and trajectories" of literature East of Delhi, Sant orature is important for several other reasons. Certainly because it has represented an important space for self-expression and community formation for many lower-caste individuals and groups since the fifteenth century. The oral transmission—through verse—of philosophical and religious ideas, of social and religious critique, and of a utopian vision has ensured that many people became, to use again Purushottam Agrawal's term, "well-listened" (*bahushrut*), whether or not they had access to education. The ventriloquism of Sant poetry also ensured that a wide range of poetic idioms became available to audiences whether or not they were literate in that language or that tradition. Further, unlike models of literary circulation that are predicated on formal translation, Sant orature shows that poetic idioms could and did circulate without translation. Typically, as we have seen, this involved "nuggets of language," particular words, images, and phrases, rather than complete lines and poems. Finally, probably because they were a form of spiritual-religious-philosophical discourse, Sant poems were deeply dialogic, in acknowledged and unacknowledged dialogue with other religious discourses and figures like the Naths and the Sufis. While in most cases the silence about who the interlocutors were means that language itself is the site where such dialogue can be retrieved, a located and multilingual approach brings to light, unusually or perhaps uniquely in the case of Malukdas, a direct acknowledgment by the Sant of the most famous Sufi of his *qasba*.

The next chapter stays with *qasbas* in Awadh but explores another "story," that of the literary education and the multilingual cultivation of Persian and Brajbhasha poetry by "local cosmopolitans." This allows us to address questions of literature as transmitted cultural capital, of patronage outside substantial courts, of the economic value and function of poetry, and of the local cultivation of cosmopolitan poetic tastes.

4

Local Cosmopolitans

Poetry and Distinction in the *Qasbas* and Small Courts of Awadh

It is 1680 in Jajmau, a very small town on the Ganges in central Awadh, during the long reign of the Mughal emperor Aurangzeb (r. 1658–1707). Sayyid Diwan Rahmatullah from the *qasba* of Bilgram is acting as deputy district administrator for his aged grandfather. Apart from knowing Persian, he is, we are told, a connoisseur of Brajbhasha, or courtly Hindi, poetry.[1] One day, when a disciple of the famous Brajbhasha poet Chintamani Tripathi recites a couplet by his master, Rahmatullah points out an error in the use of a figure of speech. The disciple reports the correction to Chintamani, who, impressed, wishes to meet the administrator-connoisseur:

> Chintamani betook himself with his family to Jajmau with the intention of bathing in the river Ganges, which flows above Jajmau, and informed the Diwan. The Diwan did all that is necessary in terms of hospitality. Chintamani remained with the Diwan for a while, and they conversed on the appropriateness of [poetic] themes. And he composed a poem (*kabitta*) in the *jhūlnā* metre in praise of the bravery and chivalry of Sayyid Rahmatullah. Here is the poem:
>
> *garaba gahi singha jyūn sabala gala gāja, mana prabala gaja-bāja-dala sāja dhāyau,*
> *bajata ika chamaka ghana ghamaka dundubhina kī taraṅga khara/ghira dhamaka bhūtala hilāyau.*
> *bīra tihi kahata hīya kampi ḍara jo risana sain kau sūra chahūn aura chhāyau.*
> *kahū chala pāī taja nāha sanāha? iha Rahamatullā saranāha āyau.*
> Proud, strong and roaring, like a lion he arrays with forceful mind his elephants, horses and army.
> Lightning strikes, blows fall fast, drums thump hard—shaking the earth.
> Hearts tremble at his anger and call him a hero, a champion who masters all directions.
> Where can I go, leaving my lord's armour? I seek refuge with Rahmatullah.

East of Delhi. Francesca Orsini, Oxford University Press. © Oxford University Press 2023.
DOI: 10.1093/oso/9780197658291.003.0004

> [Afterward t]he Diwan sent some gold coins and a heavy golden robe to the house of Chintamani as a gift for the poem, but [Chintamani] expressed the wish to appear in the exalted presence [of the Diwan] so as to be properly invested with the robe. The Diwan retorted that the robe was not really worthy of him and that [Chintamani] should accept it in secret [a polite expression]. In the end Chintamani came in the presence of the Diwan, and in front of the assembly recited the *kabitta*, put on the robe, and accepted the reward. This poem is recorded in [his collection] *Kabitta Bichāra* [Reflections on poems], after the one in praise of Sultan Zayn al-Din Muhammad, the son of Shah Shuja [i.e., grandson of the previous emperor]. (Azad Bilgrami [H 1166/CE 1752] 1913: 366)

In this ordinary encounter between a poet and a (temporary) patron, courtly practices of distinction and connoisseurship are replicated on a very small, local scale in what can hardly be called a courtly setting, between people who may be called local cosmopolitans. The practices include deference and etiquette, learned literary conversation that displays knowledge of the fine points of poetics (*nuktasanj*), handsome hospitality, and an exchange of a praise poem for gifts of money and a ceremonial robe. The hierarchy in the exchange—with the poet as supplicant and the patron as connoisseur—is the reverse of literary memory: Chintamani is remembered as one of the great Hindi poets of his age, while no one remembers Rahmatullah, who was clearly small fry.[2] Who does the anecdote exalt? Chintamani for his reward and recognition, or Rahmatullah as the knowledgeable patron, on this one occasion, of a poet who usually enjoyed much loftier, royal patronage? The rare inclusion of a Hindu Brajbhasha poet in this Persian dictionary-cum-anthology of poets (*tazkira*) clearly needs to be qualified, particularly since, as we shall see, local Brajbhasha poets who *taught* Brajbhasha poetry to the Bilgrami local cosmopolitans are left out of it. The poem in the exchange is a cleverly alliterative but fairly standard *kabitta*, or independent poem, that praises the local administrator for his extraordinary courage and military strength: before his deafening drums enemies and the earth itself tremble. *Kabittas* were the main currency of poetic exchange and connoisseurship in this Hindi courtly poetic culture (see Sengar below) and were multipurpose: in other words, poets could easily recycle them by inserting the name of a different patron.[3]

Yet, what must have been a very ordinary encounter is actually an extraordinary *textual* event. It occurs in a biographical dictionary-cum-anthology (*tazkira*) of Persian poets devoted largely to poets from the author's own town of Bilgram, written about seven decades after the event. Most unusually, this particular *tazkira* features a separate chapter on the "connoisseurs of Hindi" (*qāfiya-sanjān-i hindī*) among Bilgram Persian literati and *quotes their Hindi verses* at length, to my knowledge the only Persian *tazkira* ever to do so. Yet, although Hindu Brajbhasha poets like Chintamani occasionally crop up, only Bilgrami elite Muslims are given entries. In other words, religion and class are two major discrimens of this Persian *tazkira* archive even when it breaks with its monolingual protocol.

Earlier chapters took a located and multilingual approach to follow the currency and transformations of the *katha* genre across different languages, periods, and "communities of taste" and to explore a form of sung religious poetry that provided a powerful idiom for nonelite individuals and communities. This chapter asks what it meant to be a "local cosmopolitan," in other words to acquire poetic tastes in cosmopolitan languages that are markers of distinction, but in such a local setting. What did it mean to be a cosmopolitan not in the imperial court or capital city but in a more modest context and peripheral location? How were cosmopolitan tastes and poetic skills in Persian and Brajbhasha acquired and practiced? How multilingual were the local cosmopolitans, and how can we find out, when sources like Azad's *tazkira* are so unique even if the episode it describes seems so unexceptional?

Discussions of cosmopolitanism in world literature have, understandably, focused on wide reach and circulation. In the case of India, cosmopolitanism has been largely identified with languages, particularly Sanskrit and Persian, and literary cosmopolitanism with elite culture in royal or imperial courts.[4] But there are three problems with this identification. First, imperial courtly practices cannot simply be written onto the whole terrain of the empire, in settings where resources, personnel, and hierarchies were much more modest. "Courtly" must mean something quite different when describing the Mughal imperial camp and Rahmatullah's gathering in Jajmau. Second, as in world literature, privileging imperial centers renders invisible too much of the rest of literary culture; it produces a picture of world literature that is too thin and sparsely populated and reproduces the biased view of those at the center. The implication is that literature "out there" will not be worth exploring, that poets will be imitative and provincial—"provincial" being, after all, a term of disparagement. Finally, the term "cosmopolitan" when used for people often carries a distinct Kantian political and ethical undertone of openness that is at odds with the ideas and practices of hierarchy, distinction, and exclusion that these cosmopolitans actively engaged in.[5] This was a time, Margrit Pernau has emphasized, when social hierarchy was understood in terms of relative proximity and distance rather than of a vertical axis.[6] Indeed, references to proximity and easy access to people of high status and power, and to exclusive poetic gatherings and encounters, code elite status.

This chapter therefore seeks to nuance both "Mughal culture" and literary cosmopolitanism in terms of *scale* and *location*.[7] Being a cosmopolitan fish in a small pond involved acquiring a habitus of distinction; its particular temporality involved investing a great deal in education for possible future opportunities, and biding one's time. It also meant exploiting to the full cosmopolitan networks away from the centers, investing in hospitality (when possible), letter writing, and exchanges of texts and manuscripts. It meant mastering cosmopolitan poetic codes and inscribing oneself, one's family, and one's local place in and through those codes. It involved gathering documentary proof and writing local histories, biographical dictionaries of local poets and Sufis, or verses in praise of one's village or town. In the context of multilingual Purab, researching multilingual locals also means going against the protocols of distinction that have separated the Persian and Brajbhasha/Hindi archives and actively looking in them for traces of multilingual cultivation among local poets and connoisseurs.[8] As we shall see, the strategies they employed were quite different from those of the poets of the previous chapters.

Reconstructing a Multilingual Archive

Though the "achievements of the Mughals throw into deep shadow the kingdoms and cultures that preceded them in north India," and Persian is associated with Mughal culture, Persian literacy and poetry took root much earlier in the eastern region (Orsini and Sheikh 2015: 1). This was thanks to the judges, Sufis, and poets who settled in the garrison towns in the thirteenth century as part of the expansion and rooting of the Delhi Sultanate in the region, or who were attracted to the Jaunpur court of the Sharqi Sultans in the fifteenth century.[9] While the literary culture of the Sharqis and under the north Indian Sultanates is best described as bilingual—its expansive romances were, after all, in Hindavi (see Chapter 2)—the copious production of Persian dictionaries, Sufi treatises, biographies, and other texts shows that Persian became the main language of Sufi textuality and a cornerstone in the education of aspiring local cosmopolitans.[10]

By far the most substantial producers of Persian texts in the Sultanate period were Sufis, and Sufi hospices, or *khanqahs,* were sites where Persian poetry, and in particular the mystical verses and narratives of 'Attar (1145–1221) and Rumi (1207–1273), were regularly taught, recited, and used as illustrations in spiritual discourse (see Rukn al-Din [H 1311] 1894). Whatever their subject, the Persian texts authored by local Sufis were dotted with verse quotations from these and other poets, as well as occasional Hindi couplets, or *dohas.*[11] The order of exposition in these texts likely reflected the hierarchy of languages and textual traditions in the authors' minds: a quote from the Qur'an would come first, followed by one or more Arabic Hadith (sayings attributed to the Prophet Muhammad), then Persian verses by famous poets, which sometimes translated the Arabic phrases, followed by verses in Persian by the author, and finally by Hindi "equivalents." For example, to explain the relationship between *aṣl* (origin, essence, root) and derivation, ʿAbd al-Quddus Gangohi used a morphological and botanical simile (stem/root and declension/branch) to say that "the branch is the same as the root [or essence]" and that Allah is close to his people. He supported the point first with God's own words, "And we are nearer to Him and his life-vein" (Qur'an 50:16), then with a Hadith ("And the Prophet Muhammad says, Allah has told me that 'I am closer to you than your own being' "), followed by a Persian verse by the Indian Sufi "madman of God" (*majzub*) Malik Masʿud:

> The world is the offshoot, the Lord of the world the original substance,
> Inside your secret (*sirr*) you will find origins and offshoots.

Finally, ʿAbd al-Quddus "translated" the Persian verse with a Hindavi one, probably his own:

> Dohra:
> *belī yah saṃsār sabha, mūla so sirjanhāra*
> *herihi belī mūla sõ, būjhahu barahma bicāra*
> The entire world is a creeper, its root the creator.
> The creeper and the root are together in the heart, understand this divine thought. (Gangohi 1898: 19)[12]

In Hindi and Sanskrit poetry the creeper usually evokes other associations as one of the "stimulants" of love (*uddipanavibhavas*). But paired here with the root it offers a good equivalent for the Persian verse, with the "secret" and the heart both harborers of higher truths, echoing the use of the creeper (*belī*) as a polyvalent symbol in Yoga literature and in Sant poetry.[13]

Was this kind of bilingualism common in Sufis' oral expositions, too? Judging by the fact that ordinary people visited the hospices documented by biographies and collections of anecdotes or sayings, it seems so. Sufis' oral discourses and interactions must in fact have been largely in the vernacular, yet the protocol of Persian textuality dictates that even conversations are written down in correct Persian, with only the occasional sentence or verse in Hindavi breaking through (e.g., Rudaulvi 1909; Shah Mina 1880; Rukn al-Din [H 1311] 1894). Quite a different practice from the "quasi-Persian" of Sant orature (Chapter 3). Important "traces" though these Hindavi phrases are, they are so few and far between that it is easy to form the mistaken impression that Sufis inhabited their own Persian (and Arabic)-only world.

It is once again Sufis who figure as poets in the biographical compendia that form the main archive of Persian poets, together with teachers and well-born officials. The genre of the *tazkira* (lit. "remembrance"), first employed for Sufis and then for poets and other professionals, became very popular in Mughal India and was used to highlight networks, construct genealogies, and canonize and remember past and present Persian—and from the eighteenth century also Urdu—poets.[14] *Tazkiras* come in many sizes and reflect different purposes: some aim at being encyclopaedic, others only list poets attached to a particular patron or region or who are the disciples of a poetic master. Some are largely anthologies with the barest biographical notes; others are mostly biographical and include friends or relatives of the author or else important patrons who merely dabbled in Persian poetry. Thanks to *tazkiras,* Persianate poetic circles and networks can be traced with some precision, and even local cosmopolitans appear in relatively large numbers (see Kia 2011; Dhawan 2014; Pellò 2012).[15]

Let us return, as an example, to the *tazkira* from which the initial anecdote came, *The Free-Standing Cypress* (or *Cypress of Azad, Sarw-i Āzād*, 1752) by Sayyid Mir Ghulam 'Ali "Azad" Bilgrami (1704–1786). This was one of four *tazkiras* written by Azad Bilgrami, by then a renowned scholar of Arabic and Persian living in the Deccan, far south of his hometown of Bilgram.[16] Each *tazkira* is different, but in each Azad manages to insert a few Bilgramis among other, arguably much more famous, poets.[17] *The Free-Standing Cypress* contains biographies of 143 Persian poets (and patrons) in India from the Mughal period to his day, and as many as twenty-eight Bilgramis (Azad Bilgrami [H 1166/CE 1752] 1913)! Another *tazkira, Ma'āsir al-kirām* (Noble glories, 1753), dedicated solely to 153 "pious and learned men of Bilgram," begins at a much earlier time, with the ancestor of the clan of the Sayyids of Barha to which Azad belonged, who had originally come from Wasit in eastern Iraq and settled in Bilgram at the time of Iltutmish (d. 1236), the reputed founder of the Delhi Sultanate (Azad Bilgrami 1910).[18] *Noble Glories* ends with Azad himself. In fact, the work is divided into two sections, one on the "pious men" and the other on the "learned people," and Azad features himself in both.

As for *The Free-Standing Cypress*, the number of individuals and wealth of biographical and historical detail makes it a wonderfully rich source, and we can see how Azad's swelling the ranks of Bilgrami men of letters helped put the *qasba* on the literary map. Azad is particularly keen to note when an individual or his relatives found imperial employment, starting with one Shaikh Nizam Bilgrami "Zamir:"

> One of the old poets of this place, a connoisseur (*nuktasanjān*) of sweet pen. His residence is in mohalla Qazipura, at the foot of the elevation. He was still young when his father departed for paradise. His paternal uncle, Shaikh Sulayman, who was among the excellent servants of the court of Emperor Akbar, educated him in the seclusion of obedience. After his studies, he excelled in the practice

> of poetry (*mashq-i sukhan*) and reached high excellence in this art. . . . He spent his time with the noblemen of the time and enjoyed particular respect. And spent his life in isolated seclusion. In the end he settled in the *qasba* of Safidun near Delhi and died there in H 1003 (the date of his death transmitted in a short poem [*qit'a*] by Mubarak Khan Dihlavi). He has a *diwan* with *qasidas*, *ghazals*, *ruba'is* (quatrains) and other verse forms for a total of 15,000 couplets. Sayyid Muhammad Ashraf Dargahi has commented positively on it. . . . His poetry was in the style of the time, so with few ornamentations. Here is the beginning of a ghazal:
>
> Who, beside the mirror, can glance upon your face?
> Who, beside the shoulder, can reach out to your curl? (Azad Bilgrami [H 1166/CE 1752] 1913: 244–245)

The Shaikh is praised as a connoisseur of poetry although his style is "old-fashioned;" in other words, it did not follow the "fresh style" (*taza-gu'ī*) of the poets at the imperial court (see Kinra 2007). The other "local cosmopolitans" included in this *tazkira* are either teachers (see next section) or Sufis like Mir 'Azmatullah Bilgrami "Bekhabar," about whom Azad writes:

> The successor of the "Sayyid of seekers," Mir Sayyid Lutfullah Bilgrami. A good poet of witty speech (*namkīn kalām*), and one of those Sufis who are "masters of the language" (*ṣāḥib al-lisān*).[19] He was playful, and elite and ordinary people all came to his gatherings (*majlis*). *Bekhabar* ("unselfconscious") was the right pen-name for him, and he was consciously "without consciousness." In his own *tazkira The Unselfconscious Ship* (or The Ship of Bekhabar, *Safīna-yi bekhabar*) he mentions his encounter with Mirza 'Abd al-Qadir Bedil, which I copy here. . . .
>
> He and Azad [i.e., the author] once travelled together from Bilgram to Shahjahanabad [i.e., Delhi] and had a good time all the way. . . . He excelled in the broken cursive script (*shikasta*) and was also well versed in the art of music. His collected works consist of ca. 7,000 verses.[20] He died in Shajahanabad on 24 Dhul'Qada 1142 [10 June 1730], and was buried in the compound of Nizam al-Din Awliya. When he died the composer of these pages wrote him an ode in which every line is a chronogram, and I present it here to the connoisseurs. (Azad Bilgrami [H 1166/CE 1752] 1913: 315, 325)

As we shall see, Azad studiously copies Bekhabar's encounter with the most famous Indian Persian poet of the eighteenth century, Mirza 'Abd al-Qadir "Bedil," and the conversation is presented as one among equals, elevating the local cosmopolitan to the rank of the world-renowned poet.[21]

Azad paid multiple tributes to his grandfather Mir ʿAbd al-Jalil Bilgrami (1660–1725), who, despite a checkered career, was instrumental in catapulting the family into the much larger world of imperial service, and on whom more below.[22] Not only Mir ʿAbd al-Jalil, his son Mir Sayyid Muhammad, his other grandson Mir Muhammad Yusuf, and more—Azad inserts the whole clan in the *tazkira*, so that the cultural history of Bilgram effectively becomes the history of its Persian-educated Sayyids and shaikhs. This is where we can stop reading Azad's *tazkira* along the grain and start asking: Who is left out?

Some of those excluded were men of the same social standing as Azad, and we may assume that either he did not have enough information or he did not care for them.[23] Also excluded were women and Persian-educated Hindus.[24] As with Kara (Chapter 2), the names of Bilgram's neighborhoods in a later local history evoke, by contrast, a much more expansive and varied social world, underlining how narrow and exclusive Azad's social range is. For example, the local history mentions a Khatrana, a neighborhood where Khatris and Brahmans lived, and also a Bhatpura, a neighborhood of bards and panegyrists (*bhāṭ* or *bhaṭṭ*) and esteemed Hindi poets (*kabīshwar*) (S. Bilgrami [1883] 2008: 62).

Azad's *tazkira The Free-Standing Cypress* is exceptional, as I have mentioned, in including a full separate chapter on Bilgram's "connoisseurs of Hindi poetry," eight shaikhs and Sayyids. Brajbhasha poets from other backgrounds are either mentioned only in passing or not mentioned at all. Azad, who includes the famous Brajbhasha poet Chintamani to indirectly exalt Rahmatullah, does not include the Bilgrami Hindu poet Haribans Rai Misra, who *taught* Brajbhasha poetry and poetics to his grandfather Mir ʿAbd al-Jalil. Azad does mention Haribans's son Diwakar Misra in passing as "one of the respected Brahmans of Bilgram, and well known among everyone (*khāṣ-o-ʿām*) in the arts of Sanskrit and *Bhākā* [*bhakha*, i.e., Hindi]," which allows him to say that Mir ʿAbd al Jalil recommended Diwakar for service to one of the Sayyid brothers, who were kingmakers in Delhi in the early eighteenth century.[25] To find other Hindi poets from Bilgram, we need to turn to other archives.

There is in fact one short entry on Haribans in the earliest Hindi biographical dictionary and anthology of poets, Shiv Singh Sengar's ([1878] 1970) *Shiv Singh's Lotus* (*Śiv Siṃh Saroj*; see Chapter 5). Sengar mentions that Haribans taught Hindi poetry to Mir ʿAbd al-Jalil, but also that he was patronized by a local raja, and he quotes two of Haribans's own poems.[26] The Urdu local history names two more Bilgram Brajbhasha poets, Ghasita Rai and Rai Har Prashad: "their poems are not popular (*ʿamīyāna*) but learned and literary (*ʿālimāna* and *shāʿirāna*)." Intringuingly, this history also tells us that these Hindu poets "knew thousands of Arabic and Persian verses by heart," indicating that poetic multilingualism in Bilgram went both ways (S. Bilgrami [1883] 2008: 62).[27] A slightly later Hindi literary history that incorporates names that had cropped up during the early twentieth-century Hindi manuscript search yields yet more names of Bilgrami Hindu and Muslim poets.[28] What this growing list highlights is how even an apparently fulsome source like Azad's Persian *tazkira* is nonetheless exclusive, largely on linguistic but also socioreligious grounds, and how silence is not absence and we just need to look elsewhere.

What the chapter on Hindi poets in *The Free-Standing Cypress* does provide is a fascinating overview of the range of Hindi poetic tastes among the elite Muslim literati of Bilgram, and how these tastes changed over time. The eight entries are:

1. Shaikh Shah Muhammad Farmuli (sixteenth century)
2. "Madhonayak" (d. 1687)
3. Rahmatullah (1650–1706)
4. Mir ʿAbd al-Jalil (1660–1725)
5. Ghulam ʿAli "Raslin" (fl. 1740)
6. Sayyid Barkatullah "Pemi" (1660–1729)
7. Mir ʿAbd al-Wahid "Zauqi" Bilgrami (d. 1721)
8. Muhammad ʿArif Bilgrami (fl. 1750)

Shah Muhammad Farmuli represents the older, pre-Mughal Afghan elite.[29] His composition of Hindi poetry is linked in popular memory with his love for a quick-tongued local girl, Champa, whose name is that of a popular flower (a Plumeria). When, from horseback, he noticed her wearing a black thread ornament around her arm,

> Shaikh Shah Muhammad pointed at that ornament and said: "How pretty! It's a *bhanvar* sitting on a lotus." The *bhanvar* is what they call a black bee and the *kanval* a lotus (*nīlūfar*). He compared the black silk to the black bee and the arm to a red lotus, which is commonly used in Hindi metrical poetry (*mauzūnān*). And the love (*ʿishq*) of the black bee for the lotus is established among the connoisseurs of Hindi just like that of the nightingale for the rose, and that of the turtle-dove for cypress among the Persians. With flowery language, Champa answered: It's not a *bhanvar*, it's a *gobarvandh*. That is the black beetle that comes out of cowdung. (Azad Bilgrami [H 1166/CE 1752] 1913: 351–352)

In other words, Champa boldly and cheekily corrects Shah Farmuli, suggesting an even more earthy insect and, at the same time, a more precise word. Impressed, Shah Farmuli carries Champa off and they live happily together, exchanging poetic repartees in *doha* couplets.[30] *Dohas* have cropped up already in the previous chapters, and they were indeed ubiquitous in Hindi poetic culture, either as individual verses (*muktaka*, also called *sakhis*, or "witnesses," among Sant poets, see

Chapter 3), as part of the *doha-chaupai* stanza of narrative poems and romances (Chapter 2), or strung together in collections (*dohavali*). Collections of a hundred (*shataka*) and seven hundred (*satasai*) couplets were already popular in Prakrit and Sanskrit, and they became popular once more in courtly Hindi poetry, the most famous being Biharilal's *Satasaī*. Tulsidas (1974: 85–128), too, had a *Dohāvalī* in Brajbhasha.[31] After Farmuli and Rahmatullah (whose collection is not extant), Mubarak 'Ali (b. 1583) and Raslin produced two celebrated collections: Mubarak wrote a hundred couplets about two markers of female beauty, the mole (*Tila-sataka*) and the curl (*Alaka-sataka*); Raslin one on the woman's body from top to toe, *Aṅga darpaṇa* (A mirror to the body, 1737).[32] In other words, from Shah Farmuli onward, the *dohavali* seems to have been the favorite genre among the Brajbhasha Muslim poets of Bilgram, whose collections became more and more informed by the categories and subcategories of courtly poetics.

To go back to Azad's list of Hindi poets from Bilgram, the entries on Mir 'Abd al-Wahid and Barkatullah Pemi are evidence of the continued currency of Hindavi songs and poetry in Sufi practice.[33] Next, Sayyid Nizam al-Din "Madhonayak" shows the close connection existing, among local cosmopolitans as well as at imperial and subimperial courts, between the cultivation of Brajbhasha poetry, knowledge of Sanskrit, and musical knowledge and connoisseurship. After he became proficient in Persian verse and prose at a young age and taught "the honoured Persian books," "Madhonayak"

> turned to Hindi knowledge (*'ilm-i hindī*), and in the city of Banaras, which is the foundation of *rasa*, he studied the books of Sanskrit and *bhākā* [i.e., Hindi or Brajbhasha] and acquired great skill. He acquired knowledge of sound and rhythm (*nād* and *tāl*) in Indian music and played music (*sāngīt*) uniquely well. He became a scholar and fine expert in this art and a celebrated singer (*nāyak*) of the age. This is why he takes Madhonayak as *takhallus* (pen-name). He wrote two books: one is *Nādachandrikā* (The Moon of Sound), and the other *Madhonāyak singār* (Madhonayak's Ornament). The experts in the art of music of the time came from far away to serve him and have him solve their problems. His compositions (*naqshas*) are famous. Singers clutch their ears when they mention his name, and this is a sign of respect commonly used among Indians. (Azad Bilgrami [H 1166/CE 1752] 1913: 356–357)

Madhonayak is also mentioned in a text by another Bilgrami who proudly inscribes the town into global geography. One of the things Bilgram is famous for, he writes, is a well whose water makes one's voice melodious: "[I]f you drink its water for four days your voice and appearance improve" (Murtaza Bilgrami 1879: 156).

With Sayyid Ghulam Nabi "Raslin" (1699–1750) we are at the pinnacle of Brajbhasha courtly poetic culture. Raslin was the author of a well-regarded manual of poetics, the *Rasa prabodha* (Enlightenment of rasa, 1742) and an accomplished poet, praised by his contemporaries.[34] A military man who died fighting the Rohilla Afghans in the service of the second Nawab of Awadh, Safdar Jang, Raslin is the most famous *qasba* bilingual Persian-and-Brajbhasha poet. Azad wrote about him:

> Someone predicted at birth that he would become a poet. He was very well-versed in Arabic, Persian, and Hindi arts. He studied everything with Mir Tufail Muhammad Bilgrami. He had a very good way of arranging his poems. Especially with his Hindi verse, where he reached unparalleled heights and made the eyes of the parrots of India double up in amazement. (Azad Bilgrami [H 1166/CE 1752] 1913: 213)

The Hindi anthologist Sengar ([1878] 1970: 786) echoed this appreciation and called *Rasa prabodha* "very authoritative;" he also noted Raslin's multilingual scholarship and poetic abilities, and mentioned that he had five hundred Hindi books in his library.[35] Unfortunately neither Azad nor Sengar says with whom Raslin studied Brajbhasha poetry and poetics, though Azad tells us that among the five hundred Brajbhasha books in his library there were commentaries, poetry collections, and poetics manuals, some with his own marginalia in Brajbhasha.

The range and currency of Hindi/Brajbhasha poetry among the shaikhs and Sayyids of Bilgram raise the question of whether the elites of other *qasbas* and courtly milieus also cultivated both Persian and Brajbhasha poetry to the same degree or in the same fashion. Other *tazkira* writers are not as forthcoming about it as Azad, however. Moreover, in the second half of the eighteenth century the new fashion for Urdu poetry—i.e., for vernacular poetry modeled on Persianate forms then called Rektha or, confusingly, Hindi—seems to have elided the memory, if not the practice, of Brajbhasha poetry. Only when *tazkiras* mention particular books or genre names, or "Indian knowledge" and "Indian music," can we surmise that Brajbhasha and not Urdu is being referred to.[36]

What about the "other side," i.e., the Hindi/Brajbhasha archive in the sixteenth to eighteenth centuries? How multilingual and socially inclusive is it? Information is much patchier to start with, although biographies of Sant poets and devotees were written from the late sixteenth century, courtly poets sometimes included some account of their family and background (in a section called *kavi-vamsha*), and verses stringing together the names of prominent poets (called *namavali*) became increasingly common in the eighteenth century. Anthologies of Brajbhasha poems typically circulated without biographical notes. Anecdotes about poets were rather part of oral, family, and local lore, and it was this lore that Sengar drew on for his 1878 voluminous compilation of almost a thousand poets, in effect the first "Hindi *tazkira*." Though the book's biographical entries, placed in largely alphabetical and not chronological order, are often extremely brief, its historicizing impulse clearly met the need of the hour, and several revised editions followed in quick succession.[37] Sengar was in fact the most important source for the first ever history of Hindi literature, G. A. Grierson's (1889) *Modern Vernacular Literature of Hindustan* and for subsequent Hindi histories, as we shall see in the next chapter.

Sengar's *tazkira* reflects what Hindi literature meant for connoisseurs at the time, in other words, courtly poetry in Brajbhasha. Although he was excited at discovering early Rajasthani heroic poetry,[38] praised Tulsidas and other bhakti poets, and even included Kabir, Nanak, Malukdas, and a few other Sants, the most important genre for Sengar was definitely the *kabitta*, the stand-alone poem in syllabic meters that was, with the *savaiya* and the *doha*, the main currency of courtly Hindi literary culture from the sixteenth century on.[39] *Kabittas* lent themselves beautifully to the display of rhetorical knowledge and could be used to praise a patron or illustrate a particular figure of speech. Poetics manuals (*riti grantha*) of the period not only explained figures of speech but also deemed which topics were poetic; they categorized moods and emotions, the parts of a woman's body, and different kinds of women. *Riti granthas* worked as proofs of the author's mastery over the complexities of the poetic code, as teaching materials, as offerings to one's patron in expectation of a reward, and as frames in which one could slot one's individual verses. Practically all poets of courtly Hindi, i.e., Brajbhasha, wrote at least one such manual, often several. Within this code, innovation took place through the amplification and subtle variation within the scheme, not through breaking or dismissing the scheme (see Busch 2011). *Riti granthas* of this period are praised for the new categories of heroines (*nayikas*) added, or for using unusual meters. For example, the founder of a lineage of Brajbhasha poets (see below) in Awadh, Kalidas Trivedi, was praised for including in his *Vadhūvinoda* (The delight of women, 1692) a chapter only on wives and another only on courtesans, and for using less common meters (*bhujangapratapa*, *kundaliya*, *trotaka*, and *chaupai* instead of *kabitta*): "a most wonderful book," Sengar ([1878] 1970: 660) called it. One poem by his grandson Dulah cleverly describes the complex emotions of a woman whose lover is her neighbor's husband: while she rejoices at his return, she is also jealous, something that does not escape the attention of other women in the house:

> I hear my neighbour's one has come,
> my heart is glad. But Dulah

the poet sees the wife's state,
how her body burns and smoulders.
At home all women mock me—
"What's wrong, *bahu*, do tell us.
Other people's joys bring
joy, this heartache
is something new." (Sengar [1878] 1970: 245)

Sengar's courtly, *kabitta*- and *grantha*-centric view magnified courtly poets and sidelined, e.g., *katha* authors, so that although Sengar ([1878] 1970: 778) clearly knew about Malik Muhammad Jayasi and mentions him in the biographical section ("he composed *Padmāvat* in *bhasha*"), he included no verse example, whereas he collected *kabittas* of even "ordinary" poets if he considered them to be good. Learning to discriminate between good (*uttama*), adequate, and bad *kabittas* was, after all, a topic explicitly treated in poetics manuals. A memorable *kabitta* was one that contained both a direct and a figurative meaning (*shlesha*) and that used the *langue* of the poetic idiom to produce a new *parole*, as in this *kabitta* by Dulah, which can be read to describe both a sinuous girl and a flexible bow (the key is, as usual, in the last line):

sundara subesa madhya muṭhī meṃ samāta jāko
pragaṭo na gāta besa, bandana saṁvārī hai

The slender waist fits in your fist
The body reveals little, a mere red dot shines.
Dulah the poet says, that quiet beauty weighs
only a dram and looks molded in a frame.
The riser is soft, take it in your hand,
wholly virgin, yet victorious in battle,[40]
happy and worthy from tip to toe,
as dear to me as a bow from Multan. (246)

Sengar's Purab-centered view works in our favor, in that he includes more and a wider range of entries from the region than from, say, Rajasthan or central India.[41] His detailed entries about eastern courtly poets begin in the sixteenth century with Narhari and Gang, the first professional poets to become attached to Mughal grandees and to gain access to the imperial court, far from their birthplaces. Sengar ([1878] 1970: 678) calls both of them *bandijan*, bards and panegyrists, suggesting that this was their original occupation.[42] Heavily alliterative verses were meant to showcase the poets' talent, as in this six-liner (*chhappay*) by Gang to Mughal emperor Jahangir:[43]

dalahi calata halahalata bhūmi
thala thala jimi caladala
pala pala khala khalabhalata
bikala bāla kara kula kala

As the army pounds ahead, the earth
sways and shakes like a *pipal* leaf.
When snare-drums of war blast
like insect drones, and the pole star
smashes to the ground, the enemy,
like family peace in the hands
of a twitchy daughter, grows unnerved.
Just as, says Gang, when your mighty army
treads heavily, King Jahangir, the earth's surface,
a rising cobra, hissing, spitting
venom from its thousand cheeks. (Sengar [1878] 1970: 99)

When he was attributing such fearsomeness to Diwan Rahmatullah in Jajmau, Chintamani was exalting the small, local patron to similar dizzying heights.

Sengar also pays tribute to *acharya* (master) Chintamani,[44] his brothers Matiram and Bhushan, and other seventeenth- and eighteenth-century Brajbhasha poets from the region, including Sukhdev Misra from the ancient town of Kampila, and the lineage of Kalidas Trivedi, comprising his son Udaynath Tivari 'Kavindra' and Udaynath's son Dulah Trivedi from nearby Banpura.[45] Their trajectories show that, after traveling in search of patronage with Mughal grandees and their Rajput allies, at the end of the seventeenth century these courtly poets began to find patronage locally, in the "mud-brick courts" of the rajas of Amethi, Asothar, Arwar, and Dhaundhiya Khera. Several of these rajas became well-known Brajbhasha poets themselves.[46] For example, Kalidas Trivedi started out with the Raja of Jammu, who fought with the Mughal army, before becoming attached to Raja Himmat Singh of Amethi (Sharma 2003: 16–17). His son Udaynath began serving the local rajas of Amethi and Asothar before leaving to work for the ruler of Bundi in Rajasthan; apart from his poetic manuals, his poem of linked verses called *Jañjīrā* (Chain) became especially popular.[47] Yet one of the most famous Brajbhasha poet-scholars of this period, Bhikharidas, never left and lived all his life in the small seat of Arwar near Pratapgarh (which had been established only in the 1680s); his patron was Hindupati Singh, the brother of the local raja. Finally, Sengar included many contemporary poets, whether independent or attached to the court of the Maharaja of Banaras.

Brajbhasha elite courtly poetry is, unsurprisingly, better archived than Sant poetry. Despite the patchiness and exclusions of the Hindi archive, what it highlights is that the cultivation of not only Persian but also courtly Brajbhasha poetry became a mark of distinction, a currency of exchange, and a means to ease one's way in the world for local cosmopolitans from the region. *Tazkiras* and early anthologies attest to the great practical importance of occasional poems like the one Chintamani offered to Rahmatullah. Such praise poems fell into disrepute in the twentieth century's critical upsurge against courtly poetry and were viewed as evidence that poets sold their art instead of dedicating it to the people—*ashrit*, "patronized," is still somewhat of a dirty word in Hindi literary histories. But Hindi anthologies (like *tazkiras*) admiringly transcribe poems that made their authors famous or that were generously rewarded, like the one Kalidas Trivedi composed for Emperor Aurangzeb's conquest of Golconda Fort.

Taken together, the Persian and Hindi archives are asymmetrical, with far more information about Persian poets and their networks than about Hindi/Brajbhasha ones. The archives are also, unfortunately, generally uninterested in the poets' multilingual practices; multilingual education and poetic practice are mentioned only in passing, if at all. This largely remains the case. When literary histories recall that the Hindavi *katha* writer Nur Muhammad "Kamyab" (ca. 1750) also composed Persian poetry, or that the Brajbhasha poet Chandanray was "a good Persian poet," their Persian verses are not included or discussed (McGregor 1984: 153, 199). Besides, as I have already noted, since in Persian texts "Hindi" can refer to either Hindavi, Brajbhasha, or Urdu, only when Hindi is mentioned in connection with music or with Hindi poetic knowledge (*'ilm-i hindī*) can we assume that Brajbhasha is being referred to. As a result of these strict protocols, apart from very few exceptions it becomes impossible to see how poets practiced their bilingualism and to compare their Persian and Hindi writings. But because education was such an important marker of distinction, it is there that we can find plenty of clues about how the multilingual habitus of these literati was formed.

Studying and Strolling

Education was key to becoming a "local cosmopolitan," to social reproduction for the scribal elite, and to social mobility for the rest.[48] Unsurprisingly, teachers are among the Bilgramis most effusively praised in Azad's *Free-Standing Cypress*, even though they did not compose poetry regularly.[49] Azad singles out two in particular—Hafiz Ziyaullah and Mir Tufail Muhammad Bilgrami (1663–1739)—for having taught generations of Bilgramis, including Azad himself.[50] For those born in scholarly families, education typically began at home, continued with local teachers, and later involve travel to other *qasbas* or cities for further instruction in particular branches of knowledge.

Persian education began with Sa'di and the other "study books" (*kutub-e darsī*) in the standard curriculum of elementary education (*dabistan*).[51] The higher (*sanad*) level required, for literature, the study of lexicography and prosody. Azad Bilgrami gives us a taste of this Persian and Arabic curriculum when he writes about himself and his cousin and fellow student Mir Muhammad Yusuf:

> We studied the *kutub-i darsī* together with Ustad Mir Tufail Muhammad Bilgrami, and we were taken to *sanad* for lexicography (*lughat*), the Prophet's traditions (Hadith) and biographies (*siyar-i nabawī*) by [our grandfather] Mir 'Abd al-Jalil; we also learnt the prosody (*'urūż* and *qāfiya*) of literary arts (*funūn-i adab*) from [his son] Mir Sayyid Muhammad. . . . This is how we studied: we would read out continuously to each other two books or a single book from two places (*ba-samā't o qir'āt-i yakdīgar mī khwandīm*), and at night (*shabdīz*) we used to ride on the plain of study (*dar miżmār-i taḥṣīl mīrāndīm*); if from time to time we encountered an obstacle, we would take up a different lesson in that hiatus. During the time he stayed in Bilgram to acquire knowledge (*qasb-i 'ulūm*), [Mir Muhammad Yusuf] also spent some time teaching other students. Later Mir Muhammad Yusuf went to Delhi in order to study mathematics, geometry, accountancy, and so on from several scholars there and reached a high level in the field of mathematics (*riyāżī*). (Azad Bilgrami [H 1166/CE 1752] 1913: 307)

When sources tell us about education, then, it invariably involves learning one or more languages. In turn, learning languages meant memorizing verses that made poetic rhythms and repertoires of images and tropes part of one's body. The same was true for Hindi and Sanskrit education, in which one stored verses and texts literally "in the throat" (*kanthastha*). In both Persian and Hindi, poetic tastes were then trained and refined by reading manuals about metrics, rhetoric, and poetics and through the study of great poets. "Who learns by heart (*kaṇṭha karai*, lit. 'in the throat') this *Throat Ornament* (*kaṇṭhābharaṇa*) will find happiness, gain lustre in the assembly (*sabhā*), and be called a connoisseur of poetic ornaments," wrote Dulah about his own manual, the *Necklace for Poets* (*Kavikulakaṇṭhābharaṇa*) (Dulah 2000: 24).

In his letters home, Mir 'Abd al-Jalil, who was himself fluent in Persian, Turkish, and Arabic (he had learned the whole Arabic *Qāmūs* dictionary by heart) and had trained in "all the sciences," urged his son Mir Sayyid Muhammad to study Arabic assiduously, and was delighted when Mir Sayyid Muhammad wrote back that he had been able to cite an Arabic verse "at the right moment" (Narayana Rao and Shulman 1998). (More on these letters below.) Azad himself would go on to study Hadith further with scholars in Medina and gained the certificate allowing him to teach certain Hadith texts (Leese 2019: 54).[52]

The distinction between serious study—with books and teachers—and familiarity is one that several authors made with regard to poetic education. "Strolling," *sair*, and its attendant metaphors of scent, flowers, and bees, "hearing melodies," and "savoring" the taste or scent of poetry were common metaphors for poetic appreciation and could also indicate literary knowledge in which one was less systematically trained. About himself, Azad Bilgrami ([H 1166/CE 1752] 1913: 351, emphases added) confessed:

> I am as acquainted with the Arabic as with the Persian and Hindi languages. And I drink of all three cups as much as I can. For Arabic and Persian I *trained* for poetry (*sukhan*) for a long time and nourished (*parvardam*) the tender shoots of meaning [or of the nine *rasas: naurasān-i ma'ānī*] in the bosom of thought. Though I did not have the opportunity to train in Hindi poetry (*mashq-i sukhan-i hindī*) and I could not conquer the green pastures of this dominion, I had plenty of [opportunities] to *hear* the melodies of the nightingales of India and ample chance to *savour* the sugar-sellers of this land of flowers.

And about his revered grandfather Mir 'Abd al-Jalil, Azad wrote:

> His lofty status was too high for him to put his lips to the trifling talk of Hindi poetic themes (*lab ba turrahāt-i shā'irī-yi sīmā manẓūmāt-i hindī mī kashīd*) and contaminate his guarded (*muḥtāṭ*) tongue with unnecessary chitchat. But occasionally, if he sought to cure his heart (*jigar*) when it got too hot, he would listen to Hindi. (A. Bilgrami ([H 1166/CE 1752] 1913: 260)

Unlike the years of continuous study needed in order to master Persian and Arabic knowledge, Azad expresses the cultivation of Hindi poetry as effortless, like a natural breeze flowing into the *qasba*: "Metrical poetry (*mauzūnān*) in the Hindi language has shown itself abundant in Bilgram. And it fills the noses with the sweetness of the sandalwood of freshness and blossoming. This is why a chapter dedicated to this group was compiled separately; and that perfumed pastille is [here] entrusted into the hands of the connoisseurs of scents" (351–354). In fact, as we learned from Sengar, Mir 'Abd al-Jalil did *study* Brajbhasha poetry and poetics with the Bilgrami poet Harbans Rai Misra.

In similar terms, Puhakar, the author of the "courtly *katha*" *Rasaratan* discussed in Chapter 2, trained to be a professional scribe or Kayastha and then "reflected on" prosody and the various poetic forms (*chhanda vanda piṅgala prabandha vahu rūpa vichārana*).[53] He also "strolled through Persian poetry" and recited Persian verses (*pārasīya kāvya puni saira vidhi najamana sara aviyāta kahiya*), but when it came to his Sanskrit literary education, of which he was clearly proud, he named several poets and poeticians, from Valmiki, the author of the Sanskrit *Rāmāyaṇa,* to Kalidasa, Bana, Sriharsha, Jayadeva, Dandi, Bhanudatta, and Udayana, as well as the Rajasthani poet-bard Chand Bardai.[54]

Particularly for Brajbhasha poets from Brahman families, a grounding in Sanskrit poetry and poetics was very much the norm (see Busch 2011).[55] The manuals of poetics and prosody they wrote in such profusion doubled as teaching materials, and becoming tutors for their patrons' children was a common professional route.[56] But Sanskrit education was not just for Brahmans. The Muslim Nizam al-Din "Madhonayak" of Bilgram, as we have seen, studied Sanskrit books in order to better ground his musical knowledge.[57]

For local cosmopolitans, studying in the *qasba* had a particular temporality, which involved biding one's time before one could put that educational capital to good use in the wider world. This point is brought out particularly well in the letters, already mentioned, that Mir ʿAbd al-Jalil Bilgrami, Azad's grandfather, wrote from his post in Sindh to his son Mir Sayyid Muhammad back in Bilgram.[58] The letters carried instructions, exortations, and requests for copies of texts available in the family library or from other scholars in Bilgram.[59] "My heart was greatly delighted at the account of your intense study, and of your acquisition of accomplishments," wrote Mir ʿAbd al-Jalil (quoted in Gladwin 1798: 137).[60] In the next letter, from Delhi, he declared himself anxious to see his son but was reluctant to send for him since he had not been able to get reinstated to the post in Sindh, from which he had been suspended (141). His son clearly repeated the request, for in letter after letter Mir ʿAbd al-Jalil had to explain his objections and urge Mir Sayyid Muhammad to stay put in Bilgram until he could get an order appointing the son to his own old post in Sindh (141, 147, 151, 153, 159, 177, 213, 247). Then, at an opportune moment, Mir ʿAbd al-Jalil asked his son to rush to Delhi as quickly as possible so that his educational capital could finally translate into professional reproduction.[61]

In sum, education in early modern Awadh was necessarily multilingual and inevitably literary in a broad sense. Memorization and the reading of a few literary classics formed the basis of this education and gave the educated familiarity with one or more poetic systems, depending on family background, religious orientation, and individual taste. For some, the combination was Persian with some Arabic and/or Hindi; for others, it was Sanskrit and Brajbhasha, with some "strolling" into Persian. Indeed, it was this knowledge of Arabic and Hindi, as well as Persian, poetry that made the *qasba* literati from Bilgram stand out among the sea of provincial Indo-Persian literati. This was something that Azad emphasized, particularly in the case of his grandfather Mir ʿAbd al-Jalil and of Azad himself.[62]

There is plenty of evidence that this multilingual education remained the norm even when English education and the colonial education system eventually replaced them. Nothing shows this better than the manuscript autobiography of an ordinary Brahman clerk in the colonial toll office of Mirzapur, near Banaras, written in Hindi in 1880 (see also Orsini 2019a). Born in 1850, Bhanupratap Tiwari was raised by his grandfather in the family's ancestral village near Banaras while his father worked in nearby Mirzapur as record-keeper in the colonial superintendent's office. Bhanupratap's short manuscript autobiography reads like a catalogue of what he studied and read and with whom. With a service profession in mind, his education was geared at stacking up language skills. But because language learning consisted largely of reading literary texts, Bhanupratap's multilingual education also involved acquiring several aesthetic tastes and repertories.

First, when Bhanupratap was between three and a half and five, his grandfather made him learn by heart a large number of Hindi devotional couplets (*dohas*), which he still remembered and wrote down fifty years later. When he was five, after his tonsure ceremony and the ritual worship of study books (*pāṭh pūjā*), his grandfather taught him modern Hindi and Sanskrit, and a local learned and pious man read with him the modern Hindi prose version of Krishna's life (Lalujilal's *Premsāgar*; see Chapter 5) and most of the works by Tulsidas in both Brajbhasha and Avadhi. When Bhanupratap was eight, his father decided it was time for him to learn Persian and enrolled him at the local Chunar Mission School for three years, where he studied Shaikh Sa'di's collection of stories, the *Bostān* (The scented garden). Bhanupratap continued studying Persian privately with his father, with whom he read Sa'di's other classic, the *Gulistān* (The flower garden), and with a teacher in Mirzapur, with whom he read the fifteenth-century Timurid poet Jami's *Yūṣuf Zulaykha,* the Mughal story collection in ornate prose *Bahār-e dānish* (The spring of wisdom), and a letter-writing manual (*Inshā-e khalīfa*) (Tiwari 1880: 2).[63] Other Persian texts he studied later, piecemeal with local scholars included: Nizami Ganjavi's *masnavi Sikandarnāma,* some works by the chief intellectual of Emperor Akbar's court, Abu'l Fazl, and the poetry of Hafiz. But Bhanupratap was also keen to learn English: he started studying *Ballantyne's Primer* on his own before he managed to enroll in an English school for a couple of years, until he had to leave it when his father retired due to illness and Bhanupratap had to start working as an office clerk in his stead.[64]

Bhanupratap's autobiography is precious as a record of an ordinary multilingual education and the persistence of a multilingual habitus several decades after the East India Company had switched the languages of the administration and law courts from Persian to English and Urdu, in 1835. For Bhanupratap, too, acquiring literary taste began with learning languages and a sense of meter by memorizing large numbers of verses (in Hindi and Persian). By and large Bhanupratap shared his tastes—which involved practices of joint reading, recitation, and singing—with different people, different "communities of taste" that only partly overlapped. With some people he sang devotional songs and listened to discourses (*satsang*)—his family was initiated into one of the Sant communities, the Darya Panth (see Chapter 3). Sometimes the same people were also keen on courtly Brajbhasha verse. With other people he shared Persian poetry. It's unclear whether Bhanupratap ever developed a taste for modern Hindi literature; he was a contemporary of Bharatendu Harishchandra in Banaras, the father of modern Hindi, but does not mention reading him or reading newspapers, nor does he mention the Great Revolt of 1857 that raged across north India. Working in a colonial office with a British administrator also put Bhanupratap in direct contact with colonial scholar-administrators. As we shall see in the next chapter, he learned enough English to be able to put his multilingual skills to a new use and contribute articles and translations from Hindi and Persian to the ethnographic journal *North Indian Notes & Queries*, edited by William Crooke. Bhanupratap's example makes us think of education in this period as a portfolio that varied according to professional aim, family resources, personal interest, religious affiliation, and no doubt chance.

Practices of Distinction

There was no doubt a vast gulf between the resources available in the imperial centers and in the *qasbas* and "mud-brick courts," however much poets tried to exalt them in their eulogies. If temporally local cosmopolitanism involved an often lengthy preparation and investment in education before one left one's village or town in search of employment and renown elsewhere, spatially local cosmopolitans sought to reproduce courtly culture in local gatherings.[65] The trappings of patronage could be replicated on a much smaller, and transient, scale by adhering to protocols of etiquette and deference, as we saw in the anecdote of Chintamani and Rahmatullah. Other anecdotes invoke famous poets attesting to the mastery of the local cosmopolitans. For example, in a long section in the entry devoted to his grandfather Mir 'Abd al-Jalil, Azad Bilgrami ([H 1166/CE 1752] 1913: 260) narrates a meeting with the famed Persian poet Nasir 'Ali Sirhindi (d. 1696):

> The meeting between the late Mir 'Abd al-Jalil and Nasir 'Ali took place in Aurangabad, Deccan. He himself told me that the meeting went well, and that they conversed with each other. The session (*jalsa*) lasted from early in the day until midnight. At the time Nasir 'Ali had just recently composed his *qasida lāmiya*.[66] Its praise section (*tashbīb*) is devoted to heat, and the rest to praise of the chief of the prophets, i.e. the Prophet Muhammad. . . . He recited the whole

qasida and then asked, "Did you like it, son? (*Bete, khwūsh āmad*?)" I said, "The whole *qasida* is good." Then he insisted, "*Bete,* if you liked it you should mark out what (*bāyad nishān dād*)." I said, "One couplet." When he heard these words, a change came over his face. I asked him why and said: "It is all a pouring of pearls and they are all equally beautiful, but once in a while you hear something particularly exquisite." At this he regained colour and asked me which couplet I preferred. I said:

zi baski nam bazamīn nārasīda mī sūzad
chū sham' bar sar-i shākh ast rīshā-yi nihāl
As dew sizzling before it reaches ground
is the fiber of a young shoot, a moth atop a branch.

Nasir 'Ali was delighted and praised me saying that he also considered it the best couplet of them all.

In the anecdote Nasir 'Ali confirms Mir 'Abd al-Jalil's excellent taste and in fact depends on his approval. Further on in the conversation, Mir 'Abd al-Jalil objects to a word Nasir 'Ali had used in his *masnavi* in praise of Emperor Aurangzeb because he had also used it in the same poem to praise a horse. Nasir 'Ali agreed to take the verse out.[67] On another occasion, somebody recited half a line by the other celebrated Indian Persian poet of the time, Mirza Bedil, and asked, "Who can finish it?", and Mir 'Abd al-Jalil did so on the spot (Azad Bilgrami [H 1166/ CE 1752] 1913: 261). Even when the encounters with famous poets are less flattering, they are still testimony that the local cosmopolitan could gain an audience and get close to the great master.[68]

The long years of memorizing and training were necessary to be able to come up with an appropriate verse on the spot. Mir 'Abd al-Jalil's letters to his son offer a historically vivid sense of how poetry was used in the search for patronage as a means of attracting the attention of those in positions of power and authority. But whereas in his grandson Azad Bilgrami's account Mir 'Abd al-Jalil's story exemplifies a smooth rise to recognition and success, Mir 'Abd al-Jalil's letters tell a rather different story, as we have seen.[69] This is the story of an extremely well-educated but provincial and unconnected administrator who, after venturing all the way from Bilgram to the Deccan to the Mughal emperor's camp, struggles to get an audience and receives only a meager appointment as newswriter in a distant province with a land assignment (*jagir*) only on paper. Later, the quatrain he writes in the margin of a news report meets with his superior's disapproval, and he finds himself dismissed for the irregularity. First reinstated, then once again dismissed, Mir 'Abd al-Jalil travels to Delhi, the Mughal capital, to try to get another position and to activate his land assignment, without which he fears he will become destitute and a nobody.[70] There he becomes sick and lost at a moment of great political flux. He writes to his son:

> It is very distressing with such a body to be placed in the royal camp (*lashkar*) without employment (*bekār*), in the commencement of a reign, when none of the grandees of Alamgir's [the previous emperor, Aurangzeb] reign is in power and none of the new ones know me. Nobody asks after virtue or ability, all the old rules of government are being thrown aside, and the affairs of the people are at a standstill unless one has a lot of money. And sometimes even after people have spent a lot of money they end up injured and cover their head with dust. (Gladwin 1798: 170)

Mir ʿAbd al-Jalil hopes to get close to the kingmaker of Delhi, Amir al-Umara Husain ʿAli Khan, one of the Sayyid brothers, by bringing a "colourful page" to one of Amir al-Umara's levees. But the plan goes awry, since the fasting month of Ramadan intervenes and levees are discontinued. His second attempt, with a virtuoso felicitation poem for the Eid festival at the end of Ramadan, earns a smile and a compliment. But a desperate Mir ʿAbd al-Jalil writes to his son back in Bilgram, "What does verbal favour release? (*az meharbānī-yi zabānī che mīgushāyad*?)" (Gladwin 1798: 174).[71] When, after several months in Delhi with no prospects and no income, his only other connection leaves, Mir ʿAbd al-Jalil writes, "[I]t seems as if I had arrived at Shahjahanabad only today" (201). Without connections, the local cosmopolitan can do nothing.

Finally, Mir ʿAbd al-Jalil manages to deliver to Amir al-Umara three chronograms (*tarikh*) for his newborn son, in Arabic, Persian, *and* Hindi.[72] The Amir takes notice and inquires after his situation (*che aḥvāl-i shomā asti*) (Gladwin 1798: 202). But even this seems to sink into the sand since the Amir is about to leave for the Deccan. Luckily, one day the fateful quatrain that Mir ʿAbd alul Jalil had inserted in the news report and that had led to his dismissal is mentioned. He is asked to recite it again and relate all the circumstances. The next day, Amir al-Umara brings it to Emperor Farrukh Siyar's notice, Mir ʿAbd al-Jalil gets reinstated, and through the amir's good offices he even manages to get his *jagir* activated and increased. When the Amir asks for some Brajbhasha verse, Mir ʿAbd al-Jalil eagerly displays his ability to procure it. He quickly writes to his son:

> One day in a gathering [of Amir al-Umara's] mention came of Alam's *kabittas*, of which he is very fond. He asked me to procure some of them for him. Therefore I turn to you, whatever *kabittas* or *sīkh* [as in *nakh-shikh*, the head-to-toe description of the female body] of Alam—the two are the same thing—you can get from Harbans Misra or Diwakar, or from his son Ghasiti or from anyone else, *write them in Hindi letters*, one or two forms, whatever you can get, and

> send them quickly over to me. *In the Hindi script (dar khaṭṭ-i hindī) there are fewer scribal errors* (*taḥrīf*, clerical error), *when Hindi is written in Persian script many clerical errors occur*. But it should be good Hindi calligraphy. (Gladwin 1798: 266, emphases added)[73]

Poetry, in the form of multilingual chronograms and the ability to procure Hindi verses, has finally paid off.

Well, yes and no, as Abhishek Kaicker has shown. Although Mir ʿAbd al-Jalil did get his office and land assignment, and this became the means through which the next generation of Bilgramis could reach Mughal employment and higher notice,[74] what was supposed to be his crowning achievement, a long *masnavi* for Emperor Farrukh Siyar's wedding to the daughter of Raja Ajit Singh of Marwar in 1715, ended in failure. This failure was not because of "the impediments of the era," as his grandson Azad put it, claiming that Mir ʿAbd al-Jalil failed to make a fair copy in time before the emperor died in 1719. As Kaicker brilliantly shows, Mir ʿAbd al-Jalil's "illocutionary failure" was rather due to the fact that he narrated the wedding as the subjugation of the rebellious raja, who trembled at seeing the Mughal army led by the future Amir al-Umara, Mir ʿAbd al-Jalil's immediate patron. But by the time Mir ʿAbd al-Jalil had penned the poem, Farrukh Siyar and Amir al-Umara and his brother had fallen out, and Raja Ajit Singh had become one of the brothers' chief allies, and in fact helped them depose the emperor in 1719. A year later, Amir al-Umara himself was dead. In other words, Mir ʿAbd al-Jalil had used the narrative and descriptive conventions of such celebratory *masnavis* correctly, but failed to adapt them to the changed political reality. By praising him and humiliating Ajit Singh, Mir ʿAbd al-Jalil had played the wrong cards. It was only in 1731, after the whole episode had boiled over and Mir ʿAbd al-Jalil himself had been dead a few years, that his grandson Azad Bilgrami could edit and "publish" the *masnavi,* arguing that it had been only the "impediments of the time" that had prevented its proper, imperial recognition (Kaicker 2018: 360).

Read through his letters to his son and against the grain of Azad's tribute, Mir ʿAbd al-Jalil's story illuminates poetry in a different and more unstable and precarious location: the location of a provincial cosmopolitan who sought career promotion at a time of great political upheaval. The Bilgramis' particular skills in composing and appreciating courtly Hindi poetry—and in some cases, like Mir ʿAbd al-Jalil, his son Mir Sayyid Muhammad, and grandson Azad, also Arabic poetry—was what gave them an edge over the vast sea of Indian Persian literati. Yet they still needed networks and introductions to rise in the world. And things could always go wrong.

There are in fact many *qasbas* in Awadh with proud sons who attached the toponym to their name (*nisba*), yet the Bilgramis were the most successful in making their toponym a mark of distinction. How did local cosmopolitans manage to make their locality so visible in the cosmopolitan code?

Strategies of Local Inscription

If education and the display of mastery over codes of poetry and social etiquette were the markers of local cosmopolitans, another strategy through which they registered their participation in cosmopolitan literary culture was to inscribe themselves, their families, and their localities into grand geographic and temporal schemes. The same locale that to a distant gaze appeared provincial, uninteresting, or largely empty, in the hands of local authors became meaningful and rich with temporal and mythohistorical depth. Whether in a geographic compendium, a *tazkira,* or, later, a local history, local notables and local places were included and made visible alongside the more famous. We have already seen Azad thrust Bilgramis into his general *tazkiras* and compose some dedicated to Bilgramis alone.[75] He even theorized about the "love for one's homeland" (*ḥubb-e waṭan*) among those who, like him, had wandered away. It was God who placed the love of one's homeland the hearts of angels and of men and "created a desire for one's original place (*ḥaiz*) in the nature of all things." This desire was a natural law, like the orbit of the planets, the upward movement of fire, or the rush of spring water toward the sea. A bird in the cage is restless when it remembers its warm nest, and a fish out of water dies of thirst. This is all the more true for man, who contains all these worlds within him and whose affections are the strongest.[76] Azad's enterprise could also be viewed as carrying a particular historical significance, since questions of center and periphery, which had been less pressing in the Mughal realm in the heyday of empire, became more critical in the eighteenth century, when the old imperial hubs resisted acknowledging the growing political relevance and cultural vitality of the regional states.[77]

The local is inscribed very differently by a distant cosmopolitan gaze, as in the geographic compendium of the world called *The Seven Climes* (*Haft iqlīm,* ca. 1590), written by the Iranian émigré at Emperor Akbar's court ʿAqil Khan "Razi." In the *Seven Climes* Awadh is pointedly empty of towns and notable people. All Razi (1963: 499, 504) can rustle up is a short note on Lucknow ("[I]t is a small town and has a good climate. They make good bows") and Ayodhya ("Situated on the banks of the Sarju, it is a famous city") and generic entries on three notable men (see Orsini 2015c). From the cosmopolitan point of view of this universal Persian text, by an author who probably never traveled there, Awadh as a region registers as empty, and its readers would decode empty as unimportant.[78]

But 170 years later, a Bilgrami "local cosmopolitan" who was actually born in Peshawar and who ended up as secretary to an East India Company administrator after serving various Mughal and Awadh officials, Murtaza Husain Bilgrami (1719–ca. 1795), updated *The Seven Climes* by writing *The Seven Gardens* (*Ḥadīqat al-aqālīm*, 1778–1782). He described Awadh as teeming with many small towns, which he in all likelihood visited or resided in while on duty.

The list includes not only Ayodhya and Lucknow, but also Gorakhpur, Bahraich, Nimkhar, Khairabad, Gopamau, Pihani, and of course Bilgram. About Nimrikh, e.g., Murtaza Husain Bilgrami (1879: 153–154) tells his readers:

> **Nimkhar** also called **Misrik**, a fort on the banks of the Gomti, and near it there is a tank called Sarbab [Sartab?]. The water boils so much that if a man goes in, he floats and gets thrown up.

His description of Ayodhya (Awadh) inscribes the city not just spatially but also temporally, in the "deep time" of both Hindu and Islamic chronology, and collates the four ages (*yugas*), the *Rāmāyaṇa,* Islamic oral traditions, and contemporary religious practices:[79]

> Awadh, large town on the banks of the Ghaghra, also called Sarju, and in the books of the Hindus it is called Ajodhya. In the Satjug it was the capital of Raja Ramchandra alias Ram, and I have written about his building a bridge and crossing over to Lanka [in another section]. And after Ram, in the Kaljug (*kaliyuga*) the city was built by Kishan son of Purab son of Hind son of Jam son of Noah. In the environs of the city people sifted sand for gold. At the distance of 2 miles east of the city lies the tomb of Seth son of Adam and Job the prophet, and it is a place of pilgrimage for commoners and nobles alike. Their tombs in this place are not [what you will find] in history books. (151)

Ayodhya is thereby inscribed into Islamic sacred time-space, but Islam also gets inscribed into local time-space. Murtaza Husain's entry on Lucknow references Razi's ("Earlier it used to produce good bows, but no longer") but is more concerned with the recent developments under the nawabs of Awadh and with his own personal connections to famous inhabitants.[80] As for his "beloved home town" of Bilgram, the entry is entirely devoted to establishing the claim that it was *his* ancestor and not Imad al-Din, the person Azad Bilgrami had named in his *tazkira Ma'āṣir al Kirām*, who had "planted the flag of Islam and of *shari'a* rule" in Bilgram (156). In other words, Murtaza Husain inscribes the universal scheme in the cosmopolitan language with a thickly traversed and inhabited local world (no empty space for the insider) and uses it to bolster his own family's claim and story on the *local* place of Bilgram against other claimants. Yet in social terms his local space is as exclusive as Azad's, and no one who is not a shaikh or a Sayyid gets a mention: no nonelite Muslims and no Hindus.

Temporal inscription was important for both Sufi and courtly Brajbhasha poets to ground and exalt even small towns and villages. In Chapter 2 we saw how Malik Muhammad Jayasi praised Jais as a "holy place" from the very first *yuga*, while Puhakar (1963: 12–13) described his village in the Doab region between the rivers Ganges and Yamuna as a hidden sacred ford (*tīratha*) established by a king suffering from leprosy who was miraculously cured by its water. Sukhdev Misra praised his ancestral town of Kampila, from which he had moved to a less illustrious village, as a transhistorical abode of *dharma*.[81]

In both the Persian-Urdu and Sanskrit-Brajbhasha traditions, the word for "description" (*vaṣf/tawṣīf* and *varṇana*) also means "praise."[82] In other words, when poets and rhetors "describe" a place or a person, what is usually implied is a paean that, following established conventions, employs hyperbole and simile to elevate that person or place to a higher realm. This was of course an important function of literature—to exalt one's patron and/or subject and to transport them and the audience to a loftier realm. Besides hyperbole, similes that drew upon a repertoire of familiar symbols (the paradise of Allah or of Indra, paradisical trees like Tuba, the garden of Iram, buildings as tall as the sky or Mount Meru, etc.) and "poetic translation" (i.e., translation into a poetic code) were key elements in poetic "description." Does this mean that descriptions were completely generic, simply slotting a particular local place in an already existing paradigm? Yes and no. A few touches, or a particular combination of stock elements, could gesture to actual locations while inscribing them in the poetic codes, as with the fort high above the Ganges and the city and bazaar at the bottom for Dalmau and Ghazipur in Da'ud's *Chandāyan* and Usman's *Chitrāvalī* (see Chapter 2). When "describing" the "two bodies" of the city of Ayodhya—the visible and transient and the transcendent and eternal—devotional-courtly Brajbhasha poet Lal Das dazzled his readers with a stock praise of the city (*nagara-varnana*) filled with Brahmans, musicians, and aesthetic pastimes. This signaled that "this Ayodhya," where "bhakti and yoga keep watch as gate keepers," is the doorway to liberation and is only the "gross" body to the "subtle" city of eternal delight—or *Delight of Ayodhya*, the title of his work (*Avadhavilāsa*, 1675):

> On every side golden forts topped with bejewelled cornices
> stand like a hard test, impervious and inescapable on all sides, like illusion (*māyā*).
> Four main gates, matchless and huge, as liberation made form,
> Four doors of knowledge and detachment, where
> Bhakti and Yoga keep watch as door keepers.
> Countless bazaars and marts, a maze of lanes to get lost in,
> Streams of elephants, chariots, bulls and horses struggle to push through.
> Stories, songs, actors and *bhaṭs*, many kinds of courtesans,
> jugglers and all sorts of wonders circle all around you. (Laldas 1983: 39)

If this is *this* Ayodhya, the poet says, imagine what "that" Ayodhya, where Ram and Sita sit eternally in their celestial palace, must be like!

Literary localization in a cosmopolitan code could also work in more indirect ways, as in the narrative poem that Mir 'Abd al-Jalil Bilgrami wrote in his youth in praise of his hometown. His "description" is largely generic praise with no specific toponym or building mentioned. Yet Mir 'Abd al-Jalil does code localness, in two ways. First, he focuses on a feature that in Persian poetry was associated with India—the monsoon season—in the style of the most famous Indian Persian poet, Amir Khusrau. Second, he uses a Hindavi word for a particular red-lac insect (*bir bahuti*) that comes out in the rainy months and a poetic reference belonging to the demotic genres of Hindavi monsoon songs and poems:

> *az* ***bīr bahūṭī-e*** *dil-āvez gītī shuda yaksar arghavān-khez*
> *bar shāh-e bahār-e mulk-e nāsūt aflāk niṣār karda yāqūt*
> *afshānda zamāna tukhm-e rangīn tā gul kunad ārzū-ye derīn*
> *gītī che qadar nishāṭ andūkht k'īn tukma-ye la'l bar qabā dūkht*
> *tā khāma ze waṣf-e ōst gulchīn bar safḥa niqāt gashta rangīn*
> the entrancing **red-lac insect** has turned the world red all at once,
> the sky has scattered rubies on the lord of spring of the kingdom of humans,
> the age scatters colorful eggs till the long-lasting wish bears fruit.
> What delight the world acquired by sewing this red button on its cloak
> as the pen collects roses in its praise (*waṣf*), dots turn colorful on the page.[83]

In other words, it is not a different register, or even a local reference, that makes this poem about an intimate locale, but a specific vernacular *poetic* element inserted in what is otherwise a perfectly legible cosmopolitan code.

Parallel Cultivation

In common parlance, the multilingual and multireligious culture of Awadh is called "Ganga-Jamuni," to suggest literary and religious hybridity through the merging of the two rivers. Yet, unlike the "open" platforms and shared repertoire of motifs moving across languages that we saw in *kathas* (Chapter 2) and the equally "open" and even more dialogic "ventriloquism" of Sant orature (Chapter 3), this chapter has shown that the cultivation of Persian and Hindavi (and later Brajbhasha) poetry by local cosmopolitans involved practices of distinction, whether in terms of the marked social hierarchy of select "communities of taste" or of cultural exclusion of anyone who had not mastered the code. This, I would argue, is the reason why such sustained multilingual literary habitus, the result of multilingual education, cultivation, and simple exposure, did *not* result in the mixing of poetic idioms, nor in practices of translation across them. If the aim was to acquire and display mastery of one or more poetic codes, there was more mileage to be had from performing the codes to perfection than in breaking them, nor was there any conceivable need to translate when one could savor the taste of poetry in the original language. For this reason, while there were obvious comparable features in Persian and Brajbhasha poetry and poetics—e.g., in the double rhyme scheme (*radif* + *qafiya*, also visible in *kabittas*) or in the idioms of beauty, love, service, and praise—by and large these comparisons remained *latent* possibilities, the topic of literary conversation, perhaps, rather than written elaboration or reflection.[84] Drawing on Azad Bilgrami's discussion of the respective codes of Persian and Arabic, Simon Leese (2019) has recently argued that Persian and Arabic were conceived as separate poetic terrains, partly identified geographically with Arab and 'Ajam, to which Indian poets and scholars like Fayzi Fayyazi and Azad Bilgrami added Hind, India; these poetic terrains could be brought together, but only with caution, carefully preserving their codes. So, interestingly, even when languages were conceived as composite, within this sphere of cultivation poetic idioms remained distinct. Let us take, e.g., Bhikharidas, the greatest eighteenth-century Hindi rhetor. Bihkharidas acknowledged Persian as part of the makeup of Brajbhasha (the reading of the verse is ambiguous):

> भाषा ब्रज भाषा रुचिर कहें सुमति सब कोइ
> मिलें संस्कृत फारिसीहु सो अति प्रघट होइ
> ब्रज मागधी मिलें अमर नाग जमन भाषानि
> सैहैज पारसी हूँ मिलें षट बिधी कहति बखानि
> All people of good understanding say
> that Brajbhasha is a delightful language,
> mixing Sanskrit and Persian (*phārisī*) yet so clear.
> Braja, Magadhi (Avadhi), Sanskrit (*amara*), Naga (Prakrit?) and *jamana* (Arabic?),
> as well as simple Parsi (*pārasī*) are found [or mixed]:
> they say poetry is of six different types. (*Kāvyanirṇaya*, 1.15, Bhikharidas 1957: vol. 2, 5; see also Busch 2011: 120)

He was also the earliest to articulate a Brajbhasha poetic canon in his verse in praise of poets (*kavi-prashansa*), and included in it several Awadh poets (**in bold**), among them two of the Persophone poets from Bilgram, Raslin and Mubarak:

> Sur, Kesav[das], Mandan, Bihari, **Kalidas [Trivedi]**, Brahma,
> **Chintamani, Matiram, Bhushan**—let us learn from them.

Liladhar, Senapati, Nipat, **Niwaj,** Nidhi,
Nilkanth, **Misra Sukhdev,** Dev—let us respect them.
Alam, Rahim, Raskhan, Raslin,
Mubarak—no praise is too much for their good minds.
Do not merely consider Braj dwellers for Brajbhasha,
but learn it from the verses of such great poets.
Doha: There have been two head (*sardar*) poets—Tulsi and Gang.
In their poems you find many kinds of *bhasha*. (*Kāvyanirṇaya* 1.16–17, Bikharidas 1957: vol. 2, 5–6)[85]

Bhikharidas is an innovative scholar; his manual *Rasasārāṃśa* includes a chapter on rhyme (chapter 22), a topic not covered by other scholars, one on the ten qualities of the grapheme (*acchara*, chapter 19), and an innovative typology of figures of speech.[86] Like other eighteenth-century Brajbhasha poets of Awadh, Bhikharidas stretched courtly poetry to include popular subjects like the "song of the twelve months." Sensitive to contemporary trends in Brajbhasha, he cast lower-caste women—including the midwife, the barber's wife, the carpenter's wife, the painter's wife, the dyer's wife, the washerwoman—as go-betweens (*dūtikā*) in the love tryst.[87] Yet neither he nor any of the other Brajbhasha poets at the small Awadh courts—Kalidas Trivedi, Udaynath Tiwari, Dulah, etc.—used a Persianate register or played with Persianate vocabulary.

The same is true of Bilgram's bilingual Persian-Brajbhasha poets. The most famous of them, Ghulam Nabi "Raslin," was a contemporary of Bhikharidas. Though he also composed Persian poetry, he became famous in his own time as an accomplished Brajbhasha poet and scholar. Like Bhikharidas, and before him the poet Dev, Raslin was authoritative and innovative; e.g., he offered three different systems for the classification of heroines, or *nayikas*. He also claimed, "If you read this book [*Rasaprabodha*] from beginning to middle to end, you will not want to read any other manual on *rasa*" (*Rasaprabodha* 1.26, Raslin 1988: 8). Yet even Raslin, who used Imam 'Ali as his example for the heroic mood, or *vira rasa*, and described the quiet (*shanta*) *rasa* in terms that are clearly monotheistic,[88] did not use any Persianate words even when he praised Allah and the Prophet and his descendants and companions:

tina santati ke pagana pai, dharaū sadā sira nāya
puni tinake hitakāriyana, dehu asīsa banāya

I bow my head to the feet of the three children
and of their companions, too, may they bless me. (*Rasaprabodha* 21, Raslin 1988: 1)[89]

Just like the Hindu Persian poets who praised the holy sites of Islam or used Islamic and Persian metaphors to talk about Hindu holy sites, Raslin was perfectly adept at praising the Ganges through a "Hindu prism" (see Pellò 2012, 2014a):

> *Bishnu jū ke paga tẽ nikasa sambhu sīsa basi,*
> *Bhagīratha tapa tẽ kṛpā karī jahān paī.*
> *patitana tāribe kī rīti terī erī Ganga,*
> *pāye Rasalīna yaha tereī pramāna paī.*
>
> From Vishnu's feet to Shiva's head,
> thanks to Bhagiratha's austerities
> you graced the world. Ganges,
> ferrying sinners across is your fashion,
> as Raslin found out with proof from you.
> Yamuna's brownish, Sarasvati's reddish
> waters are shed in your snowy own,
> just as the dark and fiery qualities (*tamoguna, rajoguna*) of the world
> are purified (*karike satoguna*) and dispatched on a holy craft. (*Kabitta mutafarriq* 23, in Zaidi 1977: 72)

So if we read together the Persian and Hindi/Brajbhasha verses of Bilgrami poets like Ghulam Nabi "Raslin," we find little or no evidence of mixing or the "traffic" of poetic idioms that was such a visible characteristic of Sant poems. Even Mir 'Abd al-Jalil's multilingual chronogram did not mix idioms in the same verse but showed his parallel mastery over the different codes. In fact, Raslin earned high praise from Hindi critics because his works on poetics are written in "very pure Brajbhasha *though he was a Muslim*. There are no Persian words in them. There is no difference between his language and that of a Brahman poet" (G.B., S.B., and S. B. Mishra 1913: 392, emphasis added).

By contrast, by the 1740s some Brajbhasha poets, like Prince Savant Singh "Nagaridas" of Kishangarh who was directly related to the Mughal imperial family, were responding directly to the new Rekhta poetry which had recently taken Delhi's poetic circles by storm.[90] Instead, even when Rekhta/Urdu poetry came into fashion in the region in the 1750s, Raslin and the other Brajbhasha poets in the "mud-brick" courts of Awadh—Kalidas Trivedi, Udaynath Tiwari, Dulah, and others—did not play with the Persianate register. The fact that one of them, "Tosh," a landlord in Allahabad district, did so shows that mixing was indeed a possibility, only one of which these poets chose not to avail themselves.[91]

The same goes for translations. While we may assume that proficiency in multiple poetic codes would lead poets and literati to translate across them, in fact this was not the case until late into the nineteenth century (see Chapter 5). This was not, as I have argued elsewhere, because universal intelligibility rendered translation unnecessary, or because no translation was ever undertaken (Orsini 2020b). Rather, it was because learning a language meant learning its poetic code and being able to read poetry in that language. If poetic translation happened, as in one tantalizing instance in Bhanupratap Tiwari's autobiography, it happened only on the side (see Figure 4.1).[92]

This chapter about courtly culture on a local scale and in a peripheral location has highlighted, perhaps unsurprisingly, preparation and investment in

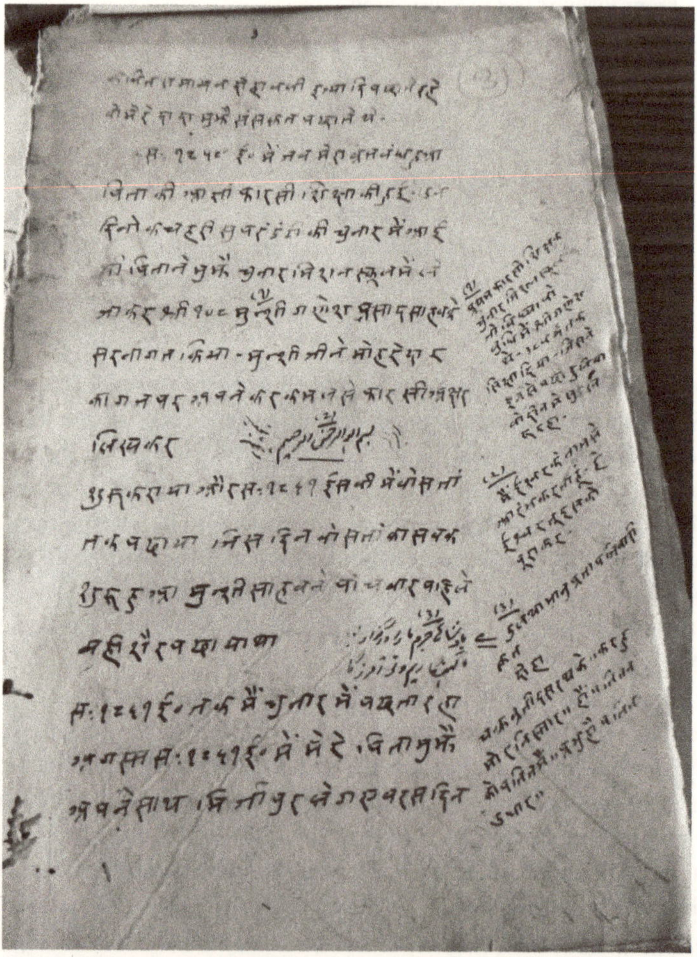

Figure 4.1 Detail of Bhanupratap Tiwari's autobiography with his translation of a Persian couplet into Brajbhasha on the side.
Source: UP Manuscript Library, Allahabad. Photograph by author.

education; the need to stand out in some way, in the case of the Bilgramis by becoming particularly multilingual; and the ways in which one could be cosmopolitan "at home." These ways included elevating one's local place through the cosmopolitan idiom, keeping select company, and playing up whatever high connections one had. The absence of a single center, fulchrum, or goal, whether the imperial court or the upper echelons of the Mughal nobility, meant that there were multiple foci of authority and validation (the gentry in the *qasbas* and the local rajas in their mud forts), multiple hierarchies, and multiple communities of taste that partly overlapped and whose historical and geographic trajectories also varied.

What distinguishes the *qasba* poets of Awadh from their loftier imperial counterparts? At the Mughal imperial court appreciation for both Persian and Brajbhasha poetry and of Sanskrit "knowledge" was what characterized patrons like the emperors Akbar and Jahangir or Mughal grandees like 'Abdur Rahim Khanekhanan.[93] By contrast, court poets, while exposed to the other languages and poetic tastes, were famed for or specialized in only one.[94] Nor was the hierarchy between Persian and Hindi ever called into question.[95]

What seems to have set the Bilgramis apart, by virtue either of their being far from the imperial court or of coming out of the multilingual *qasba* milieu, is the fact that they cultivated both Persian and Hindi *as poets*. So while from one perspective we could view the "local cosmopolitan" intellectuals of Bilgram as reproducing at a local level cosmopolitan poetic tastes in Persian and Hindi and imperial practices of connoisseurship and patronage, from another perspective what the Bilgrami literati did was quite special. As we saw, this cultivation and composition of both Persian and Hindi poetry—or in some cases Persian, Arabic, and Hindi—could make all the difference for these local cosmopolitans.

Urdu and Amnesia

One final question: What happened to this parallel cultivation of Persian and Hindavi or Brajbhasha in Awadh when the taste for Rekhta/Urdu poetry swept over north India in the eighteenth century?[96] A single-language approach tends to view change in terms of substitution, whereas a multilingual approach tends to see new fashions as rearranging rather than superseding older tastes. So while a single-language approach reads the rise of Urdu poetry as a phenomenon of vernacularization, a switch from the older cosmopolitan language of Persian, a multilingual approach reads it rather as a shift and a readjustment within a continuing multilingual literary culture.

In very broad terms, what we begin to see is a bifurcation between *qasba* and rural Awadh and urban Lucknow. In the *qasbas* and in rural Awadh the old

Persian-Brajbhasha (or Brajbhasha-only) poetic culture persisted even when Lucknow's literary culture became identified with Persian, and particularly with Urdu. A few patrons and poets in Lucknow under the nawabs continued to cultivate Brajbhasha poetry on a more limited scale, and many fewer manuals of poetics were composed in comparison with the earlier period. The taste for Brajbhasha poetry shrank to the domain of music and songs, which still required some familiarity with the aesthetics and repertoire of Brajbhasha poetry, but less intensive study. Otherwise, in the new capital Lucknow, religiously oriented toward Shi'a Iran and welcoming an influx of Persian and Rekhta poets from Delhi, Persian-Urdu bilingualism replaced the older one of Persian-Brajbhasha. The Brajbhasha poetic past was in fact quickly forgotten, and contemporary biographical dictionaries and anthologies of Urdu poets do not mention those who also wrote in Brajbhasha (e.g., Hindi 1958; Mir Hasan 1979). Instead, Lucknow Urdu poetic culture made space for demotic words and worlds within the dialogues of narrative poems (*masnavis*), the emotional dirges on the battle of Karbala (*marsiyas*), and the incipient urban theater. By contrast, in the local courts and towns of Awadh, as well as in nearby Banaras, Brajbhasha poetry remained in vogue well into the twentieth century, both at the maharaja's court and in urban, merchant-led circles, where it was superseded by modern Hindi poetry only in the 1920s and 1930s (see Ritter 2010; Orsini 2002; Busch 2011).

In fact, a located and multilingual approach to the long eighteenth century helps bring into relief the parallels between the urban cultures of Lucknow and Banaras, cities that are usually contrasted with each other, epitomizing Persian-Urdu and Sanskrit-Hindi cultures, respectively. One result of this dichotomy is that we are endlessly surprised to find the emerging Urdu musical theater in Lucknow employing so many songs in Brajbhasha and other regional dialects, or Hindi poets in and around Banaras writing Urdu verse, too (see Sengupta 1994; Ritter 2010). Moreover, the temptation is to read these acts as individual choices motivated by "syncretic" tendencies or as political reactions to colonialism.[97] Instead we do better to read them in the light of continuing practices of multilingual education (like Bhanupratap's), if this was the case, or as part of the new fashions in the urban culture of both Lucknow and Banaras, which partly continued and partly altered earlier practices of cultivation.

Such multilingual traces reflect continuing practices, in that both Lucknow and Banaras in this period saw a combination of courtly and urban culture of musical and poetic soirées at court or in the mansions of landed and merchant elites, with master-poets who held courtly positions but also taught private pupils and created individual poetic circles (see Pellò 2012). But they also signal new fashions, since in both cities public pageants, festivals, and processions were consciously devised in which the nawab in Lucknow and the maharaja in Banaras played an important ritual part, but which also saw the participation of urban elites and of the general population in a show of mutual legitimation and social cohesion (see Cole 1998; Dalmia 1997; Freitag 1989a). In both cities one visited semi-public gardens, fairs, and other open spaces to see street performers, courtesans and other "beloveds" and to be seen in one's finery, while time seems to have been regulated not by the modern clock but by the calendar of festivities and ritual events.

In both Lucknow and Banaras courtesans were at the heart of musical life and elite entertainment; they lived in the very center of the city (the Chowk) and could be glimpsed in open spaces and on public occasions. In both cities the rich variety and opulence of gold-and-silver-embroidered, woven and threaded textiles, of jewelry encrusted with precious and semi-precious stones, of perfumes and fine food and drink items, find expression in the elaborate descriptions within poetic genres, from Mir Hasan's *masnavis* (see Figure 4.2) to *rekhti* poems about clothes and ornaments and the elaborate description of the

Figure 4.2 The bazaar of Faizabad with performers.
Source: Mir Hasan's *masnavi 'Īd kī tahniyat*, New York Public Library, Spencer Coll. Indo-Pers. ms. 15, fol. 12v–13, UUID: bc58e000-c624-012f-2fd5-58d385a7bc34.

attire of the *paris* (fairies)/courtesans in Agha Hasan 'Amanat's runaway success, the play *Indarsabhā* (Indra's court, 1852–1854).[98]

A similar pattern of continuity and change is evident in the one form that was equally important in Lucknow and Banaras—indeed everywhere in north India in the eighteenth and nineteenth centuries: the song. Song collections predate this period but now experienced a veritable boom in manuscript and later in print, with capacious repertoires that included Urdu and Persian *ghazals*, Brajbhasha *khyal* and *thumri*, Brajbhasha and Purbi (Eastern) seasonal *hori* and *basant*, and Punjabi *tappas* (see also Chapter 5). Importantly for us, songs presupposed *and* created familiarity with the meters and styles of Brajbhasha, Urdu, and Persian poetry and their "structures of feeling," a familiarity that could be acquired aurally, with the help of melody, rhythm, and practice. Songs about love, devotion, the seasons, and particular events were made famous by courtesans and composed by the likes of the King of Awadh Wajid 'Ali Shah (1822–1887) and Bharatendu Harischandra (1850–1885) and were among the main attractions of nascent musical theater. Though Harishchandra is best remembered as a playwright and editor of pioneering magazines, indeed as the "Father of Modern Hindi," songs about love, devotion, the seasons, and particular events form a substantial part of his oeuvre and of his daily poetic practice. Like other elite men of his time, Harishchandra was trained in music and singing by leading courtesans and, according to an early biographer, composed as many as fifteen hundred songs; his collected works include more than ten printed song collections. The same holds true for other literati of his day.[99]

To most people today the culture of Awadh means the culture of Nawabi Lucknow, a culture of Urdu poetry, sophisticated and witty repartee, music and courtesans like Umrao Jaan, and Shi'a devotion and festivals, although in fact the Nawabi lasted a little over a hundred years, from 1722 to 1856, and Urdu poetry came into Awadh only in the second half of the eighteenth century. While the story is not "wrong," what this book shows is how such a strong identification with sophisticated Urdu has obscured *other* stories, languages, and connections. At the same time, this chapter has shown that to idealize this multilingual and multireligious culture as one of shared amity—as the unproblematic confluence of the Ganges and the Jamuna—means overlooking the very real structures of distinction and exclusion that operated in this multilingual locale. These included fault lines of rank, caste, lineage, and of course gender, as much as of political, religious, or literary and cultural affiliation. Identity was multidimensional then, too.

The next and final chapter explores what happened to this society in political, cultural, and linguistic flux, economically still ebullient despite the political upheavals of the eighteenth century, when new ideas of language, literature, and community took hold in the nineteenth century under colonial rule.

Bhanupratap Tiwari's autobiography brings home that English and the colonial education system had only a limited penetration, and this was true well into the twentieth century. But the sweep of new ideas and the impact of print and of commercial urban culture did reshuffle the literary culture, and the sense of a literary past, in very significant ways. Once again, rather than a mere substitution and supersedence, it was a reshuffling. And rather than one story, we have several.

From the perspective of world literature, the exploration of the layered and multilingual world of literature East of Delhi in the chapters so far cautions us against positing languages and literary traditions as arrayed in opposed or hostile camps, or else as harmoniously fused in a prelapsarian, precolonial whole. At the same time, narrating the emergence of literary idioms and fashions as a process of becoming, and showing the continued vitality of tastes, cautions us against thinking that when colonialism and its language, English, came, they swept this whole world away.

5
Colonial Impact and Indian Response

"Colonial impact and Indian response"—this is how the period of British colonial rule (1757–1947) is usually described, in terms that tend to frame Indian change and innovation as engineered by colonial initiatives, as a *reaction* to colonial *action*. In cultural and literary terms, colonial "impact" encompasses everything from technology (print) to institutions and systems of knowledge (schools and the education system), social figures (the salaried intellectual, college student, editor-publisher), and new ideas and modern genres of literature, particularly in prose. While historiography has come to the view of a more gradual colonial takeover and emphasizes the dynamic role played by local groups and individuals who took advantage of the political vacuum in competition and collaboration with the increasingly powerful East India Company, literary historiography still narrates the turn from precolonial to colonial culture as a complete epistemic shift. Colonialism entailed the cultural hegemony of English and the "stable subordination" in literary terms of India to the imperial center (Moretti 2006a: 120). According to this view, popular now as it was among nineteenth- and early twentieth-century critics, literary modernity could happen only by imitating, translating, and assimilating metropolitan models, whether of lyric poetry or the novel.

In addition, for a long time the "colonial encounter" and what is termed the "Bengali Renaissance" were defined by studies of Bengal or, more precisely, Calcutta. We pictured colonial intellectuals as office-going babus, suited and booted in public while donning plaited dhotis and sacred threads at home, equally comfortable with the English classics (and often also Latin and Greek) as with Sanskrit texts, even as they forged modern literature and the press in Bengali.[1] Other regions and language areas were viewed as variations on Bengal: a little more radical here, a little belated there.[2] In this paradigm, north India's later and patchwork colonization produced a literary "delay" (Sisir Kumar Das 1991: 44 called it "meta-phany"): new ideas and literary models flowed upcountry from Calcutta, and modern literature in Hindi (and to a lesser extent Urdu) played "catching up" with Bengali under the overbearing imprint of Englishness. But did British colonialism really produce a complete epistemic and aesthetic rupture? Were English education and literature "masks of conquest" that indelibly shaped modern Indian literatures in their own image? Were Indian

East of Delhi. Francesca Orsini, Oxford University Press. © Oxford University Press 2023.
DOI: 10.1093/oso/9780197658291.003.0005

writers so "crushed by English poetry" that they forgot earlier intellectual and aesthetic traditions?[3]

As I have been arguing throughout this book, perspective, language, and location do matter. So in this chapter I ask: What happens when we take a *multilingual* and *located* perspective on the "colonial impact" and try to connect the different trajectories, stories, and tastes—the shifts but also the continuities—that together make up the "(north) Indian response" to colonialism? What effects did colonial institutions, new technologies, and powerful new ideas produce on the multilingual and multilayered literary culture of Purab/Awadh? But also, what role do we see local intellectuals and institutions playing in these transformations and in the debates that accompanied them, particularly regarding Hindi and Urdu language and literature and the formation of new literary canons?

This chapter begins by outlining some of the transformations across the cities of colonial Awadh, while hinting at the multiple stories that together made up their space. New ideas of language, literature, history, community, and nation did crystallize with momentous consequences in the context of Orientalism, colonial education, western ideas of civilization and progress, and of course anticolonial nationalism. In north India, this is the familiar story of modern Hindi and Urdu and their bitter parting of ways, in which actors and institutions in Awadh played a crucial role. But where, as in Awadh, there existed strong local intellectual and literary traditions, "English culture" and the "new knowledge" (*naī vidyā* in Hindi, *na'ī roshnī* or "new light" in Urdu) of colonial modernity left a more limited imprint and failed to completely dislodge existing tastes and practices. In other words, fundamental shifts in ideas of language, literature, history, and community took place precisely at the level of ideas. These ideas produced very real effects, from institution-building to the crystallization and mobilization of communities; from the legitimate knowledge inscribed in textbooks, anthologies, and literary canons to what I call the "invention" of folk literature as separate from literature per se. But these ideas also produced a remarkable gap between what people thought and believed about language and literature and the tastes they practiced.

This gap between ideas and tastes often gets forgotten in narratives centered on Hindi, Urdu, and postcolonial English, but it becomes very visible in the continued familiarity that people (and literary characters) display with the whole range of literary idioms across Hindi and Urdu, or in the creative reuse of multilingual resources, particularly in theater, satire, parody, and for political mobilization, as we shall see. Seeking out the "multiplicity of stories and trajectories" also brings into view the different meanings that the world held at the time, from the radical "abroad" (*pardes*) of indentured coolies to the "significant geography" of Turkey for Muslim intellectuals and the discovery of world literature *through*, but *beyond*, imperial English.

Awadh as a Colonial Center

Awadh became a cultural center in the eighteenth century, when the breakaway Mughal governors (or nawabs, pl. of *nā'ib*) set up Awadh as a separate state whose capital was first Faizabad and then Lucknow. At the same time, the economic and political importance of Banaras grew, already under the shadow of the East India Company.[4] Despite the belated and patchwork annexation of Awadh and adjoining territories to the Company, and the watershed of the Rebellion of 1857, the region became a cultural and political center under colonial rule.[5] Not just Lucknow and Banaras, but also cities like Allahabad and Kanpur became vibrant hubs, connected by print, personal networks, and associations, yet each with its own distinct character and a heterogeneous set of "stories and trajectories" (Massey [2005] 2012).

The boom of print culture, the proliferation of associations, and the gradual expansion of the colonial education system gave cities a cultural centrality that depended not on the presence and patronage of a court but on the density of entrepreneurial actors and reading and studying publics. In turn, these publics helped coalesce new "imagined communities" (Anderson 1991). An overview of publishing and education shows many innovations, but also some continuities, and the existence of a "multiplicity of stories." Awadh *qasbas* became satellites of these cities, still endowed with cultural prestige but, at least in the eyes of their chroniclers, moving at a slower pace.[6] In the countryside, meanwhile, the post-1857 compact between the colonial government and the landlords, particularly the big landlords called *taluqdars*, squeezed intermediate farmers and gave rise to multiple waves of unrest (see Kumar 1984).

In the nineteenth century, Awadh cities became important multilingual publishing hubs.[7] Lucknow was the first, with several printing presses already established in the late 1830s, during Nawabi rule (see Stark 2007: 54–59). Then, only one year after the great Rebellion of 1857, while the old city was being gutted and rebuilt for the sake of colonial surveillance, newcomer Munshi Naval Kishore (1836–1895) built up, through British connections, what became one of the largest publishing houses in Asia, with an extensive national and international distribution network. Though the Naval Kishore Press printed more books in Urdu than in any other language, it also reproduced in print a very wide range of older Persian, Arabic, Sanskrit, Hindi, and Urdu literary and knowledge traditions. Its impressive catalogue shows that Naval Kishore did not try to streamline or reform knowledge but rather maximized it, publishing everything from costly Persian and Arabic tomes to flimsy Urdu and Hindi chapbooks of songs and tales. It published Persian, Urdu, Hindi, and English school textbooks as well as scientific and legal dictionaries and religious and literary works in Sanskrit, Persian, Arabic, Urdu, and Hindi (Stark 2007: 54–59).[8]

In fact, the Urdu-Hindi publishing boom of the 1870s and 1880s consisted as much of "genres reproduced" from existing oral and written traditions as of "genres introduced," like the detective novel (Orsini 2009). Newspapers, too, promoted both new and old genres. Naval Kishore's successful Urdu newspaper *Oudh Akhbār* (Awadh Newspaper, 1859), which became the first daily in northern India in 1877, pioneered the serialization of novels in Urdu.[9] Its rival, the satirical weekly *Oudh Punch* (1877), Maryam Sikander (2021) shows, brought into play and parodied all kinds of old and new verse and prose genres, from encyclopedia entries to *ghazals*, banking on Urdu readers' familiarity with them. Both newspapers catered to readers from Lucknow and to a burgeoning and cosmopolitan Urdu middle class spread out across India (Dubrow 2018).

Allahabad, too, became a major center of newsprint and publishing in English, Hindi, Urdu, and Bengali, given the significant presence of "upcountry" (*probashi*) Bengalis settled in the city.[10] The town that in 1827 had so disgusted the famous Delhi poet Ghalib had become, by 1834, a provincial capital and the seat of the High Court, and some of its lawyers became among India's most prominent politicians.[11] Like other colonial cities, Allahabad was crossed in 1859 by the railway line and developed an expansive railway colony. The railway divided the colonial city, with its Civil Lines, impressive public buildings, and genteel bungalows, from the Old Town, with its bazaars around the central Chowk and dense *mohallas*, or residential neighborhoods, sprawling down to the River Jamuna (see Mehrotra 2007).

The publishing scene in Allahabad was dominated by the Indian Press (1884), which was started by one such upcountry Bengali, Chintamani Ghosh, and which in the early twentieth century surpassed the Naval Kishore Press as the largest publisher in the province (see Ali 1989, 2007; Orsini 2002). The Indian Press brought out the most authoritative Hindi, Bengali, and English monthly magazines of the day: *Sarasvatī* (1900, edited by Mahavir Prasad Dvivedi) in Hindi and, under Ramanand Chatterjee's editorship, *Probāshī* (1901) in Bengali and *Modern Review* (1907) in English (see Ali 1989).[12] Indeed, the symbiosis between textbooks, periodicals, and books was crucial to the success of publishing conglomerates like the Indian Press. So was the circulation of print material across languages. In general, the textual material circulating between English and Hindi or Urdu, and between Bengali and Hindi, tended to be educational or reformist, but translations of Victorian sensational novelist G. W. Reynolds were bestsellers in Urdu and Hindi, and popular Bengali novels were regularly translated and adapted into Hindi (see Naim 2018; Orsini 2002: 58–60; 2009: ch. 7). The traffic between Urdu and Hindi was more intense and included tales, poems, and songs (see Orsini 2009: chs. 2, 3).

Nor was the Indian Press the only publisher in Allahabad. The concentration of schools, colleges, teachers, and students powered the Urdu publisher and bookseller Kitabistan and, on the other side of the railway tracks, a cluster of Hindi publishers specializing in textbooks.[13] Allahabad's prominent Hindi Literary Association (Hindi Sahitya Sammelan, est. 1910) was also active as a scholarly and textbook publisher, while the Belvedere Press, as we saw in Chapter 3, brought out an unequaled series of booklets of Hindi Sant poets aimed primarily at devotees. Within Allahabad itself, therefore, Kabir's words appeared in print in quite different formats—as chapbooks, in textbooks, and in scholarly editions.

By comparison with Allahabad, Banaras (or Kashi, to use the traditional name) retained a more traditional air as a major site of religious pilgrimage and Sanskrit education, but also of crafts manufactured in its populous neighborhoods.[14] With a large population of teachers, students, merchants, and pilgrims—i.e., many potential readers and writers—Banaras had many prerequisites to become a publishing center, yet until the 1870s publishing in the city remained largely tied to education and religion, with many texts printed in Sanskrit or Sanskrit with Hindi glosses.[15] But there are other stories of publishing in Banaras. For example, Banaras publishers were crucial in printing hundreds of works from the Brajbhasha courtly poetic tradition.[16] Interestingly, the city was also the center of Nepali book publishing, given the strict censorship by the Rana regime in Nepal. It also had its sprinkling of Urdu publishers.[17] And in the 1890s, entrepreneurial Hindi writers like Devkinandan Khatri and Jayramdas Gupta brought out monthlies solely dedicated to novels and founded their own presses, creating a boom in commercial novel publishing.[18]

Finally, Kanpur grew from the ashes of its large army cantonment (destroyed in the 1857 Rebellion) into a textile and leather industrial city, with a vigorous labor movement and early lower caste activism.[19] Kanpur, too, had a diverse publishing scene. Besides some of the most active Urdu presses already in the 1850s (Muhammadi, Mustafa'i, and Nizami) (see Stark 2007: 57), in the early twentieth century Kanpur hosted the important Urdu monthly *Zamāna* (The Age, edited by Dayanarayan Nigam, 1903–1942) as well as the radical Hindi nationalist newspaper *Pratāp* (Ardour, 1913) and its press, Pratap Karyalaya, run by Ganesh Shankar Vidyarthi, which published many booklets related to labor, socialism, and the Russian Revolution. The Adi Hindu Press brought out some of the earliest Dalit publications by lower-caste activists (see Narayan 2011; Beth 2016). In each city, then, a wide array of publishers maximized outreach by publishing in different languages and in new and older genres. And the monumentality of publishers like Naval Kishore and the Indian Press should not obscure the important stories represented by smaller publishers like the Belvedere Press, publisher of Sant booklets (see Chapter 3), or the early Dalit publisher Adi Hindu Press in Kanpur.

With colonialism, the cities of Awadh became educational hubs, too, home to some of the earliest and most prestigious colleges in northern India.[20] But though the colonial Education Department administered exams and oversaw degrees, government schools remained few on the ground, and what we call the colonial "system" consisted in fact of a heterogeneous array of mostly private schools and colleges receiving grants-in-aid, as well as some alternative institutions like Arya Samaj schools, or "national" (i.e., nationalist) schools and colleges (see Kumar [1991] 2005; Orsini 2002: ch. 1.4). Although the overall percentage of school-going pupils remained lower than in other regions, in the early decades of the twentieth century the number of schools and colleges multiplied.[21] As recent scholarship shows, it was then that low-caste Dalits first acquired formal education, often through missionary or cantonment schools.[22] Meanwhile, older educational institutions like the *madrasa* of Firangi Mahal (est. early eighteenth century) in Lucknow continued to thrive and in fact played an active role in contemporary politics (see Hasan 1981).

The colonial education system inscribed at all levels a two-tiered hierarchy of languages, with English at the top and the vernaculars below. Vernacular schools were more poorly endowed and charged lower fees, vernacular teachers were paid less, and so on. Knowledge was also supposed to flow unidirectionally from English into the vernaculars, through the medium of translation.[23] English poetry was held up as a model to be imitated. Colonial officers praised Shridhar Pathak's (1889) Hindi translation of Oliver Goldsmith's *The Deserted Village* as "an absolutely line by line rendering of Goldsmith, every idea punctually reproduced." They stressed the benefit of "direct[ing] the Indian mind to the beauties of nature and to the tender feelings of the heart," given that "[e]xtravagance of language and artificiality of sentiment characterize and disfigure Oriental Verse."[24] Equally warm praise was heaped on Pathak's translation of Goldsmith's *The Hermit*.[25] Both texts were staples of the English colonial curriculum and were much translated into Indian languages throughout the nineteenth century. Pathak was trained in Brajbhasha and knew Sanskrit but also had a BA and was an activist in the Hindi movement for official recognition.[26] His translations, among the earliest attempts at writing poetry in modern standard (i.e., Khari Boli) Hindi instead of Brajbhasha, are in a kind of artificial language, a mishmash of Sanskrit loanwords and neologisms awkwardly juxtaposed with occasional dialectal terms and expressions that make the meaning difficult to follow without the English original, though alliteration and rhyme help the poems flow. Though Pathak was conscious and wary of the distance between the "purely English" poem and Hindi, as a college graduate and Hindi activist he may have had the developing Hindi school curriculum in mind.[27]

But colonial schools, even girls' schools, were not just sites of colonial indoctrination. They "often became local centres of literary and political activity visited by national leaders and leading poets, and the classroom provided a space for politicization outside the curriculum" (Orsini 2002: 89). In fact, Hindi's low prestige in the colonial system gave Hindi intellectuals a free hand in designing the Hindi syllabus (see below). As Krishna Kumar ([1991] 2005: 145) has argued, Hindi was the "secret door" through which cultural nationalism entered the colonial system.

Moreover, as Bhanupratap Tiwari's example in the previous chapter showed, formal education formed only part of a student's educational portfolio and literary *habitus*, which continued to be acquired through other, informal means. This was true particularly of Persian and Sanskrit. Take the "Father of Modern Hindi," Bharatendu Harishchandra (1850–1885), heir to a wealthy merchant family, who is said to have replied to those who criticized his expenditures on many pet projects, "Wealth ate up my forefathers, now I am going to eat it up" (quoted in Dalmia 1997: 128). Educated first at home in Hindi, Urdu, and English, Harishchandra was enrolled for only a few years at Queen's College before dropping out; in the meantime he studied Sanskrit and read widely in Orientalist publications.[28] Thus, family upbringing and aesthetic tastes undercut the colonial separation and hierarchy between English and the vernaculars. Nor was Harishchandra alone or unique—many other Hindi poets in this period, such as Jagannath Das Ratnakar (1866–1932), Bhagvan Din (1876–1930), and Ayodhyasingh Upadhyay Harioudh (1865–1947), continued to cultivate Brajbhasha and Urdu poetry in parallel (see Ritter 2010). Even in the anglicized atmosphere of Allahabad University (called "the Cambridge of the East") many teachers and students straddled the English, Urdu, and Hindi literary worlds, among them Raghupati Sahai "Firaq" Gorakhpuri (1896–1982), who was a famous Urdu poet but taught English, and the English scholar and future vice chancellor Amarnath Jha (1897–1955), son of a celebrated Sanskrit scholar, active in Hindi associations, and equally proficient in English, Sanskrit, Urdu, Hindi, and Maithili (see below). Harivansh Rai Bachchan (1907–2003), a student and lecturer of English, shot to fame for his captivating Hindi poem *Madhushālā* (Wine tavern, 1935), directly inspired by FitzGerald's translation of Omar Khayyam (see Trivedi 1995: ch. 2).[29] And while students in the 1920s and 1930s lionized the new Imagist (Chhayavadi) and Progressive poets, connoisseurs (*rasiks*) continued to meet in every city and cultivate their taste for Brajbhasha poetry in private gatherings (see Orsini 2002: 33, 36).

While the most important Urdu literary associations grew outside Awadh (in Lahore, Aligarh, and Hyderabad), the Society for the Promotion of the Nagari Script (Nagari Pracharini Sabha, est. 1893) in Banaras and the Hindi Literary Association (Hindi Sahitya Sammelan) in Allahabad grew into veritable powerhouses of Hindi scholarship and activism, crucially defining modern Hindi and lobbying the colonial government, the public, and the Indian National Congress in its favor (see King 1974; Orsini 2002).

What this overview shows is that colonial "impact" and technology transfer did transform Awadh cities, but did so differently in each case, with multiple stories—like that of Dalit publishing in Kanpur, or Sant publishing in Allahabad—that dominant narratives of reform obscure. Similarly, while the dominant narrative of colonial Lucknow after 1857 is one of decay and nostalgia for the earlier Nawabi city with its pageants, celebrated courtesans, poetry, and music, Lucknow clearly remained a thriving literary center. This is not to say that colonialism did not have a profound impact, particularly at the level of ideas and institutions, and that ideas did not have consequences. If today we think that Hindi and Urdu are the languages of different peoples, if we speak of language contact in military terms as "conquest" or "surrender" and are surprised to find texts written in the "wrong" script or authors using the "wrong" language, if we read authors' intentions off the religion of their birth and consider orature the timeless and anonymous expression of village sensibility, it is because new ideas of vernacular language, literary history, and folk literature took such hold in the colonial period.

Colonial Effects and the Vernacular Problem

The materials and arguments presented in this book so far support David Lelyveld's (1993: 202) formulation that "[p]eople did not have languages; they had linguistic repertoires that varied even within a single household, let alone the marketplace, school, temple, court, or devotional circle," and that these "codes of linguistic behaviour took on the same characteristics of hierarchy that other sorts of human interaction did." Not only did speaking require shifting register and even language according to addressee and context; most literary practices entailed learning and using a separate code from that of one's spoken language—be it a koinè, as with the Sants (Chapter 3), a formalized poetic vernacular like Brajbhasha or Urdu, or a high language like Persian and Sanskrit (Chapter 4). Script was a function of one's education and profession, and it was understood that the same literary text, particularly a vernacular one, could be written in different scripts; this was as true of manuscripts of Jayasi's *Padmāvat* as of Tulsidas's *Rāmāyan* for centuries (Chapter 2). Understanding and using different linguistic repertoires was so commonplace that it hardly warrants the appellation "multilingual."[30]

It is important to reiterate these points because of the profound epistemic shift that the idea of the vernacular, intended as "one's own language" (Hindi *nij bhāshā*), the "mother tongue" (Hindi *mātṛbhāshā*, Urdu *mādarī zabān*), and "the language of the people" (Hindi *lokbhāshā*) produced.[31] Whereas till then little meaning had been attached to a person's local speech (certainly to that of one's mother!), and it was learning to be eloquent in the languages that mattered and was valued, the new vernacular ideal identified language with script, community, history, and progress in deeply consequential ways.[32]

The ideological and pragmatic advantages of having a single standard vernacular for community formation and communication cannot be doubted, as Benedict Anderson and David Gramling have pointed out. Anderson (1991) famously credited the rise of standardized "print vernaculars" with enabling people to imagine a nation ("una d'arme, *di lingua*, d'altare," or "one in army, *language*, and religion," sang Italian nationalist poet Alessandro Manzoni in "Marzo 1821," emphasis added). Gramling's (2016: 1) provocative book credits the "invention of monolingualism" (or its "scientific discovery in the seventeenth century") for affording all kinds of things, from the European Enlightenment to "mass literacy and organized anti-absolutism, for populaces who have at least a fighting chance at understanding their governments and laws, for the coalescence of modern scholarly disciplines," etc. But what interests me here are the disruptive effects that the potentially democratic idea of the vernacular had for multilingual literary culture and multilingual persons. I see four such effects.

First, the Herderian idea that a language "belongs" to a community of people and that people's thoughts and feelings find authentic expression in "their" language projected modern language definitions and ideals of literature back into history and inscribed them into a communitarian and civilizational paradigm that distinguished "Indian" from "foreign" words, languages, genres, stories, and people.[33] Second, language was territorialized in only apparently innocent scientific and/or pragmatic ways—from the need to settle on one vernacular for a region or province for educational and administrative purposes (the immediate cause of the Hindi-Urdu controversy) to language maps like those accompanying Grierson's *Linguistic Survey of India* (1898–1928), in which languages are laid out as adjacent territories. In the process, the ordinary multilingualism found in places or embodied in individuals and communities of taste was made invisible.[34]

Third, the intrinsic connection between script and language—a notion first articulated by Orientalists and taken up by campaigners for the official recognition of Nagari—denied the history of multiscriptualism in northern India, a history that meant, as we have seen, that the same text circulated among different reading communities and that different registers could be part of the same language, accessible to the same person. Finally, the idea that one vernacular should be used for *all purposes*—that a vernacular could, and should, be both immediately understandable by all and be able to carry scientific, abstract, and modern knowledge *while being true to its cultural core*—in practice discounted existing common vocabulary and encouraged instead a rush toward coinages from opposite lexical pools.

The new continuum of language-script-community was honed by British Orientalists but heartily embraced by Indian intellectuals and activists. Tasked with preparing teaching materials for East India Company trainees at Fort William College in Calcutta, in 1800 the Scottish teacher and scholar J. B. Gilchrist pronounced a new definition and classification of the north Indian vernacular. He called it Hindustani (Hindoostani) and distinguished three varieties: a highly Persianized "Court style," a middle style of educated men or "Hindustani proper" (both written in Perso-Arabic script), and a rustic style or Hindavi (Hinduwee, also called Bhakha/Bhasha) written in Nagari script. This last he called "the exclusive property of the Hindoos alone" (Gilchrist [1796] 1970: 4). Textbooks produced at Fort William College by Indian writers, or *munshis,* were named either Hindustani (Urdu) or Bhakha (Hindi), and if reprinted in the other script, their vocabulary was altered accordingly (see Pritchett n.d.).

By itself this would have been only a matter of name and register, had it not been folded into new language entities in which language came to be neatly aligned with community. Hindi in Nagari script "belonged" to the Hindus, whereas Hindustani (or Urdu, to use the term that became common in the nineteenth century) in the Perso-Arabic script "belonged" to or had been "developed" by Muslims. Undergirded by the Orientalist-colonial view of Indian history, with its Aryan-Hindu golden age, dark Middle Ages of "Muhammadan invasion," tyranny, and oppression, and the promises of the *pax Britannica,* this notion of language and community took deep roots in Indian discourse in the nineteenth century. Take Harishchandra: in his memorandum to the 1882 Hunter Commission for public education, he voiced strong support for Hindi by using the argument of Hindu majoritarianism and abused Urdu by calling it "the language of dancing girls and prostitutes" (quoted in Dalmia 1997: 208). By then he had composed a mock-elegy for Urdu, titled *Urdū kā syāpā* (Dirge for Urdu, 1874). Yet, as Vasudha Dalmia notes, Harishchandra accompanied this public projection of standard Khari Boli Hindi as the language of the province with a constant attention to the local varieties of the spoken vernacular (Purbi, Kannauji, Brajbhasha, etc.) and to variations in language use between the language spoken at home, the written language, and the language of poetry. He actually acknowledged that few spoke Khari Boli Hindi at home, and that he had himself tried many times to write poetry in Khari Boli but had found it impossible.[35] Moreover, Harishchandra also composed poetry in Urdu. This is what I mean by the gap between ideas—in this case of a single, standard community language—and practices and tastes.

The ground for public controversy around language was laid in the 1830s, when the East India Company government decided to replace Persian in the lower courts with a two-tier system of English and vernacular, and the question arose of which should be named the vernacular of a province, linking the vernacular to access to employment (see King 1994).[36] While in some provinces—such as Bengal—the choice was easy, in provinces where more than one language was widespread, or in the United Provinces where there was "one language but two scripts," it was not. Urdu was by then more established as a public language and print vernacular, but as "the language of the Hindus," Hindi had numbers on its side. Arguments were advanced, honed, hurled, and repeated in countless articles, pamphlets, petitions, and even poems and plays, particularly whenever there was a colonial consultation on the language of education and administration (as in the 1860s and 1880s), public mobilization on other issues (as for cow protection in the 1880s), or when the decision over which should be the future national language became more pressing (in the 1930s) (see King 1994; Rai 2001; Orsini 2002). In this unfolding drama, Awadh Hindi intellectuals like Bharatendu Harishchandra, Madan Mohan Malaviya, and Mahavir Prasad Dvivedi and Hindi associations like the Society for the Promotion of Nagari of Banaras and the Hindi Literary Association of Allahabad played a central role.

A whole new vocabulary of foreignness vs. Indianness and competitive antiquity, clothed in historical scientific objectivity, came into play. Although evidence for the use of Khari Boli—the common linguistic base of both Urdu and Hindi as print vernaculars—was scant before the eighteenth century, since, as the previous chapters have shown, it was Hindavi and Brajbhasha that were used, it was imperative to establish that one's vernacular had been used from the earliest times. And while the influential Orientalist linguist G. A. Grierson (1889: 7, 107) dismissed Urdu as "exotic" and having "uncertain citizenship" in India but also asserted that Hindi had been "invented" by Europeans at Fort William College,[37] Hindi and Urdu scholars instead traced a direct and linear connection between the earliest textual records and iconic literary figures and the present vernaculars. "When the Muhammadans came to India Hindi was the vernacular language of Hindustan, and the Nagari character, or its variations, the medium through which all business was carried out," Malaviya (1897: 1), the Allahabad lawyer turned politician, bluntly stated in his influential *Memorandum*, quoting colonial officers and scholars to buttress this invention of tradition.[38] Urdu scholar Hafiz Mahmud Sherani ([1930] 1966: 132, emphases added) read early vernacular traces in fourteenth- and fifteenth-century Persian texts as evidence that Muslims had created Urdu as *their* language:

> These words and expressions, in my opinion, are enough evidence for the antiquity of the Urdu language, and *in truth it can be said that this language was commonly spoken among Muslims in this period*. . . . [W]e see that *Muslim peoples (aqwām) created a special language for themselves in India* and as they spread thanks to their conquests and victories, this language spread eastward, westward, to the north and to the south as well, together with them.[39]

The language of conquest stuck even with those who tried to find a common ground, as Padmasingh Sharma did in a series of lectures on Hindi, Urdu, and Hindustani at the Hindustani Academy in Allahabad in 1932. Though Sharma foregrounded social interaction over politics to explain language creation, and argued that language contact and lexical borrowings were ordinary processes, he still employed the language of invasion and conquest. Hinting at Urdu, Sharma (1932: 4, emphases added) said:

> There is no regional language in India in which foreign words have not entered in good number. Despite that, *no foreign language has mounted such a powerful attack* on our country so as to completely uproot a local (*deśī*, lit. "of the country") language and take its place. Just as foreigners come and settle and adopt the language, culture, habits, customs, and dress of the adoptive country, outside words that come along with them also adopt the form (*raṅg-rūp*, "form and color") of the words of the adoptive country and accept the dominion of its grammar. In that way, though they have come with the victorious peoples, [these words] combine with the vocabulary of the defeated country and lose their separate existence, or rather *defeated after the continuous attack, struggle, and siege by the local language, they accept defeat and surrender,* and after being properly "purified" they take on local dress.

In such discussions, the etymology of Urdu from the Turkic word for "encampment" invariably suggested that Urdu had "come" from outside, with the "Muhammadan conquerors," if only, as Sharma put it, to be conquered by Indian languages in turn. Although Shamsur Rahman Faruqi (2001) has convincingly shown that Urdu referred to the "language of the exalted camp" (*zabān-e urdū-e muʿalla*), i.e., the imperial court in Delhi, and not to the "invading hordes," this etymology stuck and is still routinely invoked.

Nor was the proposal of a middle, common ground—also termed Hindustani—acceptable to either side (see Lelyveld 1993; Lunn 2018). Hindustani, as propounded by M. K. Gandhi and the Hindustani Academy in Allahabad (est. 1910), came to mean a widespread spoken koinè that could be written in either script. The "strategic indeterminacy" of this definition allowed many people from the worlds of Hindi, Urdu, Persian, and history holding different views about language to work together. Yet this strategic indeterminacy could neither paper over the competitive historical narratives nor satisfy the new all-encompassing ambition of the vernacular.[40]

The notion that a vernacular language should cover *all* domains of language use, spoken and written, pragmatic and literary, colloquial and specialized—work earlier performed by different languages—also invites scrutiny. The need for the vernacular to expand its terminology and textual repertoire in order to be able to convey all kinds of knowledge prompted both Hindi and Urdu associations to set up committees that produced lists of technical and scientific words, scientific textbooks, and impressively large dictionaries.[41] This need stemmed from a perceived urgency to "catch up" with modern knowledge, exemplified by English, but also from the recognition that English could not be the medium through which such knowledge reached the masses. Yet even when the stated preference was for "finding" words already in common use, in practice the experts reached out to their respective generative high languages—Sanskrit for Hindi and Arabic and Persian for Urdu—and coined and normalized terms that pushed Hindi and Urdu further apart, making them less intelligible to each other.[42] For the Society for the Promotion of Nagari, Persian and Arabic *were* foreign languages and their words should be avoided:

> [O]ur principle is this: as far as possible, *no words from Persian, Arabic, or other foreign language* should be used for which an easy and current Hindi or Sanskrit word is available, but those words from foreign languages which have become fully current, and for which no Hindi word exists or the substitution of a Sanskrit word for it means that a flaw of difficulty in comprehension is possible, those words should be used. In summary, the very first place should be given to pure Hindi words, the next to easy and current Sanskrit words, the next to ordinary and current words from Persian and other foreign languages, and the very last place should be given to non-current Sanskrit words. Difficult words from Persian and other foreign languages should never be used. (Shyamsundar Das 1957, quoted in King 1974: 309, emphasis added)

In such circumstances, it became unthinkable that Persian had been an Indian language for seven centuries; that both Hindi and Urdu *already* contained words of Sanskrit, Arabic, Persian, Turkic, English, and Portuguese origin (as Sharma argued); and that Hindi speakers already were or could become familiar with Persian words and Urdu speakers with Sanskritic words. The idea of using a single vernacular for all purposes was meant to be, and in many ways was, a democratizing move. But because it came embedded in ideas about historically appropriate word-making pools, instrumental notions of language and translation, and implicit hierarchies of knowledge, in practice the vernacular that was naturalized was hardly less artificial and exclusive than what it was meant to replace. In the process, the existing connections with other familiar and available linguistic repertoires were severed.

Although all the protagonists of the Hindi-Urdu controversy in Awadh stemmed from a multilingual milieu and acquired a multilingual habitus, they imagined the vernacular as monolingual. They approved only of culturally appropriate bilingualism (Hindi-Sanskrit, Urdu-Persian) and tried to shame multilinguals into "serving their own language:" "We request all scholars of English to grant us a favour . . . of writing useful articles in their own language. If they do not know how to write it they need not feel ashamed: if they really don't know how they only have to learn! Please fulfil your duty!" exhorted Dvivedi.[43]

Whether Hindi and Urdu are "one language, two scripts" or two languages is still a highly contested and controversial matter today, on which no objective truth but many contrasting positions exist. And because each position blames and exposes the loopholes of the other's claims while containing loopholes of its own, no satisfactory conclusion can ever be reached. My argument here has been that we need to start by scrutinizing the idea of the vernacular per se as a historical construct. We need to uncouple language from script and, as this book has done, reject the single-language monocultural historical narratives that accompany the arguments about Hindi and Urdu. It is more fitting, as this book has done, to start from the multilingual and multiscriptual context, distinguish between spoken, written, and literary language varieties, and acknowledge that people could and did cultivate more than one taste and one language. We also need to acknowledge that languages are not unchanging monoliths but rather change together with literary tastes and fashion, sometimes pretty quickly, as the case of Urdu poetry in the eighteenth century shows. Then the myth-making, exclusions, and collapsing of levels (spoken/literary, individual/community) involved in constructing Hindi and Urdu as separate and autonomous languages become evident. At the same time, because these constructions have been deeply consequential, we also need to acknowledge that over this period Hindi and Urdu *did* become, for most intents and purposes, separate languages, continuing overlaps and multilingual familiarity notwithstanding.

What bearing did the language controversy and the "separation, standardization, and historicization" of Hindi and Urdu have on literary historiography and literary memory?[44] This is the topic of the next section. Once again, Awadh intellectuals and institutions played a key role in the process.

Separate Canons

Literature, like language, was at the heart of ideological, institutional, and aesthetic transformations in the colonial context.[45] While important scholarship has emphasized the role played by English literature as a powerful model—whether as a "mask of conquest" (Vishwanathan 1989), a "crushing" influence (Chandra 1992), or a disruptive model (Pritchett 2004)—here my focus is more specifically on how, and how far, the literary traditions of multilingual Purab/ Awadh were incorporated into the Hindi and Urdu literary canons. How did the new standards of literature and views of language deal with the multilingual heritage of tastes and practices in the region, through which categories and with what emphases and exclusions? Were they enshrined in the university curricula of Hindi and Urdu departments and reproduced as "legitimate knowledge" (Bourdieu 1991) in school and college textbooks? Did curricula acknowledge or incorporate the "other" language and traditions at all? As we shall see, a comparative perspective usefully shows up parallels in the construction of two separate monolingual Hindi and Urdu literary canons, but hardly any overlap.

One important difference between the first histories of Urdu and Hindi literature was in the sources and precedents they relied upon. Urdu literary histories relied substantially on biographical dictionaries-cum-anthologies, *tazkiras*. This was true of the first literary history in Urdu, Muhammad Azad's celebrated *Water of Life* (*Āb-e ḥayāt,* 1880), written in the context of Government College Lahore, and the even earlier French history written in Paris by Garcin de Tassy (*Histoire de la littérature hindouie at hindoustanie,* 1839–1847, translated into Urdu as early as the 1840s). As a result, these histories were rich in anecdotes about individual poets and around networks of teachers and pupils; they focused on the genre that *tazkiras* privileged (like the *ghazal*), and reproduced the *tazkiras*' linguistic protocols, which overwhelmingly excluded bilingual poets, as we have seen.

By contrast, as we saw in the previous chapter, Hindi literary culture had not produced a similar biographical genre, though oral anecdotes and hagiographies supplied some personal detail.[46] The first attempt at a literary history in Hindi, Shiv Singh Sengar's *Shiv Singh's Lotus* (*Śiv siṃh saroj,* 1878), was, as we saw, really a *tazkira* that privileged the portable poetic genre favored by courtly Hindi (Brajbhasha) culture, the *kabitta.*[47] In this way, literary historiography in Hindi and Urdu began by reproducing the linguistic and literary biases of early modern compilations and archives.

But when, in 1900, inspired by a similar search for Sanskrit manuscripts, the Association for the Promotion of the Nagari Script (NPS) undertook an extensive and ambitious search for Hindi manuscripts that went on for seven decades, the search brought to light a much broader range of works than those considered by the earlier anthologies on which Sengar had relied. The manuscripts found were listed and described in detailed reports,[48] and soon scholars involved in the manuscript search, such as the Mishra brothers, produced a much more voluminous and detailed literary historical archive. Their *Miśra bandhu vinod* (The entertainment of the Mishra brothers, 1913) included as many as 3,757 poets, though still listed alphabetically, *tazkira*-like.

It fell upon another NPS associate and future Hindi professor at Banaras Hindu University, Ramchandra Shukla (1884–1941), to systematize this mass of information into a new, fourfold historical scheme that, though renewed and partly challenged since, still remains the bedrock of Hindi literary history.

Originally written as an appendix to the monumental NPS Hindi dictionary, to which he had contributed, Shukla's *History of Hindi Literature* (*Hindī sāhitya kā itihās*, 1929) answered the need of the university syllabus and has never been out of print. A literary-historical tour de force, rich in details and assured in its critical assessments that became "established notions" (*sthāpnāeṃ*), it was founded on two critical principles, one moral and the other historical. Morally, Shukla evaluated poets on the basis of whether their writing furthered the "people's taste" (*lokruchi*) and "people's *dharma*" (*lokdharma*) and strengthened the social fabric. Historically, Shukla mapped Hindi literary production onto a colonial-Hindu nationalist narrative of "Muslim oppression and Hindu resistance." He famously divided Hindi literature into four ages. The first was the heroic age of Rajasthani epics and dated from *before* the Islamic invasion. The invasion, he argued, had so demoralized the people that it had turned them inward, producing the second period, of bhakti; devotional poets like Tulsidas had heroically upheld the Hindu social and religious fabric, while Kabir and others had harmfully criticized it. Continued foreign rule and reliance on courtly patrons rather than "people's taste" had then led Hindi poets toward courtly decadence in the *riti* or courtly period, until the modern age, the age of prose under colonial rule. Religion dictated the classification of texts and the intentions of authors (what Purushottam Agrawal has called "birth determinism"). Thus Shukla discussed *kathas* at length (Chapter 2) but split them in different chapters dedicated to Sufi romances (*sufi premakhyan*), devotion to Ram (Tulsidas's *Rāmcharitmānas*), and "stray works" (like Puhakar's *Rasaratan*). The axis of Indianness vs. foreignness—*Rasaratan* was "completely Indian" in outlook, unlike the Sufi romances—rendered invisible the continuities, echoes, and dialogism across the *kathas* that I highlighted in Chapter 2 (Shukla [1929] 1988: 157). Birth determinism and, consequently, strong intentionality recur in Shukla's positive assessment of Jayasi, who as a *Muslim* writer *in Hindi* was now an oddity, like Raslin (Chapter 4): "*Though a Muslim*, he told Hindu stories in the language of the Hindus and showed complete harmony (*samañjasya*) between the touching conditions of their lives and his liberal (*udār*) heart" (101, emphasis added). While praising Jayasi's "emotional heart" (*bhāvuk hṛday*) that "recognized the beauty of the pure love of the heroine-as-wife (*svakīyā*)," Shukla could not resist a dig at the "decadence" brought in by Islamic culture: "[T]his pure Indian form of love has been disappearing because of foreign influence, particularly of Urdu poetry (*shāyirī*) and songs" (quoted in Gupta 2017: 277).

In fact, both Hindi and Urdu literary histories channeled the strong "Victorian" critique of their respective poetic traditions, which they accused of being artificial, stagnant, decadent, and obsessed with erotic love. If Azad's contemporary Altaf Husain Hali in his poem *Musaddas* (1869) had decried the "cesspools" of Persianate poetry and advocated a "return" to the purity of Arabic poetry, a similar historical-exhortative poem by Maithilisharan Gupta (1999: 131) criticized Hindi poetry for its obsession with erotic love.[49] These poems by Hali and Gupta featured prominently in Urdu and Hindi school textbooks, while Azad's book became part of the Urdu syllabus at high school and university level.[50] Curiously, some Urdu critics held up Brajbhasha poetry as more natural at the very same time that modern Hindi critics decried its artificiality.[51]

While the historical and moral judgment was damning, individual poets were still cherished; this is part of the gap between ideas and tastes that I have been referring to. For example, in their canonizing study *Nine Gems of Hindi* (*Hindī navaratna*, 1910, rev. 1924), the Mishra brothers constructed a canon that made space for both devotional *and* courtly poets; they called the former "great souls" (*mahatma*), the latter "great poets" (*mahakavi*).[52]

Almost exactly contemporary with Shukla's history, the *History of Urdu Literature* (1927), written in English by the Allahabad Urdu professor Ram Babu Saksena, and soon translated into Urdu, did a similar job of greatly expanding the purview of Urdu literary history.[53] Saksena produced a longer historical narrative that began with Amir Khusrau in the early fourteenth century, touched the Mughals, and incorporated the new researches on Deccani Urdu poetry undertaken by Maulvi Abdul Haq. Saksena's history placed greater value on the Shi'a elegies that had become so prominent in Nawabi Lucknow (though not on the racy *rekhti* poems which had also become hugely popular there). While praising Urdu as a "noble literature, the best symbol of Hindu-Muslim unity," Saksena (1927: ii) echoed denunciations of Urdu as a foreign and exotic language, and of its poetry as imitative. These terms completely reversed the logic of Persian and Urdu poetic culture: as scholars have shown, imitation of the masters had long been crucial, as a form of training, a homage, and a display of mastery (see, e.g., Losensky 1998; Zipoli 1993). As an expert on Urdu and Persian poetry, surely Saksena (1927: 23) must have known this, yet the colonial impact of ideas of originality and indigeneity produced a totally inverted discourse:

> Older Urdu poetry was not an indigenous product. It drew its inspiration from Persian and copied foreign models. It was dominated by the prosody of the Persians which had been invented by the Arabs. . . . This bondage to Persian had its strength and weakness. . . . It had no evolution such as English poetry had. Hence its range is very limited for it sank in the rut of old battered Persian themes and adorned itself with the rags of cast off imagery of Persian poetry having absolutely no relation to India, the country of its birth.

Short headings summarized the chief "defects of such imitation:" (1) it made Urdu poetry seem unreal; (2) it made Urdu poetry rhetorical; (3) it made Urdu poetry conventional; (4) it made Urdu poetry mechanical, artificial, and sensual;

(5) it made Urdu poetry unnatural (Saksena 1927: 23–25). Saksena described the gradual shift of Urdu poetic idiom along Persian lines in ambivalent terms, as "refinement" but also as "exclusion" of "obsolete" and "indigenous" Hindi words.[54] Narrated in these terms, what had been a process of literary affiliation dictated by a logic of distinction became a sign of cultural alienation and national betrayal.

These parallel but separate literary historical visions found direct expression in university syllabi, which also enshrined modern literature in the canon. If the English literature syllabus foregrounded Shakespeare's plays, Milton, Tennyson, and other poets from *The Golden Treasury,* as well as some nineteenth-century realist fiction, but also tested more students broadly on scientific discoveries and classical Greece and Rome, Urdu and Hindi literature syllabi consolidated two separate, self-contained, and largely monolingual canons *with no overlap at all.*[55] This canon and its "legitimate knowledge" percolated from the universities and literary institutions into school textbooks.

School textbooks were even more careful in exposing young minds to the dangerous allure of the respective poetic traditions and featured more modern poetry and a range of prose texts and genres.[56] For example, the poetic section of Ismail Merathi's ([1909] 1913) influential *Urdu Helper* included mostly post-reform poets (Hali, Akbar Ilahabadi, and the author himself), with only a sprinkling of the celebrated classics (Mir Taqi Mir, Atish, Sauda, Ghalib, Nasikh, Insha and Rind).[57] Again, comparing Hindi and Urdu textbooks shows parallels, some significant differences, and no overlap whatsoever. The textbooks' introductions were often sites of historical statements that directly echoed the arguments of the language controversy. For example, in his introduction to the school reader *Hindi Selections* (1927), compiled by Amarnath Jha of Allahabad University (see above), veteran Hindi scholar and colonial administrator Lala Sitaram (1927: 1) bemoaned the fact that although "the literature of our country is very old . . . and the spread of our language has increased . . . during foreign rule, out of wonder and with a view to increase their status, scores of Hindus became writers of Farsi, Urdu, and English."[58] Sitaram further compared the decline of poetry in the hands of bards (*bhats*) with that of singing in the hands of prostitutes, and inveighed against the English and Urdu education system that made (presumably Hindu) children unaware of and uninterested in their literary past. Perhaps for this reason this textbook was more oriented toward the Hindi poetic tradition—bhakti but also courtly (though judiciously excluding erotic poetry). Practically all its items, whether in verse or prose, older or contemporary, revolved thematically around characters and stories from the *Rāmāyaṇa,* the *Mahābhārata,* and the Sanskrit Puranic tradition, strengthening the identification of Hindi literature with the Indian-Hindu cultural "core," so that the textbook would reintroduce English- and Urdu-educated Hindus to "their" tradition (Jha 1927). By contrast, a poetry reader for high school, *Padya parijāt*

(Poet's heavenly tree, 1931), compiled by two teachers from Benares Hindu University's Hindi Department, Pitambar Datt Barthwal (the Sant specialist; see Chapter 3) and Keshavprasad Mishra, introduced readers to a broader spectrum of the Hindi literary canon, reproducing the BHU curriculum almost without change.[59]

The prose reader *Essence of the Hindi Language* (*Hindī bhāṣā sār,* 1916, fourth edition 1927) by two other Banaras professors long associated with the Society for the Promotion of the Nagari Script, Lala Bhagvan Din and Babu Ramdas Gaur, consciously began not with Fort William College texts but with one by Munshi Sadasukhlal from Allahabad composed in Urdu script forty years later. This choice was a rebut to Grierson's quip that Hindi literature had been brought into existence by Europeans at Fort William College. Overriding the issue of script, the editors argued that, unlike the *munshis* of Fort William College, Sadasukh Lal had written in a "natural" language free of "foreign," i.e., Persian and Urdu, words:

> *Though the script is Urdu . . .* [t]he importance of this piece lies in the fact that whereas Lallu Lalji and Sadal Misra wrote at the behest of the government, which *makes them liable to the suspicion of artificiality*, Munshiji instead wrote it for his own interest in the ordinary, colloquial Hindi *spoken* by educated Hindus from Prayag [Allahabad] to Delhi. The passage is also significant because *although he was a scholar of Arabic and Persian, the writer did not use any foreign words. . . .* Therefore the passage clearly proves that the modern style of Hindi is not artificial (*kṛtrim*) but ancient (*prāchīn*). (Bhagvan Din and Gaur 1927: 2–3, emphases added)

The second edition included the short piece *Rānī ketakī kī kahānī* (The story of Queen Ketaki, ca. 1803), a quirky linguistic experiment by the Persian and Urdu polymath Insha Allah Khan "Insha" (1772–1817) in which he had tried to write a story without any Persian and Arabic words. This minor linguistic experiment was eagerly seized upon by Hindi activists as valid textual evidence that Muslims could indeed and did write Hindi if they only wanted to!

> We have included his piece so that our Muslim brethren may consider how a celebrated Muslim living in Lucknow, a worthy writer of Persian and Urdu, intimate courtier of Nawab Sa'dat 'Ali Khan and poet laureate at his court thought about writing a book in the Hindi language. Did he think the language inferior and dead (*tucch aur murdā*) or did he consider acquiring proficiency in that language a matter of pride?! (Bhagvan Din and Gaur 1927: 6–7)[60]

The inclusion of these as well as several other Urdu prose pieces in this textbook—passages from the popular Urdu novel *The Bride's Mirror* by Nazir Ahmad

(*Mir'āt ul-'urūs*, 1869) and the editor of *Oudh Akhbār* Ratannath Sarshar's *The Story of Azad* (*Fasāna-e Āzād*, 1878–1883)—did not signify its authors' openness to Urdu. Rather, it was an instrumental appropriation as part of a polemical and competitive stance. Hindi has two styles, the authors claimed, "pure" and "mixed," just as Gujarati has "pure Gujarati" and "Parsi Gujarati:" "Urdu is but another name for mixed Hindi" (Bhagvan Din and Gaur 1927: 9).

In other words, though the separate literary canons of Urdu and Hindi (including both Brajbhasha and Hindavi) were rooted in precolonial understandings, they now indexed not just literary but also social, political, and religious group identities, and a strong moral and political tone crept into literary-critical discourse. In the process, multilingualism was invisibilized, discouraged, or misconstrued. So a taste for Urdu in a Hindi reader was perceived as thoughtless alienation at best, and culpable betrayal and separatism at worst, while Muslim poets of Hindi were praised for their "adoption" of "Indian" (i.e., Hindu) stories and of Hindi *as if it were not their own language*. Meanwhile, Urdu literary histories criticized Urdu's traditional orientation toward Persian as harmful exotic artificiality. This climate of competition, mutual accusation, self-critique, and distrust actively produced amnesia about the plural and shared literary tastes that had existed and continued to exist. In fact, it denied the possibility that such plural and multilingual tastes could exist.

There were a few dissenting voices. "It is distressing to come across Hindu graduates and under-graduates in some part of the U.P. [United Provinces] who think that their duty towards Hindi necessarily means and implies that they should exclude from their thought the language and literature in which their ancestors only a generation ago excelled," lamented Tej Bahadur Sapru in his foreword to Saksena's (1927: iii) *History*. But even books that put forth a more inclusive view of history, language, and literature now presumed ignorance and/or amnesia. *Hindi Poetry* (*Hindī shā'irī*, 1931) by Az'am Kurevi, published in Urdu by the Hindustani Academy, briefly *introduced* Urdu readers to the history of Hindi poetry before providing short biographies of the most canonized (*mustanad*) Hindi poets, with samples and comments.[61] Urdu readers, Kurevi (1931: 16) suggested, would benefit from reestablishing that familiarity and use the taste (*mazāq*) for Hindi to enrich their Urdu poetic taste: "Because we know the taste of Persian and Arabic we are attracted towards them. If we knew Hindi poetry in the same way, we would definitely incline that way, too, and it would enrich the Urdu treasure with a priceless acquisition."

Kurevi's book is particularly significant because in order to counter the Hindi-Urdu divide and show that Indian Muslims had in fact participated actively and enthusiastically in the making of Hindi literature in the past (sixteen of the thirty-three poets mentioned, and seven of fourteen biographies, are of Muslim Hindi poets), it actively recalled and brought into play the multilingual local of

Awadh. In his historical introduction, Kurevi claimed the Persian poets Amir Khusrau and Mas'ud Sa'd Salman as early *Hindi* poets, discussed romance writers Da'ud and Jayasi (Chapter 2), and even the songs and poems of the Mughal emperor Shah 'Alam II and the last King of Awadh Wajid 'Ali Shah. In fact, five of the poets Kurevi discussed were from Bilgram: Mubarak, Rahmatullah, Mir 'Abd al-Jalil, Raslin, and Pemi (Chapter 4)! In other words, within this general account of Hindi poetry for Urdu (and implicitly Muslim) readers, written in the context of the growing Hindi-Urdu divide, the multilingual cultivation of Persian and Hindavi/Brajbhasha of the *qasba* poets of Bilgram worked as a powerful memento of past familiarity.

Another important effect of the reformulation of literature and the separation of languages in the colonial context is what I call the "invention" of folk literature, i.e., the invention of the category of folk literature as separate from literature per se and as anonymous and atemporal. The real effect of this process was to render the shared repertoire of songs "homeless" and the contemporary dynamism of orature invisible.[62]

Colonial Folklore and the Invention of Folk Literature

Pahilé nám lé Alláh Miyán ká
Dújé Nabi Rasúl.
Tíjé nám lé Fátimá ká,
Jehé mukh par barsai núr.
Mithá nám hai Alláh Miyán ká
Dújé míthá Rasúl.
Tíjé míthá Sáwan Bhádon,
Jo barsai so núr.

—Bhanupratap Tiwari, "A Religious Song of the Dhobis," *North Indian Notes & Queries* (December 1891), 145.

Most of the literary texts and genres discussed in the earlier chapters of this book—from *kathas* and Sant songs to sophisticated couplets—were meant to be sung, recited, or read aloud (*bāṃchnā* in in Hindi). Indeed, in the colonial period the soundscape of northern India continued to be saturated with songs, storytelling, and performances, some specific to certain performers, communities, occasions, or sites, and others to be sung or recited as the opportunity arose (Orsini and Schofield 2015). Itinerant performers—whether Jogis or Madaris, Nats or Noniyas, Kevats or Doms, Ahirs or Dusadhs—crisscrossed the region along routes of labor, trade, and pilgrimage that stretched from Mirzapur in Purab to Nepal and Bengal, from Jaunpur to Gorakhpur and the Nepali Tarai, from Ballia to Ranchi, and from Allahabad to Calcutta.[63] From the early twentieth century, they also began to bring with them chapbooks for sale, and migrant laborers from the region who traveled to Calcutta, Burma, and the plantation colonies carried these songs and chapbooks with them. Sant poets, we saw in Chapter 3, had drawn on some of these song traditions, but so did the many amateur, often illiterate, poets who battled with words in public competitions called *dangals* or *akharas*, the terms used for wrestling grounds and contests, at the fairs and festivals that multiplied in the nineteenth century. In his book on one such song genre, the *kajli*, Harishchandra's friend Badrinarayan Chaudhri "Premghan" (see below) noted that *kajlis*, which women in Mirzapur usually sang during the spring Kajli fair, were now also being sung by bazaar singers (*gavaiyas*), who used a more generic koine instead of the local Bhojpuri. It was in fact this koine that was used in the song collections in both Hindi and Urdu scripts that flooded the north Indian print market in the late nineteenth century.[64] Nor, as we have seen, were these songs only "popular." In the early twentieth century, songs were at the heart of musical life, a staple of commercial publishing, and crucial to a whole range of musical theaters—from professional Parsi theater and its north Indian version Nautanki, to the Bhojpuri Bidesia newly devised by Bhikhari Thakur (1887–1971).[65]

But in the context of the redefinition of literature that marked new boundaries of language and taste, as the previous sections have shown, this rich repertoire of songs could not become part of either Hindi or Urdu "literature" and literary history. Neither Shukla's nor Saksena's histories made space for songs. Grierson, an avid collector of orature and the author of the first Hindi literary history, could have included them, but unfortunately he declined to do so on scholarly grounds.[66]

Instead, despite their continuing popularity and dynamism, songs came to be demarcated as folklore, or *loksahitya* (the Hindi calque for "folk literature"). This move had several important and long-lasting consequences. First, songs were delinked (and de-classed) from literature proper. (Even in music they are usually termed "light-classical.") Second, songs were folded into a discourse of the *lok* as *Volk* that confined them to the village domain and imagined them as symbols of vanishing cultural purity. In this imagination of the song as the heritage of village folk there was no space for contemporary performers and innovators, nor for hybridization through media like the stage or the chapbook. Third, since *loksahitya* pertained to the *Volk*—now imagined as Hindu-Indian—Muslim songs, customs, and performances were also implicitly excluded from Hindi *loksahitya*. As for Urdu, its self-definition was too tied to language to even register Muslim orature that was not in "chaste Urdu." Excluded on one side on religious-cultural grounds and on the other on linguistic grounds, Muslim orature became completely invisible as a result.[67]

The Hindi "invention of *loksahitya*" took place in the context of, but separately from, colonial folklore, and it is worth examining their relationship in a more detail. The rich world of north Indian orature—comprising tales, songs, proverbs, omens, epics, etc.—attracted the interest of colonial folklorists at the same time that it was animating theater and commercial publishing. As Sadhana Naithani (2010: 1) has pointed out, the impulse behind the collection of folklore in India—as in other colonies—differed from that in Europe: instead of a nationalist "engagement of middle-class intellectuals, poets, and writers with the narratives and songs that were common among the majority of the populace" of *their* society, in the colonies it was colonial administrators and missionaries (and their wives) who first collected "folklore"—ostensibly to "reveal the mind of the people."[68]

The most famous scholar-folklorist of the North Western Provinces and Oudh apart from Grierson was another Anglo-Irish, William Crooke (1848–1923), who worked in Purab between 1871 and 1896. Crooke published an appreciated *Rural and Agricultural Glossary* (1888) and in 1891 took over the journal *North Indian Notes & Queries* (*NIN&Q*), started by the Punjab scholar-administrator Richard Carnac Temple. Crooke then published two celebrated books, *The Popular Religion and Folklore of Northern India* (1892) and *The Tribes and Castes of the North Western Provinces and Oudh* (1896) (Naithani 2010: 6).

The rubrics of *NIN&Q*—"Popular Religion," "Sociology," "Folklore," "Ethnography," "Anglo-India," "Philology," and "Antiquities"—give an idea of the contours of this colonial interest, which encompassed linguistics, religion, history, and ethnography, though in fact the categories often got blurred. As its title suggests, the journal consisted largely of short notes rather than articles. In fact, long articles were chopped up and interspersed as notes or snippets, though tales were mostly printed in full. *NIN&Q* dealt with the local and the particular, with caste and custom; it registered and delighted in oddities. The snippets contributed to the systematic mapping of "castes and tribes" that went into the compendia of colonial power-knowledge, gazetteers, census reports, etc.[69] But, and this is what interests me here, they also record orature in a specific and localized way that is unavailable elsewhere. As Naithani has pointed out, scholars such as Crooke almost completely erased from their books their indispensable collaborators, like Pandit Ram Gharib Chaube.[70] But in *NIN&Q* the signatures of the Indian contributors appear clearly at the end of each note: that of Chaube himself, of Aziz ud-Din Ahmad, Abdur Rahman, M. Mirza Beg, Raj Bahadur, Pandit Kashinath, Jwala Prashad, Khairat Ali, Sawai Singh, Balkrishna Lal, and even our very own Bhanupratap Tiwari from Chunar, who contributed something almost every month between 1891 and 1893.[71] These contributors were probably teachers and clerks, like Bhanupratap, who were encouraged to record forms of orature and ritual practices around them, with a certain degree of colonial self-objectification for sure, but also with curiosity. It is here that one of the few instances of Muslim orature appears, thanks to Bhanupratap.[72] He wrote, "The following song was recited to me by an old dhobi [washerman] at Chunar. It is a curious illustration of the adoption of Muhammadan ideas by low-caste Hindus," the word "curious" marking either his own curiosity or the impact of colonial ideas of caste and religious demarcations.

Pahilé nám lé Alláh Míyán ká
Dújé Nabi Rasúl.
Tíjé nám lé Fátimá ká,
Jéké mukh par barsai núr.[73]

First repeat the name of God,
second of the Prophet.
Take third the name of Fatima,
heavenly light rains on her face.
The name of God is sweet,
sweet is the name of the Prophet;
Sáwan and Bhádhon are sweet,
they rain heavenly light.
On the day Mecca's foundation was laid,
the world knows,
the believers in Muhammad
bent their head in obeisance.
Tigers played the flute,
bears blew the trumpet.
Indra's fairies came to dance,
the Holy Prophet came to watch.
The Prophet came down,
pretending to watch the dance
he placed his foot on the ground.[74]
All believers in Mohammad
stood with their hands joined. (translated by Bhán Pratáp Tiwárí)

While the Indian folklorists encouraged by Crooke paid attention to particularities of local orature and named their informers, this was not true of what became mainstream Hindi folklore. There is no better example of this process than Ramnaresh Tripathi's pioneering folklore collection of village songs, *Grām gīt* (Village songs, 1929). Tripathi (1881–1962) had learned Urdu at his village school before he turned to Hindi, trained in Brajbhasha poetry, studied English in high school and, after a fairly peripatetic life and some nationalist activism, settled down in Allahabad as a Hindi poet, publicist, and publisher. His elegantly printed and bound five-volume poetry anthology *Kavitā kaumudī* (Moonlight, or Guide to poetry, 1929), including volumes on Hindi (Brajbhasha), Urdu, Sanskrit, and Bengali, set a high standard for such anthologies and won great acclaim. One volume pioneered the publication of oral poetry. Between 1919 and 1930 Tripathi had toured all over north India to collect folk songs, and in 1940 he brought out a three-volume anthology of "village literature" (*Grām sāhitya*), again the first of its kind in Hindi.

Grām gīt is organized according to folklore categories of life-cycle rituals and occasions (birth, harvest, spring, etc.) in unspecified "village speech," with translation into standard Hindi. It carries no indication of who the singers were, of the time and site of collection, or of particularities of language, and it has been criticized by later folklorists for the lack of proper protocols of collection and transcription.[75] But this indefiniteness is conducive to the meaning of village orature, according to Tripathi, as his lengthy and rhetorically rich introduction shows. There, Tripathi emphasizes the *distance* between the world of orature and his own, a distance that is physical (rural vs. urban) but also cultural and spiritual. Though he begins by retailing an encounter with a poor village woman, he then rhapsodizes on the village as a frozen site of cultural authenticity, a common trope at the time.[76] Tripathi uses the description or theatrical tableau, or *jhanki* (in Hindi lit. "glimpse"), to present a kind of "village sublime," a chronotope in which classical Sanskrit and Hindi devotional poets eternally live and poetic tropes of clouds and birds are animated, where people live in harmony with nature, and "natural" love leads to healthy family relationships. That village is a "country" that is distant but also accessible: "Is it far away? No, it's so close, closer than any other country can possibly be. We only have to take off the spectacles from our eyes and for once remember our soul" (Tripathi 1929b: 2). The book of village songs therefore promises to translate—in the etymological sense of "carrying over"—the modern reader into this enchanted world.

The introduction begins uncompromisingly with a statement of colonial cultural deracination that precedes the retrieval of the folk:

> Under the influence of an odd kind of education, we have moved very far away from our country. Trapped within the confines of only [a] few words from our language. Neither do we want to move beyond that precinct, nor do those words allow the inner voice (*antarnād*) to enter our boundaries. Though we live in our country we have turned into foreigners. We have strayed from the path that would have definitely taken us to the country of our world-renowned forefathers. Instead, we are walking down a broad and clean avenue and are so captivated by the charming views on both sides that we have forgotten to ask—where is this road leading us? We have thrown away the candle that

> helped us find our way with our own eyes. Now, even though we are walking in the brightest lights we are so bewildered (*chakāchauṃd*) that our eyes cannot see what lies ahead of us. And where are we going, blinded by all these lights? (Tripathi 1929b: 1)[77]

Tripathi collapses physical and historical distance to present the village as the site of cultural authenticity, a "country" where both Sanskrit poets and bhakti poet-saints eternally dwell:

> Where is the country where the souls of Valmiki, Kalidasa and Bhavabhuti dwell?[78]
>
> What is that country like, where Tulsidas speaks in every house? Where is Surdas playing in the guise of a child? Where is Kabir, sharing out the essence of his soul in the form of ambrosial nectar?
>
> Ha!
> *Koī aisī sakhī chatur na milī,*
> *Hameṃ piyā ke ghar lauṃ pahuṃch detī.*
> I have not found a clever girlfriend
> who can take me to my lover's house. . . .
>
> But are we drifting away from those whose life-stream flows, song-like, along the unbroken stream of the Ganges, bright but swift-moving, and the Yamuna's dark but deep waters?
> Amazing!
>
> *"Pās baiṭhe haiṃ magar dūr nazar āte haiṃ"*
> "We sit so close but seem so far away." (Tripathi 1929b: 2)[79]

A description of natural splendor expands into a golden-age description of plenitude, combined with a Gandhian vision of village democracy and social order and abundance.[80] Thus the village for Tripathi is a "country" where every house is surrounded by sandalwood trees and bamboo thickets, and "the shade of mango and *mahuā* trees keeps roadways cool and pleasant." "Where everyone eats in golden plates and drinks from golden glasses. Where every house has a picture gallery (*chitraśālā*), every woman is skilled in painting, and every man has the taste to appreciate the beauty of art." Here "songs spring forth from every mouth," "complex questions of politics are unpicked sentence by sentence in village assemblies," and "every kind of freedom exists, within the bounds of *dharma*." Nature and poetry meet in literalized tropes (clouds call husbands home, and cuckoos carry the message of *virahinis* that "the month of Phagun has come"). Nature (*prakṛiti*) takes an expansive character as the opposite of artificiality and stifling social conventions. So in this village, "young women choose their own spouses, and grooms select their own brides;" marriage "is undertaken not in order to fulfill one's desire but inspired by the wish to give birth to excellent offspring who are going to serve the people;" and the "natural [*akṛtrim*, lit. "nonartificial"] river of a mother's affection, the unbroken waves of a wife's passionate devotion, the watercourse of a sister's unlimited love, and the stream of nature's eternal desire (*śṛṅgāra*) never stop flowing." "Come, let us go to that country," Tripathi (1929b: 3) concludes.

Unlike other contemporaneous representations of the village as a site of poverty and of caste and economic exploitation, like Premchand's stories and novels, here what I call the chronotope of the village sublime stays well away from realism and collapses time and place in order to symbolize authentic Indian culture—distant yet tantalizingly close, timeless, both past and present, and both bhakti-devotional and Sanskrit-classical. Village songs stand for this village as residual of a cultural life force that has become invisible and inaccessible to English-educated Indians but that can be retrieved, in a very Gandhian fashion, by simply removing the alienating spectacles of western education.[81] As already mentioned, what becomes invisible in this remarkable rhetorical tour de force are the real performers, the actual performance contexts, and the ongoing dynamic transformation of performance styles.

In a rural and urban soundscape still saturated with orature and responding to colonial folklore, Hindi folklore was therefore too burdened with ideals of cultural purity and timeless authenticity to accommodate specificities of caste, location, historicity, and popular religion. The "invention" of folk literature as a separate category from literature was in fact characterized by several exclusions: of contemporary orature and performers, and of local Muslims and their folklore, those songs of Dhobis, fakirs, and Madaris or the Muslim festivals and rituals that colonial folklorists did, to a point, record. Contemporary poets and performers in those languages and traditions—Mahendar Misir (1865–1946) and Bhikhari Thakur—real innovators who composed and performed in and for their times and who traveled the world of Bhojpuri coolie laborers or *girmitiyas* across the Indian Ocean, were excluded from the purview of Hindi literature and relegated to folk literature in the regional dialect. This is still the case: Bhikari Thakur and Mahendar Misir may have been belatedly feted and honored as the "emperors of Bhojpuri," but as folk artists, or *lok kalakar*, they still stand outside Hindi literary history. Folklore collections continue to be organized by area and language and to exclude Muslim songs and tales.[82] The first conference dedicated to Urdu folklore was organized only in 1988, the second one in 2017.[83]

The amnesia about orature and the multilingual repertoires and the modern critique of earlier literary traditions that the creation of monolingual ideas of Hindi and Urdu language and literature entailed were not total, though, as the next section argues. In fact, if we shift our attention from programmatic definitions and canonizing genres (like textbooks and literary histories) to other genres that carry traces of current tastes and practices, we find plenty of evidence that familiarity with a broad set of idioms continued even after boundaries of script hardened. This evidence is to be found less in novels and more in other genres which, the next section also argues, were in fact more crucial to political mobilization and the imagining of communities. Satires, songs, and political allegories, in particular, made ample and effective reuse of multilingual resources.

Forget the Novel

So far this chapter has discussed the far-reaching impact of new ideas of language and literature. This section, prompted once again by Doreen Massey, asks: What are the *other* trajectories and stories, tastes and practices that together make up the "(north) Indian response" to colonialism? What do we exclude if we consider only the dominant narratives of literary reform and newness and believe that literary modernity simply *replaced* earlier traditions? Sure, novels did get written and read in this period and deserve attention for the complex literary and social mediations they undertake (see Mukherjee 1985; Dalmia 2017). But an exclusive focus on fiction, or on modernist poetry, occludes how other genres, such as drama, satirical skits, historical poems, songs, and the short story, are crucial for understanding literature as a site of modernity in the "colonial contact zone" (Pratt 2008). Songs in particular played an important role in imagining the nation and in inspiring and mobilizing various kinds of political communities.[84] "National" (*rashtriya*) songbooks that used popular tunes and familiar forms to carry nationalist messages fill the catalogue of publications proscribed by the colonial government. Early Dalit activists also reworked the texts of popular song genres.[85] Here I briefly focus on three examples: Parsi theater plays as archives of multilingual song idioms, political allegories that stylize characters through language, and a humorous story that shows the continuing currency of Brajbhasha and Urdu idioms of love. Echoing Aamir Mufti's (2016: 11) title *Forget English!*, to "forget the novel," then, does not mean that "it has either been or ought to be (or wants to be) forgotten." Rather, it is "to suggest the possibility, or necessity, of thinking past, around, and *about* it" (19).

At the same time as Hindi and Urdu were imagined as two distinct monolingual vernaculars, commercial publishing encouraged the proliferation of heterogeneous, multilingual aesthetics and tastes through short tales, or *qissas*, and theater and song chapbooks, printed in both scripts (see Hansen 1992; Orsini 2009).[86] Commercial publishing enjoyed a particularly symbiotic relationship with commercial theater. And though the most successful theater companies were established in the 1850s in the colonial capitals of Calcutta and Bombay by Parsi entrepreneurs (hence the name Parsi theater), these drew extensively on north Indian personnel, adopted Urdu for dialogues, incorporated Urdu and Hindi song genres already widely in circulation, adding to the repertoire, and regularly toured north Indian towns, eagerly awaited and influencing local song practices (Hansen 2004).[87]

One of the first, and extraordinarily successful, Parsi theater plays was the *Court of Indra* (*Indarsabhā*, 1852–1854), written in Lucknow by the poet 'Amanat (Hansen 2001; Taj 2007). Scholarship on the play has highlighted its debt to Urdu verse narratives (*masnavis*) current in Lucknow, like the *Magic of Speech* (*Siḥr al-bayān*, ca. 1770) by Mir Hasan, and to the music and dance soirées of courtesans and the developing musical opera called *jalsa* or *rahas*, which appears within the play as a mise-en-abîme (Hansen 2001).[88] In fact, the plot motifs in the second half of the play—the love between a human prince and a celestial woman (*pari*) who wake up together in an enchanted garden, her banishment from the king's court and wondering as a *jogan*, a female *jogi*, in search of her beloved—echo those found not just in contemporary Urdu *masnavis* but also earlier, in Hindavi *kathas* (Chapter 2). In the first half of the play, celestial beauties (*paris*) dressed in the colors of different gems, sing before the king, the god Indar (Indra). The spectacle was, by all accounts, dazzling and deeply absorbing.[89] The forty-six songs that the *paris* sing in the play represent the eclectic repertoire of songs courtesans sang—Urdu *ghazals* and *chhands*, Brajbhasha *thumris* and *horis*—but a few innovatively mix images and poetic idioms, such as the Urdu *ghazal* with the very *desi* rhyme *basanti* that plays on the yellow color of spring (*basant*).[90] Though the number of songs in Parsi theater plays gradually declined, this eclectic array, with each song carrying a particular aesthetic and affective range (the riotous merry-making of Holi, the innocent pleasure of swing songs, the teasing and longing of *thumri*, etc.), became very much part of the appeal and success of Parsi theater, replicated in each and every play regardless of topic and genre.

The success of 'Amanat's play on the Parsi stage marks a dispersion of themes, and the very real dispersion of craftsmen, musicians, singers, and dancers from the patronage of courts to the market, but also shows the powerful appeal of older stories and songs within colonial Indian society. Parsi theater's melodrama, scholars have emphasized, and its acting and staging techniques, were all new and very much part of the experience of modernity.[91] The *Indarsabhā* was staged regularly until the 1930s across India, Burma, and the Malay world (Hansen 2001; Braginsky and Suvorova 2008). From the perspective of world literature, the national and international success and impact of Parsi theater between the 1860s and 1930s highlight a different—paracolonial—circulation from that of the novel. The term "paracolonial," which signifies *beside* and *beyond*, is "immensely useful if one wishes simultaneously to acknowledge the effects of colonialism," Stephanie Newell (2011: 350) argues, and "to displace the Eurocentric and deterministic periodization of culture and history in the colonies as being precolonial, colonial and postcolonial." Parsi theater traveled along and *beside* imperial routes, but also *beyond* them, into princely states and regions where Urdu and Hindi were not spoken.[92] The aesthetics it conveyed was all but reformist.

It is useful to pause on the aesthetic and affective power of the visual and verbal exuberance of Parsi plays because we also find that power exploited in literary genres like satirical parodies and allegorical plays, my second example.[93] Harishchandra's political allegory *The Sad State of India* (*Bhārat durdaśā*, 1875), like the play by his contemporary and friend Badri Narayan Chaudhri "Premghan," *India's Fortune* (*Bhārat saubhāgya*, 1889), written for an annual session of the Indian National Congress in Allahabad in 1888, includes an assemblage of songs and spectacle that is similar to that of Parsi musical theater, but here used to cajole, arouse, and enthuse viewers and readers into *feeling* for the nation.[94] Christopher Pinney's (2002: 147) critique of Benedict Anderson's model of nationalism as "a highly cerebral construct invoking flows of discourses in a world stripped of its materiality" is pertinent here. Anderson's genres of choice are, famously, the newspaper and the novel. By contrast, Pinney argues that in the early period of Indian nationalism and "of intimacy between lithography and theater, the nation [was] invoked primarily through allegory" (133).[95] Allegorical plays, images, songs, and poems worked through a "dangerous corporeality," played with regional and caste linguistic registers for characterization, and re-accented the tunes and beats of familiar song and verse forms to embody ideas in characters one could hate or pity. In Harishchandra's *The Sad State of India*, e.g., Madira, or Wine, dressed like a courtesan, sings a *dhamar* song in Brajbhasha urging the audience, "[D]rink wine, you fools, youth wanes fast," while Laziness sings a *ghazal* to argue that striving and effort "are no good" (*nahīṃ acchā* is the rhyme scheme) (Sharma 1989: 466, 464).[96]

The great popularity of these plays and poems supports Pinney's argument that it was genres *other than the novel* that played a significant role in arousing "national feelings" and making the nation not just an idea but an entity that people could relate to and *feel for*. Speeches and discursive appeals to reasoned arguments are indeed part of the allegorical plays, but they come enclosed in a more epic and symbolic struggle between good and evil, friend and foe. Harishcandra's *The Sad State of India* opens with a yogi in a lane singing a *lavani* song with a pathetic text: "Come weep together, India's brothers! Alas, the sad state of India is not fit to be seen!" The song contrasts past glories ("we were the first" to receive wealth and power from God, to become civilized, to enjoy the arts, etc.) and present disarray and sets a tone of urgency ("under English rule we have every means of happiness/but wealth goes abroad, hence our distress") (Sharma 1989: 460). In the second scene, a Learesque India in rags (with only "half a crown") lies prostrate on an ominous cremation ground and continues the lament (Song [*Git*]: "No one grasps my hand, I have millions of sons yet I wander helpless, alas") (461–462).[97] India is taunted by Shamelessness (Nirlajjata), while Hope (Asha) makes a fleeting appearance. In the third scene India's Enemy (Bharat durdaiv), a composite figure "half in Christian and half in Muslim dress," sings and dances a dance of destruction. His commander, aptly named Destruction (Satyanash), comes dancing to attendance and boasts that the famous historical figures who brought destruction in their wake—Hulagu Khan, Chingiz Khan, and Timur—were all his servants; he then introduces other helpers who are working to finish off India, Bharat. In the fourth scene, in an "English-furnished room," the Foe of India calls on several helpers: Illness (Rog), Laziness (Alasya), Wine (Madira), and Darkness (Andhakar), who combine material and symbolic elements in their characters and speeches (468). The fifth scene, apparently more realistic but in fact parodic, is set in a library; it stages a formal meeting (*sabha*) of educated Indians, with a Bengali President (speaking strongly accented Hindi with *sh* sibilants instead of *s* sounds), a pragmatic Maharashtrian Editor, a lackadaisical Poet, and two timid north Indian (*desī*) gentlemen, all discussing how to stop the attack of the Foe of India. Their inconclusive and comical debate is disrupted in the end by Disloyalty (in English), who, dressed like a policeman and speaking with a strong English accent, arrests them all. The sixth scene shifts from the ridiculous to the sublime and pathetic in "the midst of a dense forest." Here India's friend India's Fortune (Bharatbhagya) tries in vain to raise India from its stupor with a song, "Wake Up, Wake Up Brother!" He then goes into a long soliloquy that oscillates between prose and verse and between despair and lament and pride over past glories; in (modern) tragic fashion, India's Fortune ends up killing himself with a dagger (467–471).

Harishchandra's and Premghan's plays may have been in Hindi, but the range of languages and registers they include is much wider. Premghan's *India's Fortune* also features a "foe of India" commanding an allegorical army of generals and soldiers ready to finish off India, and a "friend of India" who has a parallel but weaker set of helpers.[98] Premghan grounds his allegorical characters in familiar social types through linguistic stylization: so in the scene depicting the 1857 uprising (of which he is critical), the man who comes to save the British Memsahib and her children speaks Punjabi (Punjabi regiments on the whole did not revolt), while the rebels speak Bhojpuri, Urdu, and Marathi, the languages spoken in the epicenters of the rebellion.[99] In another scene, the character Commerce is a Marwari (a prominent merchant group) who speaks Rajasthani; Agriculture is an Avadhi-speaking peasant, while Dharma speaks highly Sanskritized Hindi. Even Empress Victoria speaks Hindi in this play.

The final act takes place in London in Parliament, and features Victoria, the Liberal MP and "friend of India" Sir Charles Bradlaugh, the Lord Chancellor, and the Secretary of State for India all speaking and singing in a Hindi heavily accented with retroflex plosives (in bold below) and missing aspirates. "Who is making all this noise?" asks Victoria, "It's the whole people of India," Bradlaugh answers. The Secretary of State chants a petition from the Indian people that reminds the empress of her promises in the 1858 Proclamation and asks for representation. She gladly consents, saying that Indians are her subjects just as the people in England (*Kaun-sī bāṭ aisī hai ismẽ, uzr ḍene se hamko ho jismẽ. Jis ṭarah hamārī riyāyā yah sārī, haīn is ṭaur ye bhī hamārī*). All the Parties in Parliament—Liberal, Conservative, Radical, the Speaker, Prime Minister Gladstone, and the Lord Bishop—join her in an "English *ghazal*" in English-accented Urdu, acclaiming, "[L]ong live the famous justice of Great Britain!" (Premghan 1949: 377, 378).

While the play stages a successful loyalism—so that, after depicting the excesses of British rule in India, getting the ear of the empress in London is enough to reverse them—accent introduces an undercurrent of humor and mockery that undercuts the seriousness of the plea and the dignity of the monarch. Whereas in other cases accent, like dress, simply identifies and locates a character (the Avadhi peasant, the Marwari trader, the Bhojpuri rebel), the British characters' English-Hindi accent and code-mixing risk sliding into mockery, and they acquire a comical tinge even when the scene is pathetic, as when the starving English children besieged during the Rebellion plead with their mother, "Well! *āmko makkan roṭī do.*" "Well, *giv mī e kap āv ṭī.*" "Well mamma! *E kaisā shor gul? Oh! kyo oṭā!*" (*Well,* give us bread and butter. *Well, give me a cup of tea. Well mamma,* what uproar is this? Oh, what is it?) The mother replies, *Av kors! koī ḍūsrā bachānevālā ikmaṭ nahīn! Sab industānī log ḍushman o gayā* (*Of course!* There is no one to save us. All Indian people is become enemy) (Premghan 1949: 330).

Even more than in Harishchandra's play, in Premghan's *India's Fortune* the songs evoke the noisy soundscape of the period, the teeming processions, gatherings or *jalsas*, English band music, devotional singing, public speechifying, dramatic soliloquy, group singing, and more. Premghan includes *kajli, holi, chaiti, khemta, dhamar, thumri,* and *ghazal* songs, and even riffs off the famous Persian *ghazal* by Hafiz, *Tāza ba tāza, nau ba nau* (Afresh and anew), a song much appreciated and copied by British music lovers in India, for a "*ghazal* in English rhythm" sung by the invading army: *hind pe jo chale haiṃ ham, tāzā ba tāzā nau ba nau. zulm kareṅge o sitam* [chorus:] *tāzā ba tāza nau ba nau* (We've come to attack India, *afresh and anew*. We'll wreak oppression and destruction [chorus:] *afresh and anew*) (Premghan 1949: 326). Premghan even uses a *kajli* song to list all the names of attending Congress delegates:

> Good days for India have come! It's time for the National Congress! (*refrain*)
> Mr Hume and Dada Bhai Naoroji are there,
> And people like Shri Raghunath Rao, Badruddin Tayyabji.
> Both Babu Umeshchander, Iyyer Subrahmanyam,
> Together with Raghav Vir, Narindar, Kashinath Tilang.
> Who planted the new seed of this country?
> The wise Raja Rampal, and Rahmatullah.
> Chairman Mandler, Humayun Jah, Norton rinsed it,
> Dr Rajinder Bar, Surendra Babu watered it. (Premghan 1949: 366)

Such multilingual play was also at work in the satirical parodies and self-parodies in mixed Hindi (or Urdu) and English that featured abundantly in Urdu and Hindi newspapers in the colonial "contact zone," of which perhaps the most famous are the poems of Akbar Ilahabadi (1846–1921).[100] In a similar poem, Harishchandra ventriloquizes a sycophantic anglicized Indian (a "complete" or Poora gentleman) who boastfully introduces himself to an Englishman while remarking on his humiliation at the hands of the Sahab's peons:

> I introduce myself to you Sir I am
> Poora Gentleman
> Take my salam, give me chair
> Honour me much if you can
> I get a chair in Lat Sahab Darbar, my
> Number is ninety-two.
> Some time they give me gardaniyā
> And tell bāhar niklo tum
> Denā na lenā muft ke āye yah haiṇ
> Baṛe darbari kī dum.
> I w'nt say any suchchee bateṇ let the
> India be barbād
> I don't believe in Hindu idols, but I
> Worship only to show
> Neither my sālā sab zāt wāla zāt se
> Bāhar kare ham ko.[101]

As Vasudha Dalmia (1997: 290) points out, the "split in language is thus also a split in the person, for the man is nothing less than two-faced." In satirical skits like "All Castes Belong to God" (*Sabai jāti gopāl kī*, 1873), instead, Harishchandra uses mock-Sanskrit to satirize Brahman pandits happy to grant certificates of high caste status to anyone in exchange for a fee.[102] In fact, they can prove that even Muslims (*miyan*) belong to the four castes, using not only Sanskrit verses (*shlokas*) but even an *Allahopaṇiṣad* singing their praises to show it (Sharma 1989: 542)!

"Brajbhasha went from being a living language to a historical relic in the 1920s," Allison Busch (2011: 239) concludes at the end of her magisterial book about courtly poetry in Brajbhasha. And indeed, if one heeds the virulent condemnations of eminent critics like Mahavir Prasad Dvivedi or Ramchandra Shukla, one cannot but agree. But the impact of their views can also be overestimated. Not only did influential Hindi magazines continue to carry columns with Brajbhasha and Urdu verse, but Brajbhasha songs and Urdu *ghazals* remained a staple of theatrical plays and substantial anthologies appeared in book form in response to a perceived demand.[103] Indeed, political mobilization *needed* songs, and public poetry meetings (*musha'iras*) magnified the popularity of Urdu poetry. In the early twentieth century *musha'iras* changed from being courtly or private recitations showcasing one's latest compositions before patrons and peers, to being large public-facing events that accompanied school and civic functions as well as large political gatherings. *Musha'iras* attracted considerable audiences, were reported and advertised in local newspapers, and turned some poets, like Hasrat Mohani, into heroes. As Ali Khan Mahmudabad (2020) shows, *musha'iras* made space both for poets composing in traditional genres and for those experimenting with new forms like free-verse *nazms*; as in the case of allegories, both old and new kinds of poetry could catalyze political emotions. According to contemporary accounts, the audiences of *musha'iras* were mixed and included both literate connoisseurs and semi-literate poetry lovers, who acquired poetic tastes through oral exposure and memorization.

We also find ample traces of the continued currency of Brajbhasha and Urdu poetry as idioms of love in early twentieth-century fiction. Let me conclude this section with one example from Pande Bechan Sharma "Ugra's" (1907–1967) highly popular and controversial short-story collection about same-sex relations, *Chocolate* ([1928] 1953). In the story "Kept Boy" (*Pālaṭ*), a group of high school boys in an unspecified north Indian city have fun together, go to the cinema to watch a Charlie Chaplin film, party, and banter and flirt openly with other boys. Though the story is written in a Sanskritized register of Hindi, it is peppered with Urdu couplets and Brajbhasha verse that the boys quote to each other. In fact, the story opens with a couplet:

'ishq kyā-kyā hamen dikhātā hai
āh! tum bhī yak nazar dekho

> Love, what wonders it shows us,
> ah! take but one look. (109)

Taking advantage of gender-indeterminacy in Urdu verse, the object of love is not specified. When one of the group of friends takes a liking to a boy glimpsed at the cinema, Urdu verse is what he immediately resorts to:

> Why do you ask me how I feel?
> Do you ever find me well?

And he elaborates:

> I too am devoted to the lock falling on someone's cheek,
> I too am prey to time, to the passing days and nights.

Another Urdu verse is needed to praise the boy's languid eyes:

> It is from those semi-open eyes
> That the bud has learnt to open, slowly.[104]

No, another friend comments, approving his taste; a Brajbhasha verse by the seventeenth-century poet Biharilal is more appropriate:

> I have never seen eyes so enchanting,
> God! Those are like the eyes of a doe.[105]

And so it goes on. While ostensibly the story and its diegetic narrator strongly condemn same-sex love, the pleasure in the exchange of verses is unmistakable, as is their broad currency.[106] These are not complex verses that require poetic knowledge beyond familiarity with the most common metaphors, unlike those in Chapter 4. But they testify to the continuing familiarity with, and enjoyment of, Urdu love poetry at a time when, supposedly, both Hindi and Urdu literature had rejected it and "moved on." Of course, once again we should not confuse plurality of tastes with pluralism. In a later celebrated novel by Muslim author Rahi Masoom Raza (*Ṭopī Shuklā*, 1969), the protagonist Topi recalls his grandmother, a Brahman woman who loved Persian poetry but hated Muslims, as an example of the paradox between social and political views and aesthetic tastes that was one of the legacies of this multilingual literary culture.

It is important to balance arguments about the hegemony of English and the separate canonization of Hindi and Urdu literature with an eye to other trends that preserved and encouraged familiarity with the "other" language. If the new ideas of literature called for a rejection of old tastes as decadent and harmful, the result was not in fact a wholesale casting-off but more often a coexistence of contradictory tastes, a new multilingualism, and a new hybridity. This realization, in turn, forces us to reconsider literary modernity as not simply the dispersion of new genres from the imperial metropoles to the colonial peripheries in a kind of centrifugal modernization, a process of colonial impact and local response. My last argument in this chapter is about the use of English, already in the colonial period, as a medium to provincialize English literature and go *beyond* it. If the curriculum remained resolutely anglocentric, magazines by the early twentieth century promoted a literary (re)orientation to the world beyond English, using English as the medium of reading and translation.

Beyond (and through) English

Whereas the school and university curriculum encouraged an English- and British-centric literary vision, Hindi and Urdu writers soon discovered through English translation other European, particularly French, Russian, and Scandinavian, writers (see Orsini 2019b). Especially with regard to the short story, the most popular genre in Hindi and Urdu print culture in the early twentieth century, the most often quoted foreign authors were Maupassant and Tolstoy. As the foremost Hindi-Urdu fiction writer of the 1920s and 1930s, Premchand (1880–1936), put it this way:

> Stories (*galpa*) are popular in all European languages, but in my view no other European language has stories of as high quality as French and Russian. In English Dickens, Wells, Hardy, Kipling, Charlotte Young, the Brontës have all written stories but they do not equal those of Guy de Maupassant or Pierre Loty. . . . In Russia, the best stories are those by Count Tolstoy. Several are based on old exemplary tales. Chekhov has written many stories and is very popular in Europe, but his stories are unexceptional, only life sketches of decadent Russian society.[107]

Premchand himself translated (via English) Anatole France's *Thaïs*, G. E. Lessing's *Nathan der Weise,* and a volume of Tolstoy's stories (see Lunn 2013). Even in the case of the novel, Hindi writers and readers looked more toward Bengal, and it was Bengali novelists like Bankimchandra Chatterjee and Saratchandra Chatterjee who provided blueprints for Hindi novelists, in a case of lateral rather than vertical literary transfer (see McGregor 1972). In other words, to consider Hindi and Urdu literature as "stably subordinated" to imperial Europe because of "colonial impact" would be a gross and disingenuous simplification.

The opening to the literary world beyond English and beyond the British Empire was partly the result of the search for more consonant political and cultural examples of modernization, like Turkey or Japan, and partly an attempt to set Indian literature alongside the great civilizations of the world. So Urdu writer Sajjad Hyder took up a Turkish nom de plume (Yildirim, i.e., Lightning) and transcreated Turkish novellas and plays of the reformist Tanzimat period, thinking that Turkey could provide Indian Muslims with a blueprint of a modernizing "Eastern" country (see Husain 1992).[108] And Urdu poet Miraji translated widely, via English, particularly from Southeast and East Asian poetry, so as to provide Urdu readers and poets with fresh models (see Orsini 2020a).

By contrast, the first book in Hindi on world literature, *Vishva-sāhitya* (World literature, 1924), originally a series of articles written in the journal *Sarasvatī* by its editor Padumlal Punnalal Bakhshi, stitched together material from heterogeneous sources to construe a narrative of world civilizations—Greece/Europe, China, Japan, and India—and literary values. Chapters on "the foundation and development of literature," poetry, drama, science, "literature and dharma," and "world language" used world literature to reflect on the basic qualities of literature. The critical discussion of Asian literatures may appear rather "thin," but this does not detract from the valiant attempt at presenting a coherent narrative of the literary world beyond English, deprovincializing Hindi readers and provincializing English (see Bakhshi 1924; Orsini 2019b).

Shifting the Lens

Let us return to the question of "colonial impact and Indian response." This underpins a model of world literature that is predicated on the "diffusion" of modern European literature (particularly the novel), on the supposed unification of the world literary system, and on the "stable subordination" of colonial literatures like those of India as peripheries to the imperial centers. In this view, the "vast and heterogeneous range of practices of writing" (Mufti 2016: 11) of the world were assimilated into the universal category of literature. While these critical statements seek to make legible the impact of colonialism and empire, they in fact obscure the complex set of processes, continuities, and discontinuities that we saw taking place. They are also not objective statements but stem from a distinct location, a distant view that privileges English over Indian languages and familiar genres over others it cannot recognize. If, as I have done in this chapter, we shift the lens to a local and multilingual perspective, the picture changes dramatically. As in the *Quarterly Statements of Publications*, the new titles and genres that became landmarks of literary modernity, like Shridhar Pathak's poems on the natural beauty of Kashmir in modern Hindi instead of Brajbhasha, appear drowned in the sea of songbooks, tales, theater chapbooks, and other genres that instead reflect the multilingual and oral-literate literary culture of the time but never made it into literary histories. English is hardly visible.

That colonialism had a profound impact on north Indian society and literature at the structural and epistemic level—from education to notions of literature—is beyond doubt. But what I have wanted to question in this chapter is the kind of "postcolonial common sense" that presents the narrative as an *Anglophone* one of "colonial impact and anticolonial resistance." It is again a question of locatedness, temporality, space, and (lack of) multilingualism. Let us take one influential recent study of colonial and postcolonial literature as an example. "I shall begin by drawing limits," Elleke Boehmer (2005: 1) writes, entirely reasonably. "This study is chiefly concerned with literature written in English, which even if to only an extent narrows the field."[109] But what effects does this conception of the colonial and postcolonial literature of the British Empire as happening entirely within English, though across different colonies and the metropole, have for her narrative? For one thing, starting the narrative only in the second half of the nineteenth century cuts out early Orientalism, which left such a considerable mark on European thought and literature, arguably transforming it (see Schwab 1984; Mufti 2016). It also looks for evidence of colonial response in Anglophone writing alone—whereas we have seen that one fundamental feature of colonial impact in India is that the transformations, debates, and responses took place overwhelmingly in Indian languages, and that apart from the radical pioneers and bilingual intellectuals in Calcutta, even those who studied and read in English overwhelmingly wrote in Hindi, Urdu, Marathi, Tamil, etc. By focusing only on Anglophone writing, the temporal framework of "impact and response" gets skewed, so that the "response" seems to occur only in the early twentieth century, with "The Stirrings of New Nationalism" (see Boehmer 2005; Chapter 3). If, by contrast, we think of English as coming into an already multilingual, layered, and dynamic literary field, our view of colonial/imperial English as fundamentally reshaping Indian languages and literature in its own image and turning India into a literary (semi-)periphery of Europe necessarily shifts. This of course does not mean that we should *not* consider English, but we need to consider it within this multilingual context and as itself comprising multiple trajectories and stories, some of them paracolonial.

In this chapter, I have traced the unmistakable impact of new ideas of language, literature, and community on the multilingual literary culture east of Delhi, in the region known as Purab and later Awadh. In particular, I have noted how competing discourses about language, and the impact on literary historiography of ideas of indigeneity vs. foreignness, and of natural and people-oriented vs. artificial and decadent poetry, led to the writing of quasi-monolingual literary histories that made invisible and irrelevant not only the "other" traditions but also contemporary orature and Muslim folklore. In the categories of literary history there was no longer space for the parallel cultivation of Persian and Brajbhasha poetry (Chapter 4) or for the coexistence of Hindi and Urdu poetic tastes that continued to be a reality for so many. The capacious repertoire of *kathas*—which partly overlapped with that of Persianate narratives (verse *masnavis* and prose *dastans* and *qissas*) and which saw tropes and stories traveling between the two and between Hindavi and Persian (Chapter 2)—was now split between "Indian" and "foreign" and slotted under different headings: Sufi, bhakti, and courtly, each implying different motivations and audiences. Nor was there space in Hindi or Urdu literary histories for *kathas* as a contemporary form, though these were still being written in Awadh, in Avadhi in Persian script, in the twentieth century. Bhakti poetry became central to the story of Hindi literature, but that of the Sants, apart from a few, was not considered "poetic enough," and most local Sants remained "three-line poets" (Chapter 3).

Redirecting attention to continuities as well as innovations shows the resilience of aesthetics and tastes even after literary and social reformers pronounce them irrelevant, decadent, or dangerous—as the case of the still-popular *ghazal* exemplifies so well. It also shows how new genres *other* than the novel, like musical theater, exploited aesthetic eclecticism and were arguably more significant to the consolidation and spread of nationalist and other ideologies.

As to the "assimilation" of either the old or new multilingual and vernacular literary repertoires into world literature, I opened this book by showing how little of that assimilation took place. Orientalist scholarship typically privileged ancient Sanskrit literature, which in compendia and histories of world literature written in European languages came to represent Indian literature as a whole, as if no literature had been composed since.[110] Whereas Sanskrit posts multiplied in European universities over the nineteenth century, only Paris had, from 1827, a professor of modern Indian languages, Garcin de Tassy (see Chapter 1).[111] Indologists like Fredric Pincott, Duncan Forbes, and Grierson knew modern Indian languages well and were acquainted with contemporary Indian writers and literary associations; they were thus ideally placed to act as "intermediaries" and introduce modern literary writing to European readers. But their attitude to modern writers was predominantly paternalistic and their language remained one of "improvement" and progress, not of aesthetic-literary appreciation. Almost without exception they preferred medieval devotional poetry or martial epics.

As a result, although the number of professional and amateur Orientalists with proficiency in one or more Indian languages was probably higher in nineteenth-century Europe than it is now, and although bibliomigrancy did occur and many books in modern Indian languages and in translation reached Europe thanks to enterprising book importers, too many "technologies of recognition" (Shih

2004) stopped these books from being read "as literature" (Damrosch 2003).[112] First was the "denial of coevalness," that "persistent and systematic tendency to place the referent(s) . . . in a Time other than the present of the producer of [here, literary] discourse" (Fabian 1983: 31). The qualifiers "Eastern" and "Oriental" (as in "Oriental novel" or "Eastern Poetry") seem to have automatically turned even contemporary works into "not modern" or "not-yet-modern." Second, modern Hindi and Urdu texts were treated as material for language pedagogy, which made them somehow unworthy to be treated as "literature." Modern Hindi and Urdu texts were indeed published and translated in Britain and in India, but they were not read "as literature." Third, European and American philologists authoritatively decried Hindi literature as a recent invention, too recent to have produced anything worthwhile yet. Fourth, implied in discussions of the "development" and "modernity" in Indian literature was the assumption that they could only come from following European models (under "British tutelage"). Fifth, even when modern Indian texts, genres, and authors were discussed, they were mentioned as a group or in passing, denied the recognition of making singular contributions. Last but not least, Indian was usually very explicitly defined as Hindu, hampering the recognition of modern Urdu literature in the eyes of most modern Indologists. Thus was modern Indian literature made invisible.

Conclusions

Thinking through Space

In this book I have tried to reassemble the "multiple stories and trajectories" (Massey [2005] 2012) of literature in a multilingual society. I have deliberately turned away from the exclusive protocols of the (patchy) early modern archives and the monolingual and communitarian thrust of modern literary histories, which tell these stories as if they had little or nothing to do with each other and as if people lived in monolingual silos.

In order to reassemble these stories and tell a different, multilingual history, of overlaps and entanglements as well as distinction and disregard, my first step has been to think heuristically through space, with Doreen Massey as a guide.[1] But rather than mapping people's regional consciousness in relation to Awadh or Purab ("the East"), or Awadh's position in relation to the political center, I have used cartography to find out which authors and texts in different languages were geographically close to each other and could have therefore had access to the same, if not written, at least oral texts. This approach worked particularly well in the case of Krishna devotionalism, which failed to register in Hindi literary history but comes into view, almost magically, as a literary phenomenon thanks to traces in *Persian* texts (see Orsini 2015b). It also works well in the case of individual towns, as with Khwaja Karak and Malukdas in Kara in Chapter 3: "reading them together" has meant that the dialogism inherent in several of Malukdas's utterances appears more starkly and his choices of poetic register make better sense, since he addresses audiences who would also hear Sufi discourses, or indirectly addresses Sufis by re-accenting their words. At the same time, the stray mentions in Khwaja Karak's biography that he listened to itinerant singers of Hindavi songs bring this otherwise "Persian" author into the vernacular world. Throughout the book I have not emphasized Purab or Awadh as markers of regional or linguistic identity but rather viewed it as a site for multilingual people, spaces, and practices.[2]

Exploring what I call the "multilingual local" also makes us conscious of the silences and erasures, and forces us to look elsewhere for the other texts, authors, and stories that dominant narratives leave out. This is the case of Bilgram in Ghulam 'Ali Azad Bilgrami's *tazkira*, which is eloquent about the cultivation of Brajbhasha poetry among local Persograph elites but silent about nonelite

East of Delhi. Francesca Orsini, Oxford University Press. © Oxford University Press 2023.
DOI: 10.1093/oso/9780197658291.003.0006

Muslim and Hindu poets of Persian and Brajbhasha in the *qasba*—not to speak of the practice of devotional singing or *katha* recitation that also probably took place there. Exploring "multilingual locals" is therefore an exercise in continuously looking for other traces and sources across language archives, always conscious that what one gets are partial accounts. Space in this sense is a good example of what working with *one* language or tradition within a multilingual environment means: one can of course work with texts in just one language, but one must remain aware that there are other languages and stories/texts around them.

Space has also been useful for thinking how literature works in a multilingual (and of course stratified and hierarchical) society in terms of the concrete spaces of literary practices—the sites and occasions of performance, training, devotional singing, and poetic cultivation, with their different communities of taste. The evidence is limited but not completely absent. In the case of the *kathas*, there are many traces of performance contexts and audiences within the texts themselves, while the material and scriptural evidence of manuscripts gives us clues about their social circulation and use (see also Orsini 2015d).[3] Qutban's *Mirigāvatī* may have started out as a sophisticated tale for the Sharqi court in exile from Jaunpur, but available copies show that it was probably local chieftains, Sufis, and merchants who read it and had it copied (Chapter 2). Conversely, considering the spaces of practices like song writing and listening reveal parallels between sites that have been kept separate, like Lucknow and Banaras in the eighteenth and nineteenth centuries (Chapter 4).

Spaces of performance and recitation are particularly important for two reasons. First, many of the texts from the early modern period—and for theater, songs, and tales in the modern period—were meant to be read aloud, recited, or performed.[4] Individual verses found their written place in poetry collections, manuals, or notebooks after they were recited or heard, part of a culture of poetic sociability and currency of exchange (Chapter 4). Second, thinking of the performance context and aural dimension of written texts helps us think beyond the apparently insurmountable boundaries of script and literacy. While script indicates who the text was copied *for* (so that copies of the same text in multiple scripts indicate that it circulated among different social groups), when performed or recited orally the same text could and did reach, and could be overheard by, other audiences, too. Here I have found it useful to distinguish between *access* and *familiarity* produced by repeated exposure—say, to preachers or reciters of the Puranas, as was probably the case for the Sufi *katha* authors (Chapter 2)—and *cultivation*, which involved learning the finer points of prosody. *Aural* cultivation—being "well-listened," or *bahushrut*, to use Purushottam Agrawal's term—could be a prerogative of illiterate people, too, as Chaturi's example in Chapter 3 shows. And people literate in only one language or script, like Malukdas and other Sants, could draw on their aural exposure to poetic idioms in languages of which they had probably only a partial grasp: their nuggets of Persianate Sufi idioms and verses in "spoken Persian" do not conform to the rules of Persian prosody, a sign that they had not studied Persian (given that its protocols were so strict). Conversely, if, when we think of all those who studied and composed in Persian in northern India, we bear in mind that they must have also spoken and understood the vernacular, the result is that they come out of their Persian silos and become part of the "multilingual local." Again, an imaginative effort is required to undo the boundaries of early modern archives that have kept apart, for example, even Sufi Persian and Hindavi authors. Even minute textual traces and occasional references help, as when we read that the Sufis mentioned in Persian *tazkiras* listened to, and occasionally composed, vernacular verses. Stacked together, these traces and references become ordinary practices that were left unremarked.

Once we bring together the multiple stories of Persian, Hindavi, and Brajbhasha textualities and the dialogism between them, what, from a distant gaze, appears as an inconsequential and provincial region before the formation of the Nawabi state in the eighteenth century is teeming with people and texts. "It is true that big imperial states often tend to be happy habitats for arts, including literature," Pankaj Jha (2019: 239) notes in his recent book on the fifteenth-century multilingual polymath Vidyapati, who lived and worked in a small village in north Bihar and was attached to a very local court, though he was heir to a long and proud lineage of Sanskrit scholars. "But it is also frequently, and erroneously, assumed that the arts are so dependent on their imperial patrons that they rarely survive without them," Jha adds. Yet even "a cursory survey of the cultural and intellectual milieu of the fifteenth century" proves otherwise. "One might as well turn the presumption on its head, and ask whether large trans-local empires find fertile ground only in pre-existing fields of well-tended 'knowledge formations'" (239).

Courts and rulers tend to grab the attention, perhaps none more so than the Mughals, where cultural trends of a period are read off the emperor's individual tastes and preferences. But (and this is a simple but important insight for world literature, too) literature does survive and even thrive outside the imperial and metropolitan centers, as long as there are communities of taste, practices of cultivation, and incentives to transmit cultural capital to the next generation. And poetic, narrative, and performance styles have the power to attract audiences again and again, whether in the centers or the peripheries.

Space has worked in this book as a way to bring together literary strands that have inhabited their own disciplinary silos: Sufi, bhakti courtly Brajbhasha, and Persian. In Hindi literary histories, bhakti and courtly (*riti*) poetry were even set up as separate and successive ages, only to oblige scholars to continuously point out exceptions.[5] For this purpose, texts and individuals have been my lenses. Sometimes several strands appear together in a single text—think of Jayasi's Hindavi narrative of Krishna, the *Kanhāvat* (Chapter 2)—or in a single individual, like Ghulam Nabi "Raslin" (Chapter 4) or Bharatendu Harishchandra (Chapter 5). For individuals, we need to move away from "birth determinism" and to think of their range of tastes as a portfolio, part of their embodied *habitus* but also linked to the fashions of the time and to individual preferences. So while literary histories constructed linguistic and communitarian narratives of Persian, Hindi, and Urdu as if the languages had always been there with airtight corpora (Chapter 5), I have preferred throughout not to use languages as historical actors but rather to think of what people did *with* them. This has allowed me to tell the literary history of Purab as composed of several strands and communities of taste, for sure, but also to note that many people routinely and unproblematically partook of several tastes, as the example of Bhanupratap Tiwari shows so well: with some people he practiced devotional poetry in *satsang*, with others he discussed Persian.

This nonessentialist view of language and community also helps us to observe (dispassionately) shifts in linguistic and literary fashions. Whereas Urdu literary scholars invested in constructing a continuous and monolingual literary history may be perturbed by the absence of any Urdu textual production in northern India before the eighteenth century, we can distinguish ordinary language use from literary/poetic use and admit that we just don't know enough about the former.[6] We can then note that Urdu poetry was first practiced in Awadh only in the early eighteenth century, though it soon became so fashionable and popular as to become *the* main story and eclipse all the others.

At the same time, we have also seen that when new fashions changed people's tastes—as that for Brajbhasha courtly poetry and the *kabitta*, or for Rekhta/Urdu poetry—often the older strands and tastes did not disappear but became more circumscribed; they survived rather than thrived. This is the case of *kathas* in the eighteenth and nineteenth centuries: manuscripts continued to be copied, and new *kathas* even continued to be composed. But the new *kathas* were inconsequential, while some of the older stories were refashioned in the new trendy genres: *Padmāvat* was rewritten as an Urdu *masnavi*, and several Urdu *Rāmāyans* were written by and for the growing community of Persian-educated Hindus (see Phillips 2010).

Doing multilingual literary history is also an exercise in relativizing the meaning of literature and systems of value. While Persian and Brajbhasha poetry came with their own systems of poetics and understandings of what made a "good poem,"[7] this was not the case for Sant poetry.[8] Yet this doesn't mean that we have to agree with *kavya*-centric views that considered the poetry of Kabir or Malukdas unpoetic. As a matter of fact, attending to the reasons why early Hindi critics did not consider Sant poetry "poetic" helps identify and relativize their own system of values. "Making space for Sant orature" (Chapter 3) means, first of all, to acknowledge that devotional practices and instructional genres can be aesthetically powerful and appealing, too. Again, this seems like an obvious point to make—we can think of the long tradition of religious songs and sermons in Europe, or of sermonizing and poetry in praise of the Prophet in the Islamic world—but too often limited notions of literature tend to push genres and forms outside its purview and deem them non- or less poetic.[9] Or, as in the case of Tulsidas in Hindi, devotional poets are said to "rise above" the mere devotional thanks to their individual artistry. Instead, devotional songs and tales and other genres of verbal art deserve attention not only in their own right, for their particular registers of language and imagery and their rhetorical strategies, but because they constitute the main literary experience for a much wider section of society than the sophisticated poetics of the highly educated. As once again Tiwari's autobiography shows, they were often the first kind of poetry that one learned by heart.

"Making space for Sant orature," as I suggested in Chapter 3, has relevance for world literature, too, which has been slow in recognizing the importance and extent of orature as an important and often widely traveled and long-lasting form of literary production and experience. But if the main obstacles to this recognition have been the emphasis on "bibliomigrancy" (Mani 2016), i.e., the circulation of literature in *book* form, and the idea that world literature is only that which is recognized "as literature" (Damrosch 2003), acknowledging Sant orature as literature yields two useful dividends. First, as already mentioned, it asks us to pluralize the understandings of "literature" rather than simply exclude what does not conform to or is not recognized as literature *by some*. Second, while circulation in world literature is usually predicated on the technologies of print and the written word, orature shows that other technologies allowed it to circulate, often very widely. Sant poetry shows that these technologies have included performance and chapbook publishing, and the same is true of other oral traditions, such as Bhojpuri songs and ballads and theater chapbooks. In many cases, it was the same publishers who printed books and chapbooks, like the Naval Kishore Press. Others, such as the Belvedere Press or the publishers of Bhojpuri chapbooks in Calcutta and Banaras or of Nautanki plays in Hathras, specialized in chapbooks alone.[10] These chapbooks followed pathways of circulation different from those of books and often reached different, and much wider, audiences.

One abiding interest in this project has been "literary contact." Did literary genres and repertoires in different languages that were present in the same space, and/or in the same person, relate to and transform each other, and if so how? In Chapter 2, I explored this question through the lens of a single genre—the *katha*—and "followed" it across time and languages as a way of understanding the dynamics of circulation in a multilingual literary culture. The focus on genre showed how a new, and sophisticated, vernacular Hindavi genre was created out of the combination of an oral story—possibly already told as an oral epic—and literary elements from three traditions: Persian romances, the song of the twelve months, and earlier poetics. Why *linguistically* the genre should carry no trace of Persian becomes an interesting historical question, a matter of choice rather than a natural state of affairs. I then noted how the authors of these Sufi romances, or *pemkathas,* delighted in intertextual allusions, particularly to the epics and the Puranas, and combined multiple levels of signification to narrate both tales of love and Sufi quests, in the process making epic and Puranic elements part of the Sufi repertoire of figurative discourses. One consequence of this was that, despite individual differences and preferences (e.g., between Usman's *Chitrāvalī* and Puhakar's *Rasaratan*), Indian and Persianate figures and motifs became aligned (celestial beauties as *apsaras* and *paris*, demons as *rakshasas* and *divs*) and created a shared pool and narrative grammar. Translations—or rather rewritings—in Persian showed authors either staying close to the Hindavi grammar of the genre or recasting the stories according to more generic codes of Persian *masnavis*. Interestingly, each text makes particular choices and has to navigate how much "Indian" detail to introduce. The Urdu *masnavis* and *dastans* that became so popular in the eighteenth and nineteenth centuries partly drew on this shared pool of motifs, but also strikingly innovated language and descriptions, and it was they, rather than *kathas*, that influenced early theater.

As for poetic idioms, Chapters 3 and 4 show that Sants and "local cosmopolitans" followed quite different strategies. Sant poets mixed poetic idioms because, I suggested (but I may be wrong!), they needed to speak to a diverse public and show their versatility. Conversely, for "local cosmopolitans" who studied and cultivated Persian and Brajbhasha poetics in the *qasbas*, it was important to show their mastery of each individual code. Otherwise we would have expected much more mixing from them, too. More mixing starts to appear in the nineteenth century, particularly in the context of theater—as we saw with the "spring ghazal" of Amanat's *Indarsabhā*, but also elsewhere.

Whereas circulation in world literature is predicated on translation (and spatial movement), the case of Awadh shows considerable circulation of poetic and narrative idioms, yet *not* through translation. Generations of students learned Persian through Sa'di's *Gulistān* and read Rumi and Hafiz, but translations into Hindi and Urdu appeared only in the nineteenth century. Translations could and did happen, but only under specific circumstances.[11] Again, traces—as in the margins of Bhanupratap's autobiography—show that translation "on the hoof" was possibly more common.[12] This suggests that, in a multilingual literary culture, translation is *not* the main medium of circulation but rather familiarity through performance or aural access or through reading in the original language.

This has consequences for our understanding of cosmopolitan and vernacular languages, too. In Sheldon Pollock's (1998a: 393) scheme, cosmopolitan and vernacular are "modes of literary (and intellectual, and political) communication directed toward two different audiences. . . . The one is unbounded and potentially infinite in extension; the other is practically finite and bounded by other finite audiences." But what happens if the audiences are bilingual and understand both? As Jha has shown, Vidyapati "chose" a particular genre and language for each text: Sanskrit for a letter-writing manual, a manual of ethics, and religious and ritual texts; Maithili for songs in the regional vernacular; and an intermediate language called Avahatta for a historical narrative. Pollock suggested that the political imaginaries and sociotextual and political communities of a cosmopolitan or vernacular language text will be different (universalistic and imperial vs. regional and bound). But when author, patron, and audience are largely multilingual, the question becomes, "[W]hat else in the social and political world is being chosen when a language-for-literature *and a genre-for-literature* is chosen?" (Jha 2019: 20). In other words, what does the choice of a particular language and genre among a range of possibilities say about the political and sociotextual community that is being addressed, but also about the cultural and political imaginary that it conveys? This is a question that needs to be asked every time we examine texts within a multilingual culture.

Moreover, we expect that, within a multilingual literary culture, one language will influence the other, and this mutual influence will be a primary engine of innovation.[13] To an extent this is the case—Brajbhasha courtly poetry and poetics were heavily influenced by Sanskrit models, and the Urdu *ghazal* drew on Persian precedents. Yet in many cases there is no smoking gun. We see startling innovation that carries strong echoes of another tradition, but there is no evidence of a connection (Behl 2007).[14] In fact, as we have seen, early modern archives can be stubbornly silent about other people and trends around them. Yet even to highlight these echoes, to look for the presence behind the absence, can yield results, as the case of Krishna bhakti in Awadh shows.

Finally, if one of the problems of recent world literature has been the rush to theorize its subject and purview through a limited number of keywords (center-periphery, circulation, recognition, translation), expanding the range of conceptual tools and critical approaches should be high on the agenda so as to make the field more robust and capacious.[15] If too much literature is *not* "world literature," what kind of world literature do we end up with? Whose world literature, and for whom? Whereas most (all?) the works theorizing world literature so far have been transnational, this book has suggested that a located and "ground-up" approach also speaks to world literature. Location and a spatial—though not just cartographic—approach; consciously looking for "other stories;" familiarity and access vs. cultivation; mixing vs. parallel cultivation; aurality, overhearing, and being "well-listened;" circulation without translation; transcodification; "language-genre choices" for authors and audiences versed in both cosmopolitan and vernacular language traditions at the same time—these are some of key terms that I have proposed and used in this book. With them I have tried to ask new questions about the location and circulation of texts, bring back together languages and literary traditions, and understand how multilingual authors and audiences work.

Notes

Chapter 1

1. All translations in the book are mine unless otherwise indicated.
2. As Aamir Mufti (2016) has argued.
3. These obstacles are what Shu-Mei Shih (2004) has called the "technologies of recognition" that empower western critics and institutions to set the standards and make critical judgments about non-western literatures.
4. Pace Venkat Mani's (2016) notion of "bibliomigrancy."
5. See below for a discussion of languages and language names.
6. There is a large scholarship on the topic, among it Breckenridge and Van dee Veer (1993), Dirks (2001), and Pennington (2005).
7. The use of the term "Hindū mind" for a Muslim poet may be read in various ways: Grierson may have been using Hindu as a synonym for "Indian" ("the Indian mind"), as was fairly common at the time. Or he did not accept Jayasi's Muslimness as the basis of his writing. Or thought that Jayasi had transcended his Muslim self to write a Hindu romance.
8. For "birth determinism," see P. Agrawal (2009).
9. For Pavie (1865: 6) and other Orientalists, the event was historical, but "indigenous writers deviate a lot from the truth." Yet he had decided to translate it "since the imagination of poets is always in harmony with the traditions of the country and the spirit of the people, of which they are brilliant interpreters; and since the medieval poetry of India is still too little known" (6).
10. More recently, controversy embroiled Sanjay Leela Bhansali's film *Padmaavat* in 2017 because even suggesting that Padmavati could have been seen and touched by the Muslim Sultan Ala'uddin was offensive to some Rajput organizations, while others objected to the film's stereotyping of Ala'uddin as a bloodthirsty and lustful Muslim ruler.
11. I thank Philip Lutgendorf for the last suggestion.
12. Malik Muhammad Jayasi, *Padmāvat*, with glosses by Shaikh Muhammad Shakir, MS Hindi 6, Rampur Raza Library.
13. For scalar literary ecologies, see Beecroft (2015).
14. "One-world thinking" is Mufti's (2016) formulation; see also Krishnan (2007) for a broader critique.
15. For a brilliant critique of the implicit hierarchy between local and global, see Gibson-Graham (2002). As Shih (2004) argues, the least we can do as scholars is not endorse the biases of the global publishing market but expose them.

16. In this respect, a located approach to world literature is aligned with Gayatri Spivak's (2003: 6) call for "nonexhaustive taxonomies" and "provisional system making."
17. For genre as encoding particular views of the world, see Conte (1994). Recently, Simon Leese (2019) has offered the concept of "poetic terrains" to describe how Indian literati versed in Persian, Arabic, Urdu, and Hindi (Brajbhasha) poetry and poetics conceived of them as separate terrains whose boundaries could be crossed only in limited ways; in Chapter 4, I examine the choice of learned poets to cultivate Persian and Brabhasha poetry in parallel.
18. "In much of classical ghazal poetry," she also notes, "references to the world have far more metaphysical rather than geographic connotation. The world is imagined in terms of the hierarchical planes of heaven and earth rather than the spherical and multicolored globe" (Burney 2019: 157).
19. There may be "*ghazal* moments" in a *masnavi*, particularly in what Suvorova (2000) calls "ballad-like"*masnavis*, but the overall logic of each genre is different. As Chapter 2 shows, verse and prose narratives (*masnavis* and *dastans*) are quite able to incorporate Indian figures, *realia*, and places from *kathas*.
20. This is why, despite its elite bias, Mir Ghulam 'Ali Azad Bilgrami's *tazkira The Free Cypress* or *the Cypress of Azad* (*Sarw-i Āzād*, 1752) is so unique in that it includes Bilgram poets who composed in Hindi (Brajbhasha), too (Chapter 4). As Pellò (2012) shows, it was largely *tazkiras* compiled by *Hindu* Persian literati that include Hindu poets of Persian, of whom there were many by the eighteenth century.
21. For aural access, see Orsini and Schofield (2015).
22. As Pankaj Jha (2019) has shown, the fifteenth-century polymath Vidyapati wrote an innovative epistolary manual and a collection of edifying stories in Sanskrit that betray awareness, if not influence, of Persian equivalents, though Vidyapati nowhere mentions them.
23. Kabir's popularly accepted dates are ca. 1398–1518, making for an improbably long life span; after considering historical evidence, David Lorenzen (1991: 14–18) concludes that Kabir was likely born around the mid-1400s and died close to the commonly accepted date of 1518; Tulsidas's dates are ca. 1530–1623.
24. "Literary capital is both what everyone seeks to acquire and what is universally recognized as the necessary and sufficient condition of taking part in literary competition. This fact makes it possible to measure literary practices against *a standard that is universally recognized as legitimate*" (Casanova [1999] 2004: 17, emphasis added). But is it?
25. Eminent linguist G. A. Grierson (1904: vol. 6, 9) considered Avadhi (also called Purbi) a dialect of Eastern Hindi: "The word 'Awadhi' means literally the language of Awadh or Oudh, and the area over which the dialect bearing this name is spoken agrees, to some extent, with the meaning of the term. Avadhī is spoken throughout Oudh, except in the District of Hardoi, in which Kanauji is the local language, and in the eastern corner of the District of Fyzabad, in which Western Bhojpuri is current. North of the Ganges, it is also spoken in the western portion of the District of Jaunpur, in the private domains of His Highness the Maharaja of Benares, which occupy a portion of the North-Gangetic area of Mirzapur, and in North-Gangetic Allahabad. It has

also crossed the Ganges, and is the language of South-Gangetic Allahabad, and of the whole of the District of Fatehpur except the country bordering on the Jamna River, in which a mixture of Bagheli and Bundeli is spoken." In modern geographic-political terms, the area corresponds to eastern Uttar Pradesh; further west, the Gangetic plain continues toward Delhi in western Uttar Pradesh, while the more sparsely cultivated and populated Madhya Pradesh (earlier Malwa) lies to the south.

26. According to the great record of the Mughal Empire, Abu'l Fazl's (1598) *Ā'īn-i Akbarī*, the *subah* of Awadh comprised the *sarkars*, or divisions, of Awadh (Ayodhya), Gorakhpur, Bahraich, Khairabad, and Lucknow; the *subah* of Allahabad those of Allahabad, Ghazipur, Banaras, Jaunpur, Manikpur, Chunar, Battha Gathora, Kalinjar, Korah and Kara (Habib 1986: vi).
27. See the pathbreaking scholarship of Madhuri Desai (2017), reversing decades of insistence on temple destruction in the city.
28. Persian local histories typically recount the towns' pre-Islamic names as they tell stories of conquest and settlement. The definition of Amethi by a colonial judge, Mr. Capper, can serve as a general description of an Awadh qasba: "A Musalman settlement in a defensible military position, generally on the site of an ancient Hindu headquarters, town or fort, where, for mutual protection, the Musalmans who had overruled seized the proprietary [*sic*?] of the surrounding villages resided; where the faujdar [military commander] and his troops, the pargana qanungo [district record keeper] and chaudhri [headman], the mufti, qazi, and other high dignitaries lived; and, as must be the case where the wealth and power of the Moslem sect was collected in one spot, a large settlement of Sayyad's mosques, dargahs [Sufi hospices], etc. sprang up. As a rule, there was little land attached, and that was chiefly planted with fruit groves, and held free of rent, whilst each man really had a free hold of the yard of his home and the land occupied by his servants and followers" (quoted in Rahman 2015: 30).
29. By comparison, Gujarat in western India acquired a strong regional identity earlier (see Sheikh 2010).
30. According to the classic distinction between high and low languages (diglossia), high languages are markers of high culture and vehicles of higher forms of knowledge, formally taught and historically the preserve of specialist individuals and groups, while low languages are used in informal, primarily spoken domains. Modern regional monikers for local vernaculars like Avadhi, Khari Boli, or Bundeli did not appear until late Mughal and early colonial philology (see Dalmia 1997).
31. For a wide-ranging collection of essays on Persian in Indian and other multilingual contexts, see Green (2019).
32. See, e.g., the brothers Chintamani, Bhushan, and Matiram in Busch (2011: 103); see also Puhakar (Chapter 2), and Bhanupratap Tiwari (Chapter 4) in this volume. Sheldon Pollock's work and his research project *Sanskrit Knowledge Systems on the Eve of Colonialism* have successfully drawn attention to the extensive and rich Sanskrit text production in the second millennium CE; Truschke (2016) documents the active patronage of Sanskrit at the imperial court, but we still lack a study of "the ordinary life" of Sanskrit in north Indian towns and villages. Kapadia (2018) suggests

that even very small chieftains and polities would hire Sanskrit poets to produce eulogistic texts when they wanted to claim a loftier pedigree.

33. Its popularity as a language and poetics needed to appreciate north Indian (Hindustani) music and songs is testified by the inclusion of descriptions of Brajbhasha in Persian musical and encyclopaedic treatises, e.g., *Tuḥfat al-Hind* (*Gift from India*, 1675; see Ziauddin 1935; Keshavmurti 2013).
34. Few of Tulsidas's works come dated: his song collections *Kṛṣṇa Gītāvalī* (ca. 1590), *Gītāvalī* and *Vinaya Patrikā*, the poems in *Kavitāvalī*, and many of the verses in the *Dohāvalī* are in Brajbhasha; his *Rāmcharitmānas* (1574), *Rāmalālanahchhū*, and *Jānakī*- and *Pārvatī-maṅgala* (1586) are in Avadhi; see McGregor (1984: 114–157).
35. For example, Dittmer (1972), King (1994), Dalmia (1997), Rai (2001), Orsini (2002), Lunn (2013).
36. "Orature" is a term coined by Ugandan linguist and literary theorist Pio Zirimu and taken up by Ngũgĩ wa Thiong'o (2007) that overturns the usual hierarchy between written and oral by claiming that written literature is only a small part of the wider world of the spoken world.
37. For *sahaskritī*, see Shackle (1978b).
38. This contrasts with the large translation projects undertaken by kings like Alfonso the Learned of Castille in the thirteenth century (Gallego 2003); Sultan Zain al-Abidin of Kashmir in the fifteenth century (Digby 2007); the Mughal emperor Akbar in the sixteenth (Truschke 2016); or his great-grandson Dara Shukoh (Gandhi 2020).
39. A brilliant discussion on the dangers of overinterpretation and underinterpretation when it comes to the Persianate register in Brajbhasha poetry is Busch (2010b).
40. See also Johns (2002) and Mallette (2005) for Sicily.
41. "[*C*]*osmopolitan* and *vernacular* can be taken as modes of literary (and intellectual, and political) communication directed toward two different audiences, whom lay actors know full well to be different. The one is unbounded and potentially infinite in extension; the other is practically finite and bounded by other finite audiences, with whom, through the very dynamic of vernacularization, relations of ever-increasing incommunication come into being. We can think of this most readily as a distinction in communicative capacity and concerns between a language that travels far and one that travels little" (Pollock 2000: 593–594; see also Pollock 1998a, 1998b, 2006). Pollock spatializes cosmopolitan and vernacular (though in abstract terms): the former is potentially universal while the latter travels little. And he links them to polities and the agency of rulers and their courts, so that empires and polities with wide ambitions choose cosmopolitan languages, while vernaculars mark the emergence of regional, more bounded polities.
42. For the "provincialization" of Persian in the fifteenth century, see Pellò (2014b).
43. In Europe, Old French spread in the Île de France, Normandy, Lorraine, Burgundy, Anjou, and of course England (Paden 2006: 151).
44. For an individual, it was education in a high language that provided access to the ideal Persian, Arabic, Sanskrit, and Hindi republics of letters necessary to become a cosmopolitan *adib*, *kavi*, or pandit, whether or not one traveled (see Chapter 4); travel, authorship, lofty patronage, and/or position increased one's position. Early modern

cities (Delhi, Agra, and Lahore) and the Mughal traveling camp-capitals were cosmopolitan sites in that they attracted and valued traders and scholars from other parts of the world.

45. Moretti (2013) forecloses the problem of "reading more literatures" by advocating "distant reading," which neatly bypasses issues of genre definition, standpoint, and the coexisting of old and new tastes. Instead, two simple "laws" of diffusion and convergence can explain the "evolution" of world literature (Moretti 2006).
46. As Conrad (2016: 133, 134, 140) puts it, "different units direct our attention to different processes"; "the forces that made each space cannot be found entirely within the unit itself;" and "the global is not a distinct sphere, exterior to national/local cases: it is rather a scale that can be referenced even when we look at individual lives and small spaces."
47. For the *qasida*, see Sperl and Shackle (1996); for the *ghazal,* Bauer and Neuwirth (2005) and Neuwirth et al. (2006); for *Punch,* Harder and Mittler (2013); for the novel, Moretti's multivolume history (2001, 2006b), which contrasts with his more streamlined and Eurocentric "laws" (2000 and 2003).
48. For an early reflection on scale in relation to world literature, see Tanoukhi (2011).
49. This has been done for modernism, with much fruitful reflection on questions of chronology; see, e.g., Stanford Friedman (2015) and Wollager and Eatough (2012).
50. It is telling that medievalists take a multilingual and layered approach that is much more similar to mine here (e.g., Mallette 2005); see also the brilliant Valdés and Kadir (2004).
51. See Moretti (2006a) and Casanova ([1999] 2004); see also Masuzawa (2005) for a similar problematic with regard to world religions.
52. "The global, I contend," writes Ganguly (2016: 21), "is an empirical category in the Saidian sense; it is the domain of territorial and empirical expansion. The novelistic world can be conceptually distinguished from the globe by a phenomenological apprehension of the work of the human in making worlds through language and through an orientation critically attuned to the *surplus* of humanness."
53. In fact, I have avoided discussing authors and topics that are already excellently served by scholarship, like Kabir (Vaudeville 1974; P. Agrawal 2009) and Tulsidas (Lutgendorf 1991), Urdu and Persian literary culture in Nawabi Lucknow (Sharar 1989; Vanita 2012; Pellò 2012), or the literary culture of Banaras (Dalmia 1997).
54. For the "intermediality" of poetic, artistic, and musical connoisseurship, see Schofield, Aitken, and Busch (2014).

Chapter 2

1. See Williams (forthcoming) for a history of Hindi literature that focuses on technologies of writing.
2. Scholars, often anthropologists, who have documented performances of narratives, note that performers, particularly of oral epics, select episodes and that no single

performance covers the whole story; e.g., Lutgendorf (1991), Smith (1990, 2005), A. Gold (1992).

3. This chapter draws substantially on Orsini (2017).
4. In fact, the same narrative could be called *qissa* or *dastan* and follow a *masnavi* meter. Shorter stories or tales, like those in Sa'di's *Gulistān*, would instead be called *hikayat*.
5. Examples include the Andalusian *muwashshah* and the Provençal and Sicilian lyric (Menocal 1987; Mallette 2005); the fortune of Petrus Alphonsi's collection of stories and anecdotes *Disciplina Clericalis* (Leone 2010); Ibn Tufayl's *Hayy ibn Yaqzan* (Aravamudan 2014); and the Italian *romanzo cavalleresco* and Elia Levita's 1507–1508 Yiddish *Bovo-bukh* (Baumgarten and Frakes 2005).
6. On "following" as a method, see Conrad (2016: 121); Chapter 1.
7. To recap from Chapter 1: the scripts used in Purab were Persian, Nagari or Devanagari, and Kaithi, a largely regional cursive script used by scribal groups (the name comes from Kayastha, the professional scribal caste) when they did not use Persian. Kaithi manuscripts are often unadorned and roughly copied and indicate nonelite circulation, though there are exceptions (see Ill. 2.4). Because we are so used to associating vernacular texts written in Persian script with Urdu, which is Khari Boli rather than Avadhi, Hindavi texts in Persian script, which never contain diacritical marks, are now extremely difficult to read. The same was clearly not the case for earlier readers, who did not need diacritics.
8. As Ramanujan (1991: 46) famously put it, "[N]o one in India ever reads the *Ramayana* or the *Mahabharata* for the first time": "[T]he cultural area in which *Ramayanas* are endemic has a pool of signifiers that include plots, characters, geography, incidents, and relationships. . . . These various texts not only relate to prior texts directly, to borrow or refute, but they relate to each other through this common code or common pool. Every author . . . dips into it and brings out a unique crystallization, a new text with a unique texture and a fresh context. . . . [N]o telling is original, no telling is a mere retelling—and the story has no closure, although it may be enclosed in a text."
9. The Puranas are voluminous Sanskrit compendia of stories of cosmogonies, gods and demons, human dynasties, caste histories, etc. For entextualization, see Barber (2007). For the oral epics of Lorik and Chanda, see Flueckinger (1989) and Pandey (1982a, 1985, and 1995).
10. "Knowledge of 'Lorik dances,'" notes McGregor (2003: 915n3), was "documented in Mithila c. 1325 in Jyotirishvar's *Varṇaratnākara*," a manual for poets. Apabhramsha (*apabhraṃśa*, lit. "corrupt") is an umbrella term used by Indian grammarians for late Middle-Aryan languages between the sixth and thirteenth centuries; Jain authors continued to write works in Apabhramsha till the sixteenth century (see de Clercq 2014).
11. The text partly follows the *Varṇaratnākara* in its description of the city and of the castes and professions of its inhabitants. By comparison, oral versions are much more concise: "Gaura is a fort with twelve villages (*pālī*), many cowherds (*ahīr*) live there" (Pandey 1982a: text, 5).
12. These are among the most attractive and original illustrated pages in the John Rylands Library copy (stanzas 143–152).

13. *Chandāyan* 25.1 (Da'ud 2018: I, 129 for caste names, I, 237 for the names of flowers). The list of trees includes *nāriyara, gobā, dāriyo dākha, nāriga, khariga, kāṭahara, tāra, jāmani, khajūri, bara, pīparā, ambilī* (I, 123).
14. Narrative-wise, *Chandāyan* focuses on only one part ("Chanda's elopement," *canvā kā uṛhār*) of the oral epic, which narrates many more battles and exploits of Lorik and segues into the adventures of his son Bhorik; see Pandey (2018: I, 80).
15. See, e.g., in the oral *Lorikāyan* the caste slurs with which a low-caste Chamar, Bantha, teases Chanda. Bantha shares the same guru with Lorik but later becomes his enemy (Pandey 1985: 55).
16. When news of Chanda's birth spread, envoys turn up from as far away as Dwarasamudra in the South, Malwa and Gujarat in central and western India, Tirhut in the Northeast, Ayodhya, Badayun, and Ujjaini: "the four worlds" (*chahuṃ bhuvana*) (Da'ud 2018: I, 137).
17. As Aditya Behl notes, the presence of this coded language should not lead us to consider the *Chandāyan,* or indeed other Sufi romances, as mere allegories.
18. See Behl (2012a), particularly chapter 3, "Creating a New Genre: The *Chandāyan,*" for an illuminating discussion; also Pandey's many articles and books on the subject.
19. As Behl (2012a: 77) notes, the Persian titles given (probably later) to these stanzas call Chanda's bodily attributes *sifat*, which evoke the attributes and names of God, divided into wrathful (*jalālī)* and gentle (*jamālī*). Chanda's attributes equally shift between destructive and restorative. The description runs from stanza 58 to 85, though the illustrator of the *Chandāyan* manuscript in the John Rylands Library gave up after a few folios.
20. The best historical overview of north India in this century is Digby (2004).
21. In fact, as Simon Digby (1967) noted, *Chandāyan* mentions paintings on the wall of Chanda's bedroom, which the John Rylands Library manuscript partly reproduces (see Figure 2.1). This can be part of the cultural aspirations that the *katha* expresses.
22. For example, *sirijanahārū* instead of *<u>kh</u>āliq* for the creator.
23. I expand on this point in Orsini (2018).
24. *Bhuvāṅgū, bhujāṅgū* in another reading: the snake makes sense in relation to poison (*hara*), but seems to become a black bee that "flies away."
25. *Ḥijāb* can refer either to "the veil of sin" (*ḥijāb-e ẓulmānī*) or to the "luminous veil" (*ḥijāb-e nūrānī*), virtuous actions which also keep one away from God; the words in bold are in red ink in the manuscript. The text, edited by M. Ehteshamuddin, has since been published by the Institute of Persian Research, Aligarh Muslim University.
26. Bilgrami's *Haqā'iq-i Hindī* instructed disciples on how to listen to Hindavi songs on female beauty, the seasons, and even Krishna and the milkmaids, in an esoteric way to draw out completely different sets of meanings; clearly such recoding could apply to a romance in much the same way; see Behl (2012a: 225–226); Orsini (2014b).
27. Two centuries later, the Mughal historian 'Abd al-Qadir Badayuni mentions *Chandāyan* and notes the great fame of this "very graphic work" in Awadh; a famous shaikh, Taqi ud-Din Rabbani, who conducted sermons in Delhi, "used to read some occasional poems of his from the pulpit, and the people used to be strangely influenced by hearing them, and when certain learned men of the time asked the

Shaiḵh saying, what is the reason for this Hindi Maṣnavī being selected? He answered, the whole of it is divine truth and pleasing in subject, worthy of the ecstatic contemplation of devout lovers, and conformable to the interpretation of some of the Āyats of the Qur'ān, and the sweet singers of Hindūstān. Moreover by its public recitation human hearts are taken captive" (translated by G. Ranking, cited in Behl 2012a: 314). A local genealogy and much later Sufi sources identify Da'ud as the father of Taqi ud-Din Rabbani and of another famous local Sufi, Shaikh Ahmad 'Abd al-Haqq; see Pandey (2018: I, 18).

28. The first group (Berlin and Lahore-Chandigarh mss.) belong to the Jaunpur-Bihar region, and the second to Central India, i.e., Malwa, Ahmadnagar, or Khandesh; see Brac de la Perrière (2008: 335); Adamjee (2011: 172–173).
29. Hasan Sijzi's Persian *masnavi 'Ishqnāma* (Tale of love, 1301) and Amir Khusrau's *Duval Rānī va Khiẓr Khān* (1314) were also set in contemporary India but were cross-religious romances; see Bednar (2014), Prakash (2019), and Gould and Tahmasebian (2021).
30. Both Adamjee and Brac de la Perrière note that other groups also commissioned illustrated manuscripts in north India in this period, notably Jains, but not in the vernacular.
31. See his son's Ruknuddin's *Laṭā'if-i quddūṣī* (Quddus's stories), quoted in Behl (2012a: 62), with translation of the only surviving stanza; see also Shahbaz (2020).
32. For example, Vishnudas's versions of the *Mahābhārata* and the *Rāmāyaṇa* in Tomar Gwalior; Damo's (1459) *Lakṣmansen-padmāvatī kathā*, about a different Padmavati; Bhima Kavi's (1493) *Ḍaṅgvai kathā*, mentioned above; and *Satyavatī kathā* (1501), which follows the trials of the virtuous wife Satyavati; for the last two, see Orsini (2015d).
33. *Padmāvat* 17.3 (Jayasi [1956] 1998: 16); *Kanhāvat* 5.1 (Jayasi 1981: 135).
34. The titles echo the names of their protagonists: Mirigavati (Doe-eyed), Padmavati, Madhumalati (Jasmine), and Kanha (i.e., Krishna).
35. For example, the tension between chieftain and sultan over one's woman, the motif of the seven-colored mare, performance scenes at court, and the grand battles.
36. Thanks to the work of Shyam Manohar Pandey, Thomas de Bruijn, Aditya Behl, Ramya Sreenivasan, Shantanu Phukan for Hindavi, Thibaut d'Hubert and Ayesha Irani for Bengali, and Christopher Shackle and Jeevan S. Deol for Punjabi.
37. And when Prince Rajkunwar, wandering as a yogi, saves a local princess from a demon: "The people of the town ran to see him.

> He has killed **Rāvaṇa** and saved **Sītā**!
> This is the **Rāma** who had killed **Vālin**.
> This is the **Kānha** who vanquished **Kāliya**.
> Here is the **Rāma** who had killed **Rāvaṇa**,
> here the **Kānhā** [= Krishna] who destroyed **Kaṃsa**.
> This is the **Bhīma** whose hands slayed **Kīcaka**,
> who smashed the arms of **Duḥśāsana**!
> This is the **man-lion** who slew **Hiraṇyakaśipu**,
> Blessed be the mother who gave birth to him!" (translated in Behl 2012b: 93)

38. For Jayasi's pervasive intertextual references to the *Rāmāyaṇa,* see de Bruijn (2010); for the gods Shiva and Parvati assisting Ram and Sita at their wedding, see Sakata (2013).

39. "I'll tell you about my great town, ever-beautiful Jais.
In *satyayuga* it was a holy place called the 'Town of Gardens.'
Then *treta* went, and when *dvāpara* came there was a great *rishi* [seer] called Bhunjaraja.
88,000 *rishis* lived here then, among dense . . . [?] and eighty-four ponds.
Bricks were baked to build solid *ghāṭs* and eighty-four wells were dug.
Here and there handsome forts were founded like stars in the night sky,
And many orchards, with temples on top.
There they sat doing penance, those human *avatāras*
Who went through this world performing sacrifices, repeating mantras night and day.
Then *kaliyuga* came and the ascetics left this world to disappear.
Once again the place became a bamboo thicket, a forest called Jaykarana.
It was in this condition when *it was resettled by Turks.*
They are good lords worthy of praise
who enjoy the taste of flowers and betel-nut and the nine kinds of offerings.
Rich and poor men live in tall houses
and the scent of incense and sandalwood,
of *meru, kumkum* and *kastūrī* wafts through.
When you see this beautiful town scented with flowers,
the closer you get you feel you're climbing mount Kailasa." (*Kanhāvat,* Jayasi 1981: 136–137, emphasis added)

40. In a similar vein, Padmavati tells the wise parrot Hiramani that she will not give herself up to Ratansen so easily:
She said: "Listen parrot to what I say.
He's so besotted, I could meet him today if I wanted to.
But he doesn't know my love's secret core (*maramu*),
only one who dies and finds union knows about love.
I think he's still immature,
he has not been dyed in the fast colour of love. . . .
Has he turned black, scorched like a bumblebee?
Has he burned on a flame like a moth (*pataṅgu*)?
Has he mastered the ichneumon's art?
Is he alive or dead?
Has his love dissolved and become one [with its object]?
Has fear left his heart?
The only instant worth its name is that spent for one's beloved." (*Padmāvat,* v. 231, Jayasi [1956] 1998: 221)

41. When Shiva, moved by Ratansen's entreaties, agrees to help him climb into Padmavati's father's palace, he uses words that apply equally to the fortified palace and to the yogi's body (*Padmāvat,* stanza 215, Jayasi [1956] 1998: 205–207).

42. Apart form Behl (2012a) and de Bruijn (2012), see also Shackle (1992).
43. "With crystal earrings (*mundrā*) in his ears, a thread (*selī*) on his head, a *rudrākṣa* rosary (*jāpa*) around his neck, a discus (*chakaru*), a yoga-belt (*jogauṭā*), a bag (*kothī*), a patchwork cloth (*kanthā*), wooden sandals on his feet (*pāvarī*), [he became] a follower of Gorakh. With ash (*vibhūti*) on his face [and] a meditation crutch (*adhārī*) held in his hand, he made his seat by sitting on a hide (*chālā*). [Carrying] a staff (*ḍaṇḍā*) [and] a bowl (*khappar*), he blows a horn (*sīṅgī*); singing lovesongs he torments himself. Then he plays the ascetic's viol (*kiṅgarī*) and conjures up an image of Chandā's face in his mind" (*Chandāyan*, v. 164, translated in Mallinson 2022: 71).
44. For example, when Krishna in Jayasi's *Kanhāvat* turns into a yogi for a fortnight; Lorik in the *Chandāyan* (v. 165.1, Da'ud 2018: I, 255) does one year of "service" (*sevā*) in a yogi establishment, but we learn nothing more about it.
45. When her father wants him to marry her and take over half his kingdom, Rajkunwar declines, saying that, as a yogi, he wants neither pleasures nor kingoms; but he can resume his quest for Mirigavati only after marrying Rupmini (and leaving her behind).
46. This becomes an opportunity for imparting a lesson: the yogi Ratansen is water and the raja is fire, and water quells fire. If the raja kills the yogi, his supporters will wage war and a huge *Mahabharata*-like conflagration will follow (*Padmāvat*, vv. 263–264, Jayasi [1956] 1998: 250–252).
47. Heidi Pauwels (2012b, 2013) has expressed doubts about attributing this text to Jayasi, given that its single manuscript dates it to the same year as the *Padmāvat* (1540). But to me the emphasis on Jais as well as similarities in phrasing and plotting support the case for Jayasi's authorship. Pauwels also interprets the *Kanhāvat* as a Sufi satire on Krishna. While recognizing the undeniable humor—rather than satire—in parts of the narrative (a feature of many episodes of Krishna's life and indeed of his personality), I rather argue that Jayasi reworks the Krishna story so as to speak to different audiences at multiple levels.
48. For differently accented utterances of "Neither Turk nor Hindu," see Orsini (2018).
49. "Exoteric knowledge, external guise" (*pragaṭa bidyā, pragaṭa bhesū*) is what Krishna calls outward religion (*Kanhāvat*, v. 346.2, Jayasi 1981: 316).
50. The term would be *tadbhava* (with the "same meaning" but different form), i.e., where the spelling of a Sanskrit word follows its historically evolved form; conversely, in the more Sanskrit-infused milieu of eastern Bengal/Arakan, the romance writer Alaol also employed a homogeneous language but in a higher register, using Sanskrit-derived words in their original, or *tatsama* ("same"), orthography.
51. An exception is the description of the Sultan's cavalry marching on Chittor in *Padmāvat*, which abounds in military terms of Persian and Turkic origin (*sirtāj, tabala, bāne, mīr, bahādur, jangī, kamānaine tīr, jebā, lejim*, etc.)
52. For example, old manuscripts of *Padmāvat, Mirigāvatī*, and *Madhumālatī* were held by the same individual in Ekadla village of Fatehpur district in Uttar Pradesh, alongside Isardas's *Satyavatī kathā* and Alam's *Mādhavānal Kāmakandalā*; see Misra's introduction to Alam (1982). Manuscripts were held in Sufi hospices or copied for individuals in north Indian towns like Gorakhpur, Amroha, Mirzapur, Ekadla,

Ghazipur, and later Banaras, without break, up to the late nineteenth century. See Table 2.2, compiled from Sreenivasan (2007); Das (1903); Plukker (1981).

53. A few manuscripts in versions in the Nagari script are also extant, e.g., a *Chandāyan* ms. copied in 1673 Vi. (CE 1616) in Joginipur, i.e., Delhi, from a Persian copy; see Pandey (2018: 108).
54. See Khosla (2015) for the illustrations.
55. An early Kaithi copy of *Madhumālatī*, though undated, indicates that this tale was copied in a non-Sufi setting and outside the Sharqi courtly milieu barely forty years after its composition, a striking evidence of parallel circulation (Plukker 1981: xxii).
56. For a historical discussion of this *Ragamala*, see Miner (2015).
57. For the Bengali versions, see d'Hubert 2018.
58. Jayasi, *Padmāvat*, MS Hindi 6, Rampur Raza Library, Rampur. I am indebted to Thibaut d'Hubert for this suggestion.
59. See Truschke (2016) on Sanskrit; Busch (2010a, 2011) on Brajbhasha poetry at the Mughal court. Agrawal (1950) wrote an early book in Hindi on Brajbhasha poets at Emperor Akbar's court, but it is fair to say that it was considered to somewhat exaggerate the case.
60. The wonderful verse autobiography by the Jain merchant and religious reformer Banarsidas (1586–1643) narrates his many business trips between Jaunpur, where he was born, Banaras, and the Mughal capital Agra (Banarsidas 1981).
61. These include Usman's (1613) *Chitrāvalī*, Puhakar's (1618) *Rasaratan*, Shaikh Nabi's *Gyāndīpak*, as well as Hamid Kalanauri's Persian *'Iṣmatnāma*, Bazmi's *Rat padam*, and *Rājkunwar*; see Tables 2.2 and 2.4.
62. Table 2.2 shows *katha* authors in this period come from a variety of social backgrounds, signaling the broad popularity of the genre: beyond the four discussed here, we find local Sants like Dharnidas and Dukhharandas, and urban literati like Surdas of Lucknow.
63. *Eka sahasa ūpara paintīsā, sana rasūla soṃ turakana dīsā. Agni [= 5] sindhu [= 7] rasa [= 6] indu [= 1] pramānā, so vikrama samvat ṭhaharānā* (*Rasaratan, Ādi khaṇḍa*, v. 28, Puhakar 1963: 42).
64. Alam does not praise either Akbar or Todarmal for their *guna*, which is surprising. The second half of the story revolves around the celebrated King Vikrama's (initially misguided) help in bringing together the two lovers, and Alam compares Todarmal to Vikrama's minister. I thank Richard Williams and the other members of the London-Oxford Brajbhasha reading group for the collective reading and translation; see also Orsini (2015d).
65. Alam includes a whole list of musical modes or *Rāgamālā* that is almost identical to Qutban's; see Myner (2015) for a comparison.
66. That Alam's *katha* was popular is testified by the large number of manuscripts, in a longer and a shorter version; its editor lists eighteen manuscripts in the Nagari Pracharini Sabha Search Reports alone (R. Misra's introduction to Alam 1982: 7). For a Persian version, *Maḥż-i 'ijāz* (The wonder of creation) by Haqiri Kashani, see Ahuja (1965) and Keshavmurti (2013).

67. The ideal caste order and heterogeneous society appear in the same line: *hindu turaka sarāhauṃ kahā, cārihu barana nagara bhari rahā* (How can I praise Hindus and Muslims [Turks], the city is full of the four *varṇas*) (*Chitrāvalī*, 26.1, Usman 1981: 7). While Brahmans are predictably intent on reciting the Vedas and performing sacrifices and ablutions, Kshatriyas (*khatrī*) and Vaishyas "are all rich" (7).
68. Usman's father, Shaikh Husain, was famous (*jaga nāūṃ*); among his brothers, his eldest, Shaikh Aziz, is well educated, an ocean of good conduct and very generous; Manullah took the path of God (*vidhi*), practices yoga, and keeps a vow of silence; Shaikh Faizullah is a great Pir who *ganai na kāhu gahe hathiyārā* (either "does not respect anyone who takes arms" or "does not consider anyone when he takes up arms"); Shaikh Hasan sings well and is acknowledged as versed in music theory by the connoisseurs (*Chitrāvalī*, 27.5, Usman 1981: 7).
69. *Nija so mathanī eka dina, mathata mathata gā phūṭi. tatvamasī puni tatva soṃ, jāya naraka saba chūṭi* (*Chitrāvalī*, 23 *doha*, Usman 1981: 6). He also uses the keyword *prema rasa*.
70. See Ricci (2019) for the multiple connotations of Ceylon, and Bocchetti (2022) for a detailed study of *Chitrāvalī* and its geographical imagination.
71. Digby (2004: 348) reads Balandip as "valandij," i.e. "holanders" or Dutch.
72. If the Bhumiganv Puhakar (1963: 13) mentions is present-day Bhogaon in Mainpuri district, not far from Kannauj, this makes him belong more to western than eastern U.P. Puhakar does not set his hometown within the framework of the four ages, or *yugas*, but rather speaks of a "secret/hidden pilgrimage place" (*tīratha gupta*, 12) established after a wandering king from the west was healed at a local pond.
73. While the patrons of the five extant copies cannot be identified, their names suggest the urban and rural milieus of landords and merchants who cultivated Brajbhasha in Awadh well into the early twentieth century (Singh 1963: 30–33).
74. Puhakar (1963: 19) writes that he first heard the story as an oral tale and then thought of meters to bind it together (*tihi para chhanda vanda hama gunī*). The editor, Shivprasad Singh (1963: 128–134), points out that some of the meter names he gives are new names for older Sanskrit meters. Apart from *savaiyas* and *chhappais*, two of the main forms of Brajbhasha courtly poetry, Puhakar uses *dohas* and *chaupais* not together in the typical stanzaic form but as separate units, sometmes in long lists. For Hindi meters, see Nagasaki (2012).
75. The last two lines are unclear: the penultimate one may be a reference to the name Jahangir gave Nur Jahan when he married her in 1611, "Nur Mahal" (Light of the palace; for very similar examples, see Busch 2010b), but she was not Jahangir's fifth wife (the nineteenth or twentieth, according to accounts). "Fifth," *pañchama*, also means "clever" and may refer to the fifth house in astrological charts or the fifth note in the musical system; its proximity to "house" (*ghara*) here suggests an astrological reference. I thank Imre Bangha and Heidi Pauwels for their help in working through this verse, which I still cannot crack.
76. "Setting his mind to it, the poet Puhakar described the nine states. The tenth state is unbearable, it cannot be done. One cannot speak of it, so I have kept it away from sight (*goi*). To speak of it makes one's tongue freeze, no poet should describe it!" (Puhakar

1963: 51). Puhakar was also the author of a short text on the various kinds of poetic heroines called *Rasaveli.*

77. Puhakar's classical bent shows when he includes set pieces of Sanskrit narrative, as when the townswomen seek a glimpse of Surasena as he leaves on parade on his elephant (*Rasaratan,* v. 3.247–252, Puhakar 1963: 82).
78. Puhakar calls his story *rasa rachita kathā rasikina ruchita ruchira nāma rasaratana* (*Rasaratan,* v. 1.20, Puhakar 1963: 9) and lists its nine *rasas.*
79. "It's a path on a sword's edge, with the Ganges and Yamuna on either side. The path of love is extremely tough, few men can manage it. The ocean of love, Puhakar, is deep and unfathomable, those who fall in hardly ever reach the shore" (*khaḍgu dhāra māraga jahāṃ, gaṅga jamuna duhuṃ ora. prema pantha ati agamu hai, nibahata hai nara thora. Puhakara sāgara prema ko, nipaṭa gahita gambhīra, ihi samudra jo nara parai, bahuri na lāgahiṃ tīra*) (*Rasaratan,* vv. 1.102–103, Puhakar 1963: 39).
80. Rambha is educated in Sanskrit and Prakrit and in music, erotics, worship, and wifely virtues; she also gets lengthy patriarchal instruction from her attendants before her wedding. This includes serving her husband, always speaking softly, and the basics of erotic science, something that Puhakar prudishly refrains from detailing. "I have described many secrets, eighty-four of them (*chāri bīsa aru chāri*), Puhakar cannot speak of them explicitly, connoisseurs can imagine them" (Puhakar 1963: 94).
81. Singh (1963: 135ff.) calls the language of *Rasaratan* "Panchali or Kannauji Brajbhasha," a Brajbhasha with Avadhi features, with also an admixture of *chāraṇ piṅgala* or Rajasthani Brajbhasha.
82. Its editor, Shivprasad Singh (1963: 2–3, emphasis added), quotes Shukla: "We find very few Hindi poets writing narrative poems on imaginary tales. Jayasi and other poets of the Sufi branch (*shākhā*) wrote works of this kind, *but their manner was not fully Indian.* From this perspective, *Rasaratan* should be given a special place within Hindi literature." Singh calls it a "Hindu *premākhyān*" (2–3); see also Chapter 5.
83. Already in the hagiographical work *Bhaktamāl* (1604) Tulsi is acclaimed as the second Valmiki.
84. Lalach (or Lalachdas), a Kayastha from "Hastigram" (present day Hathgaon) near Rae Bareilly (Lalachdas 1963), wrote his *Haricharit* in 1530. Pavie partly translated it into French (as *Krichna et sa doctrine,* 1852); according to McGregor (1984: 96n), the work was well known in the eighteenth century, and almost all the manuscript copies date from the nineteenth century.
85. Lalach's *Haricharit* was completed in 1614 by one Asanand, from a village near Rae Barelli (Dube 1967: 15; oral communication, August 2008).
86. As Philip Lutgendorf (1991) has shown in his magisterial work on the *Mānas,* Tulsi's theology is equally complex, privileging devotion to Ram as both the ineffable Highest Being and the very visible god, but also showing respect for Shiva and critiquing contemporary trends that do not pay respect to "the Vedas and Brahmans."
87. In this ordinate world, the villages, towns, and cities on the shore of the river Sarayu (in Ram's capital Ayodhya), imagined here as the lake's daughter, are the several audiences of the tale (*Mānas* 1.39 *doha,* Tulsidas 2016: 93).

88. By contrast, as we saw earlier, Jayasi's *Padmāvat* played with the Ram story as an intertext.
89. Tulsi celebrated Prayag, Chitrakut, and Ayodhya as pilgrimage sites, access to which was facilitated by Akbar's policies, such as, the abolition of the pilgrimage tax and policing of the imperial roads. I thank Philip Lutgendorf for this suggestion.
90. Desai (2017: 42–43): "[T]wo powerful Mughal *mansabdars*, Todarmal and Man Singh, owned large tracts of urban land at prime locations. Their *havelis* were significant nodes in the city, anchoring its urban life. As large complexes, they housed residential and administrative uses and were sites of production and consumption."
91. And a substantial text: *Chitrāvalī* is 614 stanzas long; by comparison, *Padmāvat* comprises 653 stanzas, *Mirigāvatī* 427, and *Madhumālatī* 539.
92. The only manuscript of *Chitrāvalī* to be found is in Kaithi script and illustrated, thus suggesting an elite but regional commission; dated 1745, it was copied by one Phakirchand, a Srivastava Kayastha of Kara Manikpur (see Chapter 3), for Hazari Ajabsingh of Chunar Fort during the reign of the Mughal emperor Muhammad Shah, and it cost Rs 101 for illustration, copying, paper, illumination, and binding (*musavvar, likhāī o kāgaz rosnāī o jildsāz*); it is housed in the library of the Maharaja of Banaras at Ramnagar, but I have been unable to see it. See Varma's introduction to Usman (1981: 6–7).
93. See Truschke (2016), Alam and Subrahmanyam (2002), Keshavmurti (2013). Amir Khusrau's *Dewalrānī wa Khizr Khān* (Bednar 2014) and Hasan Sijzi's *'Ishqnāma* (Prakash 2019) were earlier examples in the Sultanate period.
94. Hamid's (1616) *'Iṣmatnāma* and Bazmi's (1618) *Rat Padam* praise Emperor Jahangir at length in their prologues, while *Rājkunwar* was actually produced at Prince Salim's (Jahangir's name before his accession) atelier in Allahabad.
95. I am aware that I am using "transnational" anachronistically here, before the rise of nation-states, but it is to point to Persia's vast reach across several polities and empires.
96. See Pellò (2014a) for various examples of transcodification.
97. *Rājkunwar*, MS CBL In 05, Chester Beatty Library, Dublin; see Orsini (2022b) for a fuller analysis.
98. *Az nuskha-yi hindavī kunad naqal* (Bazmi 1971: 211).
99. "*Īn qissa ki kas naguft guftam*" and then "*ān shaikh-i ki būd* **'ālamash nām**." The copyist writes Madhavanal's name as Madhonal, as would be later rendered in Urdu (Ahuja 1965: 125, 126).
100. He decided to call the work *Rat padam* "because *rat* [*rata*] in Hindi means lover" (*'āshiq*, here a "weeping lover," *'āshiq-i zār*, v. 304) (Bazmi 1971: 50).
101. For example, Jayasi's description of Singhaldip in *Padmāvat* begins with a full stanza comparing it with the seven island-continents, or *jambudīpa* (<*jambudvīpa*, punning *dīpa* to mean both *dvīpa* = island and *dīpaka* = light; Jayasi [1956] 1998: 25), followed by a coded praise of the king's fort, which is made of seven precious metals, with seven gates, etc. Bazmi only says, "There is an island in the ocean called Singal, with a fort and jutting battlement (*kingra*)" (*Dāstān-i Padmāwat*, v. 317, Bazmi 1971: 51).

102. For example, *chuhchuhī, pāṃḍuka, sarau, suvā, papīhā, guḍurū, koila, bhiṅgrāja* in *Padmāvat*, each with a specific call (Jayasi [1956] 1998: 29), become "birds in the garden all sing and recite delightful poems. If one bird begins to speak, a hundred spells tweak from their beaks" (Bazmi 1971: 51).
103. For example, references to the angel Harut, as in *amūkht ba ghamza saḥr-i hārūt, vaz khanda gushād durj- yāqūt* ("she learnt in a blink Harut's magic and her laughter opened the casket of ruby" = she spoke well) (Bazmi 1971: 54). Harut and Marut were sent down to earth in human form and are considered the teachers of magic to man (Steingass 2006 [1892]: 1485).
104. For light as the key metaphor for Padmavati, see de Bruijn (2012).
105. Among the few celebrated *Indian* Persian poets were Akbar's poet laureate Fayzi Fayyazi, who composed his own Persian version of the romance of Nala and Damayanti (Alam and Subrahmanyam 2002), and Mirza Qadir Bedil (or Bidel, according to Iranian pronunciation).
106. New Hindavi *kathas* also continued to be written, though only by local poets; e.g., Shahnawaz 'Ali Saloni's *Prem chingārī* (The spark of love, 1833), 'Ali Muras's *Kunwarāvat kathā* (date?), Khwaja Ahmad's *Nūr Jahān* (1904), Kavi Nasir's *Prem Darpaṇ* (The mirror of love, 1917). See McGregor (1984); Table 2.2.
107. For a comprehensive survey of Urdu *masnavis*, see Suvorova (2000).
108. I develop this point in Orsini (2019a).
109. The manuscripts in private collections were listed and described in the Search or Khoj Reports but not collected, so a hundred years later they are mostly unavailable to us.
110. Of the *katha* authors, only Tulsidas and, very briefly, Jayasi are mentioned in Shiv Singh Sengar's (1878) compilation *Śivsiṃh saroj*. See Chapter 5; Sengar ([1878] 1970: 778).
111. "Out of 256 titles published between 1884 and 1900 by the Bharat Jiwan Press, 119 (46%) were collections of poems or songs in Braj Bhasa, mostly of *śṛṅgāra rasa*" (Orsini 2004: 119).
112. In his introduction he tells us that *Padmāvat* was part of the syllabus of BA and MA Hindi exams (Shukla 1949: 5).
113. Particularly Mataprasad Gupta, Kishorilal Gupta, Paramewshari Lal Gupta, Shivprasad Singh, Vasudev Sharan Agraval, Shivsahay Pathak, and Shyam Manohar Pandey.
114. For these, see Orsini (2015d); for Vishnudas, Bangha (2014) and McGregor (1999).

Chapter 3

1. Earlier in Tamil, and later in Kannada, Marathi, Hindi, Bangla, etc. For a chronology and history, see Hawley (2015). For saint-poets in north India, see Schomer (1987); Hawley and Juergensmeyer (1988); Lorenzen (1996).

2. Levine (2013: 219) notes, "Politically speaking, the privileging of the written over the oral is much more significant than the focus on a small proportion of novels. One of the most unevenly distributed of the world's resources is literacy itself, the skills essential to the creation and consumption of literature in the first place. UNESCO . . . estimates that about 10 percent of the world could read or write a short statement in the middle of the nineteenth century. By the 1920s the number was up to 28 percent. For most of human history, in other words, the written word was the province of a privileged minority. . . . Oral culture of some kind—narrative, religious wisdom, song, poetry—has reached nearly every human, while literacy has remained restricted to a sliver of the world's population." She adds, "[I]f world literature included oral stories, poetry, theatrical performance, and religious teaching, not to mention the oral transmission of literary texts, then we might be getting at something much broader—something like the world" (226).
3. For example, Damrosch's (2003: 6) definition of world literature, according to which a work needs, first, "to be read *as literature*" and, second, to circulate "into a broader world beyond its linguistic and cultural point of origin," acknowledges that who defines literature is a relative and loaded question. Casanova ([1999] 2004) unproblematically takes the French understanding of literature since the seventeenth century as a stable and universal definition. Beecroft (2015: 8–13) criticizes this stance; his "ecologies" emphasize the problem and allow more diversity in the definition of literature. Longxi (2009) discusses this issue in greater detail.
4. "Don't think of this as song, this is my theology" (*tumha jini jānau yaha gīta hai, yaha to nija brahma vichāra*) (Gupta, *Kabīr Granthāvalī*, 1985: 143, quoted in Agrawal 2009: 349).
5. See, e.g., Bacchan Singh (1996: 105). Even the volume dedicated exclusively to Sant poets in the sixteen-volume *Hindī sāhitya kā bṛihad itihās* (Comprehensive history of Hindi literature), which encouragingly includes a wide range of Sant poets as well as the Hindavi Sufi poets, focuses overhwelmingly on their theology, social message, lineages, and biographical details, and devotes only a short chapter at the end to aesthetics (Chaturvedi 1968: 489–502): the tone is apologetic, pointing readers away from "traditional critical methods" and toward an appreciation of the "emotional beauty" (*bhāvsaundarya*) and "simple expression of obscure meanings" of Sant poetry (501, 492, 493).
6. As Levine (2013: 17) points out, "world literature has taken its current shape from three print-based institutions—the mass literacy movements of the late nineteenth century, the publishing industry, and the university—all of which have valued writing at the expense of meaningful attention to orality."
7. For the popularity of bhakti songs in the audio-cassette boom of 1980s, see Manuel (1993) and Hess (2015).
8. See Servan-Schreiber (1999) for the circulation of Bhojpuri songs and oral epics through itinerant sellers of chapbooks.
9. Venkat Mani (2016) has proposed the term "bibliomigrancy" to indicate the material movement of texts and books in the world through libraries and commercial networks, but the concept remains anchored in the book as printed object.

10. For Shukla ([1929] 1988: 63, emphasis added), the presence of so many Persian and Arabic words in Malukdas was a drawback: "[*D*]*espite all these traits*, his language is well-formed (*suvyāvasthit*) and beautiful/pleasing (*sundar*)."
11. The fact that we know little about the "other" side, i.e., how popular Islamic or vernacular Sufi song-poems, prayers, etc. "re-accented" bhakti and popular genres, is most likely due to the dynamics of preservation; after all, they form a very substantial part of the publishing boom of the nineteenth century (see Chapter 5).
12. As we have already seen in Chapter 2, genres like the *katha* and texts like *Chandāyan* came into being precisely through a confluence of forms, tropes, and languages from both oral and written traditions rather than by a simple adoption of cosmopolitan forms in the vernacular.
13. Bhikha (2013: 12, emphasis added), e.g., tells us:

    I *wrote* many *rekhta* and *kabitta*, *sakhi* and *sabda* poems,
    I learnt, read and reflected day and night, singing Hari's praise.
    Once I heard a very unusual *dhrupad* and asked where it was from—
    it's by one who lives by Bhurkura village.

    Kabitta was a generic term for a short Brajbhasha poem that followed the rules of *kavya*; *rekhta* in a Sant context refers to a meter like that of the swinging-song or *jhulna* with a Khari Boli template and mixed Persianate vocabulary (Bangha 2010b); *sakhi* and *sabad* (*shabda*) were couplets and song-poems in Kabir's tradition; *dhrupad* was a song form that had been popular since the fifteenth century.
14. In the case of Kabir and Raidas, the earliest written attestation of their utterances and song-poems can be found in manuscripts in Punjab and the eastern region between 1570 and 1604 (Mann 2001), roughly a hundred years after their deaths; for Kabir, different textual traditions developed in Punjab, Rajasthan, and Banaras (Vaudeville 1974; Callewaert, Sharma, and Taillieu 2000) beside the oral tradition. The case is different with sectarian groups, like the Dadu-Panthis, Niranjanis, and Sikhs; there are regional differences too, with more manuscripts preserved in Rajasthan. See Mann (2001); Williams (2014, forthcoming).
15. Callewart's system of 5*, 4*, and 3* (in Callewaert, Sharma, and Taillieu 2000) to indicate the number of early manuscripts (between 1570 and 1681) in which a Kabir poem features has been mocked by Agrawal (2009) but is still crucial to gain an idea of the early attested poems.
16. "Believe one who has tried it, that the quotation of a single verse of Tulasī Dāsa or of a single pithy saying of the wise old Kabīr will do more to unlock the hearts and gain the trust of our eastern fellow-subjects than the most intimate familiarity with the dialectics of Śaṅkara or with the daintiest verse of Kālidāsa. A knowledge of the old dead language will, it is true, often win respect and admiration, but a very modest acquaintance with the treasures—and they are treasures—of Hindī literature endows its possessor with the priceless gift of sympathy, and gains for him, from those whose watchword is *Bhakti*, their confidence and their love" (Grierson 1907, quoted in Pinch 2003: 181, who offers a broad discussion of the appreciation for bhakti among missionaries and colonial administrators).

17. See Grierson (1907) and Vaudeville (1974) for the popularity of Kabir among missionaries.
18. Grierson (1920: 118), who had already compared bhakti to the reformation (with a small "r") at a 1918 lecture at the School of Oriental and African Studies, called Kabir "a Musalmān who, attracted by the reformed Hinduism, founded a sect in which Islām and it were combined." Pinch (2003: 176–177) argues that Grierson abandoned his view of the Nestorian Christian origins of bhakti after James Kennedy and J. B. Keith expressed skepticism and R. G. Bhandarkar (1913) showed evidence of the pre-Christian origin of bhakti theology in *Vaisnavism, Saivism and Minor Religious Systems*. But we see in the 1918 lecture that Christian vocabulary still governed Grierson's description of bhakti.
19. Barthwal ([1936] 1978: 15, esp. ch. 2, "The Nirguṇī's Philosophy," 18–89).
20. "Though brought up in a Muslim household," Shyamsundar Das stated, "the fact that he is steeped in Hindu ideas gestures towards the fact that Brahman, or at least Hindu, blood flowed in his veins" (introduction to *Kabīr Granthāvalī*, quoted in Agrawal 2009: 158). Hazari Prasad Dvivedi set up an elaborate scheme that accounted for the varied strands of his religious idiom: a caste of Nathpanthi householders in northern and eastern India, either weavers or beggars, had not observed caste rules and worshiped a formless god; with the coming of Islam they had gradually converted, and it was in such a family of newly converted householder *jogīs* that Kabir was brought up. The only problem, Agrawal (2009: 163) notes, is that Kabir never called himself a *jogi* but only a weaver or *julaha*, or by the caste name *kori*, or "neither Hindu nor Muslim."
21. "With the establishment of Muslim rule in the country there was no place left in the hearts of the Hindu people for pride, self-respect, and enthusiasm. Right before them their temples were destroyed, the statues of gods were demolished, and their venerable persons were humiliated, and there was nothing they could do" (Shukla [1929] 1988 : 15, quoted and translated in Gupta 2010: 268, translation slightly modified).
22. "Thus did the needs of the times find their realisation in the Nirguṇa movement initiated by Kabīr. Nānak, Dādū, Prāṇanāth, Malūkdās, Palaṭū, Jagjīvan dās, Śibdayāl, Tulasī Sāhib and a host of other Sants took up his mission from time to time and worked for the propagation of this movement for unity and equity" (Barthwal [1936] 1978: 17). Ramchandra Shukla did not share this opinion of the Sants, whom he considered—in line with Tulsidas—as spreading radical centrifugal ideas that went against the need of the hour, which was for unity among Hindus.
23. But, as A. K. Ramanujan (1973: 38) cautions, "'spontaneity' has its own rhetorical structure."
24. Multiple editions and translations of Kabir's poems are available in most major languages, and he is well represented in *The Norton Anthology* (Puchner et al. 2018: vol. 1c) and other world literature series.
25. See Hess (2015); see also Hess's introduction to her Kabir translations (in Kabir 1983) and Agrawal (2009) for aesthetic critical readings of Kabir's poetry.
26. Such songs of self-abasement are not exclusive to low-caste Sants but are found also in Surdas and Tulsidas, e.g., Tulsidas's *Kavitāvalī*.

27. See Raidas 111 in Callewaert and Friedlander (1992: 168).
28. "An Ahir is one who knows how to/carry out the Ahir's job./He leads the herd of cows and buffaloes out to graze/and keeps the calves fit" (Gulal 897, in Lal 1933: 353).
29. Barthwal ([1936] 1978: 222) singled out the Dadupanthi Sundardas as "the only educated person among them perhaps."
30. "There is no doubt that Kabir Sahab was a poet of high quality. The jewel poet of contemporary India himself, Rabindranath Tagore, has recognized him as a good poet and translated his verses (*pad*) in English. Even from reading that book of translations Kabir's literary grandeur (*gaurav*) shines through" (Mishra (1910) 1924: 511).
31. Instead, even for a staunch proponent of Kabir like Hazari Prasad Dvivedi, Agrawal (2009) notes, content was primary and poeticity was a byproduct.
32. For an explanation of these various metrical forms, see Snell.
33. Extended metaphors are one of Tulsidas's favorite devices (see Chapter 2), and the poem "I have danced enough, Gopal" (*aba hauṃ nāchyau bahuta gupāla*), which employs dance as a single extended metaphor, is one of Surdas's most famous poems; see Bryant and Hawley (2015: 692–693n400).
34. The phrase is Raheja and Gold's (1984).
35. This is a point that Agrawal (2009: 399) also makes.
36. There are relatively fewer Sufi terms in the poems by Kabir and Raidas than in those by the later Sants, which may account for why this phenomenon has been less explored. Behl (2007) commented on the "absence" of attention to this dialogism in bhakti scholarship, but now see Burchett (2019).
37. Without addressivity "the utterance does not and cannot exist" (Bakhtin, "Speech Genres," in Morson and Emerson 1990: 131). In a different context, Bryant (1978) points out that the first step, when one is listening to a Surdas poem that sets up a scene or a dialogue between characters related to Krishna, is identifying who the speaker and the addressee are.
38. What is at stake in this double-voiced discourse for Bakhtin is the "aim" or "task" of the utterance, which can be to stylize someone's idiolect or sociolect or to parody it. Assessing the aim of the Sants' double-voiced utterances is tricky because of the pitfalls of overinterpretation discussed above, e.g., to see them as "apostles of Hindu-Muslim unity."
39. For similar compositions in the Sikh scripture, the *Guru Granth,* in the section dedicated to Raga Tilanga, see Shackle (1978a) and Orsini and Pellò (2010).
40. Hindavi here is actually Khari Boli, rather than the usual mixed koinè of Sant poetry; I thank Imre Bangha for this observation.
41. "Unity of existence," the stance of Ibn al-Arabi, deemed that God could be found in all beings.
42. *Terā maĩ **dīdār-divānā***

    ghaṛī ghaṛī tujhe dekhā chāhūṃ, suna sāheba rahamānā
    *huā **almasta** khabara nahī̃ tana kī, piyā prema piyālā*
    ṭhāṛhe hoūṃ to gira gira paratā, tere raṃga matavālā
    khaṛā rahūṃ darabāra tumhāre, jyõ ghara kā bandājādā
    nekī kī kulāha sira dīye, gale pairahana sājā

taujī aura nimāja na jānūṃ, nā jānūṃ dhari rojā
bāṃg jikara tabahī se bisarī, jabase yaha dil khojā
kahaĩ Malūka aba kajā na karihaũ, dila hī saũ dila lāyā |
makkā hajj hiye mẽ dekhā, purā murasida pāyā (Malukdas 2011: 6).

See also "Crazed by pain, drunken fakir" (*Darda-divāne bāvare, almasta fakīra*, 6), "My *pīr* is without flaw, I am his servant" (*Merā pīra nirañjanā maĩ khijamatagāra*, 7) and "My dear, why will you lose" (*Ai ajīj īmān tū kāhe ko khovai*, 15), among many others.

43. *Gāphila hai bandā gunāh karai bāra bāra.*
kāma paṛe saheb dhaū kaisā pharmāvaigā.
ākhira jamāne ko ḍaratā hai merā dila
jaba jabarīla hātha gurja liye āvaigā.
khāb sī duniyā dila ko na karai sāta pāṃc
kālī pīlī āṃkhaĩ kara phiristā dikhlāvaigā.
kahatā malūka kisī mulka mẽ bacāv nahīṃ
aba kījai kirapā taba mere mana bhāvaigā. (Malukdas 2011: 27).

44. ***Laham kullahum*** *jisima kā nabī kiyā farmūda.*
nabī kiyā farmūd hadīs kī āyat māhīṃ
saba meṃ ekai jāna aura kou dūjā nāhīṃ.
khūna gosta hai eka maulavī jibaha na chhājai.
saba meṃ rosana huā nabī kā nūra birājai . . .
palaṭū jo bedaradī so kāfira mardūda
laham kullahum *jisima kā nabī kiyā farmūda.* (Paltudas 2008: vol. 1, 215)

45. Including "I belong to all and all belong to me (*sabhahina ke hama sabai hamāre*), individual beings are dear to me (*jīva mohī lāgata pyāre*), and all three worlds are [created through] my illusion, whose end no one has reached yet" (Vanshi 2006: 142).

46. *Jahā dekhaũ tahāṃ sahib merā*
kehū ghaṭa ṭhākura kehū ghaṭa cherā.
kehūṃ meṃ rām kehū rahimānā,
kehū jaivẽ kehū khātā khānā.
kehū phairai tasabī kehū japai mālā,
kehū bhae alaha miyāṃ kehū gopālā . . .
kaha malūka yaha akathā kahānī
kehū mūrakha kehū ghaṭa jñānī (Vanshi 2006: 143).

47. These include the *Mohan pothī* of 1570–1572; the *Ādi granth* of 1604, compiled within the Nanakh *panth* (also known as the Sikhs); and the 1614 *Pañchavāṇī* (Five voices) manuscript and *Sarvāṅgīs* (Complete body) by Gopaldas (1627) and by Rajab (ca. 1620?) within the Dadu community; see Callewaert, Sharma, and Taillieu (2000). For the Fatehpur ms., see Bahura (1982).

48. For these poems, see Pauwels (2009).

49. MS 4300/1247, Sherani Collection, Lahore (copied in Delhi in 1826); see also Husain (1968: vol. 2, 267, Nr. 1472); Orsini and Pellò (2010). Another *Bhagatmālā* was written by Rai Amanat Rai, a disciple of Bedil (University of Punjab Library, cat. 821P, VI 146).

50. In their respective hagiographies (*parchais*), devotees come to Banaras to see Raidas and to Kara to see Malukdas, while Malukdas is said to have traveled toward the end of his life to Kashi (Banaras), Patna, and Jagannath Puri on the coast of Orissa, where he invited the whole town for a great feast (Dikshit 1965: 66). Among the Sants, Nanak was the most traveled.
51. *Kou ujbaka kou milata chakata [hohi],*
    koi khurāsānī koi kābili [kābulī] kahāvatā
    koi kāśmīrī koi balakha bokhāre kā kahai,
    koi ṭhaṭha, bhakhara, irākūṃ āvatā.
    koi rūmī śāmī, koi habśī firaṅgī
    madha dacchhanī jāṅgar nirālā hoi janāvatā.
    pūraba baṅgālī aru uttara ke khasiyā hai
    pacchhima pachhāṃhi madhidesa mujhahi bhāvatā.
    kahata malūka saba eka hī kumbhāra gaṛhe
    aite parkara dhaū kahāṃ tẽ janāvatā. (Vanshi 2006: 144)
52. The fact that this map resembles fairly closely the one in Puhakar's *katha Rasaratan* (Chapter 2) suggests that the list had some currency in this form.
53. Simon Digby (1994a), always reliable when it comes to obscure provincial Sufis, wrote an essay on this text (of which he found a manuscript in the British Library entitled, more appropriately, *The Secrets of the those Drawn* (by God, *majẕūbīn*), and on Khwaja Karak, but his main point is that we should call him Khwaja Gurg instead!
54. Qais Manikpuri's (1916) *Tārīkh Kaṛā Manikpur* lists all the local governors during the various Sultanate dynasties (Bayly 1980).
55. The text does not mention what has become an important focus of popular devotion to Khwaja Karak: his footprints as an adult and as a child and his handprint (*panja*). Digby (1994a: 105–106) notes several encounters between Khwaja Karak with 'Alauddin Khilji and his prediction to a local official.
56. For yogis in Sufi hagiographies, see Digby (1994b).
57. Maluk had "not loved his wife" (*byāhi bahū ānī ghara māhīṃ, tāso bhagata na neha karāhīṃ*) (Dikshit 1965: 47).
58. When his father, Sundardas, dies, people tell him after the funeral, "[S]trive to maintain your family (*kuṭumbā*), look after your mother" (Dikshit 1965: 47).
59. "The fort was old, the town was old, brick and rocks were lying around" (Dikshit 1965: 51); maybe Kara did not look so different then, after all?!
60. *Dosta eka raṅga ālama ke pyāre, itane Allāha rahai na nyāre* (Dikhsit 1965: 51).
61. *Āgyākārī hākima āvai, bemukha hoi rahana na pāvai* (Dikhsit 1965: 51).
62. This section draws substantially on my essay "Booklets and Sants" (Orsini 2015a).
63. As Purushottam Agrawal (2009) has recently argued, this shows that it is wrong to consider (and champion) Kabir as a marginal and subaltern voice, a brave but failed religious reformer. Kabir was not a marginal voice but the most popular poet of trading and artisanal classes, both in his time and in the following centuries.
64. For these and other details about Kabir's printing and critical history I draw upon Vaudeville (1974: 6ff.); see also Friedlander (2012). Vaudeville (1974: 23n.) notes that

the oldest of the popular editions of Kabir was in a collection with other devotional poems edited by Shankar Haribhai in Gujarati script in 1888, and four editions in Bengali translation with commentary appeared between 1890 and 1910. The Benares Light Press in Banaras had already brought out accessible lithographed editions of Kabir, Tulsidas, and Surdas in the 1860s; see Orsini (2004).

65. The Nagari Pracharini Sabha's reports on its search for Hindi manuscripts mention not only Kabir and Raidas but also Jagjivan Das and Malukdas, thus placing them within the purview of "Hindi literature." See, e.g., the five-leaves ms. of *Kuṇḍaliyā Palaṭū Sāhab* (Nr. 222, "new"), two works by Maluk Das (Nr. 180, six and twenty-six pages, respectively), and Jagjivan Das (Nr. 122, ten pages) (Das 1903). Das's (1928) *Kabīr Granthāvalī* was based on manuscripts in the Dadu-*panthi* tradition rather than the core text of the Kabir *panth*, the *Bījak*.
66. For details, see Vaudeville (1974) and Mehrotra (2011). Peter Friedlander (2012) has argued that Sen's main sources were not oral but in fact the Belvedere Press booklets, and he changed their Radhasoami orientation into a Brahmo one and published them in the Bengali script. Amartya Sen, Sen's grandson, has vigorously challenged this claim.
67. The *Malūkdās Granthāvalī*, or *Collected Works*, only came out in 2006 (Vanshi 2006).
68. Lal (1933) is a large collection containing the *bānīs* of the Sants of Bhurkura (near Ghazipur, east of Banaras). In this volume all the poems are numbered sequentially, starting chronologically from the earlier gurus and their slim oeuvre: Banvari Sahiba (one poem), Biru Saheb (two poems), Yari Saheb (twenty), Shah Faqir (seven), and Keshodas (ten). The longer oeuvres of Biru, Bula, Jagjivan, Dulan, Gulal, and Bhikha are instead grouped by *raga* and genre (e.g., *jhulna* or swing song, *arill*), often with similar compositions by different authors next to each other, an arrangement that probably corresponded to the rhythms of communal ritual and singing.
69. Details in the family history are taken from *Agravāl Jāti kā Itihās*, pt. 2, Agrawal History Office, Bhanpura, Indore State, 1939, reproduced on the Belvedere Printing Works website, http://www.belvedereprintingworks.com/family-history.html, accessed 15 April 2014.
70. "The motivation for publishing the *Santbānī* Book Series is to save the *bānī* and message (or preaching, *upadeś*) of world-famous *mahatmas* from disappearing. Among the *bānīs* that we have printed so far, several had never been printed before and some had been printed in such fragmented (*chinn-bhinn*) and unorganised form that prevented one from extracting full benefit" (Manager, Belvedere Press [presumably Baleshwar Prasad], "Dedication," in *Gulāl Sāhib kī Bānī*, Gulal Sahab 1910: ii).
71. "In the last five years we have, with great effort and at great expense, asked for rare manuscript books and scattered verses from near and far away (*deś-deśāntar*); we either collect the originals or have copies made, and this activity is still going on. If possible we collect and print the whole texts (*granth*) and choose from their miscellaneous verses those songs (*pad*) that will be beneficial to the general public (*sarvasādhāraṇ ke upkārak*). No book is published without comparing several manuscripts and without proper emendation, unlike the books others publish without any understanding and any checking (*besamajhe aur be jāṃche*)" (Gulal Sahab 1910: ii).

72. "In correcting the songs we ask knowledgeable followers of the *panth* of the *mahatmas* who authored the texts for help, and in choosing the words we are mindful that they should be in accordance with the taste of the general public (*sarvasādhāraṇ kī ruchi*) and should be attractive and pierce the heart, so that the heart may be pure and there be no need to avert one's eye" (Gulal Sahab 1910: ii). The practice of asking respected sadhus to correct readings of texts seems to evolve at this time, as witnessed by other publishers. It contrast with Chaturi, who expounded the poems orally and who would not be recognized as an authority in print culture. I thank Imre Bangha for this observation.
73. The aims were expressed in the subtitle on the front page as well: "In which extremely attractive and devotion-fostering songs and couplets are given after correction, arranged according to main categories, with obscure words explained in footnotes."
74. These include Ramchandra Shukla's (1929 [1988]) own history as well as Parashuram Chaturvedi's *Uttar bhārat kī sant paramparā* (The Sant tradition of north India, 1950), the most comprehensive scholarly study of north Indian Sants. The first scholarly editions of Awadh Sants based on named manuscripts have been quite recent: see Callewaert and Friedlander (1992) and Vanshi (2006); Vanshi's (2014) study *Sant palṭū dās* still relies on Belvedere Press booklets.
75. Interview with Anupam Agrawal, present owner of Belvedere Printing Works, Allahabad, April 2013.

Chapter 4

1. As previously mentioned, "Brajbhasha" literally means "the language of Braj," the area around Mathura and Vrindavan between Delhi and Agra, traditionally associated with Krishna. It became a cosmopolitan literary vernacular in the second half of the sixteenth century (Pollock 1998a; Busch 2011). "Courtly Hindi" is here a moniker for poetry written following the rules and manner (Hindi, *riti*) of "poetic science" or *kavya-shastra*. Brajbhasha was also used for devotional and musical compositions that did not strictly follow these rules, though they shared much of the broader poetic grammar in relation to moods, seasons, and the depiction of love, both divine and human.
2. Sayyid Rahmatullah was the grandson of Sayyid Bhikha, one of the Bilgrami Sayyids who had found honorable employment with Mughal dignitaries under Emperor Aurangzeb. Rahmatullah was an "excellent accountant," worked with his grandfather, and managed to remain in imperial service after his grandfather died by traveling to Aurangzeb's imperial camp in the Deccan; he purportedly composed a whole text in Brajbhasha called *Pūrṇa rasa* (Complete poetic flavor), no copy of which has surfaced (Azad Bilgrami [H 1166/CE 1752] 1913: 359–363; also Zaidi 1969: 59ff.).
3. Busch (2015) shows several instances of repurposed poems.
4. For Sanskrit cosmopolitanism, see Pollock (2006); for Persian, Eaton (2019) and Green (2019); for imperial and royal courtly culture, Truschke (2016), Busch (2011),

and Sharma (2015). Note that culture in the Mughal imperial court is often taken to signify Mughal culture as a whole (e.g., Mukhia 2004).

5. By contrast, historians studying cosmopolitan *spaces* point out that cities, *darbars* or courtly assemblies, and ships or ports were crucial sites of cosmopolitan encounters, with secretaries, interpreters, merchants, poets, and spies singled out as the most likely cosmopolitans, all highly mobile, at home in several languages, and alert to different codes of behavior (see, e.g., the essays in Lefèvre, Županov, and Flores 2015). These editors in fact point to the "strategic" and sometimes "reluctant" cosmopolitanism of early modern missionaries and catholic imperial (Portuguese) outposts and the "subaltern cosmopolitanism" of soldiers and sailors. Several contributors also stress the westward traffic of ideas: news of Emperor Akbar's imperial ideology of *sulḥ-i kull* (peace with all) was carried back to a Europe torn by religious conflict and finds echo in Kant's "universal peace" (17–18).
6. Margrit Pernau, personal communication, October 2018.
7. As Kumkum Chatterjee (2009) did for the small kingdom of Bishnupur in Bengal.
8. Leese (2019) starts tracing the cultivation of Arabic poetry among Persian literati.
9. Nabi Hadi's (1995: 443) dictionary of Persian poets in India lists one 'Aziz al-Din b. 'Abd allah (d. 1413) as a known poet during the reign of Firuz Shah Tughluq (r. 1351–1388); he came from Iran, was posted by Firuz Shah as judge in Kara, and wrote several odes (*qasidas*) to him and his successor, Nasir al-Din Mahmud; his poetry collection (*diwan*) has survived but has not been studied. Malik 'Aziz ullah Bistami, also from Sistan in Iran, lived at the court of Mubarak Shah Sharqi (d. 1401), and a few of his poems have survived in literary collections (see Hadi 1995: 106). The voluminous manual for poets (*Dastūr al-shu'arā*) known as the *Jaunpur Anthology* was composed for the Jaunpur Sultan Mubarak Shah in 1400–1401 (British Museum MS Or 4110; see Rieu 1895: 232–233) and urgently awaits scholarly attention. Another poet, Mir Sayyid 'Alauddin Awadhi, came from Khurasan and settled in Ayodhya in the second half of the fifteenth century; he composed poetry under the pen name "'Ala" and was an expert in Indian music; one short poem of his, *Mā mūqimān*, became part of the elementary school syllabus and remained so till the nineteenth century (Hadi 1995: 61).
10. Stefano Pellò (2014b) has called the rooting of Persian in the regions beyond the capital Delhi in the fifteenth century the "provincialization" of Persian: this included an acknowledgment that the center of Persian was elsewhere (in Timurid Herat), and an accommodation of local knowledge and languages, attested by Hindavi synonyms and occasional lemmas in the dictionaries (see also Karomat 2014). Art historians have also highlighted this period of decentralization as the beginning of illustrated codex manuscripts and illuminated Qur'ans in north India (e.g., Brac de la Perrière 2015).
11. If we take as an example the works of Shaikh 'Abd al-Quddus Gangohi (1456–1537), who spent most of his life in a Sufi hospice in the *qasba* of Rudauli, east of Lucknow, the most quoted Persian poets are 'Attar, Rumi, and Sa'di, as well as the Indian Sufi poets Mas'ud Beg, Muhammad Qalandar, Bu 'Ali Qalandar, and Sharaf Qattal (Digby 1975: 52). 'Abd al-Quddus himself composed Persian verses with the penname

"Ahmadi" and Hindavi as "Alakhdas" (the equivalent of his Arabic name, "servant of God"). As Simon Digby (1975: 51) put it, "[H]is taste in Persian verse evidently did not incline towards the refined and ornate classical courtly tradition mainly represented by the *qasida* and the literary rather than didactic *mathnavi*." In Hindavi, too, as we saw in Chapter 3, his couplets (*dohas*) closely resemble those of his Sant contemporary Kabir; see also Orsini (2014a).

12. See Orsini (2014a) for a longer discussion.
13. The creeper can refer to the soul or the state of union with the supreme being; or to *maya* or illusion, or to the body (see Callewaert and Sharma 2009: 1523–1524).
14. As Mana Kia (2011: 259) aptly puts it, "If we regard *tazkirahs* as self-commemorations, these contemporaries turn around the figure of the author, who comes into relief in these contexts. Figures from the past function as a cultural genealogy for the self, and contemporary figures create the social context in which the self is articulated. Through the selective process of including individuals, from the past as ancestors and from the present as peers, the author creates his community, one which in turn produces this self-of-the-author-as-figure, a self relational to and indivisible from community."
15. For example, Zulfiqar 'Ali "Mast's" *tazkira*, written in Banaras in 1814, shows the author busy networking with local and more famous literati who passed through Banaras on their way to or from Calcutta; "Mast" requested verses from all of them for his *tazkira* and collected a remarkable number of *qasidas* praising him (possibly in exchange for hospitality?); in the case of one of the most famous contemporary poets, Mirza Qatil, "Mast" (1964: 72–75) was unsuccessful in acquiring any verse and so copied in extenso their polite correspondence.
16. The others are *Yād-i baiẓa* (Pure memory), *Mā's̱ir al-kirām* (1753), and *Khizāna-yi 'āmirā* (Imperial treasury, 1763). Simon Leese, who has studied Azad's Arabic textual production, notes that Azad was very careful about collecting documentary evidence for his entries, and he dates historical events and meetings as much as possible. Indeed, the chronogram, i.e., a verse that codes a date through the sum of the numerical value of Arabic letters, was his passion, and for the death of the Bilgrami Sufi Mir 'Azmatullah Bilgrami "Bekhabar," he wrote an ode (*qasida*) in which every line was a chronogram (Azad Bilgrami [H 1166/CE 1752] 1913: 325). Azad's Arabic poetic treatise *Subḥat al-marjān* (Coral rosary) also has a *tazkira*-like section, arranged chronologically, of Arabophone poets. I thank Simon Leese for this information.
17. *Khizāna-yi 'āmirā* includes 141 poets in alphabetic order, beginning with the illustrious early classic Anwari (1126–1189); canonical poets Rudaki, Khaqani, Sa'di, Amir Khusrau, and Hafiz; Mughal poet laureates Talib Amuli and Kalim Kashani; Azad's most famous contemporaries in India, both poets and *tazkira* writers (Bedil, Arzu, Sarkhwush, Anandram Mukhlis, Hazin and Walih Daghestani); his Deccani patrons, the Nawabs of Hyderabad; and six Bilgramis: himself, his grandfather Mir 'Abd al-Jalil, Bikhar, Sha'ir, Faqir, and Mir Yusuf Bilgrami (see Azad Bilgrami 2011).
18. Actually, not all the 153 figures lived in Bilgram: some only had some connection with it.

19. Lutfullah (d. 1730) was a Sufi also popularly known as Shah Laddha Bilgrami, who after an early career in the army in Bengal and Bihar turned to Sufism and spent many years in the hospice of the famous Sufi Mir Sayyid Ahmad in Kalpi before returning to Bilgram, where he lived until the age of ninety. Lutfullah composed poetry with the pen name "Ahmadi" (see Hadi 1995: 54; Azad Bilgrami 1910: 108–115). Note that *namkīn* (lit. "salty") is a positive quality.
20. Azad quotes 158 *ghazal* verses and one quatrain (Azad Bilgrami 1910: 317–325).
21. Azad also gives the biographies of Bekhabar's son and spiritual successor Mir Nawazish 'Ali and his brother Sayyid Karamullah, of Lutfullah's nephew, etc.
22. After him, Bilgramis seem to have more easily entered service in the Mughal and post-Mughal polities, including the Nawabis of Hyderabad and Lucknow and the East India Company.
23. Among other notable Bilgramis were Sayyid 'Abdullah "Qabil" (d. 1719), a poet but also a well-known calligrapher mentioned by Khushgu (Hadi 1995: 481), and Niyaz Muhyi al-Din "Vamiq," a friend of Azad Bilgrami's who served under Raja Shitab Rai of Jaunpur (ca. 1786) and left a *diwan* of verses (Hadi 1995: 615).
24. Like Fateh Chand Kayath Bilgrami (d. 1767), who traced the course of the River Gomti and wrote a book about it as well as a collection of model letters (Hadi 1995: 177).
25. See Azad Bilgrami ([H 1166/CE 1752] 1913: 370).
26. "This Brahman poet (*mahārāj kavi*) was for a long time with Raja Hanumant Singh of Amethi. I have seen a copy of the *Padmāvat* written in his own hand. He taught *bhasha* poetry to Abdul Jalil Bilgrami" (Sengar [1878] 1970: 821). The mention of him copying (or writing?) the *Padmāvat* is intriguing. Of the poems cited, one is a humorous repartee between a barley seed and *kusha* grass, the other is devotional (626).
27. It also lists several reciters of Shi'a devotional poetry (*soz* and *marsiyas*) in Persian and Urdu (S. Bilgrami [1883] 2008: 102–103).
28. These are Talib Ali "Rajnayak," Ramprasad Bandijan, Shivdin (whom Sengar [1878] 1970: 802 also mentions, as an "ordinary," *sāmānya*, poet), Jawahir Bandijan, Hariprasad Bhatt, and Newaj Jolaha (b. 1763, a weaver, i.e., nonelite Muslim) (Mishra 1913: 421, 503).
29. Shah Muhammad Farmuli was a nobleman or *amir* of Islam Shah Suri's time and a contemporary of Manjhan (see Chapter 2). According to the historical work *Afsāna-i shāhān*, "Wherever he [Islam Shah Suri] happened to be, he kept himself surrounded by accomplished scholars and poets. . . . Men like Mīr Sayyid Mañjhan, the author of *Madhumālatī*, Shāh Muḥammad Farmūlī and his younger brother, Mūsan, Sūrdās and many other learned scholars and poets assembled there and poems in Arabic, Persian and Hindi were recited" (cited in Behl 2012a: 303). Azad, however, connects Farmuli to the Mughal emperor Akbar: "The ancestors of the Farmulis of Bilgram commanded excellence and honor (*'itbār*) at the time of Akbar *pādshāh* and raised the banner of supremacy. Shaikh Shah Muhammad was a wealthy and powerful man at the time. He resided with command of the forts (*ba ḥukūmat-i aḥṣār qayām dāsht*), was a perfect master of Hindi poetry (*naẓm-i hindī*), and seized from his peers the speech of connoisseurship. All the experts of this art today recognize his mastery and

treasure his verses with their lives. They say that he was the local ruler of the area of Rapri Chandwar. One day he went out hunting with his army and by chance got separated from his retinue; he found himself by a village" (Azad Bilgrami [H 1166/ CE 1752] 1913: 352).

30. Two manuscripts of Farmuli's *Singāra sātaka* (Hundred love verses) have been found (Zaidi 1977: 100), both in the Persian script. Here is one verse that incorporates Champa's name, which can also be read as "flower-like" lamp or light:

    Round and round your light it flitters,
    Champa. A moth, my heart.
    Your face, gem-like, glitters.
    Like a wicked wife, my heart puffs up in smoke.
    mana pataṅga phiri phiri parai champā rūpa tuva joti
    ratana dīpa mukha jagamagai phūki marahi saṭha sotī. (Zaidi 1977: 101)

31. In some manuscripts, the *Dohāvalī* is extended into a *satsai.* I thank Imre Bangha for this information.
32. Raslin (1997) is a bi-scriptual edition.
33. Mir 'Abd al-Wahid, e.g., "composed poetry in Persian and Hindi, and had a good voice" (Azad Bilgrami [H 1166/CE 1752] 1913: 345); see also Orsini 2014b).
34. As we shall see, his contemporary Bhikharidas, perhaps the most famous poet-scholar of Brajbhasha poetics of the time, includes in his list of esteemed poets as many as eight poets from Awadh, and both Raslin and Mubarak from Bilgram.
35. Zaidi (1969: 92–99) gives the most informed account of his life, library, and works. Like other authors of poetics manuals in Brajbhasha (see Busch 2011: 109–120), Raslin (1969: 8) stressed his own originality: "I wrote this work in *dohas*, Raslin says [or: "I wrote in *dohas* this work full of *rasa*"] and I thought out my own definitions and created new explanations." Raslin's short work describing the parts of a woman's body (*Aṅga-darpaṇa*) dates from 1737; his longer treatise on aesthetics and varieties of heroines, *Rasaprabodha,* from 1742, is very similar to Bhikharidas's *Rasa-sārāṃśa* (1734) and exactly contemporary with Bhikharidas's treatise on metre *Chhandārṇava* (see Bhikharidas 1957).
36. For example, in his *tazkira,* Mohanlal Anis writes of Khushhal Chand Ikhlas that he studied "books of Hindi/Indian knowledge" (*'ilm-i hindī*), likely of Brajbhasha poetics (cited in Pellò 2012: 141).
37. The first three editions (two in 1878 and one 1883) contained notices of 998 poets, the fourth (1889) of 1,003. Interestingly, Sengar ([1878] 1970: 1) said he wrote the book because an earlier anthology had mistaken the Brahman clan attribution of the poet Matiram (Chintamani's younger brother): "I thought that one ought to write a book which would detail the dates, caste [*jāti*], place of residence, and poetic works of ancient and new/modern poets together with their biography." The modern editor, Dr. Kishorilal Gupta, corrected the dates of many poets because in the first edition Sengar had given their dates as *floruit* rather than birth, and had misdated one of his main sources, the anthology *Hajāra* (1–6).
38. Thanks to Tod's ([1829] 1914) *Annals and Antiquities of Rajasthan.* See Sengar's ([1878] 1970: 690–691) excited biography of Chand Bardai.

39. Even Malukdas is quoted with a *kabitta* quite out of line with his usual poems (Sengar [1878] 1970: 472).
40. When referring to the young girl, it means victorious in the battle of love.
41. He worked as police inspector in Kanta (dist. Unnao), and his library contained thousands of books and manuscripts.
42. About Narhari he wrote, "This poet was with Jalaluddin Akbar Badshah and he got the rent-free revenue of village Asni. . . . I have not heard of or seen any book by him, but I have heard many *kabittas* and *chhappays*" (Sengar [1878] 1970: 723).
43. In fact, by being in alphabetical order, *Shiv Singh's Flower* can start with Emperor Akbar himself and a few poems attributed to him (Sengar [1878] 1970: 11).
44. "This Maharaj [= Brahman] is considered among the *acharyas* (masters) of *bhasha* literature" (Sengar [1878] 1970: 692).
45. Sengar ([1878] 1970: 55, 61) includes two encomiastic poems by Kalidas Trivedi that employ very similar hyperbole to celebrate Emperor Aurangzeb's victory over Golconda Fort or his local patron Rao Bhagvantrao Khichi, whose roars of victories "open chinks in the hearts of the grandees of Delhi."
46. For example, Himmat Singh "Mahipati" (r. 1709–1731) and his son Gurudatt Singh "Bhupati" of Amethi (their noms de plume mean "king"), or Bhagvantrao Khichi of Dhaundiya Khera (d. 1735). Bhagvantrao patronized the poet Sukhdev Misra (fl. 1650–1670s), who may have returned to Awadh after serving patrons in Delhi, as well as Kalidas Trivedi, his son Udaynath Tivari, and grandson Dulah (see Sharma 2003).
47. A very popular anthology of a thousand-odd *kabittas* called *Hajārā* was long attributed to him (and was Sengar's main source) before the scholar Kishorilal Gupta (1978) showed that its date of composition must be pushed forward a hundred years. Despite the popularity of Dulah's manual *Kavikulakaṇṭhābharaṇa*, nothing is really known about his life and whereabouts (Dulah 2000).
48. One of the most striking examples of social mobility through Persian education must be that of Gaur Dhan (or is it Gobardhan?) Suraj Dhwaj, from Khari (Kara?) on the Ganges, who at the beginning of his career sat at the door of the local court (*kachehri*) copying out papers and did not even have money to buy a brass inkstand. He then got a small position in the Mughal administration and rose until he became a manager of the imperial household and personal manager of Empress Nur Jahan before he fell into disgrace. He left extensive buildings in his hometown, a temple and a water tank in Ujjain, and a neighborhood in Mathura (see Awrangabadi 1913: 572–574).
49. Of Mir Tufail, Azad only says, "Once in a while he practiced arranging verses in order to sharpen his nature and discussed the distinctions in poetry with others" (Azad Bilgrami [H 1166/CE 1752] 1913: 252).
50. According to Azad, Hafiz Ziyaullah Bilgrami had "first memorized the Qur'an as a child" and then "travelled around the qasbas of the province of Awadh to acquire knowledge from the [best] scholars of the time (*funūn-e darsī farā giraft*)" (Azad Bilgrami [H 1166/CE 1752] 1913: 250). Mir Tufail Muhammad Bilgrami had come to Bilgram from another *qaṣba* at the age of fifteen to study and "ended his journey of education in the reservoir of learning (*hauża-ye dars*) [i.e., Maulvi Sayyid Qutb

al-Din Shamsabadi]" before settling in Bilgram, where he taught for almost seventy years in the neighborhood of Maidanpura, in the sitting area, or *diwankhana*, of Mir ʻAbd al-Jalil Bilgrami, and "brought generations of students from the beginning of their studies to full master (*ustad*)" (251–252). I thank Ali Mojiz Bilgrami for taking me to see the *diwankhana* in Bilgram in February 2020.

51. This could refer to the earlier curriculum established by Fath Ullah Shirazi during Emperor Akbar's time (Alam and Subrahmanyam 2004) or to the Dars-e Nizami curriculum established by Firangi Mahal in Lucknow in the early eighteenth century (Malik 1997; Robinson 2001). A detailed list of the books and authors that an aspiring high-level Mughal administrator should study is contained in the letter that the imperial secretary (*munshi*) Chandrabhan Brahman wrote to his son; he also advised his son to read the "master poets" in his leisure time (Alam and Subrahmanyam 2004: 316–317).
52. Mir ʻAbd al-Jalil had studied under several scholars of Bilgram and other eastern *qasbas* (*qaṣbāt-i pūrab*) and "finished his studies in the circle of Shaykh Ghulam Naqshband in Lucknow" (Azad Bilgrami [H 1166/CE 1752] 1913: 253).
53. "A Kayastha's first rule is [or, First I learned the Kayastha rule] to write, document, and understand the difficult task of serving a king and of carrying out orders immediately, the twelve rules, listening to *avadānas*, and worship of the nine virtues. I reflected on metres, prosody, and the many forms of genres of composition (*prabandha*). Then I *strolled through Persian poetry* and recited various kinds of poems and couplets. Sarasvati herself came to dwell in my heart and in my mouth" (Puhakar 1963: 15, emphasis added). The editor Shivprasad Singh (1963, 9) glosses the nine virtues as patience, forgiveness, self-control, refraining from embezzlement (*asteya*), purity, control of the senses, knowledge, learning, and truth.
54. Puhakar (1963: 9): *najamana (nażm), sara (sheʻr), aviyāta (abyāt,* pl. of *bayt*, verse).
55. Sukhdev Misra, who came from a lineage of Sanskrit scholars, particularly astrologers, mentions writing "many books in Sanskrit and Prakrit" (*kiye saṃskṛta grantha jina prākṛta bahuta sameta/bhākhā vṛtta vichāra yaha, kīnhau kavikula heta*) (D. Misra 1988: 48n).
56. Sukhdev Misra was tutor for Rao Mardan Singh of Daundiya Khera, among others; as a *shakta* guru, he was also a spiritual teacher to some of his patrons (D. Misra 1988: 58–61).
57. As for the education of the early seventeenth-century Jain merchant and religious reformer Banarsidas, at age eight in Jaunpur he was sent for a year to a local school run by a Brahman pandit to learn how to "read out" and write—we assume in the vernacular, Hindavi. Then at fourteen he studied Sanskrit dictionaries of synonyms (*Nāmamālā* and *Anekārtha*) and books on poetics, astronomy, and erotic science (*Laghu kokaśāstra*) for a year with another pandit. At the same time he also acquired a taste for Persianate—if not Persian—poetry, which he expressed in Sufi-like terms: "I became a player in the game of love (*bhayau āsikabāja*) and set my mind on the path of love, suffering like a Sufi faqir" (*daradabanda jyauṃ sekha fakīra*; Banarsidas 1981: 237). A few months later, Banarsidas got seriously interested in religion and began studying religious texts with two itinerant Jain monks, as well as other Sanskrit

texts on lexicography and prosody; he even began writing one. He was living a double life, he felt, studying religious texts but composing verses on erotic love. That year he wrote a thousand-verse-long *chaupāī-dohā* work mostly on love, which he later threw into the River Gomti out of shame (Banarsidas 1981: 236–237).

58. Mir Sayyid Muhammad, who later arranged for their "publication" as "model letters." Azad Bilgrami ([H 1166/CE 1752] 1913: 291) praises him for his learning and disposition: "The Mir has a serious (*wāqar*) and intellectual disposition, and since he reads a lot the reins of his thought roam in the valley of speech. He is an expert in the Arabic, Persian, and Hindi languages and knows innumerable verses by heart in all the three languages. He often composes poetry."
59. I am grateful to Abhishek Kaicker for first showing me these wonderful letters, printed and translated by Francis Gladwin in 1798.
60. In another letter he wrote, "Exert yourself to the utmost in your studies," particularly of Quranic commentaries and Prophetic traditions (Hadith) but also jurisprudence and the sciences (Gladwin 1798: 147). In yet another letter, he advised his son not to study obscure treatises but to start with books of established reputation: "In studying the sciences it is necessary that you proceed according to method: now is the season for acquiring knowledge and this opportunity will never return" (161).
61. "Therefore it is necessary that you repair to Shahjahanabad and that quickly. . . . Bring from home only what baggage is absolutely necessary the less and lighter, with the greater ease you will travel. Please God when you get into the exercise of your offices, or arrive at Multan, you may procure whatever you require. In short, for the present come here without any incumbrance—you will be detained here a month or two whilst the papers of your Mansab and Offices are preparing. . . . The business of your Mansab and offices in the present times was a great point to accomplish" (Gladwin 1798: 248–249). Mir Sayyid Muhammad worked in the same post as his father in Sewistan, Sindh, until, after Nadir Shah's expedition there in 1740, he took leave and returned to Bilgram in 1743 to take care of family affairs and of his nephew's education (see Azad Bilgrami [H 1166/CE 1752] 1913: 290–291).
62. Azad Bilgrami ([H 1166/CE 1752] 1913: 372) quotes a Persian verse by a contemporary: "In this age, when few masters of eloquence are found, two individuals from Bilgram are masters (*ustād*) of poetry. One is the Imam of the age, Sayyid Ghulam 'Ali: no one recalls the like of him for Arabic verse. The other is a world of talent, Sayyid Ghulam Nabi [Raslin]: his nature brings Hindi verse to its aim. May God preserve them both through an Arab messenger and the God of all Glories (*bi-mursalin 'arabīyin wa-ilāhi l-amjād*)." I thank Simon Leese for his transliteration and translation of the Arabic phrase.
63. For the popularity of Jami, see d'Hubert and Paaps (2018).
64. Interestingly, the second edition of James Ballantyne's (1890) *English Primer* was printed in Banaras with a translation in easy Sanskrit, clearly to aid learners familiar with Sanskrit grammar in the study of English.
65. The terms *sabha*, *majlis*, and *darbar* are sometimes used interchangeably for assemblies or gatherings; *darbar* implies the presence of a figure of power or authority around whom others collect.

66. That is, a *qasida*, or ode, in with each line ends with the letter "l" (*lām*).
67. Ever the keen editor, Azad Bilgrami ([H 1166/CE 1752] 1913: 261) notes, "In most manuscripts it's like that, but the author has seen one manuscript in which that line is still there."
68. Bhagwan Das "Hindi," who worked for the finance minister of Lucknow state Tikait Rai, recalls in his *tazkira, Safīna-yi Hindī* (The Ship of Hindi, 1804) the story that another Bilgrami, Muhammad Sadiq "Sukhanwar" (lit. "Poet"), who came from a family of local judges (*qazis*) and pleaded before him to intercede with the minister and get his subsistence grant restored, had told him. Once "Sukhanwar" had traveled from Bilgram to Banaras with a friend and presented himself to the celebrated Iranian émigré poet Shaikh Hazin (d. 1766), who lived there in retirement: "The Shaikh was sitting on a bed with a bolster, he turned to us and gestured us to read our own verses. [My companion] recited this verse:

    dād az dil-i dard kīsh mā rā
    naguẕāsht ba ḥāl-e khwīsh mā rā
    He gave me from his painful heart
    and did not let me be to myself.

    The Shaikh was pleased and turned to me. When I, too, recited my verse, he said that the link between the words was wrong. I submitted that in the verses of the masters this kind of usage was found in abundance. The Shaikh laughed and said, 'Are you among those close to Siraj al-Din Arzu?' [who accepted Indian Persian poets as masters of language]. I said, 'I am one of his lowliest students.' The late Shaikh, by way of guidance, said, 'You both have plenty of Indian metrical verses (*mauzūn*).' But secretly he was not happy and he took leave from us" (Hindi 1958: 104).
69. See Kaicker (2018) for a full account.
70. As 'Abd al-Jalil forcefully put it, "[A] *jāgīr* [land grant] is the life of service, a servant without a *jāgīr* is in fact no servant" (Gladwin 1798: Persian text 158, English translation 159).
71. The poem goes:

    nawab falak-ruṭba amīr al-umarā
    har ḥarf zi 'īd bahre ū shud īmā
    'ain az 'aish wa yā zi yumn ast nishān
    dāl āmada zi har dawlat faiż ārā
    Amir al-Umara, lofty as the sky—
    Every letter of 'Īd nods toward him:
    'ain stands for joy, *ī* for felicity,
    dāl for every bountiful fortune. (Gladwin 1798: 174)
72. In Arabic:

    nāla amīru l-umarā ni'matan
    wa-hya qudūmu l-waladi l-mustanīr
    arrakha fī dhālika 'abdu l-jalīl
    amta'ahu llāhu bi-'umrīn kabīr
    Amir al-Umara has attained a great blessing

In the coming of [his] luminous son.
Abd al-Jalil has written a chronogram to mark the date of the occasion [1126]:
"May God grant him a long life."

In Persian:
gulī shiguft ba gulzār-i khāndān-i husain
zamāna shud bad-ū-am baqā-yi ū żamān
firishta āmīn guftā chū guftam īn tārīkh
hazār sāl shawad 'umr-i īn gul-i āman.
A flower blew in the flowerbed of Husain's family
I have become surety for its immortality
When I declared this date, "May this protected flower
bloom a thousand years," the angel said amen.

In Hindi:
putara janama sampata kahūṇ bansa seṇ mahīpa
chiranjīva juga juga sadā yaha saputara kuladīpa
I declared the year of the birth of a son
from the flock of Husain the chief.
May this son, who is the lamp of his family,
live happily in time, and in eternity. (Gladwin 1798: 206–209, translation slightly modified)

I thank Simon Leese for translating the Arabic verse.

73. Although there are many manuscripts and notebooks of Brajbhasha poetry in Persian script, testifying that the Persian-educated employed it also for Brajbhasha, this is a rare attestation that Persophone (or Persograph) literati like 'Abd al-Jalil read the Nagari script and—a small vindication for all of us who struggle when reading Brajbhasha and Avadhi in Persian script—acknowledged that it made reading clearer!
74. According to Azad, 'Abd al-Jalil "introduced Diwakar Misra son of Harbans Misra, one of the respected Brahmans of Bilgram and well known among everyone (*khāṣ-o 'ām*) in the arts of Sanskrit and Hindi (*bhākā*), into the service (*mulāzimat*) of Amir al-Umara Sayyid Husain 'Ali Khan, who made [Diwakar] one of his boon companions." Diwakar wrote a couplet in elegy for 'Abd al-Jalil:

    huvā nahī au hoegā aisau gunīn so sīla
    jaisau ahmad nanda jaga hoy gayau mīr alīla
    There never was and never will be a connoisseur
    As virtuous as Ahmad's son, the late Mir Jalil.

"By the strangeness of chances, the number that this *dohā* adds up to provided a perfect chronogram, nothing less, nothing more: he departed on 23 Rabi al-Akhir 1138 [29 December 1725]" (Azad Bilgrami [H 1166/CE 1752] 1913: 370).
75. See also the *tazkiras* by Bhagwan Das "Hindi" (1958) and Zulfiqar 'Ali "Mast" (1964), both largely dedicated to people the authors knew personally.
76. Yet longing for one's earthly home should be the prelude for longing for one's spiritual home beyond: "May this *tazkira* of my physical home gradually pull me towards that

of my spiritual home, and may it bring me from the narrowness of place to the vastness of non-place" (Azad Bilgrami 1910: 3).

77. This is an argument made by Purnima Dhavan (2014): scholars and their pupils who were employed away from the imperial hubs, like Azad Bilgrami, "appeared suddenly less connected with new trends." In this light, his anecdotes about his grandfather meeting Nasir 'Ali and finishing off a couplet by Bedil—both acknowledged masters of style—appear all the more significant. "It is in this historical moment," Dhavan continues, "that scholars like Azad Bilgrami begin to speak from the margins of the fragmenting Mughal empire, questioning the very perspective of marginality to which their own contemporary tazkirah culture could have consigned them."
78. His detailed notices of Punjab towns on the route from Kabul to Delhi (Lahore, Thanesar, Sirhind, Panipat) suggest that Razi actually visited them on his way to Delhi.
79. Many legends circulated concerning the burial sites of Seth in India and elsewhere.
80. "Lakhnau [Lucknow]: a city on the banks of the Gomti, with good climate (*āb-o hawā*) and sweet crystal sugar and *ānvlā* [myrobalan]. Earlier it used to produce good bows, but no longer. One of the author's ancestors, Qazi Muhammad, was minister of Lucknow at the end of the age of Muhammad Akbar *bādshāh*. There is an Akbari gate and a Sarai Akbari close to it, and an Akbari bridge. The gate has been renovated recently, but not the bridge, on which now butchers sit. The Wazir al-Mamalik Asaf al-Dawla Mirza Imami, son of Shuja' al-Dawla, has built a lot of new and large palaces after destroying the old houses. He has also built moorings and an Imambara and mosque on the banks of the river next to the 'Alamgiri mosque, and built them in such a way that no country of the seven climes can equal them in size and beauty. When the author worked for Abu'l Mansur Khan, he spent a lot of time in Lucknow with Raja Nawal Rai, the deputy of the province of Awadh, and met with the great men (*buzurgān*) of the time like Maulvi Nizamuddin, unmatched in knowledge and eloquence, Shah 'Abd al-Bani, etc." (Murtaza Bilgrami 1879: 155).
81. "Established by Kapila Muni on the banks of the godly river [the Ganges]. Everyday you see it crowded with poets and scholars. Men and women dwell there like gods, according to the four *varṇas*, each following their own. There are six large families of Suklas, who are gods on earth [= Brahmans], in one of which the wise Misra Sukhdev took birth" (S. Misra [S 1723] 1666), f. 3b); see also D. Misra (1988: 43).
82. The same is true of Persian and Urdu poetry praising the Prophet (*na't*). I thank Simon Leese for this comment.
83. 'Abd al-Jalil Bilgrami, *Amwāj al-khyāl* (late seventeenth century), 14, MS 8915514/16, Maulana Azad Library, Aligarh. I thank Sunil Sharma for the reference to Amir Khusrau and for his help in reading the poem. Already Razi (1963: 505) had used this strategy and quoted Khusrau's verses when praising India in the *Seven Climes*.
84. The possible and latent comparison was actualized most spectacularly in Azad Bilgrami's comparison between Arabic, Persian, and Hindi poetics and beloveds, dwelling on their *specificities*; see S. Sharma (2009).
85. The list varies slightly between different printed editions (see Chaturvedi 1962: 7). Another verse used the different purposes of poetry (*kāvya prayojana*) to divide Hindi poets:

Some acquire religious merit, such as the spiritual masters Tulsi and Sur.
Others seek wealth, in the manner of Keshavdas, Bhushan and Birbal.
Some seek only fame, like Rahim and Raskhan.
Says [Bhikhari] Das, discussing poetry always gives joy to clever people (*budhivanta*). (*Kāvyanirṇaya* 1.10, Bikharidas 1957 vol. 2:4, translated in Busch 2011, slightly altered)

86. I thank Imre Bangha for the last point.
87. The poet Dev was the first to introduce a caste typology of heroines, including lower-caste female vendors, in his *Jātivilāsa* (The delight of castes) and *Rativilāsa* (Love's delight), in intertextual relation, Nadia Cattoni (2019: esp. 151ff.) convincingly argues, with the Persian poetic genre of the *shahrashob* or "tumult in the city," a genre that delighted in describing the beauty of young urban craftsmen and vendors (Sharma 2004).
88. In fact, he prefaces his praise of God in his collection of miscellaneous poems with the title *śāntarasa kabitta* (Raslin 1969: vol. 1, 301).
89. As Busch (2010b) has noted, in doing so Raslin is close to the register of Sufi *katha* writers, but I would rather say that in the case of Raslin, who composed in two languages and mastered two poetic codes, the choice of unmixed register signals a desire to keep them separate.
90. As Heidi Pauwels (2012a, 2015) has shown, the palace library in Kishangarh has a copy of Vali's *diwan*; Savant Singh's anthology *Pada-muktāvalī* includes a few of Vali's Rekhta *ghazals*, and he began to write Vali-like poems and Rekhta *dhrupad* and *khyal* songs.
91. His manual *Sudhānidhi* (1734) contains a remarkably high number of Persianate words, phrases, and even idioms, as in this *kabitta*:

    Jamunā anhāi kai gaī maiṃ suvāhī āju
    This morning I went to the Jamuna to bathe,
    where a dusky one gave me his heart.
    He played the flute, sang many (*besa* < P *besh*) a Ragini. . . .
    Poet Tosh says, I'm dead on him (*usa para kurabāna*), my friend,
    I swear by you (*tere sira kī kasama*), he took my life away.
    He's a grand sweetheart, he and his yellow scarf,
    (*khūba mahabūba vaha jarada* [< P. *zard*] *dupaṭṭevālā*)
    But heartless—he saw me in thrall of passion and left. (Mathur 1965: 182)

    "Yellow-scarfed" (*jarada ḍupaṭṭevālā*) echoes the "red-scarfed" (*lāl ḍupattevālī*) of courtesan songs.

92. In another instance, Bhanupratap enters an Urdu verse to comment on his disappointment at having to leave his English school, and transliterates it in Nagari—another form of translation—on the side:

    qismat kī nārasāī se ṭūṭā vahīn kamand
    do-chār hāth jab ki lab-e bām rah gayā
    fate was impotent, the ladder broke just when
    the roof was just a few arms away. (Tiwari 1880: 7)

93. It is perhaps not chance that it was often royal or aristocratic patrons who became multilingual poets: apart from 'Abdur Rahim Khanekhanan, the Mughal emperor Shah 'Alam II and the Maharaja of Jodhpur Jaswant Singh.
94. There were some exceptions, like Kavindracharya, who composed in Sanskrit and Brajbhasha at the Mughal court. The proximity between Persian and Urdu in terms of poetic idiom meant that many more poets wrote or dabbled in both these languages.
95. As Jahangir's (1999) autobiography shows, he did not distinguish between Brajbhasha poets and singers. Persian poets were in another category altogether (Sharma 2015).
96. I explore this question in greater detail in Orsini (2019a), from which part of this section draws.
97. For example, Afroz Taj's (2007: 69) otherwise excellent edition of 'Amanat Lakhnavi's play *Indarsabhā* (Indra's court) states, "[L]ike any thinking person of his generation, Amanat must have been disturbed and depressed by the relative instability and political decay that was spreading around him. . . . Amanat must have also watched the expansion of the British into north central India with some dismay."
98. For *rekhti*, see Vanita (2012); for the *Indarsabhā*, Taj (2007).
99. Repertoires varied slightly: e.g., the song album compiled for the colonial resident and avid collector Richard Johnson in Lucknow (British Library, IO Islamic, 1906) includes more *tappas* and *khyals*, 'Amanat's play *Indarsabhā* has more *ghazals*, and Bhartendu's collections more seasonal songs, but all three largely overlap in terms of languages and song genres; compare with Schofield (2017) for earlier manuscript song collections.

Chapter 5

1. The literature on Bengali babus and *bhadralok* gentlemen is vast; see, e.g., Bhattacharya (2015).
2. An early wave of scholarship emphasized the similarities of response among Indian writers and intellectuals to colonial interventions in and discourses on language, literature, society, religion, history, and progress (Chandra 1992). Later regional studies have instead highlighted the importance of regional contexts and paid attention to both continuities and ruptures in terms of the relative strength and vitality of local intellectual traditions, sources of authority, and entrepreneurial cultures: see Dalmia (1997), Orsini (2002), and Pritchett (2004) for north India; Naregal (2001) and Pinto (2007) for western India; and Blackburn (2006), Ebeling (2010), and Venkatachalapathy (2012) for South India.
3. *Masks of Conquest* is the title of Vishwanathan's (1989) influential book; "Crushed by English Poetry" is the title of a chapter in Chandra (1992); *After Amnesia* is the title of Ganesh Devy's (1992) book.
4. The literature on Nawabi Lucknow is vast, but perhaps most evocative of its rich cultural life are 'Abd al-Halim Sharar's (1989, 1992) Urdu sketches on "Past Lucknow"

(*Guzishta Lakhnaū*) written between 1913 and 1920, which gained immediate renown; see also Cole (1988) and Vanita (2012).

5. The East India Company began to exert its authority in the province after it defeated the combined Awadh and Mughal army at the battle of Buxar in 1764; the Company pressured the Nawab of Oudh to cede Banaras and three other districts to the Company. More districts and divisions (Gorakhpur, Rohilkhand, Allahabad, Kanpur [Cawnpore], Etah, Etawah, Mainpuri, and southern Mirzapur) were ceded in 1801. Agra, Banda, and Hamirpur were added after the second Anglo-Maratha war (1803–1805) and the Anglo-Nepalese war of 1816. Lucknow and Oudh were annexed in 1856, just before the outbreak of the great Rebellion (or Mutiny) in 1857. Under British administration, the name of the province changed a few times: it was first called Ceded and Conquered Provinces (1805), then North-Western Provinces (1836), United Provinces of Agra and Oudh (1902), and finally United Provinces (1935); after Independence in 1947, it was renamed Uttar Pradesh (Northern Province).
6. For an absorbing and insightful meditation on the "pace" (*raftār* in Urdu) of time in the *qasbas* compared to the cities, see Robb (2021).
7. Although *qasbas* further west, toward Delhi, like Amroha or Meerut (Rahman 2015; Robb 2021), also became significant hubs of mainly Urdu and Persian publishing, authors in Awadh *qasba* seem to have sent their books to printers in the cities.
8. Details of the Naval Kishore catalogue are in Stark 2007: 181. Lucknow had several other Urdu printers, whereas contemporary Hindi literature was first published there in the 1920s by a scion of the Naval Kishore family, Dularelal Bhargava, who founded two prestigious Hindi literary monthlies and a publishing house, Ganga Pustak Mala (Nijhawan 2019). In the 1930s, former revolutionary Yashpal brought out his radical Hindi monthly *Viplav* (Upheaval, 1938).
9. The first Urdu serialized novel was editor Pandit Ratan Nath Sarshar's picaresque *Fasāna-e Āzād* (The tale of Azad or the free, 1878–1880); see Mookerjee (1992), Orsini (2009: ch. 5), Dubrow (2011), Stark (2007: 374ff.).
10. Allahabad had the greatest concentration of newspapers in the province: prominent English newspapers included the *Pioneer* (1867)—where young R. Kipling worked in the late 1880s—*Leader* (1909), and *Independent*. In Hindi there were the weekly *Abhyuday* (Rise, 1909) and monthly *Maryādā* (Dignity, 1910), both launched by Congress leader M. M. Malaviya (see Orsini 2002). Newspapers mirrored political divisions, e.g., between the *Leader*'s Liberal editor C. Y. Chintamani, Congress Hindu nationalist Malaviya, and Moderate Motilal Nehru, while revolutionaries found sympathy among students and teachers (Maclean 2015).
11. For Ghalib's letter about Allahabad, see Mehrotra (2007: 47); for colonial Allahabad and its politicians, see Bayly (1975).
12. The Indian Press was Rabindranath Tagore's Bengali publisher until he donated his copyright to his university in Shantiniketan, Vishvabharati, in 1921.
13. For Kitabistan (est. 1933–1934), see Farooqi (2012: 224).
14. The literature on colonial Banaras is vast: see, e.g., Freitag (1989b), Dalmia (1997), Dodson (2003); also Nita Kumar (1988).

15. "All in all, about twenty printing presses brought out hundreds of Sanskrit books between the 1860s and the 1880s. Most printer-publishers in Benares were in fact Brahmins—Chaubes, Tivaris and Pathaks" (Orsini 2004: 116).
16. Prominent printer-publishers included E. G. Lazarus's Benares Medical Hall Press, Gopinath Pathak's Benares Light Press, and Ramkrishna Varma's Bharat Jiwan Press, half of whose output consisted of courtly (*riti*) Brajbhasha poetry (see Chapter 4); see Orsini (2004) and Stark (2007: 64; 2015).
17. For Nepali publishing in Banaras, see Chalmers (2002). The most notable Urdu publisher in Banaras was Muhammad Hanif's Gulzar-e Benares Press (see list in Orsini 2004).
18. Khatri launched *Upanyās lahrī* (Wavelet of novels, ca. 1894) and established the Lahri Press. Jayram Das Gupta started *Upanyās bahār* (Spring of novels) in 1907; his Upanyas Bahar Press "became one of the most flourishing commercial publishers of Benares in the early twentieth century, and its books are still sold in the Chowk area of the city" (Orsini 2004: 125).
19. For a history of Kanpur, see Joshi (2003).
20. The most famous colleges include Queen's College (1791) in Banaras; Canning College (1864), Colvin Taluqdars' College, King George's Medical College, and Isabella Thoburn College for girls in Lucknow; and Muir Central College (1872), Kayastha Pathshala (1873), and Crosthwaite High School for girls (1895) in Allahabad.
21. Educational statistics for 1892 put figures for male literacy at only 5.2% (with a further 1% "learning") and 0.2% (with 0.4% "learning") for female literacy (details in Orsini 2009: 48). By the 1930s, Banaras had gained several colleges, including Theosophist Annie Besant's Central Hindu College, the imposing Benares Hindu University (est. 1915), and an alternative "national" (*rashtriya*) college, Kashi Vidyapith (est. 1920). See Orsini (2002).
22. See Rawat (2011); for Dalits in Allahabad, see Baudhacharya Nath in Narayan (2011: 79).
23. As Veena Naregal (2018: 198) has argued, the emphasis on translation from and into English as a "holdall pedagogical tool" implied an instrumental view of language, predicated on equivalence between languages and disregarding the semantic nuances of words and concepts. What was involved in fact was a "double translation," since the vernacular created for the purpose was not the one with which pupils was familiar but one they had to learn.
24. "Works such as these will not only make a valuable addition to Hindi Literature but will tell people ignorant of English what stuff English poetry is made of. They will give them insight into that fine imagery, those delicate paintings of scenes and characters which are the peculiar attractions of English poetry, they will lead them from the land of the wild, the fantastic, the supernatural, the impossible with which so much of Oriental poetry and romance abounds into the regions of reason and reality, and lastly they will give them an opportunity of setting a right value upon foreign productions instead of blindly and therefore partially deciding in favour of works of indigenous art" (*Aligarh Institute Gazette* review, 6 July 1886, quoted in Pathak 1889: iv–v). See Ritter (2011: 68–79) for an extensive analysis of this translation.

25. About "*The Solitary Yogi: a romance*, which Pandit Shridhar Pathak has translated (*ulthā kiyā*) from English into Hindi verse for the sake of Hindi and English poetry lovers" (as the cover reads), the reviewer wrote, "It is rare even in prose that so faithful a rendering is seen in the case of languages so widely different as English and Hindi, but in verse such close adherence to an original, while preserving fluency and poetic sweetness is exceedingly rare indeed" (*Opinions and Reviews*, quoted in Pathak 1889: viii).
26. He dedicated his translation of *The Deserted Village*, *Ūjaṛ Gām*, to Frederic Pincott MRAS, an "earnest advocate of the just claims of the Hindi language to official recognition" (Pathak 1889: n.p.).
27. Indeed, the standard edition of *The Traveller* and *The Deserted Village* (Goldsmith 1888) was by a professor of English literature at Elphinstone College, Bombay, Arthur Barrett, and included a substantial historical introduction and copious notes aimed at Indian students. Pathak instead tried to bring together the community of taste of Brajbhasha connoisseurs (*rasikas*) and that of the English educated and described his readers as "always tasting anew the nectar of the pleasures of verse/ bees drinking the honey of new poetry, lovers of new flowers" (translated in Ritter 2011: 70).
28. Though now justly famous for his inventive plays, Harishchandra's prodigious published output—periodicals, plays, essays, antiquarian and religious works, poems, song collections, etc.—spans the whole range of "genres reproduced" and "genres introduced," and he saw to it that even his songs and poems (largely in Brajbhaṣha, though he also experimented with Urdu) appeared in print (see Dalmia 1997).
29. Bachchan used a Sanskritic diction almost devoid of Perso-Urdu words, and the frisson and novelty generated by the contrast between diction and content praising wine-drinking, together with the musicality of the poem, proved immensely popular with Hindi audiences. According to Trivedi (1993: 34), the book has been continuously reprinted and by 1990 had sold over 100,000 copies.
30. As Andrew Ollett put it, "Why call it multilingual? It is *the* pre-modern" (personal communication, October 2019). My contention in this book, however, is that it is not *just* the premodern.
31. The scholarship on the topic is vast: e.g., King (1994), Dalmia (1997), Rai (2001), Faruqi (2001), Brass (1974). Preetha Mani (2022) writes that colonial-era vernacularization was new and positioned English as *the* paradigmatic vernacular. There is actually no term in Hindi or Urdu that combines the natural-colloquial and all-encompassing aspects of the English term "vernacular," which are, however, evident in the Hindi and Urdu discourse about language in this period: *bolchāl kī bhāshā* or *zabān* emphasizes the colloquial at the expense of the all-encompassing. For a recent discussion of the term "vernacular" comprising quite different positions, see the special issue edited by Shankar (2020).
32. "Progress in one's *own language* (*nij bhāshā*) is the root/source of all progress, your heart's distress will not be removed without knowing your language," Bharatendu Harishchandra famously said in a verse speech titled "The Progress of Hindi" (*Hindī unnati par vyākhyān*, 1877), in Sharma (1989: 228). "A man's mother tongue is as

important as his mother and motherland are. . . . One who does not respect one's language, who does not love it and does not enrich its literature, can never improve the state of his country. His dream of self-rule, his vow of improving the country and praise for patriotism are but shallow," echoed Mahavir Prasad Dvivedi in a speech to the Hindi Literature Association in 1923 (*Sammelan Patrikā,* October 1923), quoted in Orsini (2002: 128n).

33. See Dharwadker (1993) for a discussion in the context of Indian languages and literatures.
34. In his recent books on the *Linguistic Survey*, Javed Majeed (2019) has stressed the instability of Grierson's nomenclature and irresolution with regard to language boundaries, but in my view Grierson's blindness to historical and embodied multilingualism, which translated, e.g., into the erasure of Persian and Urdu, are more glaring.
35. Harishchandra, *Hindī bhāshā* (Hindi language, 1883–1884), in Dalmia (1997: 213, 214).
36. This was the time of the Anglicist vs. Orientalist controversy about the language of education, in which Macaulay wrote the famous 1835 Minute: "I have read translations of the most celebrated Arabic and Sanscrit works. I have conversed both here and at home with men distinguished by their proficiency in the Eastern tongues. I am quite ready to take the Oriental learning at the valuation of the Orientalists themselves. I have never found one among them who could deny that a single shelf of a good European library was worth the whole native literature of India and Arabia. The intrinsic superiority of the western literature is, indeed, fully admitted by those members of the Committee who support the Oriental plan of education." The speech is available on the Columbia University website: http://www.columbia.edu/itc/mealac/pritchett/00generallinks/macaulay/txt_minute_education_1835.html. In practice, in education and in the administration a two-tier system was established, with English at the top and the regional vernacular at the lower levels.
37. He was echoed by Allahabad University historian and leading spokesman for Hindustani Dr. Tara Chand (1944: 5), who wrote, "Hindi is 135 years old."
38. In an earlier document, the educationist Raja Shiva Prasad (like his contemporaries, highly multilingual) had made a similar case and argued that the use of Urdu in education and administration "thrusts a Semitic element in the bosom of Hindus and alienates them from Aryan speech" (*Memorandum: Court Characters in the Upper Provinces*, 1868, cited in Goswami 2004: 173). Both Shiva Prasad and Malaviya called Urdu part of Hindi as well as foreign: "The *Persianized dialect of Hindi, known as Urdu* . . . was, and still is, by reason of the preponderance of Persian, Arabic, and Turkish words, and the fact of it being written in the Persian characters, *practically foreign* and unintelligible to the vast majority of the people of these Provinces" (Malaviya 1897: 5, emphases added). The colonial officers and scholars he quoted variously used the terms "Nagari," "Hindi," and "Hindu" for script and language.
39. Datla (2013) carefully historicizes the positions of key Urdu scholars like Hafiz Mahmud Sherani and Maulvi Abdul Haq. She shows that Abdul Haq on the whole preferred to advance Urdu's claim on the basis of its geographic spread, its currency across religious communities, and its ability to incorporate *modern* knowledge; based

in the Princely state of Hyderabad in the Deccan, Haq traced the early use of Urdu (also called Dakkhini) there.

40. The best-known Hindustani Academy interventions in the language debate were Padmasingh Sharma's lectures *Hindī, urdū, aur hindustānī*, already quoted, and Dr. Tara Chand's (1936) *Influence of Islam on Indian Culture*. Besides a scholarly journal in both Hindi and Urdu (*Hindustānī*) and a substantial library, the other notable enterprise of the Academy was a series of translations into Hindi and Urdu. But, as Lunn (2013) has shown, even its secretary Dhirendra Varma, the long-standing Hindi professor at Allahabad University, did not think that Hindustani was viable because it had no literature (see also Lunn 2018).
41. The Society for the Promotion of Nagari of Banaras produced a Hindi glossary of scientific terms in 1906, a dictionary of legal terms in 1932, and a multivolume Hindi dictionary (King 1974). About the impressive Urdu translation program at Osmania University, Datla (2009: 1143) notes that many more new terms were coined for science textbooks (56,407 words for 175 books on science subjects vs. 6,288 new coinages for about 185 art and social science books).
42. Datla (2009: 1124) quotes a story about "coining" vs. "discovering" words in the translation bureau of Osmania University in Hyderabad, the first vernacular (Urdu)-medium university: in "Mass Education Possible through Mother Tongue Alone," Sayyid Ross Masood (Sir Sayyid Ahmad Khan's son) recounted that when he and his fellow translators were thinking about an Urdu word for the geographical term "watershed," the committee of Orientalists coined one that sounded very difficult to him, the Persian *fāsil-i āb*. A few weeks later, when touring a district, another member asked a farmer, "What do you call such hills?," and was told a common word, *pandhal*, in fact a literal translation of "watershed." "In this way we were able to discover a precious term. Perhaps, I ought not to say that we 'discovered' it, for, it had been in use for hundreds of years and we were ignorant of it, simply because we had not paid attention to our vernacular." Arguably this was an ideal rather than a practice; for a similarly rare example, see Singh (2015).
43. Dvivedi, *Hindustāniyoṃ ke ke aṅgrezī lekh* (English articles by Indians), *Sarasvatī* (1914), quoted in Bhatnagar (1951: 332).
44. The phrase is Dalmia's (1997: 148).
45. Again, the scholarship is plentiful even just on Hindi and Urdu: see Sharma (1973), Chandra (1992), Dalmia (1997), Gupta (2001), Orsini (2002), Pritchett (2004), and Ritter (2011).
46. For example, see Lutgendorf (1994) for the "ancient biography" of Tulsidas that helpfully "resurfaced" in the 1920s.
47. As we saw in Chapter 4, the alphabetical structure and *kabitta*-centrism of Sengar's *Shiv siṃh saroj* were reproduced by Grierson (1889) in his *A Vernacular Literary History of Hindustan*.
48. See Das (1903); see also Dube (2009) for a history of the project.
49. See Majeed and Shackle (1997) for the *Musaddas*.
50. See *Calendars* of Calcutta University (Matriculation and BA, 1919, 1937) and of Allahabad University (BA 1928 and 1929).

51. In Azad's metaphorical explanation of how Urdu poetry had come into being—from Indian soil and Persian breeze and color—Brajbhasha stood for naturalness, while Persianate metaphors represented artifice and excess: "[A]lthough the tree of Urdu grew in the ground of Sanskrit and Bhasha, it has flowered in the breezes of Persian. . . . If the color [of Persian metaphors and similes] had come only like cosmetic paste rubbed into the face, or like collyrium in the eyes, it would have enhanced both attractiveness and vision. But alas—its intensity caused severe harm to the eyes of our power of expression. And it made the language merely a show (*svāng*) of imaginary effects and illusions. As a result, Bhasha and Urdu became as different as earth and sky. . . . [W]hatever thing the Bhasha language mentions, it explains to us with every detail the features that are encountered in seeing, hearing, smelling, tasting, or touching that particular thing. Although this description lacks the force of exaggeration, or the pomp and grandeur of tumult and tempest, the hearer receives the same pleasure that he would have received from seeing the real thing itself. The poets of Persia, by contrast, never show clearly the good or bad features of anything they depict" (Azad, Pritchett, and Faruqi 2001: [49–50]).
52. In the first edition, only Tulsidas (who came first) and Surdas were included among bhakti poets; Kabir was introduced only in the revised edition. The courtly poets included were Dev, Biharilal, two of the Tripathi brothers (Bhushan and Matiram, but not Chintamani; see Chapter 4), and Keshavdas; then came the earlier poet of heroic *rasau,* Chand Bardai, and finally Bhartendu Harishchandra, the only modern gem. See Mishra ([1910] 1934).
53. Azad had focused exclusively on the *ghazal* and on poets from north India, particularly Delhi, thus excluding large swaths of Urdu literary production; see Pritchett and Faruqi's introduction in Azad, Pritchett, and Faruqi (2001). Saksena (1927: 1) opted for a lucid but comprehensive historical account without textual selections, inspired by Saintsbury's *Short History of English Literature.*
54. "The literary Urdu of to-day is replete with such *borrowed foreign* constructions. It must be admitted that the influence of Persian raised the dialect to [the] dignity of a language though it is to be deplored that it destroyed much of what was valuable in the dialect which it had obtained from the parent tongue [i.e., Western Hindi]" (Saksena 1927: 4, emphasis added). Persian is still considered a foreign language here. As Ralph Russell (1999) put it in his playful and perceptive essay, "How Not to Write a History of Urdu Literature": If you don't like a literature, don't write its history!
55. The Urdu BA syllabus at Allahabad University foregrounded works by the modern reformers (Azad, Hali, and Sayyid Ahmad Khan), but also some of the poetic culture of Nawabi Lucknow. Fiction featured more prominently than in the Hindi syllabus (though only at the MA level), with texts from the satirical magazine *Oudh Punch*, Mirza Hadi Ruswa's delightful novel about a Lucknow courtesan, *Umrāo jān adā* (1899), and Sarshar's picaresque *Fasāna-e Āzād* (1878–1883). As for poetry, elegies (*marsiyas*) were preferred to *ghazals* and encomiastic *qasidas*, while the MA course included special papers on two canonical poets, Mirza Ghalib and the contemporary Muhammad Iqbal. The BA Hindi syllabus at Allahabad University featured two poetic "classics," the devotional Tulsidas (see Chapter 3) and courtly Keshavdas, and the

contemporary reformist reworking of Krishna's beloved Radha by Harioudh. It also established a modern Hindi canon, with two plays by Bharatendu Harishchandra, a critical essay by Mahavir Prasad Dvivedi, and short stories by Premchand. Hindi students were also tested in literary history and in translation from English and Sanskrit (Urdu students from English and simple Persian) (*Calendar of Allahabad University* 1928: 340–342). On Hindi textbooks and the establishment of Hindi within the education system, see also Orsini (2002: ch. 1.4).

56. For example, Ismail Merathi's ([1909] 1913) influential *Kumak-e-urdū* (Urdu helper) began with a lively dialogue by Nazir Ahmad (1831–1912), whose novels had been a staple of Urdu education since the 1870s, and interspersed inspirational and instructive prose passages by the author himself and other figures of the Urdu reformist movement (Sayyid Ahmad Khan, Muhammad Husain Azad, Altaf Husain Hali, etc.) with short passages from a travelogue (by Shibli Nu'mani) and Azad's historical account of Emperor Akbar's court, etc. Ismail Merathi (1844–1917) was a Persian teacher at Agra Government Normal School (a teachers' training institution) and is remembered as a writer dedicated to poetry for children (see Nawaz 2017).
57. If the range of poetic genres in this textbook is quite wide, the content is studiously edifying. Poems include descriptive, emotive, and didactic *masnavis,* Hali's "A traveller remembering his homeland (*watan*)," as well as the section on education from his celebrated *Musaddas* and the satirical poems by Akbar Ilahabadi. The *qasida* section includes only poems in praise of Queen Victoria's Jubilee by Akbar Ilahabadi and Nazir Ahmad and Akbar's innovative poem in praise of paternal love (Merathi [1909] 1913; see also Nawaz 2017).
58. Lala Sitaram's (1923) own multivolume anthology *Hindi Selections* accompanied Hindi's inclusion as a subject at university level at Calcutta University.
59. This textbook included Kabir (see Chapter 3), Jayasi (Chapter 2), Surdas and Tulsidas (Chapter 3), but also contemporary Brajbhasha poet Jagannath Das Ratnakar from Banaras and modern Khari Boli Hindi poets Shridhar Pathak, Harioudh, Maithilisharan Gupta, and the young Chhayavadis Prasad, Pant, and Nirala. The textbook also included several poets of courtly Hindi like Rahim and Biharilal, and a "sampling" for "connoisseurs of *rasa*" (*rasajña*). Not one woman was included, however; neither the devotional Mirabai nor the contemporary Mahadevi Varma (Barthwal and Misra 1931).
60. Shyamsundar Das (1928) had published the book for the Society for the Promotion of the Nagari Script with a similar introduction.
61. Interestingly, Hindi poetry is here taken as one, without the careful distinction between bhakti and courtly that Hindi literary histories emphasized.
62. The expression "homeless texts" is from Tavakoli-Targhi (2001).
63. Servan-Schreiber (1999, 2003, 2010) details the repertoires and circuits of these singers: Naths were itinerant, ascetic followers of Shiva, Madaris followers of the heterodox Sufi Shah Madar, Nats jugglers and performers, Noniyas makers and sellers of saltpeter, Kevats boatmen; Doms took care of dead carcasses, Ahirs bred cattle, and Dusadhs pigs.

64. Premghan (1949), *Kajlī kutūhal* (The wonder of *kajli*); see also Orsini (2009: ch. 3) and Yang (1998) for the proliferation of fairs.
65. For Nautanki, see Hansen (1992).
66. "One omission must be mentioned with regret. I have refrained from including the large number of anonymous folk-epics and of folk-songs (such as *kaj'ris*, *jat'sars*, and the like) current throughout Northern India. These can only be collected on the spot from the mouths of the people, and, so far as I am aware, that has only been systematically done in the province of Bihar. I have therefore, after some hesitation, determined to exclude all mention of them from the work, as any attempt to describe them as a whole could only have been incomplete and misleading" (Grierson 1889: vii).
67. Unlike Bengal; see Karim and Sharif (1964).
68. She rightly refuses to straitjacket their impulses in a simple paradigm of colonial power-knowledge, though: "In the colonial context, there are many cycles of motivation—from macro to micro level, and from state to individual level" (Naithani 2010: 18). Colonial collectors worked individually but were often in contact with colleagues elsewhere in the empire or with the Folk-Lore Society in London, "where folklore from the whole Empire could be put on the same table and discussed" (6). For a parallel reflection on the ideology of folklore in Europe, see Neubauer (2006).
69. Like William Bennett's *Gazetteer of the Province of Oudh* (1877) or Crooke's *Popular Religion and Folklore of Northern India*.
70. Sadhana Naithani (2002, 2007) has reestablished Ram Gharib Chaube's proper authorship by reassembling and publishing the stories he collected.
71. Tiwari made use of his multilingual knowledge, detailed in his 1890 Hindi manuscript autobiography (see Chapter 4), to contribute a wide range of material to *NIN&Q*: he translated from Persian a historic letter by John Coryate (items Number 464, 1891) and botanical information (N. 696, 1891). He also reported ethnographically on the "customs" of local Shi'as, Sayyids, the Kahar caste ("tribe," items Number 344, 348, 1892), and Rauniyar Baniyas; he wrote on local festivals and on a local Sufi shaikh of Chunar. He also contributed and translated popular songs and charms, songs by Guru Nanak and about local history, as well as poems by local Brajbhasha poets, like Kashtajiva Swami from Banaras and Raja Raghuraj Singh of Rewa; see *NIN&Q* 1891–1893.
72. Other regular contributors on Muslim folklore were Munshi Karam-ud-din of Mirzapur, M. Mahmud Beg, and Abdul Rahman.
73. *Míthá nám hai Alláh Miyán ká*
Dújé míthá Rasúl.
Tíjé mıthá Sáwan Bhádon,
Jo barsai so núr.
Jehi din newá parí Makké men
Jánat muluk Jahán,
Jitné ummat rahé Muhammad ké
Sab jhuk, jhuk karat salám.
Bágh bajáwat bansuri,
Bhálu bajáwat túr,

Náchat áwain Indar kí pariyán,
Dekhat awain pák Rasúl.
Nách baháne miyan utren Nabijí,
Díye dhartí men gor,
Jitné ummat rahain Muhammad ké
Sab kharé bhaé kar jor. (NIN&Q December 1891: 145–146)

74. Tiwari translates *gor* as "foot," though it means "grave." He also wrote the translation in prose, whereas I have formatted it in verse and slightly modified it. For some reason, tales are always recorded with the name of the teller, whereas the singers of songs are left unnamed.
75. Upadhayay (1964) criticizes Tripathi's sloppiness and writes that he changed the title of his book from *Bhojpūrī grāmgīt* to *lokgīt* (Folk songs rather than Village songs) after he realized that folk songs were very much part of the urban soundscape. Tripathi's bibliography lists a large number of colonial folklore collections, showing his awareness of the discipline.
76. Interestingly, this life-changing encounter on a country road with an old woman (an echo of "grandmother," or *ṭhākurmā,* that became a crucial trope in Bengali folklore; see Adhya, in progress) while he was traveling on a horse-drawn cart (Tripathi 1929b: 1). Though in fact she did not sing or tell any tale, his conversation with her opened his eyes to the destitution and human simplicity of that rural world and his own ignorance of it—though he admits that he was born and lived in a village until the age of eighteen.
77. And later, further in this vein: "Our eyes are here, yet we seem to wake up in Europe. Our ears are here, yet we can only hear European voices and sounds. Our minds and hearts are here, yet we seem to only be able to dream of the West. What is the matter? Who has carried us away so far and so easily?" (Tripathi 1929b: 2).
78. Tripathi later quotes several medieval Sanskrit verses on poverty within villages, which here seem to enact a double move: they suture the past of Sanskrit with the present of Hindi, and they show that the "golden country" of classical Sanskrit poetry is no longer happy and bountiful, a reflection of the colonial present:

    vṛddhondhaḥ patireṣa mañcakagataḥ sthūṇavaśeṣaṃ gṛhaṃ
    kālo'bhyarṇajalāgamaḥ kuśalinī vatsasya vārtāpi no
    yatnātsañcitatailavindu ghaṭikā bhagneti paryākulā
    dṛṣtvā garbhabharālasāṃ nijavadhuṃ śvaśruściraṃ roditi

    The old and blind husband is lying on a cot. Only the posts are left of the roof.
    The four rainy months are coming, and there is no news of the son who left.
    The pot holding oil collected drop by drop has broken—worried
    and watching her heavily pregnant daughter-in-law, the mother-in-law weeps.
    (Tripathi 1929b: 10)

    For this genre of Sanskrit village poetry, see Knutson (2014).
79. Interestingly, an Urdu line is invoked to convey this particular mood.
80. "The life that has been flowing from time immemorial in the thick *dhak* forests, in the dense and cool shade of mango, *mahua, pipal,* tamarind and neem trees, alongside rippling waterways, near altars of *tulsi* scented by jasmin, *madhavi, kamini* and *malati*

blossoms, surrounded by birds chirping and cuckoos calling their tune, with fields swaying in the eastern (*purva*) breeze" (Tripathi 1929b: 2).

81. The trope of village India as untouched by historical change and the onslaught of modernity was also a colonial trope; see Inden (1990).
82. Catherine Servan-Schreiber's excellent work on Bhojpuri singers, genres, booklets, and networks of circulation, extending all the way to coolie colonies like Mauritius, is an exception.
83. For the first, see Rais (1990); the second was organized at Jawaharlal Nehru University by Dr. Mazhar Hussein and Yousuf Saeed on 8–10 September 2017; see http://www.tasveereurdu.in/schedule.html.
84. See the wide range of Hindi and Urdu poems anthologized in Nijhawan (2010).
85. For nationalist songs, see Shaw and Lloyd (1985) and Pandey (1975). For Dalit songs, see, e.g., the *kajri* "Rama, what injustice Sants' children have met with (*Rāmā santõ kī santānõ pe julm kyā ḍhāyā re harī*). First they called us *śūdras*, then they made us serve them. First they despised us, then they oppressed us" in Prabhu Dayal's (1927: 12) *Bārahmāsā achhūt pukār* (Twelve month song of an untouchable's cry). I am grateful to Ram Rawat for sharing this text with me.
86. Songbooks, songs of the twelve months (*barahmasas*), and *qissa* tales—all "genres reproduced"—were the most widely printed genres in both Hindi and Urdu in the 1870s and 1880s (see Orsini 2009).
87. Former narrator of religious *kathas* (*kathavachak*) and successful Parsi theater playwright Radheshyam Kathavachak (2001, translated in Hansen 2011: 113) recalls in his autobiography the excitement surrounding the annual tours of Parsi theater companies in his hometown. People immediately learned the songs by heart, and he set ritual and devotional songs to their tunes, a practice still current with film songs.
88. Prince Gulfam prevails upon the Green Pari to let him watch the all-female musical performance at the court of King Indar of Singhaldip, of which she is part, but when they are discovered he is imprisoned in Kuh-e Kaf (a toponym of Persian narratives), while she is banished to Earth with her wings clipped. A staple character of Persian narratives, the *div*, or demon, acts here as a helper. 'Amanat's own commentary (*sharh*) on the play offers a wonderful visual and aural sense of its contemporary performance, from firecrackers and lights to curtains, music, and sound effects (text and translation in Taj 2007: 427–519).
89. Narayan Prasad "Betab" (1872–1945), later a famous playwright for Parsi theater companies, thus described his first visit to the theater in his autobiography (2002: 32): "I started to see in the theatre all the things for which Paradise is called Paradise. Its actors were Gods, the boys playing the part of the [heroine's] girlfriends were Apsaras, the singers were Gandharvas and the actors Yakshas and Kinnaras [semi-divine beings]. Such a veil this *Indar sabhā* threw over my mind that I became entranced by those witches by day and fairies by night. But to reach there for a pauper like me was difficult."
90. Topaz (Pukhraj) Pari sang two spring (*basant*) songs, one in the koine we may call "bazaar Brajbhasha" and the other a "*basant* ghazal":

    Ruta āʾī basanta 'ajaba bahāra
    khile jarda phūla baron kī ḍāra. (refrain of *basant* song, Taj 2007: 208)

Basant is here, that wonderful season
yellow flowers spring on tree branches.
Hai jalwa tan se dar-o-dīwār basantī
poshāk jo pahne hai mĕrā yār basantī. (Taj 2007: 210)
his body's splendour tinges walls and doors of spring
as his clothes are the colour of spring.

In the former, the "rustic" words *ruta* (< Skt. *ṛtu*) for "season" and *baron* for "trees," and the localized phonology of *jard* for *zard* (P "yellow") are enough to mark the idiom as Brajbhasha and the speaker as one in a group of girlfriends enjoying the flowers of the new season. In the latter, the common Persian compound *dar-o-dīwār* and the term *yār* for "beloved," as well as the rhyme scheme (*-ār basantī*), take the viewer to the different emotional landscape of the *ghazal*, that of a courtesan performing love through the subtle play of poetic effects. In other words, the "Basant ghazal" and "Sawan ghazal" mix Urdu ghazal aesthetics with motifs and the emotional content of seasonal songs.

91. As Anuradha Kapur (2006: 211–212) has put it, "These new stylistics were in the melodramatic mode and their defining features were a *structure of* extravagance or *excess* at the level of scenography, stage effects, music, sound, language, suspense and colour. By investing the stage with a *surplus of pleasures*, and by creating narratives that plotted love in taut opposition to higher forms of duty (towards one family or one's country), the Parsi theatre created a hugely popular modern commercial entertainment that produced an ever expanding audience."
92. Davesh Soneji has found "Parsi songs" in Urdu/Hindi but in Tamil script, as well as in Tamil language, performed by companies in Thanjavur in South India that testify to their appeal (personal communication). See Cohen (2001) for the impetus touring Parsi theater had in the creation of local musical theater in Java, called *Komedie Stamboul*.
93. For satirical parodies, see Sikander (2021).
94. This influence is notable since Harishchandra professed to despise Parsi theater and once walked out of a Parsi play in Banaras in which Ram's wife Sita spoke Urdu and strutted like a courtesan (Hansen 1989).
95. Allegory thrived as a "performative domain" in "the conjunction between the space of the lithograph and the space of the theatre stage . . . a world of semiotic and affective intensity in which content (and increasingly, form) became layered with 'national feeling' " (Pinney 2002: 125).
96. Allegory created associations and produced a "semiotic infrastructure" and "affective intensities" that underwrote the later, more condensed focus on icons such as Mother India and Gandhi, Pinney (2002: 133) argues: "Once allegory has done its laborious work, figure can transform these associations into immediate identifications."
97. India is here still identified as Bharat, a male king, rather than as the female Mother India.
98. Premghan's *India's Fortune* features many allegorical characters, particularly among the enemies of India: the principal villains are India's Ill Fortune (*Badiqbal-e Hind*) and his Queen Ignorance (*Jahalat*); his helpers are named Destruction (*Markat*,

Lutlat, Tortar, Phunkpar), and their wives are Helplessness, Ruin, Violence, Injustice; his officials Enmity, Strife, Division; his Residents *Bakbak, Jhakjhak, Thakthak* and *taktak* and their wives, who have double Urdu-English names: *Kahili urf* Idleness, *Beparvai urf* Ease, *Aiyashi urf* Luxury, *Kamhimmati urf* Cowardice, *Lamazhabu urf* Free Thinking, etc. See Premghan (1949).

99. For example, the Bhojpuri rebel says, "भला तो अगववँ कुछु कहिहा? कि डेरवाय-डेरवाय हमनी के मार लिहल चाहाल, रौआँ ओजाँ रहलीं हाँ कि सुन लीं?" *(Bhalā to agvavaṃ kuchhu kahihā? Ki ḍervāy-ḍervāy hamnī ke mār lihal chāhāl, rauāṃ ojāṃ rahlī hāṃ ki sun lī?)* (So, will you say something? Or . . .) (Premghan 1949: 332). I thank Aishwarj Kumar for his translation.

100. See also the parodies and bilingual puns in Indian *Punches* in Dubrow (2018) and Sikander (2021).

101. Some time they take me by the collar
  And tell, "Just get out.
  He's got nothing to give or take,
  what did he come for,
  this useless nincompoop.
  I w'nt say anything true, let the
  India be ruined.
  I don't believe in Hindu idols, but I
  Worship only to show.
  Neither my brother-in-law nor my fellow caste men
  will throw me out of my caste. (Transliterated from *Hariśchandra's Magazine*, May 1874, in Dalmia 1997: 288, 290)

102. He uses macaronic Sanskrit in several other skits, too.

103. For example, Brajbhasha column in *Mādhurī*; the most popular Hindi journal of the 1920s, *Chānd* (Moon, 1923), from Allahabad, regularly published Urdu verses by Akbar Ilahabadi and other poets in the regular column *Kesar kī kyārī* (Saffron flowerbed); and the Brajbhasha and Urdu volumes of Ramnaresh Tripathi's *Kavitā kaumudī* (1929a and 1929c), mentioned above.

104. *"hāl kyā pūchh-pūchh jāte ho,*
  kabhī pāte bhī ho bahāl mujhe?"
  "kisī ke kākuloṇ rukh ke nisār ham bhī haiṇ
  śikār gardiś-e lailo-nihār ham bhī haiṇ"
  "khilnā kam-kam kali ne sīkhā hai
  uskī āṁkhoṇ kī nīm-khwābī se." (Ugra [1928] 1953: 192, 193; translation by Vanita in Ugra 2009: 21, 22)

105. *baru jīteṇ sara nainake aise dekhe maiṇ na*
  harinī ke naināna te hari! nīke ye naina. (Ugra [1928] 1953: 193; translation by Vanita in Ugra 2009: 22)

106. The argument about the continuing relevance and use of multiple idioms and languages of love is one I make in Orsini (2006).

107. Premchand, "Kahānī kalā" (The art of the short story), reprinted in Premchand (1992: 27–28).

108. I am grateful to Sumaira Nawaz for these references. See also Dubrow (2021) for the special issue on Japan by the Urdu journal *Sāqī* (The cupbearer, 1936).
109. The other languages she mentions are all imperial ones: French, Spanish, Dutch, and Portuguese (Boehmer 2005: 1–2).
110. "At first, oriental scholars devoted themselves to Sanskrit alone, and then, under the guidance of Burnouf, attacked Pali. In later years the classical Prakrits have attracted students," wrote Grierson (1889: x) in the preface of his *Modern Vernacular Literature of Hindustan*. For example, Albrecht Weber's 1852 history, titled *Akademische Vorlesungen über indische Literaturgeschichte*, was translated into English and published by Trübner as *The History of Indian Literature* in 1878, with several reprints; it began with the Vedas and ended with the Brāhmaṇas, wholly within Sanskrit. This purview could not but influence early histories of world literature: Paul Wiegler's (1914) *Geschichte der Weltliteratur* (History of world literature), John Macy's (1925) *The Story of the World's Literature*, and Hanns van Eppelsheimer's (1937) *Handbuch der Weltliteratur* (Handbook of world literature) all present Indian literature as Sanskrit literature.
111. Modern Hindi and Urdu (or Hindustani) were taught at the East India Company colleges and at Kings College London from the 1860s and 1870s (together with Bengali, Gujarati, Marathi, Hindi, and Hindustani), and in Trinity College Dublin from 1881, but unlike Sanskrit they were taught instrumentally (Mishka Sinha, personal communication).
112. These following points are illustrated in greater detail in Orsini 2020c.

Conclusions

1. I was delighted when, after I had written to her "out of the blue," she replied expressing her pleasure that I had used her work: "It is lovely indeed to see one's work travelling and mingling in other disciplines" (email, February 2015). This was shortly before she died.
2. As one of the anonymous readers noted, though there was and is an Avadhi *boli*, or language (which is what we now understand the Hindavi *kathas* to have been composed in), it has a weaker projection of its geographic domain than, say, Brajbhasha as *brajabhumi*, or the land of Krishna. The strongest regional identity came with Nawabi Awadh, whose main literary language was Urdu.
3. In the case of Tulsidas's Ram *katha*, there is plentiful evidence of its recitation and performance in the modern period (Lutgendorf 1991) but none for the first two centuries after its composition. In this case, it is the immediate renown of the poet and internal evidence that suggest a performance context.
4. See arguments and plentiful examples in Orsini and Schofield (2015).
5. Already Busch (2011) lamented the tight separation (and indeed opposition) between bhakti and courtly poetry and pointed out that many *riti* poets also wrote devotional poetry, starting with Keshavdas himself.

6. Unlike those assured pronouncements about what the "common language" of north India had been, from the time before and after the coming of Islam! See discussion of Malaviya and Tara Chand in Chapter 5.
7. For example, Chintamani's definitions of a "top," "medium," and "lowly" *kabitta* (see Chapter 3).
8. Though it is the case for other, more "learned" bhakti poets, like Nanddas and Sundardas; see McGregor (1984, 2003).
9. For medieval Europe, see LeClercq and Mizrahi (1982); for the rhetoric and aesthetic of Arabic poetry in praise of the Prophet, see Stetkevych (2010); and of Islamic sermons in Bengal, Petievich and Stille (2017).
10. For Bhojpuri chapbooks, Servan-Schreiber (1999); for Nautanki chapbooks, Hansen (1992).
11. I develop this point in Orsini (2020b).
12. Examination of the genre of poetic notebooks, or *bayaz*, could throw light on this possibility.
13. In Pollock's (1998a) theory of vernacularization, a vernacular becomes literary through a process of superimposition, by adopting the poetics of the cosmopolitan language.
14. Jha (2019) is particularly good at working through this question with regard to Vidyapati's generic innovations: the letter manual and ethics treatise already had a long and distinguished Persian pedigree, though Vidyapati was outside the sphere of Persian influence and mentions no Persian antecedent.
15. As the essays in Ganguly (2021) do admirably.

Bibliography

Adamjee, Qamar. 2011. "Strategies for Visual Narration in the Illustrated *Chandayan* Manuscripts." PhD dissertation, Institute of Fine Arts, New York University.

Adhya, Raahi. 2022. "The Fantastic World of the Bengali *Roopkatha*: Unpacking Gender, Generation & Genre." PhD dissertation, SOAS, University of London.

Agrawal, Purushottam. 2009. *Akath kahānī prem kī: Kabīr kī kavitā aur unkā samay* [The untold story of love: Kabir's poetry and his time]. New Delhi: Rajkamal Prakashan.

Agrawal, Saryu Prasad. 1950. *Akbarī darbār ke hindī kavi* [Hindi poets at Akbar's court]. Lucknow: Lucknow Vishvavidyalaya.

Ahuja, Yoga Dhyan. 1965. *Haqīriya's Masnavī* The True Miracle *(Mādhavānal Kāmakandalā)*. Delhi: Delhi University.

Alam. 1982. *Ālamkṛt Mādhavānala Kāmakandalā* [Alam's *Mādhavānala Kāmakandalā*]. Edited by Rajkumari Misra. Allahabad: Ratnakumari Svadhyay Sansthan.

Alam, Muzaffar. 1991. *The Crisis of Empire in Mughal North India: Awadh and the Punjab, 1707–48*. New Delhi: Oxford University Press.

Alam, Muzaffar. 2009. "The Mughals, the Sufi Shaikhs and the Formation of the Akbari Dispensation." *Modern Asian Studies* 43.1: 135–174.

Alam, Muzaffar, and Sanjay Subrahmanyam. 2002. "Love, passion and reason in Faizi's *Nal-Daman*." In *Love in South Asia: a cultural* history, edited by Francesca Orsini. Cambridge: Cambridge University Press, 109–141.

Alam, Muzaffar, and Sanjay Subrahmanyam. 2004. "The Making of a Munshi." *Comparative Studies of South Asia, Africa and the Middle East* 24.2: 61–72.

Ali, Mushtaq. 1989. *Hindī sāhitya ke itihās mẽ ilāhābād kā yogdān, iṇḍiyan pres ke viśiṣṭ sandarbh mẽ* [The contribution of Allahabad to the history of Hindi literature, in the specific context of the Indian Press]. PhD dissertation, University of Allahabad.

Ali, Mushtaq. 2007. *Iṇḍiyan pres* [The Indian Press]. Allahabad: Sangrahalay Prakashan.

Amin, Shahid. 2015. *Conquest and Community: The Afterlife of Warrior Saint Ghazi Miyan*. New Delhi: Orient Longman.

Anderson, Benedict. 1991. *Imagined Communities: Reflections on the Origin and Spread of Nationalism*. London: Verso.

Aravamudan, Srinivas. 2014. "East-West Fiction as World Literature: The Hayy Problem Reconfigured." *Eighteenth-Century Studies* 47.2: 195–231.

Auerbach, Erich. (1946) 1953. *Mimesis: The Representation of Reality in Western Literature*. Translated by W. R. Task. Princeton, NJ: Princeton University Press.

Awrangabadi, Shahnavaz Khan. 1913. *The Maaṣiru-l-umarā: Being biographies of the Muḥammadan and Hindu Officers of the Timurid Sovereigns of India from 1500 to about 1780 A.D.* Calcutta: Asiatic Society.

Azad, Muhammad Husain, Frances Pritchett, and Shamsur Rahman Faruqi. 2001. *Āb-e Ḥayāt: Shaping the Canon of Urdu Poetry*. Translated by Frances W. Pritchett and Shamsur Rahman Faruqi. New Delhi: Oxford University Press. http://dsal.uchicago.edu/books/PK2155.H8413/index.html.

Azad Bilgrami, Ghulam 'Ali. 1910. *Mā'sir al-kirām* [Noble glories]. Agra: Matba' Mufid-e Alam.

Azad Bilgrami, Ghulam 'Ali. (H 1166/CE 1752) 1913. *Sarw-i Āzād* [The free cypress/The cypress of Azad]. Hyderabad: Kutubkhana-i Asafiya.

Azad Bilgrami, Ghulam 'Ali. 2011. *Khizāna-yi 'āmira* [Imperial treasury]. Edited by Nasir Nikubakht and Shakil Aslam Beg. Teheran: Pizhuhishgah-i 'Ulum-i Insani va Mutala'a-i Farhangi.

Bahura, Gopal Narayan, ed. 1982. *Pada Sūrasadāsajī kā: The Padas of Surdas*. With an essay by Ken Bryant. Jaipur: Maharaja Sawai Man Singh II Museum.

Bakhshi, Padumlal Punnalal. 1924. *Viśvasāhitya* [World literature]. Lucknow: Ganga Pustak Mala.

Bakhtin, Mikhail. 1986. *Speech Genres and Other Late Essays*. Translated by by Vern W. McGee. Edited by Caryl Emerson and Michael Holquist. Austin: University of Texas Press.

Bakhtin, Mikhail. 1992. *The Dialogic Imagination: Four Essays*. Translated by Caryl Emerson and Michael Holquist. Edited by Michael Holquist. Austin: University of Texas Press.

Ballantyne, James R. 1890. *Dr. Ballantyne's English Primer. With Translation in Easy Sanskrit by Krishṇárám Páṭhak, etc.* Banaras. 2nd ed.

Banarsidas. 1981. *Ardhakathānak. Half a Tale: A Study in the Interrelationship between Autobiography and History*. Edited and translated by Mukund Lath. Jaipur: Rajasthan Prakrit Bharati Sansthan.

Bangha, Imre. 2010a. "Kabīr Reconstructed." *Acta Orientalia* 63.3: 249–258.

Bangha, Imre. 2010b. "Rekhta: Poetry in Mixed Language." In *Before the Divide: Hindi and Urdu Literary Culture*, edited by F. Orsini. New Delhi: Orient Blackswan, 21–83.

Bangha, Imre. 2014. "Early Hindi Epic Poetry in Gwalior." In *After Timur Left: Culture and Circulation in Fifteenth-Century North India*, edited by F. Orsini and S. Sheikh. New Delhi: Oxford University Press, 365–402.

Bangha, Imre. 2019. "Shifts in Kabīr Contexts and Texts from Mughal to Modern Times." In *Early Modern India: Literatures and Images, Texts and Languages*, edited by M. Burger and N. Cattoni. Heidelberg: CrossAsia-eBooks, 125–172. https://hasp.ub.uni-heidelberg.de/catalog/book/387.

Barber, Karin. 2006. "African Histories of Textuality." In *Studying Transcultural Literary History*, edited by G. Lindberg-Wada. Berlin: Walter de Gruyter, 66–75.

Barber, Karin. 2007. *The Anthropology of Texts, Persons and Publics*. Cambridge: Cambridge University Press.

Barthwal, Pitambar Datt. (1936) 1978. *Traditions of Indian Mysticism, Based upon the Nirguna School of Hindi Poetry*. New Delhi: Heritage.

Barthwal, Pitambar Datt and Keshavprasad Misra. 1931. *Padya parijāt* [Verse families]. Banaras: Indian Press.

Bauer, Thomas, and Angelica Neuwirth. 2005. *Ghazal as World Literature*. Vol. 1: *Transformations of a Literary Genre*. Beirut: Orient-Institut Beirut/Ergon Verlag.

Baumgarten, Jean, and Jerold. C. Frakes. 2005. *Introduction to Old Yiddish Literature*. Oxford: Oxford University Press.

Bayly, Christopher A. 1975. *The Local Roots of Indian Politics: Allahabad 1880–1920*. Oxford: Clarendon Press.

Bayly, Christopher A. 1980. "The Small Town and Islamic Gentry in North India: The Case of Kara." In *The City of South Asia: Pre-modern and Modern*, edited by K. Ballhatchet and J. Harrison. London: Curzon Press, 20–48.

Bayly, Christopher A. 1983. *Rulers, Townsmen and Bazaars: North Indian Society in the Age of British Expansion 1770–1870*. Cambridge: Cambridge University Press.

Bazmi, 'Abd al-Shakur. 1971. *Dāstān-i padmāvat* [The story of Padmavat]. Edited by A. H. Abidi. Tehran: Intisharat-i Bunyad-i Farhang-i Iran.

Bednar, Michael B. 2014. "The Content and the Form in Amīr Khusraw's *Duval Rānī va Khiẓr Khān*." *Journal of the Royal Asiatic Society* 24.1: 17–35. doi:10.1017/S1356186313000588.

Beecroft, Alexander. 2015. *An Ecology of World Literature: From Antiquity to the Present Day*. London: Verso Books.

Behl, Aditya. 2007. "Presence and Absence in Bhakti: An Afterword." *International Journal of Hindu Studies* 11.3: 321–322.

Behl, Aditya. 2012a. *Love's Subtle Magic: An Indian Islamic Literary Tradition, 1379–1545*. Edited by W. Doniger. New York: Oxford University Press. http://dx.doi.org/10.1093/acprof:oso/9780195146707.001.0001.

Behl, Aditya, trans. 2012b. *The Magic Doe: Quṭban Suhravardī's* Mirigāvatī. Edited by W. Doniger. New York: Oxford University Press.

Bennett, W. C. 1870. *A Report on the Family History of the Chief Clans of the Roy Bareilly District*. Lucknow: Oudh Government Press.

"Betab," Narayan Prasad. 2002. *Betāb charit*. New Delhi: National School of Drama. Originally published in Urdu in 1937.

Beth, Sarah. 2016. *Hindi Dalit Literature and the Politics of Representation*. New Delhi: Routledge.

Bhagvan Din, Lala, and Ramdas Gaur. 1927. *Hindī bhāṣā sār* [Essence of the Hindi language]. Allahabad: Hindi Sahitya Sammelan.

Bhatnagar, Ram Ratan. 1951. *The Rise and Growth of Hindi Journalism*. Allahabad: Kitab Mahal.

Bhattacharya, Tithi. 2015. *The Sentinels of Culture: Class, Education, and the Colonial Intellectual in Bengal (1848–85)*. Delhi: Oxford University Press.

Bhikha. 2013. *Bhikhā sāheb kī bānī* [The oeuvre of Bhikha Saheb]. Allahabad: Belvedere Press.

Bhikharidas. 1957. *Bhikhārīdās granthāvalī* [The collected works of Bhikharidas]. 2 vols. Edited by V. P. Misra. Varanasi: Nagari Pracharini Sabha.

Bilgrami, Mir 'Abd al-Jalil. *Amwāj al-khyāl* [Waves of thought] (late seventeenth century). MS 8915514/16, Maulana Azad Library, Aligarh.

Bilgrami, Mir 'Abd al-Wahid. 2010. *Haqā'iq-i Hindī* [Indian Truths]. Edited by M. Ehtehshamuddin. Aligarh: Institute of Persian Research, Aligarh Musim University.

Bilgrami, Murtaza Husain. 1879. *Ḥadīqat al-aqālīm* [The Seven Gardens]. Lucknow: Naval Kishore Press.

Bilgrami, Safir. (1883) 2008. *Tārīkh-e Bilgrām* [History of Bilgram]. Nazimabad (Karachi): Al-Muqaid Press. Originally published Arrah: Matba' Nur al-Anwar.

Blackburn, Stuart H. 2006. *Print, Folklore, and Nationalism in Colonial South India*. New Delhi: Orient Blackswan.

Bly, Robert, trans. 1977. *The Kabir Book : 44 of the Ecstatic Poems of Kabir*. Boston: Beacon Press.

Bocchetti, Annalisa. 2022. "Multilingual Cultures, Cosmopolitan Visions, and Regional Colours: The Narration of the Early Modern Indo-Persian World in the Citrāvalī by Usmān." PhD dissertation, Università L'Orientale di Napoli.

Boehmer, Elleke. 2005. *Colonial and Postcolonial Literature: Migrant Metaphors*. Oxford: Oxford University Press.

Bourdieu, Pierre. 1984. *Distinction: A Social Critique of the Judgement of Taste*. Translated by R. Nice. Cambridge, MA: Harvard University Press.

Bourdieu, Pierre. 1991. *Language and Symbolic Power*. Translated by G. Raymond and M. Adamson. Cambridge, MA: Harvard University Press.

Brac de la Perrière, Éloïse. 2008. *L'Art du livre dans l'Inde des sultanats*. Paris: Presses de l'Université Paris-Sorbonne.

Brac de la Perrière, Éloïse. 2015. "Le coran de Gwalior: Nouvelles perspectives sur l'histoire des corans enluminés dans l'inde pré-moghole." *Journal of Islamic Manuscripts* 6: 219–238.

Braginsky, Vladimir, and Anna Suvorova. 2008. "A New Wave of Indian Inspiration: Translations from Urdu in Malay Traditional Literature and Theatre." *Indonesia and the Malay World* 36.104: 115–153. doi:10.1080/13639810802017867.

Brass, Paul. 1974. *Language, Religion and Politics in North India*. Cambridge: Cambridge University Press.

Breckenridge, Carol A., and Peter Van Der Veer, eds. 1993. *Orientalism and the Postcolonial Predicament: Perspectives on South Asia*. Philadelphia: University of Pennsylvania Press.

Bryant, Kenneth E. 1978. *Poems to the Child God: Structures and Strategies in the Poetry of Sūrdās*. Berkeley: University of California Press.

Bryant, Kenneth E. 1979. "Sant and Vaisnava Poetry: Some Observations on Method." In *Sikh Studies: Comparative Perspective on a Changing Tradition*, edited by Mark Juergensmeyer and N. G. Barrier. Berkeley: Religious Studies Series, Graduate Theological Union, 65–74.

Bryant, Kenneth E., and John Stratton Hawley, eds. and trans. 2015. *Surdas. Sur's Ocean. Poems from the Early Tradition*. Murty Classical Library of India. Cambridge, MA: Harvard University Press.

Burchett, Patton E. 2019. *A Genealogy of Devotion: Bhakti, Tantra, Yoga, and Sufism in North India*. New York: Columbia University Press.

Burney, Fatima. 2019. "Locating the World in Metaphysical Poetry: The Bardification of Hafiz." *Journal of World Literature* 4.2: 149–168.

Busch, Allison. 2010a. "Hidden in Plain View: Brajbhasha Poets at the Mughal Court." *Modern Asian Studies* 44.2: 267–309.

Busch, Allison. 2010b. "*Riti* and Register: Lexical Variation in Courtly Braj Bhasha Texts." In *Before the Divide: Hindi and Urdu Literary Culture*, edited by F. Orsini. New Delhi: Orient Black Swan, 84–120.

Busch, Allison. 2011. *Poetry of Kings: The Classical Hindi Literature of Mughal India*. New York: Oxford University Press.

Busch, Allison. 2015. "Listening for the Context: Tuning in to the Reception of Riti Poetry." In *Tellings and Texts: Singing, Story-telling and Performance in North India*, edited by F. Orsini and K. Butler Schofield. Cambridge, UK: Open Book Publishers, 249–282.

Calendar of Allahabad University. 1928. Allahabad: Allahabad University.

Callewaert, Winand M., and Peter G. Friedlander. 1992. *The Life and Works of Raidās*. New Delhi: Manohar.

Callewaert, Winand M., and Mukund Lath. 1989. "Musicians and Scribes." In *Hindi Songs of Namdev*. Delhi: Motilal Banarsidass, 55–117.

Callewaert, Winand M., with Swapna Sharma. 2009. *Dictionary of Bhakti: North Indian Bhakti Texts into Khaṛī Bolī Hindī and English*. 4 vols. New Delhi: D. K. Printworld. https://kuleuven.academia.edu/WinandCallewaert.

Callewaert, Winand M., with Swapna Sharma and Dieter Taillieu. 2000. *The Millennium Kabīr Vāṇī*. New Delhi: Manohar.

Casanova, Pascale. (1999) 2004. *The World Republic of Letters*. Translated by M. DeBevoise. London: Verso. Originally published as *République mondiale des lettres*.

Cattoni, Nadia. 2019. *Dev, l'artisan-poète du 18ème siècle et la "nāyikā" dans le "Rasavilāsa": Circulation et échanges, intertextualité et transformations*. Berlin: De Gruyter.

Chalmers, Rhoderick. 2002. "Paṇḍits and Pulp Fiction: Popular Publishing and the Birth of Nepali Print-Capitalism in Banaras." *Studies in Nepali History and Society* 7.1: 35–98.

Chānd (Moon). 1923–. Monthly edited by Ramrakh Singh Sahgal. Allahabad: Chand Karyalay.

Chand, Tara. 1936. *Influence of Islam on Indian Culture*. Allahabad: The Indian Press.

Chand, Tara. 1944. "The Problem of Hindustani." Allahabad: Indian Periodicals Ltd. http://www.columbia.edu/itc/mealac/pritchett/00urduhindilinks/tarachand/tarachand.html.

Chandra, Sudhir. 1992. *The Oppressive Present: Literature and Social Consciousness in Colonial India*. New Delhi: Oxford University Press.

Chatterjee, Kumkum. 2009. "Cultural Flows and Cosmopolitanism in Mughal India: The Bishnupur Kingdom." *Indian Economic & Social History Review* 46.2: 147–182.

Chaturman Saxena Kaisth, Rai. 2011. *Chahār Gulshan (Akhbār al-nawādir): An Eighteenth-Century Gazetteer of Mughal India*. Edited and annotated by Chander Shekhar. New Delhi: National Mission for Manuscripts, Prakashika Series & Dilli Kitab Ghar.

Chaturvedi, Jawaharlal. 1962. *Kāvyanirṇaya* [Poetic judgement]. Varanasi: Kalyandas.

Chaturvedi, Parashuram. 1950. *Uttar bhārat kī sant paramparā* [The Sant tradition of North India]. Allahabad: Bharati Bhandar.

Chaturvedi, Parashuram, ed. 1968. *Hindī sāhitya kā bṛhad itihās. Khaṇḍ 4: Bhaktikāl (Nirguṇ bhakti)* [A comprehensive history of Hindi literature. Vol. 4: The Bhakti period (Nirgun Bhakti)]. Kashi: Nagari Pracharini Sabha.

Cheah, Pheng. 2015. *What Is a World? On Postcolonial Literature as World Literature*. Durham, NC: Duke University Press.

Cohen, Matthew I. 2001. "On the Origin of the Komedie Stamboel: Popular Culture, Colonial Society, and the Parsi Theatre Movement." *Bijdragen tot de Taal-, Land- en Volkenkunde* 157.2. 313–357. http://www.kitlv-journals.nl.

Cole, Juan R. 1988. *Roots of North Indian Shīʿism in Iran and Iraq: Religion and State in Awadh, 1722–1859*. Berkeley: University of California Press.

Conrad, Sebastian. 2016. *What Is Global History?* Princeton, NJ: Princeton University Press.

Conte, Giovanni Biagio. 1994. *Genres and Readers: Lucretius, Love Elegy, Pliny's Encyclopedia*. Baltimore, MD: Johns Hopkins University Press.

Court, Henry. 1889. *The Nas̱r-i-Benaẓīr or the Incomparable Prose of Mīr Ḥasan, Literally Translated into English*. Calcutta: Baptist Mission Press.

Dalmia, Vasudha. 1997. *The Nationalization of Hindu Traditions: Bharatendu Harishchandra and Nineteenth Century Banaras*. Delhi: Oxford University Press.

Dalmia, Vasudha. 2017. *Fiction as History: The Novel and the City in Modern North India*. Ranikhet: Permanent Black.

Damrosch, David. 2003. *What Is World Literature?* Princeton, NJ: Princeton University Press.

Das, Shyamsundar. 1903. *Annual Report on the Search for Hindi Manuscripts for the Year 1900*. Allahabad: UP Government Press.

Das, Shyamsundar. 1928. *Kabīr granthāvalī* [The collected works of Kabir]. Kashi: Nagari Pracharini Sabha.

Das, Shyamsundar. 1957. *Merī ātmakahānī* [My autobiography]. Allahabad: Indian Press.

Das, Sisir Kumar. 1991. *A History of Indian Literature*. Vol. 8: *1800–1910: Western Impact, Indian Response*. New Delhi: Sahitya Akademi.

Datla, Kavita. 2009. "A Worldly Vernacular: Urdu at Osmania University." *Modern Asian Studies* 43.5: 1117–1148.

Datla, Kavita. 2013. *Language of Secular Islam: Urdu Nationalism and Colonial India*. Honolulu: University of Hawai'i Press.

Da'ud, Maulana. 2018. *Chandāyan*. 2 vols. Edited by S. M. Pandey. Allahabad: Sahitya Bhavan.

de Bruijn, Thomas. 2010. "Dialogism in a Medieval Genre: The Case of the Avadhi Epics." In *Before the Divide: Hindi and Urdu Literary Culture*, edited by F. Orsini. New Delhi: Orient Black Swan, 121–141.

de Bruijn, Thomas. 2012. *Ruby in the Dust: Poetry and History of the Indian Padmavat by the Sufi Poet Muhammad Jayasi*. Leiden: Leiden University Press.

de Clercq, Eva. 2014. "Apabhramsha as a Literary Medium in Fifteenth-Century North India." In *After Timur Left: Culture and Circulation in Fifteenth-Century North India*, edited by F. Orsini and S. Sheikh. New Delhi: Oxford University Press, 339–364.

Desai, Madhuri. 2017. *Banaras Reconstructed: Architecture and Sacred Space in a Hindu Holy City*. Seattle: University of Washington Press.

Devy, Ganesh. 1992. *After Amnesia: Tradition and Change in Indian Literary Criticism*. London: Sangam Books.

Devy, Ganesh. 1999. "Literary History and Translation: An Indian View." In *Post-Colonial Translation*, edited by S. Bassnett and H. Trivedi. London: Routledge, 82–88.

Dharwadker, Vinay. 1993. "Orientalism and the Study of Indian Literatures." In *Orientalism and the Postcolonial Predicament*, edited by C. A. Breckenridge and P. van der Veer. Philadelphia: University of Pennsylvania Press, 158–188.

Dhavan, Purnima. 2014. "Method in the Margins: Azad Bilgrami and Changes in Eighteenth-Century Tazkirah Scholarship." Paper presented at workshop on Polyvocal Hindustan: Literatures, Languages, and Publics, Stanford University, March 6–7.

d'Hubert, Thibaut. 2018. *In the Shade of the Golden Palace: Alaol and Middle Bengali Poetics in Arakan*. New York: Oxford University Press.

d'Hubert, Thibaut, and Alexandre Papas, eds. 2018. *Jāmī in Regional Contexts*. Leiden: Brill.

Digby, Simon. 1967. "The Literary Evidence for Painting in the Delhi Sultanate." *Bulletin of the American Academy of Benares* 1.1: 47–58.

Digby, Simon. 1975. "Abd al-Quddus Gangohi (1456–1537 A.D.): The Personality and Attitudes of a Medieval Indian Sufi." In *Medieval India: A Miscellany*, edited by K. A. Nizami, and Irfan Habib. Vol. 3. Aligarh: Aligarh Muslim University, 1–66.

Digby, Simon. 1994a. "Anecdotes of a Provincial Sufi of the Dehli Sultanate: Khwāja Gurg of Kara." *Iran* 32: 99–109.

Digby, Simon. 1994b. "To Ride a Tiger or a Wall? Strategies of Prestige in Indian Sufi Legend." In *According to Tradition,* edited by by W. Callewaert and R. Snell. Wiesbaden: Harrassowitz, 99–129.

Digby, Simon. 2004. "Before Timur Came: Provincialization of the Delhi Sultanate through the Fourteenth Century." *Journal of the Economic and Social History of the Orient* 47.3: 298–356.

Digby, Simon. 2007. "Between Ancient and Modern Kashmir: The Rule and Role of Sultans and Sufis (1200/1300–1600)." In *The Arts of Kashmir,* edited by Pratapaditya Pal. New York: Asia House, 114–125.

Digby, Simon. 2014. "After Timur Left: North India in the Fifteenth Century." In *After Timur Left: Culture and Circulation in Fifteenth-Century North India,* edited by F. Orsini and S. Sheikh. New Delhi: Oxford University Press, 47–59.

Dikshit, Triloki Narayan. 1965. *Sant kavi Malūkdās.* Allahabad: Sant-Sufi Sahitya Sansthan.

Dirks, Nicholas B. 2001. *Castes of Mind: Colonialism and the Making of Modern India.* Princeton, NJ: Princeton University Press.

Dittmer, Kerrin. 1972. *Die Indischen Muslims und die Hindi-Urdu Kontroverse in den United Provinces.* Wiesbaden: Otto Harrassowitz.

Dodson, Michael. 2003. *Orientalism, Sanskrit Scholarship, and Education in Colonial North India, ca. 1775–1875.* Cambridge: Cambridge University Press.

Dube, Uday Shankar. 1967. "Lālachdās kṛt *Haricharit* grantha kī ek prāchīn prati" [An ancient copy of Lalalchdas's work *Haricharit*]. *Maru-Bhāratī.*

Dube, Uday Shankar. 2009. *Hastalikhit hindī granthoṃ kī khoj kā itihās* [History of the search for Hindi manuscripts]. Allahabad: Hindustani Academy.

Dubrow, Jennifer. 2011. *From Newspaper Sketch to "Novel": The Writing and Reception of "Fasana-e Azad" in North India, 1878–1880.* PhD dissertation, The University of Chicago.

Dubrow, Jennifer. 2018. *Cosmopolitan Dreams: The Making of Modern Urdu Literary Culture in Colonial South Asia.* Honolulu: University of Hawai'i Press.

Dubrow, Jennifer. 2021. "Looking East: Japan, *Saqi,* and the World of Urdu Modernism in 1930s South Asia." SOAS, University of London. http://mulosige.soas.ac.uk/looking-east-saqi-and-the-world-of-urdu-modernism-webinar/.

Dulah. 2000. *Rīti yugīn āchārya kavi dūlaha kṛta kavikulakaṇṭhābharaṇa* [*Kavikulakaṇṭhābharaṇa* by the riti-period master poet Dulah]. Edited by Atmaram Sharma. Delhi: Bhagyavanti Prakashan.

Dvivedi, Hazari Prasad. 1964. *Kabīr: Kabīr ke vyaktittva, sāhitya aur dārśanik vichārõ kī ālochanā* [Kabir: a critical assessment of Kabir's personality, literature, and philosophy]. Bombay: Grantha Ratnakar.

Eaton, Richard M. 2019. "The Persian Cosmopolis (900–1900) and the Sanskrit Cosmopolis (400–1400)." In *The Persianate World,* edited by A. Ashraf. Leiden: Brill, 63–83.

Ebeling, Sascha. 2010. *Colonizing the Realm of Words: The Transformation of Tamil Literature in Nineteenth-Century South India.* Albany, NY: SUNY Press.

Eppelsheimer, Hanns van. 1937. *Handbuch der Weltliteratur.* Frankfurt: Klostermann.

Ernst, Carl W. 2013. "Indian Lovers in Arabic and Persian Guise: Āzād Bilgrāmī's Depiction of Nāyikas." *Journal of Hindu Studies* 6.1: 37–51.

Fabian, Johannes. 1983. *Time and the Other: How Anthropology Makes Its Object*. New York: Columbia University Press.

Farooqi, Mehr Afshan. 2012. *Urdu Literary Culture: Vernacular Modernity in the Writing of Muhammad Hasan Askari*. Basingstoke: Palgrave Macmillan.

Faruqi, Shamsur Rahman. 2001. *Early Urdu Literary Culture and History*. New Delhi: Oxford University Press.

Flueckiger, Joyce B. 1989. "Caste and Regional Variants in an Oral Epic Tradition." In *Oral Epics in India*, edited by Stuart Blackburn. Berkeley: University of California Press, 33–54.

Freitag, Sandria. 1989a. *Collective Action and Community: Public Arenas and the Emergence of Communalism in North India*. Berkeley: University of California Press.

Freitag, Sandria, ed. 1989b. *Culture and Power in Benares*. Berkeley: University of California Press.

Friedlander, Peter G. 2012. "Kabīr and the Print Sphere: Negotiating Identity." *Thesis Eleven* 113.1: 45–56.

Gallego-Garcia, Maria Àngeles. 2003. "The Languages of Medieval Iberia." *Medieval Encounters* 9.1: 107–139.

Gandhi, Supriya. 2020. *The Emperor Who Never Was: Dara Shukoh in Mughal India*. Cambridge, MA: Harvard University Press.

Gangohi, 'Abd al-Quddus. 1898. *Rushdnāma*. Edited by Ghulam Ahmad Khan. Jhajjhar: Muslim Press.

Ganguly, Debjani. 2016. *This Thing Called the World: The Contemporary Novel as Global Form*. Durham, NC: Duke University Press.

Ganguly, Debjani, ed. 2021. *The Cambridge History of World Literature*. 2 vols. Cambridge: Cambridge University Press.

Garcin de Tassy, Joseph Héliodore Sagesse Vertu. 1874. *La Langue et la littérature hindoustanies de 1850–1869: Discours d'ouverture du cours d'hindoustani*. Paris: Librairie orientale de Maisonneuve.

Gibson-Graham, J. K. 2002. "Beyond Global vs. Local: Economic Politics outside the Binary Frame." In *Geographies of Power: Placing Scale*, edited by A. Herod and M. W. Wrights. Oxford: Blackwell, 25–60.

Gilchrist, John Borthwick. (1796) 1970. *A Grammar of the Hindustani Language*. Menston, Yorkshire: Scolar Press.

Gladwin, Francis, ed. 1798. *The Oriental Miscellany Consisting of Original Productions and Translations*. Vol. 1: *Original Letters &c*. Calcutta.

Gold, Ann Grodzins. 1992. *A Carnival of Parting: The Tales of King Bharthari and King Gopi Chand as Sung and Told by Madhu Natisar Nath of Ghatiyali, Rajasthan, India*. Berkeley: University of California Press.

Gold, Daniel. 1992. "What the Merchant-Guru Sold: Social and Literary Types in Hindi Devotional Verse." *Journal of the American Oriental Society* 112.1: 22–35.

Goldsmith, Oliver. 1888. *The Traveller and The Deserted Village*. Edited with introduction and notes by Arthur Barrett. Bombay: Macmillan.

Goswami, Manu. 2004. *Producing India: From Colonial Space to National Economy*. Chicago: University of Chicago Press.

Gould, Rebecca, and Kayvan Tahmasebian. 2021. "The Temporality of Desire in Ḥasan Dihlavī's *'Ishqnāma*." *Journal of Medieval Worlds* 2.3–4: 72–95.

Gramling, David. 2016. *The Invention of Monolingualism*. London: Bloomsbury.

Green, Nile, ed. 2019. *The Persianate World: The Frontiers of a Eurasian Lingua Franca*. Berkeley: University of California Press. doi:https://doi.org/10.1525/luminos.64.

Grierson, George A. 1889. *The Modern Vernacular Literature of Hindustan*. Calcutta: Asiatic Society.

Grierson, George A. 1904. *Linguistic Survey of India*. Vol. 6: *Indo-Aryan Family, Mediate Group*. Specimens of the Eastern Hindi Language. Calcutta: Office of the Superintendent of Government Printing.

Grierson, George A. 1907. "Modern Hinduism and Its Debt to the Nestorians." *Journal of the Royal Asiatic Society of Great Britain and Ireland* (April): 334–335.

Grierson, George A. 1920. "The Popular Literature of Northern India." *Bulletin of the School of Oriental Studies, University of London* 1.3: 87–122.

Gulal Sahab. 1910. *Gulāl Sāhib kī bānī, jīvan-charitra sahit* [Gulal Sahib's oeuvre, with his biography]. Allahabad: Belvedere Press.

Gunner, Liz. 2018. "Ecologies of Orality." In *The Cambridge Companion to World Literature*, edited by B. Etherington and J. Zimbler. Cambridge: Cambridge University Press, 116–129.

Gupta, Charu. 2001. *Sexuality, Morality and Community*. New Delhi: Permanent Black.

Gupta, Kishorilal. 1978. *Hajārā*. Allahabad: Smriti Prakashan.

Gupta, Maithilisharan. 1999. *Bhārat bhāratī*. Allahabad: Indian Press.

Gupta, Mataprasad, ed. 1985. *Kabīr granthāvalī* [The collected works of Kabir]. Allahabad: Sahitya Sadan.

Gupta, Navina. 2017. "The Politics of Exclusion? The Place of Muslims, Urdu and Its Literature in Rāmcandra Śukla's *Hindī Sāhitya kā Itihās*." In *Literature and Nationalist Ideology: Writing Histories of Modern Indian Language*, edited by H. Harder. New Delhi: Social Science Press, 259–281.

Habib, Irfan. 1986. *An Atlas of the Mughal Empire: Political and Economic Maps with Detailed Notes, Bibliography and Index*. Delhi: Oxford University Press.

Hadi, Nabi. 1995. *Dictionary of Indo-Persian Literature*. New Delhi: IGNA and Abhinav.

Hanks, William F. 1989. "Text and Textuality." *Annual Review of Anthropology* 18.1: 95–127.

Hansen, Kathryn. 1989. "The Birth of Hindi Drama in Banaras, 1868–85." In *Culture and Power in Benares*, edited by S. Freitag. Berkeley: University of California Press, 62–92.

Hansen, Kathryn. 1992. *Grounds for Play. The Nautanki Theatre of North India*. Berkeley: University of California Press.

Hansen, Kathryn. 2001. "The Indarsabha Phenomenon: Public Theatre and Consumption in Greater India (1853–1956)." In *Pleasure and the Nation: The History, Politics, and Consumption of Public Culture in India*, edited by R. Dwyer and C. Pinney. New Delhi: Oxford University Press, 76–114.

Hansen, Kathryn. 2004. "Language Community and the Theatrical Public: Linguistic Pluralism in Nineteenth-Century Parsi Theatre." In *India's Literary History: Essays on the Nineteenth Century*, edited by S. Blackburn and V. Dalmia. New Delhi: Permanent Black, 60–86.

Hansen, Kathryn. 2011. *Stages of life: Indian Theatre Autobiographies*. Ranikhet: Permanent Black.

Harder, Hans, and Barbara Mittler, eds. 2013. *Asian Punches: A Transcultural Affair*. Berlin: Springer.

Hasan, Mushirul. 1981. "Religion and Politics: The Ulama and Khilafat Movement." *Economic and Political Weekly* 16.20: 903–912. www.jstor.org/stable/4369836.

Hawley, J. S. 1979. "The Early Sūr Sāgar and the Growth of the Sūr Tradition." *Journal of the American Oriental Society* 99.1: 64–72.

Hawley, J. S. 1988. "Author and Authority in the Bhakti Poetry of North India." *Journal of Asian Studies* 47.2: 269–290.

Hawley, J. S. 2005. *Three Bhakti Voices: Mirabai, Surdas, and Kabir in Their Time and Ours*. New Delhi: Oxford University Press.

Hawley, J. S. 2015. *Storm of Songs*. Cambridge, MA: Harvard University Press.

Hawley, J. S., and Mark Juergensmeyer. 1988. *Songs of the Saints of India*. New York: Oxford University Press.

Hess, Linda. 2015. *Bodies of Song: Kabir Oral Traditions and Performative Worlds in North India*. New York: Oxford University Press.

Hindi, Bhagwan Das. 1958. *Safīna-yi Hindī* [The boat of Hindi]. Patna: Institute of Post-Graduate Studies and Research in Arabic & Persian.

Hofmeyr, Isabel. 2004. *The Portable Bunyan: A Transnational History of The Pilgrim's Progress*. Princeton, NJ: Princeton University Press.

Husain, Bashir. 1968. *Fihrist-i makhṭūṭāt-i maḥmūd sherānī* [List of the manuscripts of Mahmud Sherani]. Lahore: Idarah-yi Tahququat-i Pakistan, Danishgah-i Panjab.

Husain, S. 'Abid Husain. 1885. *Tārīkh-i Jā'is* [The history of Jais]. Allahabad: Matba' Jalali.

Husain, Surayya. 1992. *Sajjad Hyder Yildirim*. New Delhi: Sahitya Akademi.

Inden, Ron. 1990. *Imagining India*. Oxford: Blackwell.

Insler, Stanley. 1989. "Les dix étapes de l'amour (daśa kāmāvasthāḥ) dans la littérature indienne." *Bulletin d'Études Indiennes* 6: 307–328.

Ishrat. n.d. *Padmāwat-e urdu* [Urdu *Padmāvat*]. Lucknow: Matba' Durga Parshad.

Jahangir. 1999. *The Jahangirnama: Memoirs of Jahangir, Emperor of India*. Translated by W. M. Thackston. Washington, DC: Freer and Arthur M. Sackler Gallery and Oxford University Press.

Jain, Gyan Chand. 1998. "Urdū naṣr 1600 tak" [Urdu prose till 1600]. In *Tārīkh-e-adab-e urdū 1700 tak* [History of Urdu literature till 1700], vol. 2, edited by G. C. Jain and S. Ja'far. New Delhi: National Council for the Promotion of Urdu, 243–374.

Jayasi, Malik Muhammad. (1956) 1998. *Padmāvat: Malik Muhammad Jāyasī kṛt mahākāvya* [*Padmāvat*: Malik Muhammad Jayasi's epic]. Edited by Vasudev Sharan Agraval. Chirgaon: Sahitya Sadan.

Jayasi, Malik Muhammad. 1981. *Kanhāvat*. Edited by Parameshvari Lal Gupta. Varanasi: Annapurna Prakashan.

Jayasi, Malik Muhammad. 1995. *Il poema della donna del loto (Padmâvat)*. Translated by Giorgio Milanetti. Venezia: Marsilio.

Jha, Amarnath. 1927. *Hindi Selections*. Allahabad: Indian Press.

Jha, Pankaj. 2019. *A Political History of Literature: Vidyapati and the Fifteenth Century*. New Delhi: Oxford University Press.

Johns, Jeremy. 2002. *Arabic Administration and Norman Kingship in Sicily: The Royal Dīwān*. Cambridge: Cambridge University Press.

Joshi, Chitra. 2003. *Lost Worlds: Indian Labour and Its Forgotten Histories*. New Delhi: Orient Blackswan.

Julien, Eileen. 2006. "Arguments and Further Conjectures on World Literature." In *Studying Transcultural Literary History*, edited by Gunilla Lindberg-Wada. Berlin: Walter de Gruyter, 122–132.

Juergensmeyer, Mark. 1987. "The Radhasoami Revival of the Sant Tradition." In *The Sants: Studies in a Devotional Tradition of India*, edited by Karine Schomer. Delhi: Motilal Banarsidass, 329–355.

Kabir. 1983. *The Bījak of Kabir*. Translated by Linda Hess and Shukdev Singh. San Francisco: North Point Press.

Kabir. 2004. *The Weaver's Songs*. Translated by Vinay Dharwadker. New Delhi: Penguin India.

Kaicker, Abhishek. 2018. "An Ode to a Troubled Marriage: On Poetry and Politics in the Late Mughal Empire." *JESHO* 61: 327–360.

Kapadia, Aparna. 2018. *In Praise of Kings: Rajputs, Sultans and Poets in Fifteenth-Century Gujarat*. Cambridge: Cambridge University Press.

Kapur, Anuradha. 2006. "Love in the Time of Parsi Theatre." In *Love in South Asia: A Cultural History*, edited by F. Orsini. Cambridge: Cambridge University Press, 211–227.

Karim, Abdul, and Ahmed Sharif. 1964. *A Descriptive Catalogue of the Bengali Manuscripts in Munshi Abdul Karim's Collection*. Translated by Syed Sajjad Husain. Dacca: Asiatic Society of Pakistan.

Karomat, Dilorom. 2014. "Turki and Hindavi in the World of Persian: Fourteenth- and Fifteenth-Century Dictionaries." In *After Timur Left: Culture and Circulation in Fifteenth-Century North India*, edited by F. Orsini and S. Sheikh. New Delhi: Oxford University Press, 130–165.

Keshavmurti, Prashant. 2013. "Ḥaqīrī Kāšānī, Maṯnawī-i mādhavānal-kāmakandalā mausūm ba maḥẓ-i i'jāz'" [Haqiri Kashani, The *masnavi Mādhavānal-Kāmakandalā* called *The pure miracle*] Perso-Indica. http://perso-indica.net/work.faces?idsec=16&idw=122.

Khan, 'Abd al-Qadir. *Tārīkh-i Jā'is* [History of Jais]. Ms, mid-18th c. Lucknow: Nadwat al-'Ulama.

Khosla, Preeti. 2015. "A Study of the Visual Language of the Indigenous Styles of Book Painting in North India during the Sultanate Period (1414–1525 AD)." PhD dissertation, SOAS, University of London.

Kia, Mana. 2011. *Contours of Persianate Community, 1722–1835*. PhD dissertation, Harvard University.

Kia, Mana. 2014. "*Adab* as Ethics of Literary Form and Social Conduct: Reading the *Gulistān* in Late Mughal India." In *No Tapping around Philology: A Festschrift in Honor of Wheeler McIntosh Thackston Jr.'s 70th Birthday*, edited by Alireza Korangy and Daniel J. Sheffield. Wiesbaden: Harrassowitz, 281–308.

King, Christopher. 1974. "The Nagari Pracharini Sabha of Benares, 1893–1914: A Study in the Social and Political History of the Hindi Language." PhD dissertation, University of Wisconsin.

King, Christopher. 1994. *One Language, Two Scripts: The Hindi Movement*. New Delhi: Oxford University Press.

Kinra, Rajiv. 2007. "Fresh Words for a Fresh World: Taza-Gu'i and the Poetics of Newness in Early Modern Indo-Persian Poetry." *Sikh Formations* 3.2: 125–149.

Knutson, Jesse R. 2014. *Into the Twilight of Sanskrit Court Poetry: The Sena Salon of Bengal and Beyond*. Berkeley: University of California Press.

Kolff, Dirk. 2002. *Naukar, Rajput, and Sepoy: The Ethnohistory of the Military Labour Market of Hindustan, 1450–1850*. Cambridge: Cambridge University Press.

Kopf, David. 1969. *British Orientalism and the Bengal Renaissance: The Dynamics of Indian Modernization 1773–1835*: Berkeley: University of California Press.

Krishnan, Sanjay. 2007. *Reading the Global: Troubling Perspectives on Britain's Empire in Asia*. New York: Columbia University Press.

Kumar, Kapil. 1984. *Peasants in Revolt: Tenants, Landlords, Congress and the Raj in Oudh, 1886–1922*. New Delhi: Manohar.

Kumar, Krishna. (1991) 2005. *Political Agenda of Education: A Study of Colonialist and Nationalist Ideas*. New edition. New Delhi. Sage Publications India.

Kumar, Nita. 1988. *The Artisans of Banaras: Popular Culture and Identity, 1880–1986*. Princeton: Princeton: Princeton University Press.

Kurevi, Az'am. 1931. *Hindī shā'irī* [Hindi poetry]. Allahabad: Hindustani Academy.

Laachir, Karima. 2016. "The Aesthetics and Politics of 'Reading Together' Moroccan Novels in Arabic and French." *Journal of North African Studies* 21.1: 22–36.

Laachir, Karima, Sara Marzagora, and Francesca Orsini. 2018. "Significant Geographies: In Lieu of World Literature." *Journal of World Literature* 3: 290–310.

Lahauri, M. 'Ali Isma'il "Sajjan." 1893. *Asrār al-makhdūmīn* [The secrets of the lords]. Fatehpur: Nasim-i Hind Press.

Lalachdas. 1963. *Haricharit (Lālachdās kṛt avadhī-kāvya)* [*Haricharit* (an Avadhi poem by Lalachdas)]. Edited by Nalinimohan Sharma. Patna: Bihar-Rashtrabhasha-Parishad.

Lal, Ram Lagan, ed. 1933. *Mahātmāõ kī bānī* [The oeuvre of the great souls]. Bhurkura. Ghazipur: Ram Baran Das.

Laldas. 1983. *Avadhavilāsa*. Edited by Chandrika Prasad Dikshit. Banda: Chanddas Sahitya Shodh Sansthan.

Laloy, Louis. 1922. *Padmâvatî: Opéra-ballet en deux actes*. Paris: A. Durand et fils.

Leclercq, Jean, and Catharine Misrahi. 1982. *The Love of Learning and the Desire for God: A Study of Monastic Culture*. New York: Fordham University Press.

Leese, Simon. 2019. "Longing for Salmá and Hind: (Re)producing Arabic Literature in 18th and 19th Century North India." PhD dissertation, SOAS, University of London.

Lefèvre, Corinne, Ines G. Županov, and Jorge Flores. 2015. *Cosmopolitismes en Asie du Sud: Sources, itinéraires, langues (XVIe–XVIIIe siècles)*. Paris: Collections Purushartha.

Lelyveld, David. 1993. "The Fate of Hindustani." In *Orientalism and the Postcolonial Predicament*, edited by C. A. Breckenridge and P. van der Veer. Philadelphia: University of Pennsylvania Press, 189–214.

Leone, C. 2010. *Disciplina clericalis: Sapienza orientale e scuola delle novelle*. Rome: Salerno editrice.

Levine, Caroline. 2013. "The Great Unwritten: World Literature and the Effacement of Orality." *Modern Language Quarterly* 74.2: 217–237.

Longxi, Zhang. 2009. "What Is Literature? Reading across Cultures." In *Teaching World Literature*, edited by D. Damrosch. New York: Modern Language Association of America, 61–72.

Lorenzen, David N. 1991. *Kabir Legends and Ananta-das's Kabir Parachai*. Albany, NY: SUNY Press.

Lorenzen, David. 1996. "Kabir's Most Popular Songs." In *Praises to a Formless God: Nirguni Texts from North India*. Albany, NY: SUNY Press, 205–224.

Lorenzen, David. 2006. "Marco della Tomba and the Brahmin from Banaras: Missionaries, Orientalists, and Indian Scholars." *Journal of Asian Studies*, 45.1: 115–143.

Losensky, Paul E. 1998. *Welcoming Fighānī: Imitation and Poetic Individuality in the Safavid-Mughal Ghazal*. Costa Mesa, CA: Mazda.

Lukács, György. 1971. *The Theory of the Novel: A Historico-Philosophical Essay on the Forms of Great Epic Literature*. Boston: MIT Press.

Lunn, David. 2013. "Looking for Common Ground: Aspects of Cultural Production in Hindi/Urdu, 1900–1947." PhD dissertation, SOAS, University of London.

Lunn, David. 2018. "Across the Divide: Looking for the Common Ground of Hindustani." *Modern Asian Studies* 52.6: 2056–2079.

Lüpke, Friederike. 2016. "Uncovering Small-Scale Multilingualism." *Critical Multilingualism Studies* 4.2: 35–74.

Lutgendorf, Philip. 1991. *The Life of a Text: Performing the* Rāmcaritmānas *of Tulsidas.* Berkeley: University of California Press.

Lutgendorf, Philip. 1994. "The Quest for the Legendary Tulsidas." In *According to Tradition: Hagiographical Writing in India,* edited by Winand Callewaert and Rupert Snell. Wiesbaden: Harrassowitz, 65–86.

Macaulay, Thomas B. 1835. "Minute on Indian Education." Columbia University. 2 February. http://www.columbia.edu/itc/mealac/pritchett/00generallinks/macaulay/txt_minute_education_1835.html.

Maclean, Kama. 2015. *A Revolutionary History of Interwar India: Violence, Image, Voice and Text.* London: Hurst.

Macy, John. 1925. *The Story of the World's Literature.* New York: Boni & Liveright.

Mahmudabad, Ali Khan. 2020. *Poetry of Belonging: Muslim Imaginings of India, 1850–1950.* New Delhi: Oxford University Press.

Majeed, Javed. 2019. *Nation and Region in Grierson's Linguistic Survey of India.* New Delhi: Routledge.

Majeed, Javed, and Christopher Shackle. 1997. *Hali's Musaddas: The Flow and Ebb of Islam.* Delhi: Oxford University Press.

Malaviya, Madan Mohan. 1897. *Court Character and Primary Education in the N.W. Provinces and Oudh.* Allahabad: Indian Press.

Malik, Jamal. 1997. *Islamische Gelehrtenkultur in Nordindien: Entwicklungsgeschichte und Tendenzen am Beispiel von Lucknow.* Leiden: Brill.

Malla, Kalyana. 2015. *Suleiman Charitra.* Translated by A. N. D. Haksar. New Delhi: Penguin India.

Mallette, Karla. 2005. *The Kingdom of Sicily, 1100–1250: A Literary History.* Philadelphia: University of Pennsylvania Press.

Mallinson, James. 2022. "Nath Yogis and Their 'Amazing Apparel' in Early Material and Textual Sources." In *Objects, Images, Stories: Simon Digby's Historical Method,* edited by F. Orsini. New Delhi: Oxford University Press, 65–95.

Malukdas. 2011. *Malūkdās kī bānī* [The oeuvre of Malukdas]. Allahabad: Belvedere Press.

Mani, B. Venkat. 2016. *Recoding World Literature: Libraries, Print Culture, and Germany's Pact with Books.* New York: Fordham University Press.

Mani, Preetha. 2022. *The Idea of Indian Literature: Gender, Genre, and Comparative Method.* Evanston, IL: Northwestern University Press.

Manikpuri, 'Abdullah 'Alavi Qais. 1916. *Tārīkh Kaṛā Manikpur* [The history of Kara Manikpur]. Allahabad: Kaiser-e Hind Press.

Mann, Gurinder Singh. 2001. *The Making of Sikh Scripture.* New Delhi: Oxford University Press.

Manuel, Peter. 1993. *Cassette Culture: Popular Music and Technology in North India.* Chicago: University of Chicago Press.

"Mast," Zulfiqar 'Ali. 1964. *Riyāż al-wifāq* [The garden of harmony]. Tabriz: Chap-i Azarbayijan.

Massey, Doreen. (2005) 2012. *For Space.* 6th edition. London: Sage.

Masuzawa, Tomoko. 2005. *The Invention of World Religions: or, How European universalism was preserved in the language of pluralism*. Chicago: University of Chicago Press.

Mathur, Surendra. 1965. *Kavi toṣa aur uskī sudhānidhi* [The poet Tosh and his *Treasury of nectar*]. Kashi: Nagari Pracharini Sabha.

McGregor, R. S. 1972. "Bengal and the Development of Hindi, 1850–80." *South Asian Review* 5.2: 137–146.

McGregor, R. S. 1984. *Hindi Literature from the Beginnings to the Nineteenth Century*. Wiesbaden: Harassowitz.

McGregor, R. S. 1999. "Viṣṇudās and His Rāmāyan-Kathā." In *Studies in Early Modern Indo-Aryan Languages, Literature, and Culture: Research Papers, 1992–1994*, edited by Alan Entwistle. Delhi: Manohar, 239–248.

McGregor, R. S. 2003. "The Progress of Hindi. Part I." In *Literary Cultures in History: Reconstructions from South Asia*, edited by Sheldon Pollock. Berkeley: University of California Press, 912–957.

McKeon, Michael. 2002. *The Origins of the English Novel, 1600–1740*. Baltimore, MD: Johns Hopkins University Press.

Mehrotra, Arvind Krishna. 2007. *The Last Bungalow*. New Delhi: Penguin India.

Mehrotra, Arvind Krishna. 2011. *Songs of Kabir*. New York: New York Review of Books.

Menocal, Maria Rosa. 1987. *The Arabic Role in Medieval Literary History: A Forgotten Heritage*. Philadelphia: University of Pennsylvania Press.

Merathi, Ismail. (1909) 1913. *Kumak-e-urdū* [Urdu helper]. Lucknow: Naval Kishore Press.

Miner, Allyn. 2015. "Raga in the Early Sixteenth Century." In *Tellings and Texts: Music, Literature and Performance in North India*, edited by F. Orsini and K. Butler Schofield. Cambridge, UK: Open Book Publishers, 385–406.

Minkowski, Christopher. 2006. "King David in Oudh: A Bible Story in Sanskrit and the Just King at an Afghan court." Inaugural Lecture for the Boden Professorship, University of Oxford, 7 March. http://users.ox.ac.uk/~ball2185/Minkowski.Inaugural.pdf.

Mir Hasan. 1979. *Taẕkirā-e sho'arā-e hind* [*Tazkira* of the poets of India]. Edited by Akbar Haidari Kashmiri. Lucknow: Urdu Publishers.

Mishra, Ganesh Bihari, Shyam Bihari, and Sukhdev Bihari. (1910) 1924. *Hindī-Navaratna* [The nine gems of Hindi]. Edited by Dularelal Bhargava. Lucknow: Ganga Pustak Mala.

Mishra, Ganesh Bihari, Shyam Bihari, and Sukhdev Bihari. 1913. *Miśra-bandhu-vinod* [The entertainment of the Mishra brothers]. Prayag: Hindi Grantha Prasarak Mandali.

Misra, Durgashankar. 1988. *Sukhdev miśra: jīvan tathā kṛtiyāṃ* [Sukhdev Mishra: life and works]. Allahabad: Vasumati Prakashan.

Misra, Sukhdev. (S 1723) 1666. *Fājila alī prakāśa* [The light of Fazil Ali]. MS H 1291, Houghton Library, Harvard University.

Mookerjee, Firoze. 1992. *Lucknow and the World of Sarshar*. Karachi: Saad.

Moretti, Franco. 1987. *The Way of the World: The Bildungsroman in European Culture*. London: Verso.

Moretti, Franco. 2000. "Conjectures on World Literature." *New Left Review* 1: 54–68.

Moretti, Franco, ed. 2001. *Il romanzo*. 5 vols. Torino: Einaudi.

Moretti, Franco. 2003. "More Conjectures." *New Left Review* 23: 73–81.

Moretti, Franco. 2006a. "Evolution, World-Systems, *Weltliteratur*." In *Studying Transcultural Literary History*, edited by Gunilla Lindberg-Wada. Berlin: Walter de Gruyter, 113–121.

Moretti, Franco, ed. 2006b. *The Novel.* 2 vols. Princeton, NJ: Princeton University Press.

Moretti, Franco. 2013. *Distant Reading.* London: Verso Books.

Morson, Gary Saul, and Caryl Emerson. 1990. *Mikhail Bakhtin: Creation of a Prosaics.* Stanford, CA: Stanford University Press.

Mufti, Aamir. 2016. *Forget English!* Cambridge, MA: Harvard University Press.

Mukherjee, Meenakshi. 1985. *Realism and Reality: The Novel and Society in India.* Delhi: Oxford University Press.

Mukhia, Harbans. 2004. *The Mughals of India.* Oxford: Blackwell.

Mukta, Parita. 1994. *Upholding the Common Life: The Community of Mirabai.* New Delhi: Oxford University Press.

Nagasaki, Hiroko. 2012. "Hindi metre: origins and development." In *Indian and Persian Prosody and Recitation*, edited by Hiroko Nagasaki. Delhi: Saujanya Publications, 107–130.

Naim, C. M. 2018. "Homage to a 'Magic-Writer': The Mistrīz and Asrār Novels of Urdu." In *Indian Genre Fiction: Pasts and Future Histories,* edited by B. Chattopadhyay, A. Mandhwani, and A. Maitye. New Delhi: Routledge, 38–56.

Naithani, Sadhana, ed. 2002. *Folktales from Northern India: William Crooke and Pundit Ram Gharib Chaube.* Santa Barbara, CA: ABC-CLIO.

Naithani, Sadhana. 2006. *In Quest of Indian Folktales: Pandit Ram Gharib Chaube and William Crooke.* Bloomington: Indiana University Press.

Naithani, Sadhana. 2010. *The Story-Time of the British Empire: Colonial and Postcolonial Folkloristics.* Jackson: University Press of Mississippi.

Narayan, Badri. 2011. *The Making of the Dalit Public in North India: Uttar Pradesh, 1950–Present.* New Delhi: Oxford University Press.

Narayana Rao, Velcheru, and David Shulman. 1998. *A Poem at the Right Moment: Remembered Verses from Premodern South India.* Berkeley: University of California Press.

Naregal, Veena. 2001. *Language Politics, Elites and the Public Sphere.* Delhi: Permanent Black.

Naregal, Veena. 2018. "Translation and the Indian Social Sciences." In *A Multilingual Nation: Translation and Language Dynamic in India,* edited by Rita Kothari. New Delhi: Oxford University Press, 196–221.

Nawaz, Sumaira. 2017. "Making of the Sharif Child: Muslim yet Not Islamic." MA thesis, SOAS, University of London.

Neubauer, John. 2006. "Rhetorical Uses of Folk Poetry in Nineteenth-Century Eastern Europe." In *Studying Transcultural Literary History,* edited by G. Lindberg-Wada. Berlin: Walter de Gruyter, 88–97.

Neuwirth, Angelika, Michael Hess, Judith Pfeiffer, and Börte Sagaster, eds. 2006. *Ghazal as World Literature.* Vol. 2: *From a Literary Genre to a Great Tradition. The Ottoman Gazel in Context.* Würzburg: Orient-Institut Istanbul/Ergon Verlag.

Newaj. 1864. *Śakuntalā nāṭak* [Shakuntala, the play]. Banaras: Bharat Jivan Press.

Newell, Stephanie. 2000. *Ghanaian Popular Fiction: "Thrilling Discoveries in Conjugal Life" and Other Tales.* London: James Currey.

Newell, Stephanie. 2011. "'Paracolonial' Networks: Some Speculations on Local Readerships in Colonial West Africa." *Interventions* 3.3: 336–354. doi:10.1080/713769068.

Ngũgĩ wa Thiong'o. 1993. *Moving the Centre: The Struggle for Cultural Freedoms.* Oxford: James Currey.

Ngũgĩ wa Thiong'o. 2007. "Notes towards a Performance Theory of Orature." *Performance Research*. 12.3: 4–7. doi:10.1080/13528160701771253.

Nijhawan, Shobna, ed. 2010. *Nationalism in the Vernacular: Hindi, Urdu, and the Literature of Indian Freedom*. Ranikhet: Permanent Black.

Nijhawan, Shobna. 2019. *Hindi Publishing in Colonial Lucknow: Gender, Genre, and Visuality in the Creation of a Literary "Canon."* New Delhi: Oxford University Press.

Nirala, Suryakant Tripathi. 1983. *Nirālā Rachnāvalī* [The collected works of Nirala]. Volume 4. Edited by Nandkishor Naval. New Delhi: Rajkamal Prakashan.

Novetzke, Christian L. 2007. "Bhakti and Its Public." *International Journal of Hindu Studies* 11.3: 255–272.

Novetzke, Christian L. 2008. *Religion and Public Memory: A Cultural History of Saint Namdev in India*. New York: Columbia University Press.

Novetzke, Christian L. 2015. "Note to Self: What Marathi Kirtankars' Notebooks Suggest about Literacy, Performance and the Travelling Performer in Pre-colonial Maharashtra." In *Tellings and Texts: Music, Literature and Performance in North India*, edited by F. Orsini and K. Butler Schofield. Cambridge, UK: Open Book Publishers, 169–184.

Ollett, Andrew. 2017. *Language of the Snakes: Prakrit, Sanskrit, and the Language Order of Premodern India*. Berkeley, CA: Luminos.

Orsini, Francesca. 1998. "Tulsīdās as a Classic." In *Classics in Indian Literature*, edited by R. Snell. Wiesbaden: Harrassowitz, 119–141.

Orsini, Francesca. 2002. *The Hindi Public Sphere, 1920–1940: Language and Literature in the Age of Nationalism*. New Delhi: Oxford University Press.

Orsini, Francesca. 2004. "Pandits, Printers and Others: Publishing in Nineteenth-Century Benares." In *Print Areas: Book History in India*, edited by A. Gupta and S. Chakravorty. New Delhi: Permanent Black, 103–138.

Orsini, Francesca, ed. 2006. *Love in South Asia: A Cultural History*. Cambridge: Cambridge University Press.

Orsini, Francesca. 2009. *Print and Pleasure: Commercial Publishing and Entertaining Fictions in Colonial North India*. New Delhi: Permanent Black.

Orsini, Francesca. 2014a. "Echoes of a Multilingual World: Hindavi in Persian Texts." In *After Timur Left: Culture and Circulation in Fifteenth-Century North India*, edited by F. Orsini and S. Sheikh. New Delhi: Oxford University Press, 411–444.

Orsini, Francesca. 2014b. "'Krishna Is the Truth of Man': Mir 'Abdul Wahid Bilgrami's *Haqā'iq-i Hindī (Indian Truths)* and the Circulation of Dhrupad and Bishnupad." In *Culture and Circulation: Literature in Motion in Early Modern India*, edited by T. de Bruijn and A. Busch. Leiden: Brill, 222–246.

Orsini, Francesca. 2015a. "Booklets and Sants: Religious Publics and Literary History." *South Asia: Journal of South Asian Studies* 38.3: 435–449.

Orsini, Francesca. 2015b. "Inflected Kathas: Sufis and Krishna Bhakti in Awadh." In *Religious Interactions in Mughal India*, edited by V. Dalmia and M. Faruqui. New Delhi: Oxford University Press, 195–232.

Orsini, Francesca. 2015c. "The Multilingual Local in World Literature." *Comparative Literature* 67.4: 345–374.

Orsini, Francesca. 2015d. "Texts and Tellings: Kathas in the Fifteenth and Sixteenth Centuries." In *Tellings and Texts: Music, Story-Telling and Performance in North India*, edited by F. Orsini and K. Butler Schofield. Cambridge, UK: Open Book Publishers, 327–358.

Orsini, Francesca. 2017. "The Social History of a Genre: Kathas across Languages in Early Modern North India." *Medieval History Journal* 20.1: 1–37.

Orsini, Francesca. 2018. "*Na Turk na Hindu*: Shared Languages, Accents, and Located Meanings." In *A Multilingual Nation*, edited by Rita Kothari. New Delhi: Oxford University Press, 50–69.

Orsini, Francesca. 2019a. "Between Qasbas and Cities: Language Shifts and Literary Continuities in North India in the Long Eighteenth Century." *Comparative Studies of South Asia, Africa and the Middle East* 39.1: 68–81. doi:10.1215/1089201X-7493788.

Orsini, Francesca. 2019b. "World Literature, Indian Views: 1920s–1940s." *Journal of World Literature* 4.1: 56–81.

Orsini, Francesca. 2020a. "From Eastern Love to Eastern Song: Re-translating Asian Poetry." *Comparative Critical Studies* 17.2: 183–203. doi:10.3366/ccs.2020.0358.

Orsini, Francesca. 2020b. "Poetic Traffic in a Multilingual Literary Culture: Equivalence, Parallel Aesthetics, and Language-Stretching in North India." In *Prismatic Translation*, edited by Matthew Reynolds. Cambridge, UK: Legenda, 51–71.

Orsini, Francesca. 2020c. "Present Absence: Book Circulation, Indian Vernaculars and World Literature in the Nineteenth Century." *Interventions* 22.3: 310–328. doi:10.1080/1369801X.2019.1659169.

Orsini, Francesca. 2022a. "Literary Activism: Hindi Magazines, the Short Story and the World." In *The Form of Ideology and the Ideology of Form*, edited by F. Orsini, N. Srivastava, and L. Zecchini. Cambridge, UK: Open Book Publishers, 99–136. https://www.openbookpublishers.com/product/1411.

Orsini, Francesca. 2022b. "Translation, Circulation, Inflection: A Hindavi Tale in Persian Garb." In *Objects, Images, Stories: Simon Digby's Historical Method*, edited by F. Orsini. New Delhi: Oxford University Press, 364–387.

Orsini, Francesca, and Stefano Pellò. 2010. "Bhakti in Persian." Unpublished paper.

Orsini, Francesca, and Katherine Butler Schofield, eds. 2015. *Tellings and Texts: Music, Literature and Performance in North India*. Cambridge, UK: Open Book Publishers.

Orsini, Francesca, and Samira Sheikh, eds. 2014. *After Timur Left: Culture and Circulation in Fifteenth-Century North India*. New Delhi: Oxford University Press.

Orsini, Francesca, and Laetitia Zecchini, eds. 2019. "The Locations of (World) Literature: Perspectives from Africa and South Asia." *Journal of World Literature* 4.1: 1–12. doi:https://doi.org/10.1163/24056480-00401003.

Paden, William D. 2006. "The State of Medieval Studies in Occitan and French Literature." *Journal of English and Germanic Philology* 105.1: 137–155.

Paltudas. 2008. *Palṭūdās kī bānī* [The oeuvre of Paltudas]. 3 vols. Allahabad: Belvedere Press.

Pandey, Gyanendra. 1975. "Mobilization in a Mass Movement: Congress 'Propaganda' in the United Provinces (India), 1930—34." *Modern Asian Studies* 9.2: 205–226.

Pandey, Shyam Manohar. 1982a. *The Hindi Oral Epic Canainī (The Tale of Lorik and Candā)*. Allahabad: Sahitya Bhawan.

Pandey, Shyam Manohar. 1982b. *Madhyayugīn premākhyān* [Medieval romances]. Allahabad: Lokbharati.

Pandey, Shyam Manohar. 1985. "Candāyan aur lorikāyan" [*Chandāyan* and *Lorikāyan*]. In *Lok mahākāvya lorikāyan* [*Lorikāyan*: a folk epic]. Allahabad: Sahitya Bhavan, 54–67.

Pandey, Shyam Manohar. 1995. *The Hindi Oral Epic Tradition: Bhojpurī Lorikī*. Allahabad: Sahitya Bhawan.

Pandey, Shyam Manohar, ed. 2018. *Chandāyan*. Allahabad: Sahitya Bhavan.

Pathak, Shridhar. 1889. *Ūjaṛ Gām* [The deserted village]. Benares: Medical Press.

Pathak, Shridhar. 1931. *Ekāntvāsī Jogī: Ek premkahānī* [The hermit: a romance]. 5th edition. Allahabad: Ram Dayal Agrawal.

Pauwels, Heidi. 2009. "Imagining Religious Communities in the Sixteenth Century: Harirām Vyās and the Haritray." *International Journal of Hindu Studies* 13.2: 143–161. doi:10.1007/s11407-009-9073-4.

Pauwels, Heidi. 2012a. "Literary Moments of Exchange in the 18th Century: The New Urdu Vogue Meets Krishna Bhakti." In *Indo-Muslim Cultures in Transition*, edited by A. Patel and K. Leonard. Leiden: Brill, 61–85.

Pauwels, Heidi. 2012b. "Whose Satire? Gorakhnāth Confronts Krishna in *Kanhāvat*." In *Indian Satire in the Period of First Modernity*, edited by M. Horstmann and H. Pauwels. Wiesbaden: Harrassowitz, 35–64.

Pauwels, Heidi. 2013. "When a Sufi Tells about Krishna's Doom: The Case of the Kanhāvat (1540?)." *Journal of Hindu Studies* 6: 21–36.

Pauwels, Heidi. 2015. *Cultural Exchange in Eighteenth-Century India*. Berlin: EB Verlag.

Pauwels, Heidi. 2021. "Cultivating Emotion and the Rise of the Vernacular: The Role of Affect in 'Early Hindi-Urdu' Song." *South Asian History and Culture* 12.2–3: 146–165. doi:10.1080/19472498.2021.1878787.

Pavie, Thedore Marie, trans. 1852. *Krichna et sa doctrine*. Paris: B. Duprat.

Pavie, Thedore Marie. 1865. *La légende de Padmanî, reine de Tchitor [par Djaṭmal], d'aprèsles textes hindis et hindouis*. Paris: Imprimerie impériale.

Pellò, Stefano. 2012. *Ṭūṭiyān-i Hind: Specchi identitari e proiezioni cosmopolite indo-persiane (1680–1856)*. Florence: Società Editrice Fiorentina.

Pellò, Stefano. 2014a. "Drowned in the Sea of Mercy: The Textual Identification of Hindu Persian Poets from Shi'i Lucknow in the Taẕkira of Bhagwān Dās Hindī." In *Religious Interactions in Mughal India*, edited by V. Dalmia and M. Faruqi. New Delhi: Oxford University Press, 135–158.

Pellò, Stefano. 2014b. "Local Lexis? Provincializing Persian in Fifteenth-Century North India." *In After Timur Left: Culture and Circulation in Fifteenth-Century North India*, edited by F. Orsini and S. Sheikh. New Delhi: Oxford University Press, 166–185.

Pellò, Stefano. 2018. "Black Curls in a Mirror: The Eighteenth-Century Persian Kṛṣṇa of Lāla Amānat Rāy's Jilwa-yi ẕāt and the Tongue of Bīdil." *International Journal of Hindu Studies* 22.1: 71–103.

Pennington, Brian K. 2005. *Was Hinduism Invented? Britons, Indians, and the Colonial Construction of Religion*. New York: Oxford University Press.

Péri, Benedek. 2017. "Turkish Language and Literature in Medieval and Early Modern India." In *Turks in the Indian Subcontinent, Central and West Asia: The Turkish Presence in the Islamic World*, edited by I. Poonawala. Oxford: Oxford University Press, 227–262.

Petievich, Carla, and Max Stille. 2017. "Emotions in Performance: Poetry and Preaching." *Indian Economic & Social History Review* 54.1: 67–102.

Phillips, Robert. 2010. "Garden of Endless Blossoms: Urdu *Ramayans* of the Nineteenth and Early Twentieth Century." PhD dissertation, University of Wisconsin–Madison.

Phukan, Shantanu. 2000. "Through a Persian Prism: Hindi and Padmavat in the Mughal Imagination." PhD dissertation, University of Chicago.

Phukan, Shantanu. 2001. "'Through Throats Where Many Rivers Meet': The Ecology of Hindi in the World of Persian." *Indian Economic and Social History Review* 38.1: 33–58. http://dx.doi.org/10.1177/001946460103800102.

Pinch, Vijay. 2003. "*Bhakti* and the British Empire." *Past & Present* 179.1: 159–196.
Pinney, Christopher. 2002. "'A Secret of Their Own Country:' Or, How Indian Nationalism Made Itself Irrefutable." *Contributions to Indian sociology* 36.1–2: 113–150.
Pinto, Rochelle. 2007. *Between Empires: Print and Politics in Goa*. Delhi: Oxford University Press.
Plukker, D. F. 1981. *The Miragāvatī of Kutubana: Avadhi Text with Critical Notes*. PhD thesis, University of Amsterdam. http://gretil.sub.uni-goettingen.de/gretil/3_nia/hindi/kutmir_u.htm.
Pollock, Sheldon. 1998a. "The Cosmopolitan Vernacular." *Journal of Asian Studies* 57.1: 6–37.
Pollock, Sheldon. 1998b. "India in the Vernacular Millennium: Literary Culture and Polity, 1000–1500." *Daedalus* 127.3: 41–74.
Pollock, Sheldon. 2000. "Cosmopolitan and Vernacular in History." *Public Culture* 12.3: 591–625.
Pollock, Sheldon. 2006. *The Language of the Gods in the World of Men: Sanskrit, Culture, and Power in Premodern India*. Berkeley: University of California Press.
Prabhu Dayal. 1927. *Bārahmāsā achhūt pukār* [The Twelve months of the untouchable's cry]. Kanpur: Adi Hindu Press.
Prakash, Pranav. 2019. "'Īsq-nāma." In *Perso-Indica: An Analytical Survey of Persian Works on Indian Learned Traditions*, edited by F. Speziale and C. W. Ernst. http://www.perso-indica.net/work/isq-nama.
Pratt, Mary-Louise. 2008. *Imperial Eyes: Travel Writing and Transculturation*. London: Routledge.
Premchand. 1992. *Kuchh vichār* [Some thoughts]. Allahabad: Hans Prakashan.
"Premghan," Badrinarayan Chaudhri. 1949. *Premghan sarvasva* [The collected works of Premghan]. Prayag: Hindi Sahitya Sammelan.
Prendergast, Christopher, ed. 2004. *Debating World Literature*. London: Verso.
Pritchett, Frances. n.d. "Selected Publications of Fort William College, Calcutta." Columbia University. http://www.columbia.edu/itc/mealac/pritchett/00urdu/baghobahar/BBFORTWM.pdf.
Pritchett, Frances. 1991. *The Romance Tradition in Urdu: Adventures from the Dastan of Amir Hamzah*. New York: Columbia University Press.
Pritchett, Frances. 2004. *Nets of Awareness: Urdu Poetry and Its Critics*. New York: Columbia University Press.
Puchner, Martin, Suzanne Conklin Akbari, Wiebke Deneke, and Barbara Fuchs, eds. 2018. *The Norton Anthology of World Literature*. Vol. 1c. London: W. W. Norton.
Puhakar. 1963. *Rasaratan* [A jewel of taste]. Edited by Shivprasad Singh. Kashi: Nagari Pracharini Sabha.
Pulitano, Elvira. 2009. "Writing in the Oral Tradition: Reflections on the Indigenous Literatures of Australia, New Zealand, and North America." In *Teaching World Literature*, edited by D. Damrosch. New York: Modern Language Association of America, 216–231.
Raheja, Gloria Godwin, and Ann Grodzins Gold. 1984. *Listen to the Heron's Words: Reimagining Gender and Kinship in North India*. Berkeley: University of California Press.
Rahman, M. Raisur. 2015. *Locale, Everyday Islam, and Modernity: Qasbah Towns and Muslim Life in Colonial India*. New Delhi: Oxford University Press.
Rai, Alok. 2001. *Hindi Nationalism*. New Delhi: Orient Longman.

Rais, Qamar, ed. 1990. *Urdū men lok adab* [Folklore in Urdu]. New Delhi: Simant Prakashan.

Ramanujan, A. K. 1973. *Speaking of Śiva*. London: Penguin Books.

Ramanujan, A. K. 1991. "Three Hundred Ramayanas: Five Examples and Three Thoughts on Translation." In *Many Ramayanas: The Diversity of a Narrative Tradition in South Asia*, edited by Paula Richman. Berkeley: University of California Press, 22–49.

Raslin, Ghulam Nabi. 1969. *Raslīn granthāvalī* [The collected works of Raslin]. Edited by Sudhakar Pandey. Kashi: Nagari Pracharini Sabha.

Raslin, Ghulam Nabi. 1988. *Rasaprabodha* [How to perceive *rasa*]. Rampur: Rampur Raza Library.

Raslin, Ghulam Nabi. 1997. *Aṅga darpaṇa* [A mirror to the body]. Rampur: Rampur Raza Library.

Rawat, Ramnarayan S. 2011. *Reconsidering Untouchability: Chamars and Dalit History in North India*. Bloomington: Indiana University Press.

Raza, Rahi Masoom. 1969. *Ṭopī śukla*. New Delhi: Rajkamal Prakashan.

Raza, Rahi Masoom. 2005. *Topi Shukla*. Translated by Meenakshi Shivram. New Delhi: Oxford University Press.

Razi, Amin Ahmad. 1963. *Haft iqlīm*. Edited by M. Ishaque. Vol. 2. Calcutta: The Asiatic Society.

Richman, Paula, ed. 1991. *Many Ramayanas: The Diversity of a Narrative Tradition in South Asia*. Berkeley: University of California Press.

Ricci, Ronit. 2019. *Banishment and Belonging: Exile and Diaspora in Sarandib, Lanka and Ceylon*. Cambridge: Cambridge University Press.

Rieu, Charles. 1895. *Supplement to the Catalogue of the Persian Manuscripts in the British Museum*. London: British Museum.

Ritter, Valerie. 2010. "Networks, Patrons, and Genres for Late Braj Bhasha Poets." In *Before the Divide: Hindi and Urdu Literary Culture*, edited by F. Orsini. Delhi: Orient Blackswan, 249–276.

Ritter, Valerie. 2011. *Kama's Flowers: Nature in Hindi Poetry and Criticism, 1885–1925*. Albany, NY: SUNY Press.

Rizvi, S. A. A. 1983. *A History of Sufism in India*. 2 vols. New Delhi: Munshiram Manoharlal.

Robb, Megan E. 2021. *Print and the Urdu Public: Muslims, Newspapers, and Urban Life in Colonial India*. New York: Oxford University Press.

Robinson, Francis. 1974. *Separatism among Indian Muslims: The Politics of the United Provinces and Muslims, 1860–1923*. Cambridge: Cambridge University Press.

Robinson, Francis. 2001. *The'Ulama of Farangi Mahall and Islamic Culture in South Asia*. Delhi: Permanent Black.

Rudaulvi, 'Abd al-Haqq Ahmad. 1909. *Anwār al-'uyūn fī asrār al-maknūn* [The lights of the eyes or the hidden secrets]. Lucknow: Matba'-i Mujtabai.

Rukn al-Din ibn 'Abd al-Quddus Gangohi. (H 1311) 1894. *Laṭā'if-e Quddūsī* [The stories of Quddus]. Delhi: Matba'-i Mujtabai.

Russell, Ralph. 1999. *How Not to Write the History of Urdu Literature: And Other Essays on Urdu and Islam*. New York: Oxford University Press.

Sakata, Teiji. 2013. "Shiva and Parvati Assist Young Couples in Their Marriage as Referred to in Hindi Devotional Literature and Folk Songs." In *Bhakti beyond the Forest: Current Research on Early Modern Literatures in North India, 2003–2009*, edited by I. Bangha. New Delhi: Manohar, 127–136.

Saksena, Ram Babu. 1927. *A History of Urdu Literature*. Allahabad: Ram Narain Lal.

Schimmel, Annemarie. 2004. *The Empire of the Great Mughals: History, Art and Culture*. London: Reaktion Books.

Schofield, Katherine Butler. 2015. "Learning to Taste the Emotions: The Mughal Rasika." In *Tellings and Texts: Music, Literature and Performance in North India*, edited by F. Orsini and K. Butler Schofield. Cambridge, UK: Open Book Publishers, 407–422.

Schofield, Katherine Butler. 2017. "'Words without Songs:' The Social History of Hindustani Song Collections in India's Muslim Courts c. 1770–1830." In *Theory and Practice in the Music of the Islamic World: Essays in Honour of Owen Wright*, edited by R. Harris and M. Stokes. London: Routledge, 173–198.

Schofield, Katherine Butler, Molly Aitken, and Allison Busch. 2014. "Modernity's Challenge to India's Aesthetic Traditions." Round-table discussion, King's College London, 23 October.

Schomer, Karin. 1983. *Mahadevi Varma and the Chhayavad Age of Modern Hindi Poetry*. Berkeley: University of California Press.

Schomer, Karin, ed. 1987. *The Sants: Studies in a Devotional Tradition of India*. Delhi: Motilal Banarsidass.

Schwab, Raymond. 1984. *The Oriental Renaissance: Europe's Rediscovery of India and the East, 1680–1880*. Translated by G. Patterson-Black and V. Reinking. New York: Columbia University Press.

Segre, Cesare. 1997. "What Bakhtin Did Not Say: The Medieval Origins of the Novel." *Russian Literature* 41.3: 385–409.

Sengar, Shiv Singh. (1878) 1970. *Śiv Siṃh Saroj*. Edited by Kishorilal Gupta. Allahabad: Hindi Sahitya Sammelan.

Sengupta, Sagaree. 1994. "Krsna the Cruel Beloved: Harishcandra and Urdu." *Annual of Urdu Studies* 9: 82–102.

Servan-Schreiber, Catherine. 1999. *Chanteurs itinérants en Inde du Nord: la tradition orale bhojpuri*. Paris: Editions L'Harmattan.

Servan-Schreiber, Catherine. 2003. "Tellers of Tales, Sellers of Tales: Bhojpuri Peddlers in Northern India." In *Society and Circulation: Mobile People and Itinerant Cultures in South Asia, 1750–1950*, edited by Markovits, Claude, Jacques Pouchepadass, and Sanjay Subrahmanyam. Ranikhet: Permanent Black, 275–305.

Servan-Schreiber, Catherine. 2010. *Histoire d'une musique métisse à l'île Maurice: chutney indien et séga Bollywood*. Paris: Riveneuve.

Seth, Vikram. 1993. *A Suitable Boy*. London: Phoenix.

Shackle, Christopher S. 1978a. "Approaches to Persian Loans in the *Adi Granth*." *BSOAS* 41.1: 73–96.

Shackle, Christopher S. 1978b. "The Sahaskritī Poetic Idiom in the Ādi Granth." *Bulletin of the School of Oriental and African Studies* 41.2: 297–313.

Shackle, Christopher S. 1992. "Transition and Transformation in Varis Shah's Hir." In *The Indian Narrative*, edited by C. Shackle and R. Snell. Wiesbaden: Otto Harrassowitz, 241–264.

Shah Mina. 1880. *Malfūẓāt-i Shāh Mīnā* [The sayings of Shah Mina]. Lucknow: Matba'-i Marqa-'alam Harduni.

Shahbaz, Pegah. 2020. "Čandāyan." In *Perso-Indica: An Analytical Survey of Persian Works on Indian Learned Traditions*, edited by F. Speziale and C. W. Ernst. http://www.perso-indica.net/work/candayan.

Shankar, Subrahmanyam. 2012. *Flesh and Fish Blood: Postcolonialism, Translation, and the Vernacular*. Berkeley: University of California Press.

Shankar, Subrahmanyam. 2020. "The Vernacular: An Introduction." *South Asian Review* 41.2: 191–193. doi:10.1080/02759527.2020.1725224.

Sharar, Abdul Halim. 1989. *Lucknow: The Last Phase of an Oriental Culture*. Translated and edited by E. S. Harcourt and Fakhir Hussain. New Delhi: Oxford University Press.

Sharar, 'Abd al-Halim. 1992. *Guẕishta-e Lakhnaū* [Lucknow's past]. 2nd edition. New Delhi: Maktaba Jamia.

Sharma, Hemant, ed. 1989. *Bhāratendu samagra* [The collected Bharatendu]. Banaras: Pracharak Granthavali.

Sharma, Padmasingh. 1932. *Hindī, urdū, aur hindustānī* [Hindi, Urdu, and Hindustani]. Allahabad: Hindustani Academy.

Sharma, Ramanand. 2003. *Rītikālīn kavi kālidās trivedī granthāvalī* [The collected works of the *riti* period poet Kalidas Trivedi]. Ghaziabad: Pachauri Prakashan.

Sharma, Ramanand. 2007. *Udaynāth kavīndra granthāvalī* [The collected works of Udaynath Kavindra]. Delhi: Lokhit Prakashan.

Sharma, Ramvilas. 1973. *Āchārya Rāmchandra Śukla aura hindī ālochna* [Acharya Ramchandra Shukla and Hindi criticism]. New Delhi: Rajkamal Prakashan.

Sharma, Sunil. 2004. "The City of Beauties in Indo-Persian Poetic Landscape." *Comparative Studies of South Asia, Africa, and the Middle East* 24.2: 73–81.

Sharma, Sunil. 2015. "Reading the Acts and Lives of Performers in Mughal Persian Texts." In *Tellings and Texts: Singing, Story-Telling and Performance in North India*, edited by Francesca Orsini and Katherine Butler Schofield. Cambridge, UK: Open Book Publishers, 283–302.

Sharma, Sunil. 2017. *Mughal Arcadia*. Cambridge, MA: Harvard University Press.

Shaw, Graham, and Mary Lloyd. 1985. *Publications Proscribed by the Government of India: A Catalogue of the Collections in the India Office Library and Records and the Department of Oriental Manuscripts and Printed Books, British Library Reference Division*. London: British Library.

Sheikh, Samira. 2010. *Forging a Region: Sultans, Traders, and Pilgrims in Gujarat, 1200–1500*. New Delhi: Oxford University Press.

Sherani, Muhammad Hafiz. (1930) 1966. "Urdu fiqre aur dohre āṭhvīn aur navīn ṣadī ḥijrī kī fārsī taṣnīfāt se" [Urdu sentences and couplets from Persian works of the eighth and ninth centuries Hijri]. In *Maqālāt-e Ḥāfiz Maḥmūd Sherānī*. Vol. 1. Lahore: Majlis Taraqqi-e Adab, 102–131. Reprinted from *Oriental College Magazine* (May).

Shih, Shu-Mei. 2004. "Global Literature and the Technologies of Recognition." *PMLA* 119.1: 16–30.

Shirreff, A. G., trans. 1944. *Padmavati*. Calcutta: Royal Asiatic Society.

Shukla, Ramchandra, ed. 1949. *Jāyasī granthāvalī* [The collected works of Jayasi]. 4th edition. Kashi: Nagari Pracharini Sabha.

Shukla, Ramchandra. (1929) 1988. *Hindī sāhitya kā itihās* [A history of Hindi literature]. Kashi: Nagari Pracharini Sabha.

Sikander, Maryam. 2021. "Upstart Punches: Humour and Satire in Urdu Literature." PhD dissertation, SOAS, University of London.

Singh, Bacchan. 1996. *Hindī sāhitya ka dūsrā itihās* [Another history of Hindi literature]. New Delhi: Radhakrishna Prakashan.

Singh, Charu. 2015. "Science, Hindi Print and Agricultural Improvement in Colonial North India." PhD dissertation, Jawaharlal Nehru University, New Delhi.

Singh, Namwar. 1982. *Dūsrī paramparā kī khoj* [In search for another tradition]. Delhi: Rajkamal Prakashan.

Singh, Shivprasad. 1963. "Introduction." In Puhakar, *Rasaratan*. Kashi: Nagari Pracharini Sabha, 1–151.

Sitaram Lala. 1927. "Introduction" to *Hindi Selections*. Compiled by Jha, Amarnath. Allahabad: Indian Press, 1–3.

Smith, John D. 1990. *The Epic of Pābūjī: A Study, Transcription and Translation*. Cambridge: Cambridge University Press.

Smith, John D. 2005. *The Epic of Pabuji*. New Delhi: Katha.

Slater, Candace. 1982. *Stories on a String: The Brazilian Literatura de Cordel*. Berkeley: University of California Press.

Snell, Rupert. *Braj Bhasha Reader*. Hindi Urdu Flagship. http://hindiurduflagship.org/resources/learning-teaching/braj-bhasha-reader/. Originally published London: School of Oriental and African Studies.

Sperl, Stefan, and Christopher Shackle, eds. 1996. *Qasida Poetry in Islamic Africa and Asia*. 2 vols. Leiden: E. J. Brill.

Spivak, Gayatri Chakravorty. 2003. *Death of a Discipline*. New York: Columbia University Press.

Sreenivasan, Ramya. 2007. *The Many Lives of a Rajput Queen: Heroic Pasts in India, c. 1500–1900*. New Delhi: Permanent Black.

Sreenivasan, Ramya. 2014. "Warrior-Tales at Hinterland Courts in North India, c. 1370–1550." In *After Timur Left: Culture and Circulation in Fifteenth-century North India*, edited by F. Orsini and S. Sheikh. New Delhi: Oxford University Press, 242–272.

Stanford Friedman, Susan. 2013. *Planetary Modernisms: Provocations on Modernity across Time*. New York: Columbia University Press.

Stark, Ulrike. 2007. *An Empire of Books*. New Delhi: Permanent Black.

Stark, Ulrike. 2011. "Associational Culture and Civic Engagement in Colonial Lucknow: The Jalsah-e Tahzib." *Indian Economic and Social History Review* 48.1: 1–33.

Stark, Ulrike. 2015. "Benares Beginnings: Print Modernity, Book Entrepreneurs and Cross-Cultural Ventures in a Colonial Metropolis." In *Founts of Knowledge*, edited by A. Gupta and S. Chakravorty. Delhi: Orient Blackswan, 15–73.

Stasik, Danuta. 2009. "Perso-Arabic lexis in the Rāmcaritmānas of Tulsīdās." *Cracow Indological Studies* 11: 67–86.

Statement of Particulars regarding Books, Maps etc. Published in the North Western Provinces & Oudh . . . fourth quarter of 1879. 1880. Allahabad: N.-W. P and Oudh Government Press.

Steingass, Francis. 2006 [1892]. *A Comprehensive Persian-English Dictionary. Including the Arabic Words and Phrases to be Met with in Persian Literature*. New Delhi: Manohar.

Stetkevych, Susan Pinckney. 2010. *The Mantle Odes: Arabic Praise Poems to the Prophet Muhammad*. Bloomington: Indiana University Press.

Suvorova, Anna. 2000. *Masnavi: A Study of Urdu Romance*. Karachi: Oxford University Press.

Tagore, Rabindranath. 1915. *A Hundred Poems of Kabir*. London: Macmillan.

Taj, Afroz. 2007. *The Court of Indar*. New Delhi: Anjuman Taraqqi Urdu (Hind).

Taj, Imtiyaz 'Ali. 1975. *Ṭālib banārsī ke ḍrāme* [The plays of Talib Banarsi]. Lahore: Majlis-e Taraqqi-e Adab.

Talwar Oldenburg, Veena. 1984. *The Making of Colonial Lucknow: 1856–1877*. Princeton, NJ: Princeton University Press.

Tanoukhi, Nirvana. 2011. "The Scale of World Literature." In *Immanuel Wallerstein and the Problem of the World: System, Scale, Culture*, edited by D. Palumbo-Liu, B. Robbins, and N. Tanoukhi. Durham, NC: Duke University Press, 78–137.

Tavakoli-Targhi, Mohamad. 2001. "The Homeless Texts of Persianate Modernity." *Cultural Dynamics* 13.3: 263–291.

Tiwari, Bhanupratap. 1880. *Paṇḍit bhānupratāp tivārī chunār nivāsī kā sañchhep jīvancharit va satsaṅg vilās* [The brief autobiography of Pandit Bhanupratap Tiwari of Chunar, with the Pleasure of *satsang*]. Ms Hindi 11035, UP State Archive, Manuscript Library, Allahabad.

Tiwari, Bhanupratap. 1891. "A Religious Song of the Dhobis." *North Indian Notes & Queries* (December): 145–146.

Tod, James. (1829) 1914. *Annals and Antiquities of Rajast'han, Or, the Central and Western Rajpoot States of India*. London: G. Routledge & Sons.

Tripathi, Ramnaresh. 1929a. *Kavitā kaumudī* [Moonlight, or guide to poetry]. Vol. 1: *Hindī ke prāchīn kavi* [Ancient Hindi poets]. Allahabad: Hindi Mandir.

Tripathi, Ramnaresh. 1929b. *Kavitā kaumudī*. Vol. 2: *Grām gīt* [Village songs]. Allahabad: Hindi Mandir.

Tripathi, Ramnaresh. 1929c. *Kavitā kaumudī*. Vol. 4: *Urdū*. Allahabad: Hindi Mandir.

Trivedi, Harish. 1995. *Colonial Transactions: English Literature and India*. Manchester: Manchester University Press.

Truschke, Audrey. 2016. *Culture of Encounters: Sanskrit at the Mughal Court*. New York: Columbia University Press.

Tulsidas. 1974. *Tulsīdās granthāvalī* [The collected works of Tulsidas]. Kashi: Nagari Pracharini Sabha.

Tulsidas. 2016. *The Epic of Ram* [*Rāmcharitmānas*]. Vol. 1. Translated by Philip Lutgendorf. Cambridge, MA: Harvard University Press.

"Ugra," Pandey Bechan Sharma. (1928) 1953. *Chocolate*. Calcutta: Tandon Brothers.

"Ugra," Pandey Bechan Sharma. 2006. *Chocolate and Other Stories of Male-Male Desire*. Translated by Ruth Vanita. Delhi: Oxford Unversity Press.

Upadhyay, Krishnadev. 1964. *Bhojpūrī lokgīt* [Bhojpuri folksongs]. Patna: Bhojpuri Academy.

Usman. 1981. *Usmān kavi kṛt Chitrāvalī* [*Chitrāvalī* by the poet Usman]. Edited by Jaganmohan Varma. Kashi: Bharat Jivan Press.

Valdés, Mario J., and Djelal Kadir. 2004. *Literary Cultures of Latin America: A Comparative History*. New York: Oxford University Press. 3 vols.

Vanita, Ruth. 2012. *Gender, Sex and the City*. New Delhi: Orient Blackswan.

Vanshi, Baldev, ed. 2006. *Malūkdās granthāvalī* [The collected works of Malukdas]. New Delhi: Parmeshwari Prakashan.

Vanshi, Baldev. 2014. *Sant palṭū dās*. [Sant Paltu Das]. New Delhi: Rashtriy Pustak Nyas Bharat.

Vaudeville, Charlotte. 1974. *Kabir*. Oxford: Clarendon Press.

Venkatachalapathy, A. R. 2012. *The Province of the Book: Scholars, Scribes, and Scribblers in Colonial Tamilnadu*. Ranikhet: Permanent Black.

Viitamäki, Mikko. 2015. "Poetry in Sufi Practice: Patrons, Poets and Performers in South Asian Sufism from Thirteenth Century to the Present." Helsinki: University of Helsinki.

Vishwanathan, Gauri. 1989. *Masks of Conquest: Literary Study and British Rule in India*. New York: Columbia University Press.

Walkowitz, Rebecca. 2015. *Born Translated: The Contemporary Novel in an Age of World Literature*. New York: Columbia University Press.

Warwick Research Collective. 2015. *Combined and Uneven Development: Towards a New Theory of World-Literature*. Liverpool: Liverpool University Press.

Weber, Albrecht. 1852. *Akademische Vorlesungen über indische Literaturgeschichte*. Berlin: Dümmlers Verlagsbuchhandlung.

Wiegler, Paul. 1914. *Geschichte der Weltliteratur*. Berlin: Ullstein.

Williams, Tyler W. 2014. "Sacred Sounds and Sacred Books: A History of Writing in Hindi." Ph.D. dissertation, Columbia University.

Williams, Tyler W. Forthcoming. *"If All the World Were Paper:" A History of Writing in Hindi*.

Wink, André. 1990. *Al-Hind the Making of the Indo-Islamic World: The Slave Kings and the Islamic Conquest: 11th–13th Centuries*. Vol. 2. Leiden: Brill.

Wollager, Mark, and Matt Eatough, eds. 2012. *The Oxford Handbook of Global Modernisms*. New York: Oxford University Press.

Yang, Anand. 1998. *Bazaar India: Markets, Society, and the Colonial State in Gangetic Bihar*. Berkeley: University of California Press.

Zaidi, Shailesh. 1969. *Bilgrām ke musalmān hindī kavi* [The Muslim Hindi poets of Bilgram]. Kashi: Nagari Pracharini Sabha.

Zaidi, Shailesh. 1977. *Hindī ke katipay musalmān kavi* [Some Muslim Hindi poets]. Aligarh: University Publishing House.

Ziauddin, M., trans. 1935. *Tuḥfat al-Hind* [The gift of India]. Calcutta: Vishva Bharati Bookshop.

Zipoli, Riccardo. 1993. *The Technique of the Ǧawāb: Replies by Nawā'ī to Ḥāfiẓ and Ǧāmī*. Venice: Cafoscarina.

Index

For the benefit of digital users, indexed terms that span two pages (e.g., 52–53) may, on occasion, appear on only one of those pages.

1857, 11, 12–13, 134–35, 154, 156, 159, 182–83, 236n.5

Abdul Haq , Maulvi, 168, 239–40n.39
absent presence, 1–2
Abu'l Fazl, 134, 203n.26
  Ā'īn-i Akbarī, 203n.26
Adi Hindu Press, 156. *See also* dalit
Afghan, 11, 33, 34, 103–4, 124, 126
Agrawal, Purushottam, 75–76, 79–80, 87–88, 94, 114–15, 166–67, 193–94, 221n.63
Akbar, Emperor Jalaluddin, 10, 50–51, 52, 56, 57, 64, 68–69, 103, 121–22, 139, 147, 204n.38, 211n.59, 211n.64, 214n.89, 224n.5, 226–27n.29, 228n.42, 228n.43, 233n.80, 242n.56
Akbar Ilahabadi, 169–70, 184, 242n.57, 247n.103
Alam, 51, 52, 66, 211n.64, 211n.65
  Mādhavānal Kāmakandalā, 48*t*, 50–51, 62, 211n.66
Ala'uddin Khilji, Sultan of Delhi, 1, 2, 3, 67–68, 72, 103, 201n.10, 221n.55
Allahabad, 9–10, 12–14, 18, 50, 64, 77–78, 100–1, 102–3, 145–46, 154, 155–56, 159, 163, 172–73, 175–76, 181, 236n.5, 236n.10, 236n.11, *See also* Prayag
  print culture in, 154–56, 236n.10
  subah of, 203n.26
  University, 158, 168, 169–70, 240n.50
allegory, 181, 246n.95, 246n.96
'Amanat, Agha Hasan, 149–50, 180–81, 235n.97, 245n.88
  Court of Indra (*Indarsabhā*) 149–50, 180–81, 197, 235n.99, 245n.88, 245–46n.90
Amethi, 42, 129, 203n.28
  raja of, 42, 129, 228n.46
Anderson, Benedict, 154, 160, 181
Apabhramsha, 24, 30, 41, 79, 206n.10
Arabic, 14–15, 17, 18, 19, 26, 31–32, 33, 41, 77–78, 97–98, 119–20, 121–22, 126, 131, 132, 133, 137, 138, 142–43, 147, 154, 163–64, 167–68, 170, 171, 202n.17, 204–5n.44, 226–27n.29, 230n.58, 230n.62, 231–32n.72, 233n.84, 239n.36, 239n.38, 249n.9
archive, 3–4, 8, 21–22, 50, 60, 62, 72, 75–76, 79–80, 105, 117–30, 166, 179, 192–94, 198
Attar, Fariduddin, 119–20, 224–25n.11
  The Conference of Birds, 35
Aurangzeb 'Alamgir, 68–69, 116, 129–30, 136, 137, 223n.2, 228n.45
Avadhi, 9–10, 15, 182–83, 202–3n.25, 203n.30, 248n.2
Avahatta, 19, 198
Awadh (Oudh), 4, 9–14, 22, 50, 139–40, 147–48, 150, 153, 154, 159, 192, 197–98. *See also* Purab
  Nawabs of, 12, 126, 140, 150, 154, 170, 236n.5
  subah of, 9–10, 203n.26
Ayodhya (also Awadh), 9–10, 43, 78*t*, 101, 139–40, 141–42, 213n.87, 214n.89, 224n.9
Azad, Muhammad Husain
  Water of Life (Āb-e ḥayāt) 166, 241n.51
"Azad" Bilgrami, Sayyid Mir Ghulam 'Ali, 117, 121, 122, 123, 126, 130, 131, 132, 133, 135, 136–37, 138, 139, 140, 142–43, 202n.20, 226n.20, 226n.21, 226n.23, 230n.62, 231n.67, 232n.74
  education, 131, 132, 232–33n.76, 233n.77
  tazkiras, 118, 121, 123–24, 225n.16
    Free-Standing Cypress (or Cypress of Azad, Sarw-i Āzād), 118, 121, 122, 123, 130, 192–93, 202n.20
    Imperial treasury (*Khizāna-yi 'āmirā*) 225n.16, 225n.17
    Noble glories (Ma'āṣir al-kirām), 121, 140, 225n.18

Badal, 2, 3, 42–43, 67–68
bahushrut (*bahuśrut*, well-listened), 94, 114–15
Bakhshi, Padumlal Punnalal, 188
  Viśva sāhitya (World literature), 188

Bakhtin, Mikhail, 18, 25–26, 77–78, 91–92, 94–95, 219n.37, 219n.38
Banaras, 10, 12–15, 55–56, 78*t*, 83, 108–9, 125, 134–35, 148–50, 154, 156, 193, 221n.50, 225n.15, 236n.5
  Mughal, 61
  print culture in, 156, 196, 221–22n.64, 237n.15, 237n.16, 237n.18
  raja of, 69, 70, 110, 129, 234n.92
Banarsidas, 24, 211n.60
  education of, 229–30n.57
barahmasa (*bārahmāsā*, song of the twelve months), 30, 66, 67–68, 91–92, 111*t*, 140, 196–97, 245n.86
Barber, Karin, 76
Barthwal, Pitambar Datt, 82, 87, 169–70
  Traditions of Indian Mysticism, Based upon the Nirguna School of Hindi Poetry, 81–82, 87, 169–70, 218n.22, 219n.29
Bayly, Christopher A. 102–4
Bazmi, Mulla 'Abd al-Shakur, 64, 66, 67–68
  Dāstān-i Padmāwat (*Rat Padam*), 64, 67–68, 71–72, 211n.61, 214n.94, 214n.100, 215n.102
"Bedil," Mirza 'Abd al-Qadir, 122, 136, 215n.105, 225n.17, 233n.77
Beecroft, Alexander, 26, 216n.3
Behl, Aditya, 2, 28, 30–32, 35, 37, 42, 70–71, 198, 207n.17, 207n.19
"Bekhabar," Mir 'Azmatullah Bilgrami, 122, 225n.16, 226n.21
Belvedere Press, 108–9, 110, 155–56, 196
  booklets, 82–83, 101–2, 110–12, 112*f*, 113, 114*f*, 155–56, 196, 222n.66
  Santbānī Pustakmālā, 110, 111*t*, 112*f*, 222n.70, 222n.71, 223n.73
"Betab," Narayan Prasad, 245n.89
Bhāgavata Purāṇa, 59
Bhagvan Din, Lala, 76, 158, 170
bhajan. See devotional songs
bhakha (*bhāṣā*, language), 15, 123, 161. *See also* Hindi
bhakti, 8–9, 26, 49, 50–51, 58–59, 60, 61, 75–76, 86, 100–1, 106, 141, 177, 178
  in Hindi literary histories, 81–82, 87, 127, 166–67, 169–70, 189–90, 241n.52, 249n.6
  Krishna, 8–9, 24, 40, 59, 192, 198
  orature and poetry, 9, 76–77, 89, 91–92, 93–94, 100–1, 194–95, 216n.7
  philology, 79–80
  public sphere, 75–76
  in Purab/Awadh, 8–9, 50–51, 198
  See also Grierson's views on bhakti; Sants
Bhikha, 78*t*, 87–88, 91–92, 111*t*, 112, 217n.13, 222n.68
Bhikharidas, 129, 143, 144, 227n.34, 227n.35
Bhikhari Thakur, 172–73, 178
bhoga (enjoyment), 38–39, 40, 53
Bhojpuri, 12, 112, 113, 172–73, 178, 182–83, 196, 202–3n.25
Bhushan, 129, 144
bibliomigrancy, 190–91, 196, 201n.4, 216n.9
Bihar, 10, 34, 55–56, 59, 72, 109, 194, 243n.66
Biharilal, 124–25, 144, 157–86, 241n.52, 242n.59
Bilgram, 10–11, 116, 121, 122, 125, 131, 132, 133, 136–37, 140–41, 192–93, 226–27n.29
  literati and poets of, 117–18, 121, 123–25, 126, 133, 140, 144, 147, 171–72, 225n.18, 227n.34
Bilgrami, Hafiz Ziyaullah, 130, 228–29n.50
Bilgrami, Mir 'Abd al-Jalil, 123–24, 131, 133, 136–38, 228–29n.50, 231n.70, 232n.74
  chronogram in three languages, 137, 231–32n.72
  education, 229n.52
  and Hindi, 132, 137–38, 232n.73
  letters to his son, 131, 133, 135, 136–38
  masnavi for Farrukh Siyar, 138
  masnavi on Bilgram (*Amwāj al-khyāl*, Waves of Thought) 142–43, 225n.17
  meeting with Nasir 'Ali Sirhindi, 135–36
Bilgrami, Mir 'Abd al-Wahid, 124, 125, 227n.33
  Haqā'iq-i Hindī (Indian Truths), 32, 207n.26
Bilgrami, Mir Sayyid Lutfullah, 122, 226n.19
Bilgrami, Mir Tufail Muhammad, 126, 130, 228n.49, 228–29n.50
Bilgrami, Murtaza Husain 139–40
  The Seven Gardens (*Ḥadīqat al-aqālīm*) 139–41, 233n.80
birth determinism, 2–3, 81–82, 166–67, 194–95
Blackburn, Stuart, 79
Boehmer, Elleke, 189
booklets, 108, 110, 113–14. *See also* Belvedere Press
Bourdieu, Pierre, 8, 9, 21–22, 165–66
Brahman, 62, 67–68, 74, 83, 85–86, 105, 123, 133–34, 141, 145, 184–85, 212n.67, 213n.86, 218n.20, 226n.26, 227n.37, 228n.44, 229–30n.57, 232n.74, 233n.81
Brajbhasha, 10–11, 12–13, 15, 17, 18, 19, 23, 26, 43, 45–46, 49, 50, 51, 79, 116, 118–19, 125, 130, 157, 159, 161, 162, 185, 194–95, 213n.81, 223n.1, 241n.51
  poetics (see *rīti grantha*)

poetry, 10–11, 12, 50, 56, 57, 62, 70, 71–72, 115, 118, 125, 126, 127, 129–30, 132, 134, 137, 140–41, 147–48, 156, 167–68, 175–76, 179, 185, 186, 195–96, 212n.74, 247n.103
poets, 117–18, 123–24, 125, 126, 127, 129, 130, 133, 140–41, 144, 145–46, 146*f*, 171–72, 192–93, 235n.95, 242n.59, 243n.71
songs, 150, 180, 181–82, 185, 245–46n.90
See also *kabitta*; *kavya*; *riti*
Bryant, Kenneth, 89, 93
Bundelkhand, 9–10
Burney, Fatima, 6–7, 202n.18
Busch, Allison, 11, 15, 45–46, 57–58, 127, 133, 185, 204n.39, 248n.5

Calcutta, 12–13, 74, 152–53, 179–80, 189, 196, 225n.15
Callewaert, Winand, 79–80
capital (cultural, educational, literary, etc.) 8, 9, 21–22, 115, 133, 194, 202n.24
Casanova, Pascale, 5, 202n.24, 216n.3
caste, 2–3, 30, 31, 53, 56, 74, 75–77, 78, 82–87, 94, 144, 150–51, 156, 174–75, 178, 181, 184–85, 207n.13, 212n.67, 218n.20, 227n.37, 234n.87, 243n.71, 247n.101
Sant poetry and, 83–87, 89, 94, 114–15, 212n.67, 218n.26, 219n.28
See also Brahman; *dalit*; Kayastha
caupāī, 41, 42, 60. See also *chaupai*
center, 5, 9–10, 11, 12–13, 14, 20–21, 50, 62, 118–19, 135, 139, 147, 152, 154, 188–89, 192, 194, 198–99, 224n.10
Ngũgĩ Wa Thiong'o's definition of, 20
See also located, location
Ceylon, 1, 55–56. *See also* Lanka
Chand Bardai, 56, 132–33, 227n.38, 241n.52
Chandra, Sudhir, 165–66, 235n.3
Chatterjee, Bankimchandra, 187
Chatterjee, Ramanand, 155
Chatterjee, Saratchandra, 187
Chaturi, 74–77, 82, 85–86, 91, 94, 113, 193–94, 223n.72
Chaube, Pandi Ram Gharib, 174–75, 243n.70
chaupai (*chaupāī*, Hindi verse of four "feet"), 25–26, 28, 57, 59, 61, 124–25, 127, 212n.74
chaupal (*chaupāl*, village assembly), 24
Cheah, Pheng, 21, 23
China, 68, 188
Chintamani Tripathi, 116, 117–18, 123, 129–30, 135, 144, 203–4n.32, 227n.37, 241n.52, 249n.7
circulation, 4, 7, 17, 20–21, 22–23, 26, 72, 77–78, 100–1, 114–15, 118, 155, 198–99
of booklets and chapbooks, 77, 108–15, 172–73, 196, 216n.8, 245n.82
of books, 1–2, 3–4, 108, 196 (*see also* bibliomigrancy)
global, 5, 26, 100
of *kathas*, 25–26, 27, 34, 68, 71–72, 193, 196–97, 206n.7, 211n.55
paracolonial, 180–81
of Sant orature, 100–1, 108, 114–15
of songs, 15, 23
technologies of, 77, 108
colonial contact zone, 179, 184
colonial impact, 13–14, 23, 151, 152, 153, 168, 186–87, 188–89
composite culture, 18. *See also* Ganga-Jamni
connoisseur, 31–32, 36, 41, 67, 116, 117, 118–19, 121–22, 123, 124, 127, 131, 132, 147, 158, 185, 205n.54, 211n.58, 213n.80, 230n.59, 232n.74, 238n.27, 242n.59
Conrad, Sebastian, 20–21, 22–23, 205n.46, 206n.6
convivencia, 18
cosmopolitan, 12–13, 19–20, 26, 27, 45–46, 50–51, 56, 62–63, 66, 68, 71–72, 79, 141, 155, 198, 204n.41, 204–5n.44, 224n.5
local, 114–15, 117, 118–19, 122, 125, 129–30, 133, 135, 136, 137, 138, 139, 142–43, 146–47, 197
See also cosmopolitan vernacular
court, 8, 11, 12, 16, 42, 43, 117, 118, 125, 146–47, 148, 170, 180–81, 193, 194
"mud-brick," 9, 129, 135, 144, 145–46
Mughal, 9, 12, 50–51, 54, 56, 62, 68–69, 71, 121–22, 139, 194, 203–4n.32, 211n.59, 223–24n.4
poetry (see *riti*)
Court, Major Henry, 69–70
Crooke, William, 134–35, 174–76
cultivation, poetic, 14–15, 16–17, 23, 26, 50, 115, 118–19, 125, 126, 129–30, 132, 142–43, 147, 148–49, 172, 192–93, 198–99, 212n.73
parallel, 23, 33, 77–78, 142–47, 158, 172, 189–90, 192–93, 235n.94

dalit, 156–57, 179, 245n.85
Dalmau, 31
Dalmia, Vasudha, 158, 161, 184–85, 240n.44
Damrosch, David, 1–2, 5, 68, 113–14, 190–91, 196, 216n.3
Das, Shyamsundar, 164, 218n.20, 242n.60

Das, Sisir Kumar, 152–53
dastan (*dāstān*, Persian or Urdu narrative, usually long), 25–26, 69, 71–72, 189–90, 196–97, 202n.19, 206n.4
Datla, Kavita, 235n.1, 239–40n.39, 240n.42
Da'ud, 28, 30, 31, 33, 38, 207–8n.27
  Chandāyan, 28–34, 42–43, 141, 171–72, 207n.14, 207–8n.27
  circulation of, 33
  See also Gangohi's translation
de Bruijn, Thomas, 2, 37, 70–71, 209n.38, 215n.104
Delhi, 12–13, 14, 15, 42, 43, 55–56, 57, 123, 131, 133, 136–37, 147–48, 163, 170, 204–5n.44, 207–8n.27, 211n.53, 228n.45, 228n.46, 233n.78, 241n.53
Desai, Madhuri, 61, 203n.27, 214n.90
description (*varṇana, vaṣf/ tawṣīf*), 30–31, 33, 41, 52, 57–58, 60, 61, 65, 140, 141, 142, 150, 176, 177–78, 196–97, 207n.13, 207n.19, 210n.51, 214n.101, 241n.51, 244–45n.80
  of Chanda's bedroom in the *Chandāyan*, 29, 207n.21
  of food, 30
  of Govar, 28, 206n.11
  in *Varṇaratnākara*, 206n.10, 206n.11
Devy, Ganesh, 235n.3
  translating consciousness, 16–17
Dhavan, Purnima, 233n.77
d'Hubert, Thibaut, 30, 37
dialogism, 8, 18, 25–26, 31–32, 34, 38, 50–51, 53, 71, 77–78, 91–92, 94–95, 98, 99–100, 101, 107, 114–15, 142–43, 166–67, 192, 194, 219n.36, 219n.37
Digby, Simon, 10–11, 33, 34, 207n.21, 212n.71, 221n.53, 224–25n.11, 229n.55
diglossia, 19–20, 203n.30
  multiple, 14, 19
distinction, 10–11, 21–22, 117, 118–19, 129–30, 138, 150–51, 168–69, 192
doha (couplet), 25–26, 28, 41, 57, 60, 61, 89, 119–20, 124–25, 134, 172, 224–25n.11, 227n.35, 232n.74
dohavali, 124–25, 227n.31
dunyā (world), 6–7, 202n.18
Dvivedi, Hazariprasad, 82–83, 94–95, 218n.20, 219n.31
Dvivedi, Mahavir Prasad, 155, 161–62, 164–65, 185, 238–39n.32, 241–42n.55

East India Company, 11, 12–13, 15–16, 134–35, 139, 152, 154, 161–62, 226n.22, 236n.5
ecology, literary, 4, 26
education, 12–13, 14–15, 23, 74, 118–19, 130, 133, 134–35, 139, 157–58, 159, 229n.53
  colonial, 151, 152, 153, 154, 156–57, 158, 162, 169–70, 176–77, 178, 189, 204–5n.44 (*see also* Persian education)
  literary, 8, 23, 115, 132–33
  multilingual, 17, 130, 131, 132, 133–34, 142–43, 148–49, 158, 213n.80, 229–30n.57
  Sanskrit, 14–15, 132–33, 156, 158, 229n.55, 229–30n.57
  University syllabi, 169, 241–42n.55
English, 12–13, 17, 21–22, 55–56, 155, 157, 158, 163–65, 168, 169, 181–82, 183, 184, 186–87, 188–89, 238n.27, 238n.31
  translations, 52, 87, 109, 134–35, 152–53, 237n.23, 237n.24, 238n.25, 238n.26, 241–42n.55, 248n.110
  See also colonial education
equivalence, 8, 19, 63, 96, 119–20, 141, 237n.23

Fabian, Johannes, 190–91
Faizabad, 97–98, 101, 107, 149*f*, 154, 202–3n.25
familiarity, 8, 14, 17, 18, 25–26, 27–28, 67, 69, 99–100, 133, 147–48, 150, 153, 155, 171–72, 179, 186–87, 198–99
Farmuli, Shah Muhammad, 124–25, 226–27n.29, 227n.30
Farrukh Siyar, Emperor, 137, 138
"Firaq" Gorakhpuri, Raghupati Sahay, 158
folk literature (H *loksāhitya*), 153, 173, 178, 243n.66, 244n.75, *See also* folklore
  invention of, 169, 172–79
folklore, 174–76, 178, 189–90, 243n.72, 245n.88, *See also* folk literature
"following," 20–21, 22–23, 26, 27, 118, 201n.6
Forbes, Duncan, 190
Fort William College, 12–13, 69–70, 108–9, 161, 162, 170
Friedlander, Peter, 222n.66

Gang, 11–12, 128, 129, 144
Ganges, Ganga, 9–10, 31, 52, 61, 101, 103–4, 116, 141, 145, 150–51, 177, 213n.78, 233n.81
Ganga-Jamni culture, 18, 142–43, 150–51
Gangohi, 'Abd al-Quddus, 33–34, 65, 99–100, 119–20, 224–25n.11
  lost translation of *Chandāyan*, 29, 208n.31
Ganguly, Debjani, 21, 205n.52
Garcin de Tassy, Joseph Héliodore Sagesse Vertu. 1, 166, 190
  Histoire de la littérature hindouie at hindoustanie, 166

Gaur, Babu Ramdas, 170–71
genre
cosmopolitism, 27, 62–63, 64, 67
localization, 27, 62–63, 64, 67, 142
See also *ghazal*; *katha*; *masnavi*
geographical imagination, 6–7, 30, 49, 50–51, 55–56, 69, 101, 139, 212n.70, 214n.101
Ghasita Rai, 123–24
ghazal, 6–7, 18, 20–21, 67, 68–69, 121–22, 150, 155, 166, 180, 181, 183–84, 185, 190, 197, 198, 202n.18, 202n.19, 205n.47, 234n.90, 235n.99, 241n.53, 241–42n.55, 245–46n.90
Ghazipur, 52, 53, 141, 203n.26, 210–11n.52, 222n.68
Ghosh, Chintamani, 155
Gilchrist, John B. 161
Goody, Jack, 79
Gora, 2, 3, 42–43, 67–68
Gorakhnath, 40
Gramling, David, 160
Grierson, George A., 2–3, 70, 82, 162, 170, 173, 174, 190, 201n.7, 202–3n.25
Linguistic Survey of India, 160, 239n.34
A Vernacular Literary History of Hindustan, 126–27, 240n.47, 248n.110
views on bhakti, 81–82, 217n.16, 218n.18
Gulal, 78, 78*t*, 85–86, 87–88, 91–92, 111*t*, 112, 222n.68
guna (*guṇa*, talent, musical knowledge), 51, 52, 211n.64

Hadith, 97–98, 119–20, 131, 230n.60
Hafiz Shirazi, 134, 183–84, 197–98, 225n.17
Hali, Altaf Husain, 169–70, 241–42n.55, 242n.56
Musaddas, 167–68
Hans Kabi, 43
Haqiri Kashani, 66
Maḥż-i 'ijāz (The wonder of creation) 211n.66
Harioudh, Ayodhyasingh Upadhyay, 158, 237n.19, 241–42n.55
Harishchandra, Bharatendu, 18, 70, 150, 158, 182–83, 184–85, 194–95, 238n.28, 241n.52, 246n.94
education, 158
satirical poem, 184–85
The Sad State of India (Bhārat durdaśā), 181–83
views on language, 161–62, 238–39n.32
Hazin, Shaikh, 231n.68
heroes (*nāyak*), 42–43, 69
Lorik, 28, 42–43, 207n.14, 210n.44
Madhavanal, 51
Manohar, 36, 42–43, 54
Rajkunwar, 36, 37, 38, 42–43, 54, 65, 66–67, 210n.45
Ratansen, 1, 2, 3, 35–36, 38–39, 42–43, 54, 72, 210n.46
Sujan, 54–56
Surasena, 56–57, 58
heroines (*nāyikā*), 36
Chanda, 28, 30–31
Chandravali, 39, 40
Chitravali, 54–55
description of (*nakh-shikh, sarapa*), 30–31, 57–58
Kamakandala, 51
Madhumalati, 36, 54, 208n.34
Maina, 30
Mirigavati, 36, 37, 54, 84–85
Padmavati, 1–2, 30–31, 35–36, 54, 67–68, 72, 201n.10, 209n.40, 215n.104
Rambhavati (Rambha), 56–58, 213n.80
Rupmini, 38, 54–55, 66–67, 210n.45
types of (*nāyikā bheda*) 57–58, 127, 144, 166–67, 213n.77, 234n.87
Hess, Linda, 79–80, 86, 93
translations of Kabir, 109–10, 218n.25
Hindavi, 15, 16, 19–20, 25–26, 28, 31–32, 33, 41, 43, 49, 59, 61, 64, 66–67, 94–95, 106, 119, 120, 125, 126, 142–43, 161, 162, 171, 190, 192, 194, 206n.7, 219n.40, 224n.10, 224–25n.11, *See also* Hindi
Hindi, 2–3, 12–13, 15, 16, 56, 161, 162, 163–65, 170–71, 182–83, 194–95
See also language debates; literary history
"Hindi," Bhagwan Das, 231n.68
tazkira Safīna-yi Hindī (The Ship of Hindi) 231n.68
Hindi Literary Association (Hindi Sahitya Sammelan), 155–56, 158, 161–62
Hindustani, 28, 163, 248n.111
Hindustani Academy, 163, 240n.40
history
global, 20–21
literary (*see* literary history)
local, 3–4, 102–3, 118–19, 123, 124, 139, 203n.28, 221n.54
Hofmeyr, Isabel, 100
Humayun, Emperor, 34

Iltutmish, 121
Independence, 14
Indian National Congress, 13–14, 158, 181, 184

Indian Press, 155–56. *See also* Ghosh, Chintamani
"Insha," Insha Allah Khan, 169–70
Rānī ketakī kī kahānī, 170
interlanguage, 16–17
intertextuality, 8, 25–26, 27, 34, 35, 42, 54, 58, 62–63, 64, 66–68, 71, 196–97, 208n.37, 209n.38, 214n.88
invisibilization, 1–2, 4–5, 7, 8, 12, 21–22, 118, 160, 171, 172, 173, 189–91

Jahangir, Emperor, 50, 56, 57, 62, 68–69, 129, 147, 214n.94, 214n.95, *See also* Salim, Prince
Jais, 2, 35, 38, 59, 209n.39, 210n.47
Jajmau, 116
Jamuna (also Jamna, Yamuna) 9–10, 52, 67, 141, 145, 155, 177, 202–3n.25, 213n.79, 234n.91
Japan, 188
Jaunpur, 10, 40, 41, 51, 172–73, 202–3n.25, 203n.26, 211n.60
Sharqi Sultans of, 51, 71–72, 119, 193, 224n.9
Jayasi, Malik Muhammad, 2–4, 34, 35, 36, 42, 43–45, 59, 66, 67–68, 72, 99–100, 128, 140–41, 166–67, 171–72, 194–95, 201n.7, 213n.82, 215n.102, 242n.59
Kahnhāvat, 34, 39, 40, 42, 59, 99–100, 194–95, 210n.44, 210n.47
Padmāvat, 1–3, 6, 34, 35, 43–45, 70–71, 72, 209n.38
manuscripts, of,, 3–4, 43, 47*t*, 72, 159
translations and versions of, 43–45, 64*t*
Jha, Amarnath, 158, 169–70
Jha, Pankaj, 19, 194, 198, 202n.22, 249n.14
jogi. *See* yogi

Kabir, 3, 9, 12, 15, 19, 23, 74–77, 78, 78*t*, 79–83, 84, 85–86, 87–88, 92–93, 100–1, 108, 109–10, 111*t*, 127, 166–67, 177, 195–96, 202n.23, 216n.4, 217n.14, 217n.15, 217n.16, 218n.17, 218n.18, 218n.22, 218n.25, 219n.30, 219n.36, 221n.63, 222n.65
critical views on, 81–82, 87–88, 219n.30
works in print, 109–10, 155–56, 218n.24, 221–22n.64, 241n.52, 242n.59
kabitta (poem), 70, 71–72, 79, 111*t*, 116, 117, 127, 128, 137–38, 142–43, 166, 195, 217n.13, 228n.39, 228n.42, 234n.88, 234n.91
Kaicker, Abhishek, 138
Kaithi script, 15, 42, 46*f*, 47*t*, 59, 62, 205–6n.2
Kalidasa, 132–33, 177, 217n.16
Kanpur, 12–14
Kapadia, Aparna, 203–4n.32
Kara, 4–5, 77–78, 78*t*, 97–98, 100, 101–5, 102*f*, 103*f*, 104*f*, 123, 192, 203n.26, 210n.50, 214n.92, 221n.59, 224n.9
Karak Shah, Khwaja, 102–3, 103*f*, 104–5, 106–7, 192, 221n.53, 221n.55
Katha (*kathā*, story), 2, 22–23, 24–28, 48*t*, 49, 50–51, 58–59, 61, 70, 71–72, 118, 130, 192–93, 196–97, 208n.32, *See also* Alam: *Mādhavānala Kāmakandalā*; Jayasi: *Kanhāvat*; Jayasi: *Padmāvat*; Lalach: *Haricharit*; Manjhan: *Madhumālatī*; Puhakar: *Rasaratana*; Qutban: *Mirigāvatī*; romance; Tulsidas: *Rāmcharitmānas*; Usman: *Chitrāvalī*
authors, 48*t*, 128, 193–94, 211n.62, 215n.106
Harikatha, 59, 93 (*see also* Lalach)
manuscripts, 47*t*, 48*t*, 210–11n.52, 211n.53, 211n.55, 211n.66, 214n.92
Mughal, 50–62
Ramkatha, 58, 59, 61
social mediations of, 27, 49, 71
Sultanate, 28–49
See also intertextuality; manuscripts: illustrated; translation
Kathavachak, Radheshyam, 245n.87
Kavya (*kāvya*, poetry in verse or prose) 79, 195–96
shastra (*śāstra*, science) 76–77, 79, 132–33, 142–43, 144, 223n.1
Kayastha, 56, 84–85, 132–33, 206n.7, 213n.84, 229n.53, 234n.92
Khan Mahmudabad, Ali, 184
Khari Boli, 15–16, 157, 161, 162, 203n.30, 206n.7, 217n.13, 219n.40, 242n.59
Khusrau, Amir, 25–26, 33, 68, 142, 168, 171–72, 208n.29, 225n.17, 233n.83
Kia, Mana, 120–21, 225n.14
Kipling, Rudyard, 12–13
Krishna (also Kanha), 8–9, 18, 25–26, 39, 40, 59, 67, 81, 93, 98, 99–100, 134, 207n.26, 208n.36, 210n.44, 210n.47, 219n.37, 223n.1, 241–42n.55
See also bhakti
Kurevi, Az'am, 171–72
Hindi Poetry (*Hindī shā'irī*) 171–72

Lalach, 213n.84
Haricharit, 59
Lal Das, 141
Delight of Ayodhya (*Avadhavilāsa*), 118–42

Laloy, Louis, 1, 72
Padmâvatî, 1
language, 2–3, 7–8, 12–14, 15, 16–17, 18, 19–20, 21–22, 23, 31–32, 38, 62–63, 79, 99–100, 114–15, 157, 159–61, 163–64, 165, 176, 194–95, 198, 237n.23
contact, 18
debates on Hindi and Urdu, 16, 160–63, 165, 169–71, 239n.37, 239n.38, 239–40n.39
ideologies, 18, 176–77, 237n.23
natural, 16, 170
register, 18, 19–20, 25–26, 27, 41, 61, 112, 144, 145–46, 180–81, 182–83, 193, 195–96, 204n.39, 210n.50, 234n.89
See also Avadhi; *bhakha*; Brajbhasha; cosmopolitan; *diglossia*; Hindi; Hindustani; linguistic economy; Maithili; Persian; Urdu; vernacular
Leese, Simon, 14–15, 131, 142–43, 202n.17, 224n.8, 225n.16
Lelyveld, David, 16, 159, 163
Levine, 23, 216n.2, 216n.6
linguistic economy, 8, 9, 14–20
literary associations, 13–14, 154, 158, 161–62, 163–64. *See also* Hindi Literary Association (Hindi Sahitya Sammelan); Nagari Pracharini Sabha
literary canon, 23, 26, 78, 116, 144, 153, 165–72, 241–42n.55
literary history, 4, 7, 8, 11, 13–14, 16, 23, 50–51, 70–71, 76–77, 86, 130, 152, 165, 166, 167–68, 171, 179, 189–90, 192, 194–95, 248n.110
monolingual, 7, 8, 21–22, 23, 189–90, 192, 195
multilingual, 8, 9, 17, 26, 71, 72, 114–15, 195–96
Ramchandra Shukla's 70–71, 166–67
located, location, 4–5, 7, 9–10, 20, 21–22, 23, 26, 27, 31–32, 61, 72, 77–78, 95, 98, 100, 101, 108, 114–15, 118–19, 141, 142, 146–47, 148, 153, 178, 188–89, 198–99, 202n.16
social, 22–23, 27, 31, 34, 45–46, 50–51, 62–63, 68–69, 138
loksahitya. *See* folk literature
Lorenzen, David, 79–80, 109, 202n.23
Lucknow, 12–14, 100–1, 139, 140, 167–68, 229n.51, 233n.80, 236n.5
Nawabi, 14, 69, 147–51, 154, 159, 168, 180, 193, 203n.26, 226n.22, 235–36n.4, 241–42n.55
print culture in, 154–55, 236n.8
Lunn, David, 163, 187, 240n.40
Macaulay, Thomas Babington, *Minute on Indian Education*, 239n.36
"Madhonayak," Sayyid Nizam al-Din, 124, 125, 133
Madhumālatī. *See* Manjhan
magazines, 12–13, 14, 75, 155, 185, 186–87
Mahābhārata, 28, 35, 68, 169–70, 206n.8, 208n.32
Maithili, 19, 158, 198
Majeed, Javed, 239n.34
Malaviya, Madan Mohan, 161–62
definition of Hindi, 16, 162, 239n.38
Malukdas, 4–5, 6–7, 48*t*, 55, 75–76, 77–78, 78*t*, 79, 82, 85–86, 87–88, 90, 91–93, 95, 96, 97–98, 99–102, 102*f*, 103, 105, 106–7, 108, 111*t*, 112, 114–15, 127, 192, 193–94, 195–96, 217n.10, 218n.22, 221n.50, 221n.57, 222n.65, 228n.39
hagiography of, 6, 102–3, 105–7, 221n.50
Mani, B. Venkat, 196, 201n.4, 216n.9
Mani, Preetha, 236n.13
Manikpur, 102–3, 203n.26, 214n.92
Manjhan, 35, 36, 226–27n.29
Madhumālatī, 24, 34, 35–36, 47*t*, 48*t*, 54, 56–57 (see also *pemkatha*, romance)
manuscripts of, 47*t*, 210–11n.52, 211n.55
Persian translations of, 64*t*
manuscripts, 1–2, 27, 159, 232n.73
illustrated, 8, 10, 29*f*, 33, 42, 44*f*, 45*f*, 46*f*, 208n.30, 224n.10
kathas, 3–4, 27, 33, 34, 42, 43, 47*t*, 48*t*, 70–71, 72, 193, 195, 206n.7, 210–11n.52, 211n.53, 211n.66
of Sant poets, 79–80, 100–2, 108–9, 110–12, 217n.14, 217n.15, 220n.47, 222n.65, 223n.74
searches for, 27, 70, 106, 109–10, 170
"many Ramayanas," 27–28
map, mapping, 5, 6–7, 21, 101, 161, 174–75, 192. *See also* geographical imagination
masnavi (Persian or Urdu verse narrative), 6–7, 25–26, 27–28, 30, 33, 62–63, 67, 69, 71–72
Massey, Doreen, 4–5, 7, 11–12, 50–51, 72, 154, 179, 192
Matiram, 129, 144, 203–4n.32, 227n.37, 241n.52
Mehrotra, Arvind Krishna, 155
Songs of Kabir, 109–10
Merathi, Ismail, 169–70
Urdu Helper (*Kumak-e Urdu*), 169–70, 242n.56
meter, 18, 25–26, 28, 41, 57, 60, 61, 89, 127, 134–35, 212n.74, 217n.13
Mirabai, 3, 79–80, 242n.59

Mir Hasan, 147–48, 149*f*, 150, 180
masnavi Siḥr al-bayān (The Magic of Eloquence), 69–70
Mir Sayyid Muhammad Bilgrami, 123, 133, 138, 230n.58, 230n.61
as student and teacher, 131, 133, 230n.61
Mirigāvatī. *See* Qutban
Mishra brothers (Ganesh Bihari, Shyam Bihari, and Sukhdev Bihari), 70–71, 82, 87
Hindī navaratna (Nine gems of Hindi) 87, 168, 219n.30, 241n.52
Miśra bandhu vinod, 166
Misir, Mahendar, 178
Misra, Diwakar, 123, 137–38, 232n.74
Misra, Harbans Rai, 123–24, 137–38, 226n.26, 232n.74
Misra, Sukhdev, 129, 229n.55, 229n.56, 233n.81
mole, 30–32, 33, 37, 124–25
Moretti, Franco, 20–21, 152, 205n.45, 205n.47
Mubarak ʿAli, 124–25, 144, 171–72, 227n.34
Mufti, Aamer, 179, 188–89, 201n.2, 201n.14
Mughal
culture, 23, 26, 43, 50, 51, 52, 54, 56, 57–58, 62–63, 68–69, 71, 118–19, 147, 171–72, 194, 223–24n.4
empire, 9–10, 11, 19, 34, 50–51, 55, 61, 102–3, 139, 203n.26
patronage, 12, 128, 129, 147, 235n.93
See also court
Mukhlis, Anandram, 43, 45, 48*t*, 54, 62–63, 66, 68–69, 211n.59
multilingual
local, 4–5, 22, 118–19, 150–51, 171–72, 192–94
traces, 4–5, 8, 27, 65, 66, 67, 95–96, 97–98, 120, 185, 192–94, 197–98
See also literary history; multilingualism
multilingualism, 16, 18, 19–20, 21–22, 42, 171
mushaʿiras (gatherings for Urdu poetic recitation) 185
music, 42–43, 50–51, 52, 57–58, 66–67, 104–5, 122, 125, 126, 147–48, 149–50, 159, 172–73, 204n.33, 205n.54
musician, 51, 53, 80, 90, 180–81

Nagari (or Devanagari) script, 15, 16, 45*f*, 47*t*, 56, 91–92, 161, 206n.7, 232n.73, 239n.38
Nagari Pracharini Sabha (Association for the Promotion of the Nagari Script), 70, 109–10, 112, 158, 162, 166–67, 170, 240n.41, 242n.60
definition of Hindi, 163–64
search for Hindi Manuscripts, 70–71, 166, 216n.5
Nagmati, 43, 67–68
Naithani, Sadhna, 174–75, 243n.68, 243n.70
Narayanan, Vivek, 91, 97
Naregal, Veena, 237n.23
Narhari, 11, 128, 228n.42
Nasir ʿAli Sirhindi, 135–36
Nautanki, 172–73, 196
Naval Kishore, 12–13, 154–55, 236n.8
Naval Khisore Press, 69, 154, 155, 156, 195–96
Nazir Ahmad, 170–71, 236n.7, 242n.56
Newaj, *Śakuntalā nāṭak*, 70
Newell, Stephanie, 180–81
Ngũgĩ wa Thiong'o, 20, 76, 204n.36
NIN&Q (*North Indian Notes & Queries*) 134–35, 174–75
Nirala, Suryakant Tripathi, 74–75, 76–77, 82, 242n.59
Nizam Bilgrami "Zamir," Shaikh, 121–22
Nizami of Ganja, 25–26, 33, 134, 156
Khusrau Shīrīn, 36
North-Western Provinces, 15–16, 236n.5
novel, 20–21, 72, 152, 155, 156–57, 178, 179, 181, 187, 188–89, 190–91, 236n.9, 240n.47
and world literature, 21–22, 216n.2
Novetzke, Christian, 75–76, 79, 80
NPS. *See* Nagari Pracharini Sabha

oral epics, 28, 30, 72, 108, 113–14, 196–97, 205–6n.2, 206n.9, 207n.14, 216n.8
orality, 17, 76, 79, 216n.6
oral-literate genre, 17, 24, 188–89
orature, 17, 23, 72–73, 76–77, 79, 113–14, 159, 172, 173–75, 176, 178–79, 189–90, 204n.36
Muslim, 173, 174–75, 178, 189–90
Sant, 72–73, 76–79, 81, 83, 84–85, 86, 98, 100, 110–12, 113, 114–15, 120, 142–43
aesthetics of, 87–94
and print (*see* booklets)
religious dialogism, 94–100
and world literature, 76–77, 108, 113, 196, 204n.36
See also circulation; ventriloquism
and world literature, 1–2
Orientalist, 1–3, 7, 72, 81, 108–9, 158, 160–61, 162, 190–91, 239n.36
Oriental literature, 1–2
Oudh. *See* Awadh
overhearing, 17, 27, 95, 96, 193–94, 198–99

pad (song, lit. "foot"), 74–76, 106, 219n.30, 222n.71

Padmāvat, 1–3, 21
by Jatmal, 3, 43, 72 (*see also* Jayasi)
Persian translations and versions of, 2–4, 64*t*, 67–68, 69
Paltudas, 74, 76, 78, 78*t*, 85–86, 87–89, 90, 91–92, 93, 94, 95, 97–98, 99–100, 101, 107, 108, 111*t*
Pandey, Shyam Manohar, 30, 54, 207n.14, 207–8n.27
paracolonial, 180–81, 189
Paris, 1, 21, 72, 190
Parsi theater, 172–73, 179–81, 245n.87, 245n.89, 246n.91, 246n.92
patron, patronage, 8, 12, 23, 26, 33, 69, 71, 115, 117, 120–21, 129, 147–48, 154, 166–67, 180–81, 194, 212n.73, 228n.46
Mughal, 10, 12, 129, 147, 203–4n.32
Sultanate, 33, 42
Pauwels, Heidi, 99–100, 210n.47, 234n.90
Pavie, Théodore, 1, 43, 72
La Légende de Padmanî, reine de Tchitor, 1, 3
Pellò, Stefano, 62, 120–21, 145, 148–49, 202n.20, 204n.42, 224n.10
Pemi, Barkatullah, 124, 125, 171–72
pemkatha (*pemkathā*, romance), 25–26, 28, 34–49, 51, 56–57, 58, 71–72, 196–97. See also *katha*; romance
Sufi, 28–34, 58, 71–72
Persian, 3–4, 7, 8–9, 10–11, 12–13, 14–15, 16, 18, 19–20, 21–22, 23, 25–26, 27–28, 33, 37, 41, 62–63, 68–70, 71, 118–20, 147–48, 154, 164, 192, 241n.51
education, 14–15, 24, 31–32, 43, 50, 56, 123, 130–31, 132, 134–35, 147–48, 158, 224n.9, 228n.48, 228–29n.50, 229n.51, 229n.52
poetry and poets, 17, 25–26, 27, 30, 33, 35, 56, 62, 119–20, 122, 126, 129–30, 133, 136, 141, 142–43, 144, 150, 167–68, 171–72, 183–84, 186, 192–93, 197, 202n.17, 208n.29, 215n.109, 224n.9, 224–25n.11, 235n.94 (see also *tazkiras*)
provincialization of, 19, 204n.42, 224n.10
script, 15, 33, 42, 44*f*, 47*t*, 206n.7, 239n.38
spoken, 95, 96, 193–94
translations and retellings, 3–4, 33–49, 54, 62–64, 64*t*, 65, 66–69, 71–72, 99, 119–20, 196–97
See also cosmopolitan; cultivation; patronage, poetic idioms; "quasi-Persian"; Persianate
Persianate, 7, 14, 15–16, 56, 69–70, 77–78, 87, 91–92, 94–95, 98, 120–21, 126, 144, 145–46, 167–68, 189–90, 193–94, 196–97, 204n.39, 217n.13, 229–30n.57, 234n.91, 241n.51
Phukan, Shantanu, 19
Pinch, William, 218n.18
Pincott, Fredric, 190, 238n.26
Pinney, Christopher, 181
poetic idioms, 15, 17, 18, 23, 33, 76–78, 85, 87–88, 91–92, 93, 114–15, 128, 142–43, 168–69, 180, 193–94, 197, 235n.94
poetic traffic, 18, 27–28, 77–78, 98, 145
Pollock, Sheldon, 15, 17, 19, 26, 79, 198, 203–4n.32, 204n.41, 223–24n.4, 249n.13
portrait, 54–55, 56–58
Prasad, Bhaleshwar, 108, 110–12
See also Belvedere Press: *Santbani Pustakmālā*
Prayag, 55–56, 61, 170, 214n.89, *See also* Allahabad
Premchand, 178, 187, 241–42n.55
on the short story, 187
"Premghan," Badrinarayan Chaudhri, 172–73, 181
India's Fortune (Bhārat saubhāgya) 181, 182–84, 246–47n.98
Kajlī kautuhal, 173
print culture, 12–14, 70, 154–56, 187
See also Allahabad; Banaras; Lucknow
Pritchett, Frances, 165–66, 241n.53
Puhakar, 56, 132–33, 141, 212n.72, 212n.74, 212–13n.76, 229n.53
Rasaratan (Jewel of *rasa*), 6–7, 50–51, 54–55, 56–58, 61, 62, 70, 71–72, 196–97, 213n.82
Purab (East) 4, 8–10, 11–12, 18, 22, 33–34, 50, 101, 128, 140, 172–73, 189–90, 192, 194–95. *See also* Awadh
Puranas; Puranic, 35–36, 43, 56–57, 58, 66–68, 94–95, 169–70, 193–94, 196–97, 206n.9
purbi, Purbiya (eastern), 11–13, 43, 45–46, 49, 72, 150, 161, 202–3n.25

qasbas, 10–11, 12–14, 23, 42, 50, 95, 99–100, 115, 126, 130, 133, 135, 138, 147–48, 154, 192–93, 197, 203n.28, 236n.6, 236n.7, *See also* Bilgram; Jais; Kara
qissa (*qiṣṣa*, story, narrative), 25–26, 27–28, 62–63, 69, 71–72, 179–80, 189–90, 206n.4
quasi-Persian, 17, 96, 120
quasi-Sanskrit (*sahaskritī*), 17
Qur'an, 14–15, 67–68, 119–20, 224n.10, 228–29n.50

Qutban, 34, 35, 36, 41, 42–43, 48*t*, 52, 65–67
Mirigāvatī (*The Magic Doe*), 24, 34, 42–43, 47*t*, 52, 64, 70
Persian translation of, 64–67 (see also *Rājkunwar*)

Radhasoami, 110–12, 222n.66
ragamala (*rāgamālā*, garland of *ragas*), 42–43, 66–67, 211n.65
Rahmatullah, Sayyid Diwan, 116, 117, 118, 123, 124, 125, 129–30, 135, 171–72, 223n.2
Raidas, 12, 78, 78*t*, 83, 84, 85–86, 100–1, 108, 217n.14, 219n.36, 221n.50, 222n.65
Rai Har Prashad, 123–24
raja(s), 11, 23, 29, 31, 34, 42, 70, 129, 147. *See also* Amethi; Banaras
Rājkunwar (Persian translation of Qutban's *Mirigāvatī*), 63, 64–68
Rajput, 2–3, 11, 42, 50, 53, 67–68, 72, 129
Ramanujan, A. K., 27–28, 206n.8
Rāmāyaṇa, 3, 28, 35, 58–59, 133, 140, 169–70, 195, 206n.8, 208n.32, 209n.38
rasa (flavor, juice) 24, 30–32, 36, 39, 40, 41, 53, 58, 60, 125, 132, 144, 213n.78, 215n.111, 227n.35
prema, 36, 37, 41, 58, 212n.69
rasika. *See* connoisseur
Raslin, Sayyid Ghulam Nabi, 124–25, 126, 144–46, 166–67, 171–72, 194–95, 227n.34, 227n.35, 230n.62, 234n.89
Raza, Rahi Masoom, *Ṭopī Śuklā*, 18, 186–87
Razi, 'Aqil Khan, 139
The Seven Climes (*Haft iqlīm*) 139–40, 233n.78, 233n.83
re-accenting, 18, 30–32, 39, 40, 77–78, 87–88, 91–93, 95, 99–100, 192
reading aloud (*bāṃchnā*), 24, 172–73, 193–94
recognition, 1–2, 4, 5, 9, 21, 43, 76, 87, 100–1, 136–37, 202n.24
obstacles to, 76–77, 79–83, 190–91, 196
technologies of, 7, 20, 76, 79, 155, 201n.3
red-lac insect (*bīṛ bahūṭī*) 142
region, 4, 9–14, 139–40, 154, 194, 203n.29
Rekhta, 15–16, 18, 19, 111*t*, 145–46, 147, 148, 195, 217n.13, 234n.90, *See also* Urdu
rekhti, 150, 168
riti (*rīti*, courtly) 57, 58, 71–72, 82, 127, 166–67, 224n.5
manuals (*rīti-granth*) 71–72, 126, 127, 227n.35
poetry, 57–58, 79, 87–88, 126, 166–67, 194–95, 198, 223n.1, 237n.16 (*see also* Brajbhasha poetry)
romance, 25–26, 28. See also *pemkatha*
Sufi, 28–34, 53, 58, 72–73
Roussel, Albert, *Padmâvatî*, 1–2
Rumi, Jalaluddin, *Masnavī*, 68–69, 119–20, 197–98, 224–25n.11
rupa (*rūpa*, form, embodiment), 40, 54

Sa'di, 131, 224–25n.11, 225n.17
Bostān, 134
Gulistān, 197–98, 206n.4
Saksena, Ram Babu, 168, 173
History of Urdu Literature, 168–69, 171, 173, 241n.53, 241n.54
Salim, Prince, 50, 64, 66, 214n.94, *See also* Emperor Jahangir
Sanskrit, 3, 7, 12, 14–15, 17, 19–20, 29, 30, 36, 38, 41, 50, 56, 57–59, 68–69, 79, 81, 91–92, 123, 124–25, 132–33, 141, 143, 147, 152–53, 154, 156, 163–64, 175–76, 177, 178, 184–85, 190, 194, 198, 203–4n.32, 229n.55, 235n.94, 237n.15, 241n.51, 248n.110, *See also* cosmopolitan; education; "quasi-Sanskrit"
village poems, 244n.78
Sant (saint-poet), 17, 23, 59, 72–73, 74, 75–76, 80–81, 82. *See also* caste; Kabir; Malukdas; Paltudas; Raidas; *satsang*
poetry, 12, 74–76, 78, 81, 82, 87–88, 91–92, 93, 95, 112, 114–15, 189–90, 197, 216n.5 (*see also* Belvedere Press; booklets; circulation; dialogism; orature; *pad*)
of Purab/"three-line poets" 78, 78*t*
satsang (*satsaṅg*, gathering and singing of devotional songs), 59, 60, 76–77, 89, 94, 134–35, 194–95
scale, 4, 21, 117, 118–19, 135, 146–47, 205n.46
script(s), 4, 8, 15, 42, 44*f*, 45*f*, 46*f*, 47*t*, 137–38, 159, 160–61, 162, 163, 165, 170, 179, 193–94, 206n.7, 232n.73, 239n.38, 246n.92, *See also* Nagari; Kaithi; Persian
Sen, Kshitimohan, 108–10, 222n.66
Sengar, Shiv Singh, 123–24, 126–27, 166, 228n.41
Shiv Singh's Lotus (*Śiv Siṃh Saroj*) 123–24, 126–29, 132, 166, 215n.110, 226n.26, 227n.37, 228n.43, 228n.44, 228n.45
Servan-Schreiber, Catherine, 113, 216n.8, 242n.63, 245n.82
Seth, Vikram, *A Suitable Boy*, 14
Shah Jahan, Emperor, 68–69
shaikhs. *See* Sufi
Shakir, Shaikh Muhammad, 43, 47*t*, 67–68
Sharar, 'Abd al-Halim, 205n.53, 235–36n.4

Sharma, Padmasingh, 163
Sharma, Sunil, 45–46, 68–69
Sharqi, Sultan Husain Shah, 41, 42–43
Sherani, Hafiz Mahmud
definition of Urdu, 16, 162, 239–40n.39
Shih, Shu Mei, 76, 190–91, 201n.3, 201n.15
Shirreff, A. G. 3
Shukla, Ramchandra, 25–26, 58, 61, 70–71, 77–78, 213n.82
History of Hindi Literature (*Hindī sāhitya kā itihās*) 70, 81–82, 166–67, 173, 185, 218n.21, 223n.74
on Sufi romances, 2–3, 25–26, 31–32, 166–67, 213n.82
views of Sant poetry, 77–78, 82, 109–10, 217n.10, 218n.22
significant geographies, 6–7, 20–21, 22, 55, 69, 153
silences, 3–4, 27, 114–15, 123–24, 192–93
singers, 8–9, 23, 32, 50, 51, 72, 74, 80, 104–5, 124–25, 172–73, 176, 178, 180–81, 192, 242n.63, 245n.89, *See also* songs
Singh, Shivprasad, 213n.81, 213n.82
Sitaram, Lala, 169–70
songs, 10–11, 15, 17, 18, 19, 23, 24, 26, 30, 91–92, 113, 125, 148, 150, 166–67, 171–73, 178–79, 192, 196, 207n.26, 234n.90, 235n.99, 243n.66, 243n.71, 244n.75, See also *pad*
Dalit, 179, 245n.85
devotional, 23, 59, 74–77, 85, 87–88, 91–92, 93, 195–96, 216n.8, 222n.71, 223n.73
theater, 180, 181, 183–84, 185, 245n.87, 245–46n.90, 246n.92
village (*see* Ramnaresh Tripathi: *Grām gīt*)
space, 4–5, 6–7, 8–9, 17, 20–22, 26, 72, 75–76, 102–3, 106–7, 140–41, 149–50, 153, 157–58, 189, 192–94, 198–99, 205n.46, 246n.95, *See also* location; located; mapping; Massey; scale
Spivak, Gayatri Chakravorty 202n.16
Sreenivasan, Ramya, 2–3, 28, 42, 72
storytelling, storytellers (*kathāvāchak*), 24, 72
Sufi, 4–5, 10–11, 23, 25–26, 30, 32, 33, 34, 40, 43, 50–51, 53, 71, 77–78, 81–82, 84, 92, 94–95, 96–, 99–100
authors, 2–3, 17, 31, 36, 42, 71–72, 198 (*see also* 'Abd al-Wahid Bilgrami; Da'ud; Gangohi; Jayasi; Manjhan; Qutban)
hospices or *khanqahs*, 107, 119–20, 203n.28
shaikhs, 16, 52–53, 104–5, 122, 123, 126
tazkiras, 120–21, 194
texts, 14–15, 19, 32, 119–20 (see also *pemkathas*; kathas; romances)
Sultanate, 26, 33, 45–49, 95, 102–3, 119–20
Delhi, 10, 11, 31, 119
North Indian, 10–11, 12 (*see also* Sharqi, Suri)
Suri, Islam Shah, 34, 226–27n.29
Suri, Sher Shah, 34, 51
Suvorova, 6–7, 202n.19

Tagore, Rabindranath, 74, 87, 108–10, 236n.12
Taj, Afroz, 235n.97
Tara Chand, 239n.37, 240n.40
taste(s), 8, 9, 13–14, 18, 60, 154, 166–67, 173, 177–78, 186
communities of, 7, 9, 12, 33, 58–59, 72–73, 75–77, 118, 134–35, 142–43, 147, 160, 193, 194–95, 238n.27
literary, 5, 7, 13–14, 23, 131, 132, 171, 229–30n.57
multilingual, 17, 132, 133–35, 142–43, 147, 158, 165, 171, 179–80, 189–90
shifts in, 10–11, 26, 45–46, 50–51, 66, 71–72, 93–148, 153, 165, 186–87
See also connoisseur; cultivation; distinction; *rasa;* transmission
tazkira (biographical dictionary of poets, Sufis, or other notable people), 8, 10–11, 117–18, 120–21, 126–27, 129–30, 139, 166, 193–94, 225n.14, 225n.15, 227n.36, 231n.68, 232n.75, 233n.77
See also Azad *tazkiras*; Sufi *tazkiras*
temporality, 6–7, 21, 35, 60, 89, 93, 118–19, 133, 139, 140, 141, 149–50, 177, 178, 190–91
textbooks, 155, 167–68, 169–70, 179, 242n.56, 242n.59
Tiwari, Bhanupratap, 17, 133–34, 158, 172, 194–95, 234n.92
autobiography, 134–35, 146–47, 146*f*, 150–51, 197–98
contributions to *North Indian Notes & Queries*, 172, 174–75, 243n.71
Tiwari, Udaynath, 129, 144, 145–46, 228n.46
Tod, Colonel James, *Annals and Antiquities of Rajasthan*, 72
Todarmal, 10, 51, 61, 211n.64
Tosh, 145–46, 234n.91
transcodification, 24, 27–28, 49, 63, 63*t*, 67–68, 214n.96
translation, 3, 7, 18, 41, 48*t*, 62, 63, 77–78, 141, 157, 197–98, 237n.23, 240n.42
Hindi translations of Oliver Goldsmith, 157, 188–89, 237n.24, 238n.25, 238n.26, 238n.27
of *kathas*, 27–28, 33–34, 64*t*, 66, 68
transmission, 7, 22–23, 26, 42, 108–9, 197–98
oral, 17, 80, 114–15, 216n.2

Tripathi, Ramnaresh, 175–76, 177–78, 244n.76, 244n.78
Grām gīt (Village Songs), 175–76
Kavitā kaumudī (Moonlight, or Guide to Poetry) 175–76
Trivedi, Dulah, 116, 127, 128, 129, 144, 145–46, 228n.46
Necklace for Poets (Kavikulakaṇṭhābharaṇa) 131
Trivedi, Kalidas, 127, 129–30, 144, 145–46, 228n.45, 228n.46, 228n.47
Trivedi, Udaynath, 129, 144, 145–46, 228n.46
Tulsidas, 3, 9, 12, 15, 50–51, 58–59, 204n.34, 213n.83
Rāmcharitmānas or *Mānas* (The Holy Lake of Ram's Deeds), 6, 12, 50–51, 58–60, 62, 70–71, 72–73, 213n.86, 248n.3
in print, 70
Turk, 11, 35, 40, 106
Turkey, 153, 188
Turki, 14, 41, 131, 164

"Ugra," Pande Bechan Sharma, 185
Chocolate, 185–86
Unnao, 74
U.P. (Uttar Pradesh), formerly United Provinces of Agra and Oudh, 14, 59, 162
Upadhyay, Krishnadev, 244n.75
Urdu, 2, 3–4, 6–7, 8, 12–13, 14, 15–16, 19, 23, 25–26, 43, 69–70, 71–72, 120–21, 141, 148, 152–53, 154–55, 156, 158, 159, 161–62, 163–64, 165–66, 172–73, 179–80, 182–83, 184, 188, 189, 190–91, 233n.82, 238n.31, 239n.38, 239–40n.39, 240n.40
literary histories, 166, 167–69, 171, 189–90, 194–95, 241n.54
poetry (*shā'irī*) 101, 107, 126, 145–46, 147–48, 150, 166–68, 175–76, 180, 185, 186, 195, 196–97, 206n.7, 234n.92, 235n.94
Usman, 52, 53, 54, 58, 212n.68
Chitrāvalī, 50–51, 54–57, 62, 70, 71–72, 141, 196–97

Valmiki, 59, 132–33, 177, 213n.83
Vanita, Ruth, 69
ventriloquism, 76–77, 87–88, 91–92, 93, 94, 96, 97, 114–15, 142–43, 184
Verma, Babu Ramkrishna, Bharat Jiwan Press, 70, 215n.111
vernacular, 14, 15–16, 19–20, 26, 33, 57, 58–59, 62–63, 120, 204n.41, 238–39n.32
cosmopolitan, 10–11, 15, 19, 43, 50
vernacularization, 19, 26, 147–48, 204n.41, 238n.31, 249n.13
Vidyapati, 19, 55–56, 194, 198, 249n.14
village, 12–13, 23, 24, 74, 133–34, 141, 159, 173, 176, 177–78, 203n.28, 206n.11, 245n.81
chronotope of, 176, 178
songs (*see* Tripathi, Ramnaresh: *Grām gīt*)
viraha (longing in separation), 30–31, 38, 54, 57–58, 66, 67–68, 92
Viswanathan, Gauri, 165–66, 235n.3

waḥdat al-wujūd (unity of existence), 40, 96
Warwick Research Collective, 5
world, 6–7, 8, 20, 21, 26, 53, 54, 55–56, 57, 120, 139, 151, 188, 201n.14
See also *dunyā*
worlding, 23
world literature, 5, 7, 9, 18, 20, 21–22, 23, 26, 54–55, 76, 77, 100, 113–14, 118, 153, 180–81, 188, 190, 194, 196, 197–98, 202n.16, 205n.45
anthologies and histories of, 3, 9, 248n.110

Yamuna. *See* Jamuna
yogi, 40, 53, 54–55, 58, 92, 105, 181–82, 209n.41, 210n.43
lover as, 2, 28, 35, 36, 38–39, 58, 66, 92, 208n.37, 210n.44, 210n.45, 210n.46
yuga (age), 35, 52, 140, 141, 166–67, 209n.39, 212n.72

Zaidi, Shailesh, 227n.35